THE O'LEARY SERIES

Microsoft® Excel 2013: A Case Approach

Timothy J. O'Leary

Professor Emeritus,
Arizona State University

Linda I. O'Leary

McGraw-Hill Irwin

THE O'LEARY SERIES MICROSOFT® OFFICE EXCEL 2013: A CASE APPROACH
Published by McGraw-Hill/Irwin, a business unit of The McGraw-Hill Companies, Inc., 1221 Avenue of the
Americas, New York, NY, 10020. Copyright © 2014 by The McGraw-Hill Companies, Inc. All rights reserved.
Printed in the United States of America. No part of this publication may be reproduced or distributed in any
form or by any means, or stored in a database or retrieval system, without the prior written consent of The
McGraw-Hill Companies, Inc., including, but not limited to, in any network or other electronic storage or
transmission, or broadcast for distance learning.

Some ancillaries, including electronic and print components, may not be available to customers outside the
United States.

This book is printed on acid-free paper.

1 2 3 4 5 6 7 8 9 0 RMN/RMN 1 0 9 8 7 6 5 4 3

ISBN   978-0-07-740022-4
MHID   0-07-740022-4

Senior Vice President, Products & Markets: *Kurt L. Strand*
Vice President, Content Production & Technology Services: *Kimberly Meriwether David*
Director: *Scott Davidson*
Senior Brand Manager: *Wyatt Morris*
Executive Director of Development: *Ann Torbert*
Development Editor II: *Alaina G. Tucker*
Digital Development Editor: *Kevin White*
Marketing Manager: *Tiffany Russell*
Project Manager: *Marlena Pechan*
Senior Buyer: *Michael R. McCormick*
Designer: *Jana Singer*
Senior Content Licensing Specialist: *Jeremy Cheshareck*
Media Project Manager: *Brent dela Cruz*
Media Project Manager: *Cathy L. Tepper*
Typeface: *11/13 Times LT Std Roman*
Compositor: *Laserwords Private Limited*
Printer: *R. R. Donnelley*

All credits appearing at the end of the book are considered to be an extension of the copyright page.

Library of Congress Cataloging-in-Publication Data

O'Leary, Timothy J., 1947-
    Microsoft Office Excel 2013 : a case approach / Timothy J. O'Leary, Professor Emeritus, Arizona
State University, Linda I. O'Leary.
      pages cm.—(The O'Leary series)
    Includes index.
    ISBN-13: 978-0-07-740022-4 (alk. paper)
    ISBN-10: 0-07-740022-4 (alk. paper)
    1. Microsoft Excel (Computer file) 2. Business—Computer programs. 3. Electronic spreadsheets.
I. O'Leary, Linda I. II. Title.
HF5548.4.M523O3543 2014
005.54—dc23

                                                                            2013003946

The Internet addresses listed in the text were accurate at the time of publication. The inclusion of a website does
not indicate an endorsement by the authors or McGraw-Hill, and McGraw-Hill does not guarantee the accuracy
of the information presented at these sites.

www.mhhe.com

Brief Contents

Contents

LAB 2 ENHANCING THE WORKSHEET WITH GRAPHICS AND CHARTS EX2.1

LAB 3 MANAGING AND ANALYZING A WORKBOOK — EX3.1

WORKING TOGETHER: LINKING AND EMBEDDING BETWEEN WORD 2013 AND EXCEL 2013 — EXWT.1

Acknowledgments

We would like to extend our thanks to the instructors who took time out of their busy schedules to provide us with the feedback necessary to develop the 2013 edition of this text. The following professors offered valuable suggestions on revising the text:

Anne Acker
Jacksonville University

Jack Alanen
California State University–Northridge

Ken Araujo
Francis Marion University

Tahir Aziz
J. Sargeant Reynolds Community College

Lois Blais
Walters State Community College

Bob Clary
Patrick Henry Community College

Robert Doyle
Dona Ana Community College

Michael Dunklebarger
Alamance Community College

Jeffrey Finch
Kanawha Valley Community & Technology College

Kimberly Fish
Butler County Community College

Bob Forward
Texarkana College

Terry Griffin
Midwestern State University

Dexter Harlee
York Technical College

Tina Johnson
Midwestern State University

Dee Joseph
San Antonio College

Philip Kim
Walsh University

Ben Martz
Northern Kentucky University

Theresa McDonald
Texarkana College

David McNair
Jefferson College

Barb Norstrom
Kaskaskia College

Terry Rooker
Germanna Community College

Victor Suich
Walters State Community College

Lakeisha Vance
Alamance Community College

Barbara Wells
Central Carolina Technical College

Jensen Zhao
Ball State University

We would like to thank those who took the time to help us develop the manuscript and ensure accuracy through painstaking edits: Barbara Norstrom of Kaskaskia College, Robert Doyle of Dona Ana Community College, Candice Spangler of Columbus State Community College, and Kate Scalzi.

Finally, we would like to thank team members from McGraw-Hill, whose renewed commitment, direction, and support have infused the team with the excitement of a new project. Leading the team from McGraw-Hill are Wyatt Morris, Senior Brand Manager; Tiffany Russell, Marketing Manager; and Alaina Tucker, Developmental Editor II.

The production staff is headed by Marlena Pechan, Project Manager, whose planning and attention to detail have made it possible for us to successfully meet a very challenging schedule; Jana Singer, Designer; Michael McCormick, Senior Buyer; Kevin White, Digital Developmental Editor; Jeremy Cheshareck, Senior Content Licensing Specialist; Betsy Blumenthal and Chet Gottfried copy editors; Sharon O'Donnell and Peter DeLissovoy, proofreaders—team members on whom we can depend to do a great job.

The 20th century brought us the dawn of the digital information age and unprecedented changes in information technology. There is no indication that this rapid rate of change will be slowing—it may even be increasing. As we begin the 21st century, computer literacy is undoubtedly becoming a prerequisite in whatever career you choose.

The goal of the O'Leary Series is to provide you with the necessary skills to efficiently use these applications. Equally important is the goal to provide a foundation for students to readily and easily learn to use future versions of this software. This series accomplishes this by providing detailed step-by-step instructions combined with careful selection and presentation of essential concepts.

Times are changing, technology is changing, and this text is changing too. As students of today, you are different from those of yesterday. You put much effort toward the things that interest you and the things that are relevant to you. Your efforts directed at learning application programs and exploring the web seem, at times, limitless.

On the other hand, it's easy to be shortsighted, thinking that learning the skills to use the application is the only objective. The mission of the series is to build upon and extend this interest by not only teaching the specific application skills but by introducing the concepts that are common to all applications, providing students with the confidence, knowledge, and ability to easily learn the next generation of applications.

Instructor's Resource Center

The Online **Instructor's Resource Center** contains access to a computerized Test Bank, an Instructor's Manual, Solutions, and PowerPoint Presentation Slides. Features of the Instructor's Resource are described below.

- **Instructor's Manual** The Instructor's Manual, authored by the primary contributor, contains lab objectives, concepts, outlines, lecture notes, and command summaries. Also included are answers to all end-of-chapter material, tips for covering difficult materials, additional exercises, and a schedule showing how much time is required to cover text material.

- **Computerized Test Bank** The test bank, authored by the primary contributor, contains hundreds of multiple choice, true/false, and discussion questions. Each question will be accompanied by the correct answer, the level of learning difficulty, and corresponding page references. Our flexible EZ Test software allows you to easily generate custom exams.

- **PowerPoint Presentation Slides** The presentation slides, authored by the primary contributor, include lab objectives, concepts, outlines, text figures, and speaker's notes. Also included are bullets to illustrate key terms and FAQs.

Online Learning Center/Website

Found at **www.mhhe.com/oleary**, this site provides additional learning and instructional tools to enhance the comprehension of the text. The OLC/website is divided into these three areas:

- **Information Center** Contains core information about the text, supplements, and the authors.

- **Instructor Center** Offers the aforementioned instructional materials, downloads, and other relevant links for professors.

- **Student Center** Contains data files, chapter competencies, chapter concepts, self-quizzes, additional web links, and more.

SimNet Assessment for Office Applications

SimNet Assessment for Office Applications provides a way for you to test students' software skills in a simulated environment. SimNet is available for Microsoft Office 2013 and provides flexibility for you in your applications course by offering:

Pretesting options
Posttesting options
Course placement testing
Diagnostic capabilities to reinforce skills
Web delivery of tests
Certification preparation exams
Learning verification reports

For more information on skills assessment software, please contact your local sales representative, or visit us at **www.mhhe.com**.

Computing Concepts

Computing Essentials 2014 offers a unique, visual orientation that gives students a basic understanding of computing concepts. *Computing Essentials* encourages "active" learning with exercises, explorations, visual illustrations, and screen shots. While combining the "active" learning style with current topics and technology, this text provides an accurate snapshot of computing trends. When bundled with software application lab manuals, students are given a complete representation of the fundamental issues surrounding the personal computing environment.

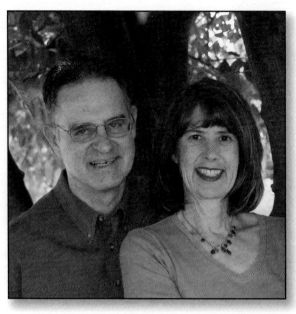

Tim and Linda O'Leary live in the American Southwest and spend much of their time engaging instructors and students in conversation about learning. In fact, they have been talking about learning for over 25 years. Something in those early conversations convinced them to write a book, to bring their interest in the learning process to the printed page. Today, they are as concerned as ever about learning, about technology, and about the challenges of presenting material in new ways, in terms of both content and method of delivery.

A powerful and creative team, Tim combines his 30 years of classroom teaching experience with Linda's background as a consultant and corporate trainer. Tim has taught courses at Stark Technical College in Canton, Ohio, and at Rochester Institute of Technology in upstate New York, and is currently a professor emeritus at Arizona State University in Tempe, Arizona. Linda offered her expertise at ASU for several years as an academic advisor. She also presented and developed materials for major corporations such as Motorola, Intel, Honeywell, and AT&T, as well as various community colleges in the Phoenix area.

Tim and Linda have talked to and taught numerous students, all of them with a desire to learn something about computers and applications that make their lives easier, more interesting, and more productive.

Each new edition of an O'Leary text, supplement, or learning aid has benefited from these students and their instructors who daily stand in front of them (or over their shoulders). The O'Leary Series is no exception.

About the Contributor

Kathleen Stewart has authored Access and Excel textbooks for McGraw-Hill's Professional Approach series (later the Lesson Approach) since its inception. She has a master's degree in education as well as an MBA. After a couple of years teaching at a suburban high school, Kathleen became Department Chairperson and Professor of Information Management Systems at Moraine Valley Community College in suburban Chicago, working with students with many interests, skill levels, and backgrounds. In addition, as president of her own training and consulting company, she and her staff delivered individual and classroom instruction and help-desk support in the public and private sectors. Kathleen is retired from her position at the college but remains active in Illinois with organizations that address higher education issues.

Dedication

We dedicate this edition to our parents, Irene Perley Coats, Jean L. O'Leary, and Charles D. O'Leary, for all their support and love. We miss you.

Introduction to Microsoft Office 2013

Objectives

After completing the Introduction to Microsoft Office 2013, you should be able to:

1 Describe the Office 2013 applications.

2 Start an Office 2013 application.

3 Use the Ribbon, dialog boxes, and task panes.

4 Use menus, context menus, and shortcut keys.

5 Use the Backstage.

6 Open, close, and save files.

7 Navigate a document.

8 Enter, edit, and format text.

9 Select, copy, and move text.

10 Undo and redo changes.

11 Specify document properties.

12 Print a document.

13 Use Office 2013 Help.

14 Exit an Office 2013 application.

What Is Microsoft Office 2013?

Microsoft's Office 2013 is a comprehensive, integrated system of programs designed to solve a wide array of business needs. Although the programs can be used individually, they are designed to work together seamlessly, making it easy to connect people and organizations to information, business processes, and each other. The applications include tools used to create, discuss, communicate, and manage projects. If you share a lot of documents with other people, these features facilitate access to common documents. Additionally, Office 2013 allows you to store and share files in the cloud on SkyDrive or SharePoint. The **cloud** refers to any applications and services that are hosted and run on servers connected to the Internet. This version is designed to work with all types of devices, including desktops, laptops, tablets and hybrid tablet/laptops.

Microsoft Office 2013 is packaged in several different combinations of programs or suites. The major programs and a brief description are provided in the following table.

Program	Description
Word 2013	Word processor program used to create text-based documents
Excel 2013	Spreadsheet program used to analyze numerical data
Access 2013	Database manager used to organize, manage, and display a database
PowerPoint 2013	Graphics presentation program used to create presentation materials
Outlook 2013	Desktop information manager and messaging client
OneNote 2013	Note-taking and information organization tools

The four main components of Microsoft Office 2013—Word, Excel, Access, and PowerPoint—are the applications you will learn about in this series of labs. They are described in more detail in the following sections.

Word 2013

Word 2013 is a word processing software application whose purpose is to help you create text-based documents such as letters, memos, reports, e-mail messages, or any other type of correspondence. Word processors are one of the most flexible and widely used application software programs.

WORD 2013 FEATURES

The beauty of a word processor is that you can make changes or corrections as you are typing. Want to change a report from single spacing to double spacing? Alter the width of the margins? Delete some paragraphs and add others from yet another document? A word processor allows you to do all these things with ease.

Edit Content

Word 2013 excels in its ability to change or **edit** a document. Basic document editing involves correcting spelling, grammar, and sentence-structure errors and revising or updating existing text by inserting, deleting, and rearranging areas of text. For example, a document that lists prices can easily be updated to reflect new prices. A document that details procedures can be revised by deleting old procedures and inserting new ones. Many of these changes are made easily by cutting (removing) or copying (duplicating) selected text and then pasting (inserting) the cut or copied text in another location in the same or another document. Editing allows you to quickly revise a document, by changing only the parts that need to be modified.

To help you produce a perfect document, Word 2013 includes many additional editing support features. The AutoCorrect feature checks the spelling and grammar in a document as text is entered. Many common errors are corrected automatically for you. Others are identified and a correction suggested. A thesaurus can be used to display alternative words that have a meaning similar or opposite to a word you entered. The Find and Replace feature can be used to quickly locate specified text and replace it with other text throughout a document. In addition, Word 2013 includes a variety of tools that automate the process of many common tasks, such as creating tables, form letters, and columns.

Format Content

You also can easily control the appearance or **format** of the document. Perhaps the most noticeable formatting feature is the ability to apply different fonts (type styles and sizes) and text appearance changes such as bold, italics, and color to all or selected portions of the document. Additionally, you can add color shading behind individual pieces of text or entire paragraphs and pages to add emphasis. Other formatting features include changes to entire paragraphs, such as the line spacing and alignment of text between the margins. You also can format entire pages by displaying page numbers, changing margin settings, and applying backgrounds.

To make formatting even easier, Word 2013 includes Document Themes and Styles. Document Themes apply a consistent font, color, and line effect to an entire document. Styles apply the selected style design to a selection of text. Further, Word 2013 includes a variety of built-in preformatted content that helps you quickly produce modern-looking, professional documents. Among these are galleries of cover page designs, pull quotes, and header and footer designs. While selecting many of these design choices, a visual live preview is displayed, making it easy to see how the design would look in your document. In addition, you can select from a wide variety of templates to help you get started on creating many common types of documents such as flyers, calendars, faxes, newsletters, and memos.

Insert Illustrations and Videos

To further enhance your documents, you can insert many different types of graphic elements. These include drawing objects, SmartArt, charts, pictures, clip art, screenshots, and videos. The drawing tools supplied with Word 2013 can be used to create your own drawings, or you can select from over 100 adjustable shapes and modify them to your needs. All drawings can be further enhanced with 3-D effects, shadows, colors, and textures. SmartArt graphics allow you to create a visual representation of your information. They include many different layouts such as a process or cycle that are designed to help you communicate an idea. Charts can be inserted to illustrate and compare data. Complex pictures can be inserted in documents by scanning your own, using supplied or purchased clip art, or downloading images from the web. Additionally, you can quickly capture and insert a picture, called a screenshot, from another application running on your computer into the current document. Finally, you can easily find and insert videos from different online sources to enhance your document.

Collaborate with Others

Group collaboration on projects is common in industry today. Word 2013 includes many features to help streamline how documents are developed and changed by group members. A comment feature allows multiple people to insert remarks in the same document without having to route the document to each person or reconcile multiple reviewers' comments. You can easily consolidate all changes and comments from different reviewers in one simple step and accept or reject changes as needed. Finally, if you save your documents online, you can review and edit simultaneously with others. The changes are accessible to the entire group. If someone does not have Office installed on his or her computer, you can send the individual a link to your document allowing him or her to follow along in a browser.

Two documents you will produce in the first two Word 2013 labs, a letter and flyer, are shown here.

A letter containing a tabbed table, indented paragraphs, and text enhancements is quickly created using basic Word features

January 9, 2015

Dear Adventure Traveler:

Imagine camping under the stars in A[...] Costa Rica, or following in the footsteps of the [...] Picchu. Turn these thoughts of an adventure i[...] Tours on one of our four new adventure tours[...]

To tell you more about these exciting[...] These presentations will focus on the features[...] places you will visit and activities you can part[...] attend one of the following presentations:

Date	Time
February 5	7:00 p.m.
February 18	7:30 p.m.
March 7	1:00 p.m.

In appreciation of your past patronag[...] the new tour packages. You must book the tri[...] letter to qualify for the discount.

Our vacation tours are professionally[...] everything in the price of your tour while givir[...] these features:

➢ All accommodations and meals
➢ All entrance fees, excursions, transfer[...]
➢ Professional tour manager and local g[...]

We hope you will join us this year on [...] Travel Tours each day is an adventure. For res[...] Travel Tours directly at 1-800-555-0004.

Adventure Travel Tours

NEW ADVENTURES

Attention adventure travelers! Attend an Adventure Travel presentation to learn about some of the earth's greatest unspoiled habitats and learn how you can experience the adventure of a lifetime. This year Adventure Travel Tours is introducing four new tours that offer you a unique opportunity to combine many different outdoor activities while exploring the world.

Safari in Tanzania

India Wildlife Adventure

Costa Rica Rivers and Rainforests

Inca Trail to Machu Picchu

Presentation dates and times are January 5 at 7:00 p.m., February 3 at 7:30 p.m., and March 8 at 7:00 p.m. All presentations are at convenient hotel locations. The hotels are located in downtown Los Angeles, in Santa Clara, and at the LAX airport.

Call Adventure Travel Tours at 1-800-555-0004 for presentation locations, a full color brochure, and itinerary information, costs, and trip dates. Student Name will gladly help with all of your questions.

Visit our Web site at www.adventuretraveltours.com

A flyer incorporating many visual enhancements such as colored text, varied text styles, and graphic elements is both eye-catching and informative

Excel 2013

Excel 2013 is an electronic spreadsheet, or **worksheet**, that is used to organize, manipulate, and graph numeric data. Once used almost exclusively by accountants, worksheets are now widely used by nearly every profession. Nearly any job that uses rows and columns of numbers can be performed using an electronic spreadsheet. Once requiring hours of labor and/or costly accountants' fees, data analysis is now available almost instantly using electronic spreadsheets and has become a routine business procedure. This powerful business tool has revolutionized the business world. Typical uses include the creation of budgets and financial planning for both business and personal situations. Marketing professionals record and evaluate sales trends. Teachers record grades and calculate final grades. Personal trainers record the progress of their clients.

EXCEL 2013 FEATURES

Excel 2013 includes many features that not only help you create a well-designed worksheet, but one that produces accurate results. The features include the ability to quickly edit and format data, perform calculations, create charts, and print the worksheet. Using Excel 2013, you can quickly analyze and manage data and communicate your findings to others. The program not only makes it faster to create worksheets, but it also produces professional-appearing results.

Enter and Edit Data

The Microsoft Excel 2013 spreadsheet program uses a workbook file that contains one or more worksheets. Each worksheet can be used to organize different types of related information. The worksheet consists of rows and columns that create a grid of cells. You enter numeric data or descriptive text into a cell. These entries can then be erased, moved, copied, or edited.

Format Data

Like text in a Word document, the design and appearance of entries in a worksheet can be enhanced in many ways. For instance, you can change the font style and size and add special effects such as bold, italic, borders, boxes, drop shadows, and shading to selected cells. You also can use cell styles to quickly apply predefined combinations of these formats to selections. Additionally, you can select from different document themes, predefined combinations of colors, fonts, and effects, to give your workbooks a consistent, professional appearance.

Unlike the Word application, Excel includes many formatting features that are designed specifically for numeric data. For example, numeric entries can be displayed with commas, dollar signs, or a set number of decimal places. Special formatting, such as color bars, can be applied automatically to ranges of cells to emphasize data based on a set of criteria you establish and to highlight trends.

Analyze Data

The power of a spreadsheet application is its ability to perform calculations from very simple sums to the most complex financial and mathematical formulas. Formulas can be entered that perform calculations using data contained in specified cells. The results of the calculations are displayed in the cell containing the formula. Predefined formulas, called functions, can be used to quickly perform complex calculations such as calculating loan payments or performing a statistical analysis of data.

Analysis of data in a spreadsheet once was too expensive and time-consuming. Now, using electronic worksheets, you can use what-if or sensitivity analysis by changing the values in selected cells and immediately observing the effect on related cells in the worksheet. Other analysis tools such as Solver and Scenarios allow you to see the effects of possible alternative courses of action to help forecast future outcomes.

Chart Data

Using Excel, you also can produce a visual display of numeric data in the form of graphs or charts. As the values in the worksheet change, charts referencing those values automatically adjust to reflect the changes. You also can enhance the appearance of a chart by using different type styles and sizes, adding three-dimensional effects, and including text and objects such as lines and arrows.

Two worksheets you will produce using Excel 2013 are shown below.

A worksheet showing the quarterly sales forecast containing a graphic, text enhancements, and a chart of the data is quickly created using basic Excel 2013 features

A large worksheet incorporating more complex formulas, conditional formatting, and linked worksheets is both informative and attractive

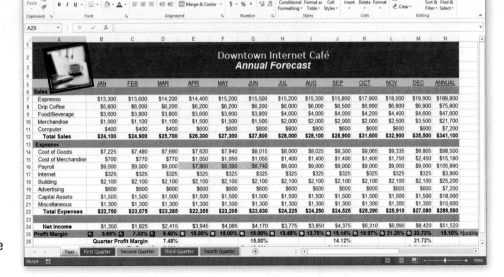

Access 2013

Access 2013 is a relational database management application that is used to create and analyze a database. A **database** is a collection of related data. **Tables** consist of columns (called **fields**) and rows (called **records**). Each row contains a record, which is all the information about one person, thing, or place. Each field is the smallest unit of information about a record.

In a relational database, the most widely used database structure, data is organized in linked tables. The tables are related or linked to one another by a common field. Relational databases allow you to create smaller and more manageable database tables, since you can combine and extract data between tables.

For example, a state's motor vehicle department database might have an address table. Each row (record) in the table would contain address information about one individual. Each column (field) would contain just one piece of information, for example, zip codes. The address table would be linked to other tables in the database by common fields. For example, the address table might be linked to a vehicle owner's table by name and linked to an outstanding citation table by license number (see example below).

Address Table

Name	License Number	Street Address	City	State	Zip
Aaron, Linda	FJ1987	10032 Park Lane	San Jose	CA	95127
Abar, John	D12372	1349 Oak St	Lakeville	CA	94128
Abell, Jack	LK3457	95874 State St	Stone	CA	95201

key fields linked — key fields linked

Owner's Table

Name	Plate Number
Abell, Jack	ABK241
Abrams, Sue	LMJ198
Abril, Pat	ZXA915

Outstanding Citation Table

License Number	Citation Code	Violation
T25476	00031	Speed
D98372	19001	Park
LK3457	89100	Speed

ACCESS 2013 FEATURES

Access 2013 is a powerful program with numerous easy-to-use features including the ability to quickly locate information; add, delete, modify, and sort records; analyze data; and produce professional-looking reports. Some of the basic Access 2013 features are described next.

Find Information

Once you enter data into the database table, you can quickly search the table to locate a specific record based on the data in a field. In a manual system, you can usually locate a record by knowing one key piece of information. For example, if the records are stored in a file cabinet alphabetically by last name, to quickly find a record, you must know the last name. In a computerized database, even if the records are sorted or organized by last name, you can still quickly locate a record using information in another field.

Add, Delete, and Modify Records

Using Access, it is also easy to add and delete records from the table. Once you locate a record, you can edit the contents of the fields to update the record or delete the record entirely from the table. You also can add new records to a table. When you enter a new record, it is automatically placed in the correct organizational location within the table. Creation of forms makes it easier to enter and edit data as well.

Sort and Filter Records

The capability to arrange or sort records in the table according to different fields can provide more meaningful information. You can organize records by name, department, pay, class, or any other category you need at a particular time. Sorting the records in different ways can provide information to different departments for different purposes.

Additionally, you can isolate and display a subset of records by specifying filter criteria. The criteria specify which records to display based on data in selected fields.

Analyze Data

Using Access, you can analyze the data in a table and perform calculations on different fields of data. Instead of pulling each record from a filing cabinet, recording the piece of data you want to use, and then performing the calculation on the recorded data, you can simply have the database program perform the calculation on all the values in the specified field. Additionally, you can ask questions or query the table to find only certain records that meet specific conditions to be used in the analysis. Information that was once costly and time-consuming to get is now quickly and readily available.

Generate Reports

Access includes many features that help you quickly produce reports ranging from simple listings to complex, professional-looking reports. You can create a simple report by asking for a listing of specified fields of data and restricting the listing to records meeting designated conditions. You can create a more complex professional report using the same restrictions or conditions as the simple report, but you can display the data in different layout styles, or with titles, headings, subtotals, or totals.

A database and a report that you will produce using Access 2013 are shown on the next page.

A relational database can be created and modified easily using basic Access 2013 features

Job Position Report

For Landis

Employee ID	First Name	Last Name	Position
12703	Jeff	Bader	Fitness Instructor
12389	Jennifer	Blackman	Sales Associate
05015	Scott	Briggs	Personal Trainer Director
12501	Elizabeth	DeLuca	Personal Trainer
12855	Kimberly	Fachet	Sales Associate
13484	Stephanie	Franklin	Food Service Server
12914	Alfonso	Gomez	Cleaning
22469	Ryan	Hogan	Personal Trainer
13303	Chris	Jensen	Greeter
13027	Kimberly	Kieken	Food Service Server
07650	Chris	Lamm	Sales Director
22085	Kristina	Lindau	Child Care Provider
13635	Juan	Martinez	Fitness Instructor
03225	Dan	Morgan	Food Service Director
99999	Student	Name	Human Resources Administrator
12420	Allison	Player	Maintenance
13005	Emily	Reilly	Assistant Manager
22297	Patricia	Rogondino	Greeter
07287	Anita	Roman	Child Care Director
12918	Carlos	Ruiz	Assistant Manager
00212	Chad	Schiff	Club Director
12583	Marie	Sullivan	Greeter

Page 1 of 2

A professional-looking report can be quickly generated from information contained in a database

WWW.MHHE.COM/OLEARY

Office 2013

PowerPoint 2013 is a graphics presentation program designed to help you produce a high-quality presentation that is both interesting to the audience and effective in its ability to convey your message. A presentation can be as simple as overhead transparencies or as sophisticated as an on-screen electronic display. Graphics presentation programs can produce black-and-white or color overhead transparencies, 35 mm slides, onscreen electronic presentations called **slide shows**, web pages for web use, and support materials for both the speaker and the audience.

POWERPOINT 2013 FEATURES

Although creating an effective presentation is a complicated process, PowerPoint 2013 helps simplify this process by providing assistance in the content development phase, as well as in the layout and design phase. PowerPoint includes features such as text handling, outlining, graphing, drawing, animation, clip art, and multimedia support. In addition, the programs suggest layouts for different types of presentations and offer professionally designed templates to help you produce a presentation that is sure to keep your audience's attention. In addition, you can quickly produce the support materials to be used when making a presentation to an audience.

Develop, Enter, and Edit Content

The content development phase includes deciding on the topic of your presentation, the organization of the content, and the ultimate message you want to convey to the audience. As an aid in this phase, PowerPoint 2013 helps you organize your thoughts based on the type of presentation you are making by providing both content and design templates. Based on the type of presentation, such as selling a product or suggesting a strategy, the template provides guidance by suggesting content ideas and organizational tips. For example, if you are making a presentation on the progress of a sales campaign, the program would suggest that you enter text on the background of the sales campaign as the first page, called a **slide**; the current status of the campaign as the next slide; and accomplishments, schedule, issues and problems, and where you are heading on subsequent slides.

Design Layouts

The layout for each slide is the next important decision. Again, PowerPoint 2013 helps you by suggesting text layout features such as title placement, bullets, and columns. You also can incorporate graphs of data, tables, organizational charts, clip art, and other special text effects in the slides.

PowerPoint 2013 also includes professionally designed themes to further enhance the appearance of your slides. These themes include features that standardize the appearance of all the slides in your presentation. Professionally selected combinations of text and background colors, common typefaces and sizes, borders, and other art designs take the worry out of much of the design layout.

Deliver Presentations

After you have written and designed the slides, you can use the slides in an onscreen electronic presentation or a web page for use on the web. An onscreen presentation uses the computer to display the slides on an overhead projection screen. As you prepare this type of presentation, you can use the rehearsal feature that allows you to practice and time your presentation. The length of time to display each slide can be set and your entire presentation can be completed within the allotted time. A presentation also can be modified to display on a website and run using a web browser. Finally, you can package the presentation to a CD for distribution.

A presentation that you will produce using PowerPoint 2013 is shown below.

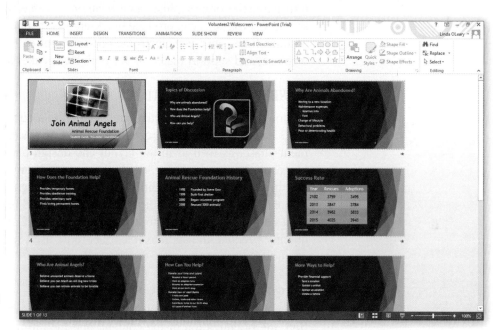

A presentation consists of a series of pages or "slides" presenting the information you want to convey in an organized and attractive manner

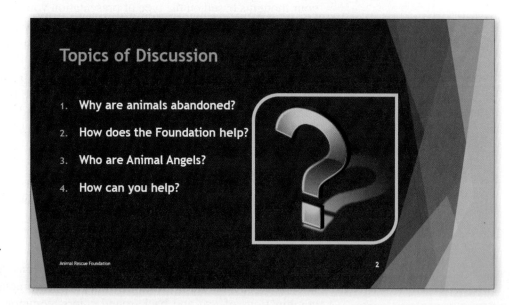

When running an on-screen presentation, each slide of the presentation is displayed full-screen on your computer monitor or projected onto a screen

Instructional Conventions

As you follow the directions in the upcoming hands-on section and in the application labs, you need to know the instructional conventions that are used. Hands-on instructions you are to perform appear as a sequence of numbered steps. Within each step, a series of bullets identifies the specific actions that must be performed. Step numbering begins over within each topic heading throughout the lab.

COMMANDS

Commands that are initiated using a command button and the mouse appear following the word "Click." The icon (and the icon name if the icon does not include text) is displayed following "Click." If there is another way to perform the same action, it appears in an Another Method margin note when the action is first introduced as shown in Example A.

Example A

1

- Select the list of four tours.

- Open the Home tab.

- Click B Bold in the Font group.

Another Method

The keyboard shortcut is Ctrl + B.

Sometimes, clicking on an icon opens a drop-down list or a menu of commands. Commands that are to be selected follow the word "Select" and appear in black text. You can select an item by pointing to it using the mouse or by moving to it using the directional keys. When an option is selected, it appears highlighted; however, the action is not carried out. Commands that appear following the word "Choose" perform the associated action. You can choose a command by clicking on it using the mouse or by pressing the Enter key once it is selected. (See Example B.)

Example B

1

- Click A ▾ Font Color in the Font group of the Home tab.

- Select Green.

- Choose Dark Blue.

FILE NAMES AND INFORMATION TO TYPE

Plain green text identifies file names you need to select or enter. Information you are asked to type appears in blue and bold. (See Example C.)

Example C

1

- Open the document wd01_Flyer.

- Type Adventure Travel presents four new trips

Common Office 2013 Features

Now that you know a little about each of the applications in Microsoft Office 2013, you will take a look at some of the features that are common to all Office 2013 applications. In this hands-on section you will learn to use the common user interface and application features to allow you to get a feel for how Office 2013 works. Although Word 2013 will be used to demonstrate how the features work, only features that are common to all the Office applications will be addressed.

COMMON INTERFACE FEATURES

All the Office 2013 applications have a common **user interface**, a set of graphical elements that are designed to help you interact with the program and provide instructions as to the actions you want to perform. These features include the use of the Ribbon, Quick Access Toolbar, task panes, menus, dialog boxes, and the File tab.

Starting an Office 2013 Application

To demonstrate the common features, you will start the Word 2013 application. There are several ways to start an Office 2013 application. The most common method is to click a tile on the Windows 8 Start screen for the program if it is available.

Additional Information

The procedure to start Excel, Access, and PowerPoint is the same as starting Word, except that you must select the appropriate application tile.

Having Trouble?

If you are using Windows 7, click [icon] Start and choose Word 2013. If you

do not see the program name on the Start menu, select All Programs, choose Microsoft Office 2013, and then choose Word 2013.

1

Click the [Word 2013 tile] **tile**
on the **Start screen.**

Having Trouble?

If a tile for the application you want to open is not on the Start Screen, right-click the Start screen, click [All apps], then click on the appropriate application tile.

Touch Tip

On a touch device, tap on the [Word 2013 tile] tile to start the application.

Your screen should be similar to Figure 1

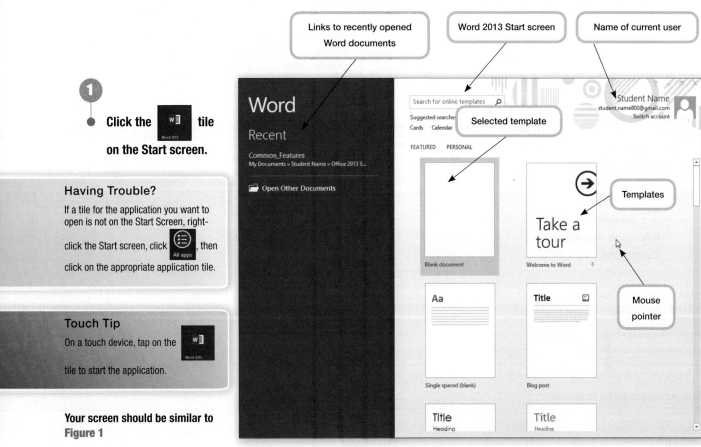

Links to recently opened Word documents

Word 2013 Start screen

Name of current user

Selected template

Templates

Mouse pointer

Figure 1

The Word 2013 program is started and the Start screen is displayed in a window on the desktop. A list of links to recently opened Word documents is displayed in the left column. A gallery of thumbnail images of available templates is displayed in the main window area. A **template** is a professionally designed document that is used as the basis for a new document. The Blank document thumbnail is selected by default and is used to create a new Word document from scratch.

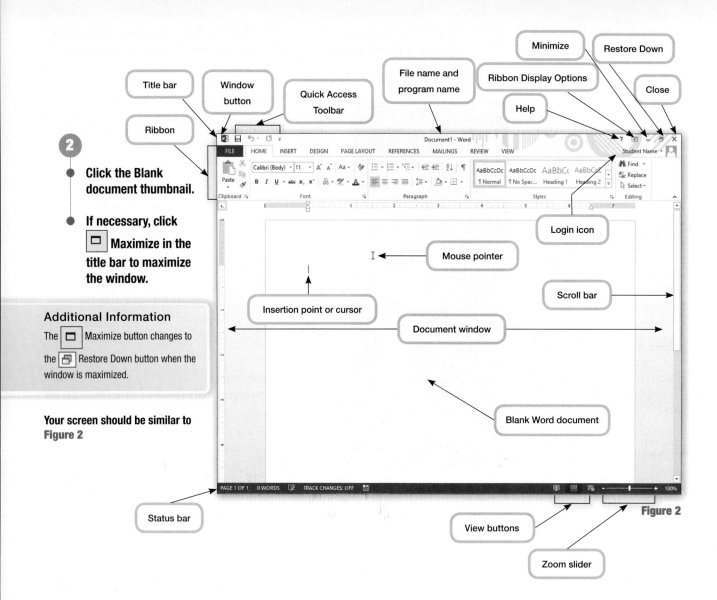

Figure 2

2

- **Click the Blank document thumbnail.**

- **If necessary, click** 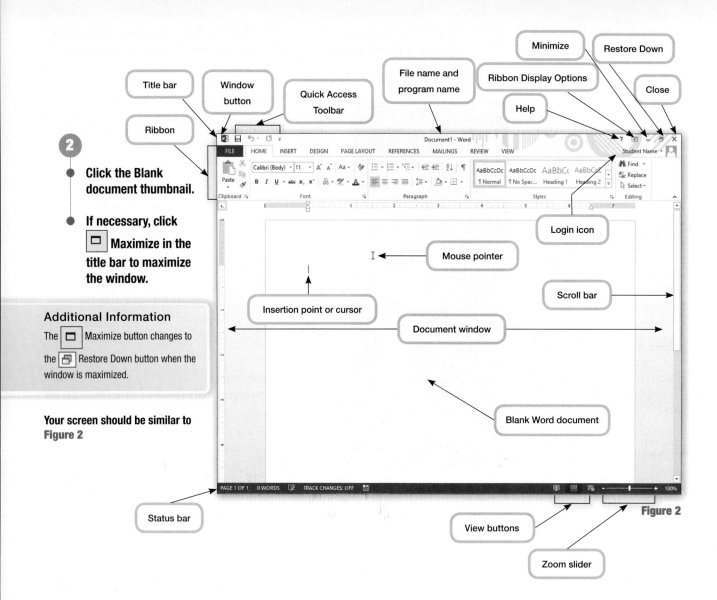 **Maximize in the title bar to maximize the window.**

Additional Information

The ⬜ Maximize button changes to the ⧉ Restore Down button when the window is maximized.

Your screen should be similar to Figure 2

Additional Information

Application windows can be sized, moved, and otherwise manipulated like any other windows on the desktop.

The blank document template is open and displays in the Word 2013 application window. The center of the title bar at the top of the window displays the file name followed by the program name, in this case Word. Both ends of the title bar contain **buttons**, graphical elements that perform the associated action when you click on them using the mouse. At the left end of the title bar is the [W] Window button. Clicking this button opens a menu of commands that allow you to size, move, and close the window. To the right of the [W] Window button is the **Quick Access Toolbar** (QAT), which provides quick access to frequently used commands. By default, it includes the 🖫 Save, ↶ Undo, and ↻ Repeat buttons, commands that Microsoft considers to be crucial. It is always available and is a customizable toolbar to which you can add your own favorite buttons. The right end of the title bar displays five buttons. The [?] Help button accesses the program's Help system. The [⬚] Ribbon Display Options button controls the display of the tabs and ribbon, allowing more content to be displayed in the application window. The last three buttons are shortcuts to the [W] Window button menu commands that are used to size,

Office 2013

move, and close the application window. The buttons on the title bar are the same in all the Office 2013 programs: — Minimize, ⊟ Restore Down/□ Maximize, and ✕ Close.

Below the title bar is the **Ribbon**, which provides a centralized location of commands that are used to work in your document. The Ribbon has the same basic structure and is found in all Office 2013 applications. However, many of the commands found in the Ribbon vary with the specific applications. You will learn how to use the Ribbon shortly. At the right end of the Ribbon is the login icon that indicates if you are logged into Microsoft's online services for file storage and collaboration. It consists of your user name and Microsoft account photo. You can click the photo to adjust your account settings, swap in a new picture, or even switch accounts.

Additional Information

You will learn about opening existing files shortly.

The large center area of the application window is the **document window** where open application files are displayed. In this case, because you selected the Blank document template, a new blank Word document named Document1 (shown in the title bar) is open, ready for you to start creating a new document. In Excel, a new, blank workbook named Book1 would be opened and in PowerPoint a new, blank presentation file named Presentation1 would be opened. In Access, however, a new blank database file is not opened automatically. Instead, you must create and name a new database file or open an existing database file.

The **cursor**, also called the **insertion point**, is the blinking vertical bar that marks your location in the document and indicates where text you type will appear. Across all Office applications, the mouse pointer appears as an I I-beam when it is used to position the insertion point when entering text and as a ⇗ when it can be used to select items. There are many other mouse pointer shapes that are both common to and specific to the different applications.

Additional Information

You will learn about other mouse pointer shapes and what they mean as you use the specific application programs.

On the right of the document window is a vertical scroll bar. A **scroll bar** is used with a mouse to bring additional information into view in a window. The vertical scroll bar is used to move up or down. A horizontal scroll bar is also displayed when needed and moves side to side in the window. The scroll bar is a common feature to all Windows and Office 2013 applications; however, it may not appear in all applications until needed.

At the bottom of the application window is another common feature called the **status bar**. It displays information about the open file and features that help you view the file. It displays different information depending upon the application you are using. For example, the Word status bar displays information about the number of pages and words in the document, whereas the Excel status bar displays the mode of operation and the count, average, and sum of values in selected cells. All Office 2013 applications include **View buttons** that are used to change how the information in the document window is displayed. The View buttons are different for each application. Finally, a **Zoom Slider**, located at the far right end of the status bar, is used to change the amount of information displayed in the document window by "zooming in" to get a close-up view or "zooming out" to see more of the document at a reduced view.

Displaying ScreenTips

You are probably wondering how you would know what action the different buttons perform. To help you identify buttons, the Office applications display Screen-Tips when you point to them.

1

● Point to the 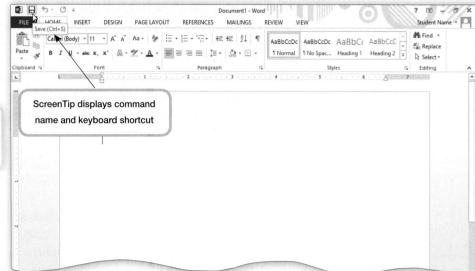 Save button in the Quick Access Toolbar.

Your screen should be similar to Figure 3

ScreenTip displays command name and keyboard shortcut

Figure 3

A **ScreenTip**, also called a **tooltip**, appears displaying the command name and the keyboard shortcut, Ctrl + S. A **keyboard shortcut** is a combination of keys that can be used to execute a command in place of clicking the button. In this case, if you hold down the Ctrl key while typing the letter S, you will access the command to save a file. ScreenTips also often include a brief description of the action a command performs.

Using Menus

Notice the small button ⏷ at the end of the Quick Access Toolbar. Clicking this button opens a menu of commands that perform tasks associated with the Quick Access Toolbar.

1

● Point to the ⏷ button at the end of the Quick Access Toolbar to display the ScreenTip.

● Click ⏷ to open the menu.

Your screen should be similar to Figure 4

Click to open menu

Menu of commands for Quick Access Toolbar

Check indicates feature is on

Figure 4

The first 11 items in the menu allow you to quickly add a command button to or remove a command button from the Quick Access Toolbar. Those commands that are already displayed in the Quick Access Toolbar are preceded with a checkmark.

The last two commands allow you to access other command features to customize the Quick Access Toolbar or change its location.

Once a menu is open, you can select a command from the menu by pointing to it. As you do the selected command appears highlighted. Like buttons, resting the mouse pointer over the menu command options will display a ScreenTip. Then to choose a selected command, you click on it. Choosing a command performs the action associated with the command or button. You will use several of these features next.

2

Point to the commands in the Quick Access Toolbar menu to select (highlight) them and see the ScreenTips.

Click on the Open command to choose it and add it to the Quick Access Toolbar.

Point to the 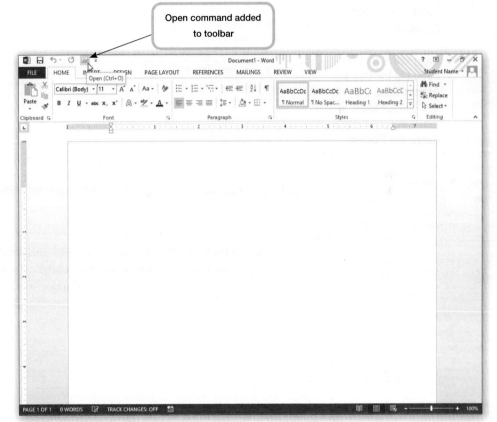 **Open button on the Quick Access Toolbar to display the ScreenTip.**

Your screen should be similar to Figure 5

Open command added to toolbar

Figure 5

The command button to open a document has been added to the Quick Access Toolbar. Next, you will remove this button and then you will change the location of the Quick Access Toolbar. Another way to access some commands is to use a context menu. A **context menu**, also called a **shortcut menu**, is opened by right-clicking on an item on the screen. This menu is context sensitive, meaning it displays only those commands relevant to the item or screen location. For example, right-clicking on the Quick Access Toolbar will display the commands associated with using the Quick Access Toolbar and the Ribbon. You will use this method to remove the Open button and move the Quick Access Toolbar.

3

- Right-click on the 📁 **Open button** on the Quick Access Toolbar to display the context menu.

- Click on the **Remove from Quick Access Toolbar** command to choose it.

- Right-click on any button in the Quick Access Toolbar again and choose **Show Quick Access Toolbar Below the Ribbon**.

Another Method

You also can type the underlined letter of a command to choose it or press [Enter] to choose a selected command.

Your screen should be similar to Figure 6

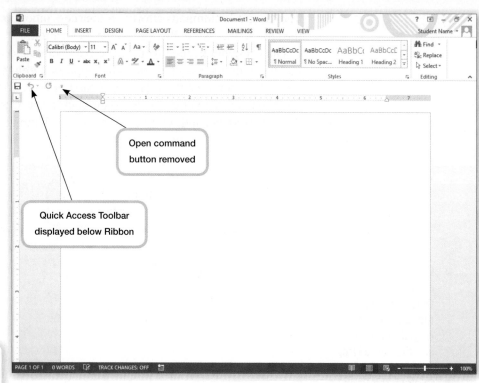

Open command button removed

Quick Access Toolbar displayed below Ribbon

Figure 6

The Quick Access Toolbar is now displayed full size below the Ribbon. This is useful if you have many buttons on the toolbar; however, it takes up document viewing space. You will return it to its compact size.

4

- Display the Quick Access Toolbar menu.

- Choose **Show Above the Ribbon**.

Your screen should be similar to Figure 7

Quick Access Toolbar displayed above Ribbon again

Figure 7

The Quick Access Toolbar is displayed above the Ribbon again.

Using the Ribbon

The Ribbon has three basic parts: tabs, groups, and commands (see Figure 8). **Tabs** are used to divide the Ribbon into major activity areas. Each tab is then organized into **groups** that contain related items. The related items are **commands** that consist of command buttons, a box to enter information, or a menu. Clicking on

IO.20   Introduction to Microsoft Office 2013   WWW.MHHE.COM/OLEARY

Office 2013

a command button performs the associated action or displays a list of additional options.

The Ribbon tabs, commands, and features vary with the different Office applications. For example, the Word Ribbon displays tabs and commands used to create a text document, whereas the Excel Ribbon displays tabs and commands used to create an electronic worksheet. Although the Ribbon commands are application specific, many are also common to all Office 2013 applications. In all applications, the Ribbon also can be customized by changing the built-in tabs or creating your own tabs and groups to personalize your workspace and provide faster access to the commands you use most.

Opening Tabs

The Word application displays the File tab and eight Ribbon tabs. The Home tab (shown in Figure 7), consists of five groups. The tab name appears in blue and is outlined, indicating it is the open or active tab. This tab is available in all the Office 2013 applications and because it contains commands that are most frequently used when you first start an application or open a file, it is initially the open tab. In Word, the commands in the Home tab help you perform actions related to creating the text content of your document. In the other Office 2013 applications, the Home tab contains commands related to creating the associated type of document, such as a worksheet, presentation, or database. To open another tab you click on the tab name.

Additional Information

Because the Ribbon can adapt to the screen resolution and orientation, your Ribbon may look slightly different. Additionally, the Ribbon may display an Add-Ins tab if your application setup specifies that add-in applications be made available in the Add-Ins tab.

Additional Information

The File tab is not a Ribbon tab. You will learn about the File tab shortly.

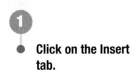

1

Click on the Insert tab.

Your screen should be similar to Figure 8

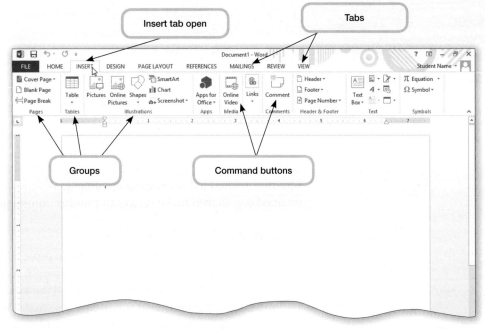

Figure 8

This Insert tab is now open and is the active tab. It contains 10 groups whose commands have to do with inserting items into a document. As you use the Office applications, you will see that the Ribbon contains many of the same tabs, groups, and commands across the applications. For example, the Insert tab is available in all applications except Access. Others, such as the References tab in Word, are specific to the application. You also will see that many of the groups and commands in the common tabs, such as the Clipboard group of commands in the Home tab, contain all or many of the same commands across applications. Other groups in the common tabs contain commands that are specific to the application.

To save space, some tabs, called **contextual tabs** or **on-demand tabs**, are displayed only as needed. For example, when you are working with a picture, the Picture Tools tab appears. The contextual nature of this feature keeps the work area uncluttered when the feature is not needed and provides ready access to it when it is needed.

2

● **Click on each of the other tabs, ending with the View tab, to see their groups and commands.**

Additional Information

If you have a mouse with a scroll wheel, pointing to the tab area of the Ribbon and using the scroll wheel will scroll the tabs.

Touch Tip

On a touch device you can swipe the Ribbon tab to scroll the tabs.

Your screen should be similar to Figure 9

Figure 9

Each tab relates to a type of activity; for example, the View tab commands perform activities related to viewing the document. Within each tab, similar commands are grouped together to make it easy to find the commands you want to use.

Displaying Enhanced ScreenTips

Although command buttons display graphic representations of the action they perform, often the graphic is not descriptive enough. As you have learned, pointing to a button displays the name of the button and the keyboard shortcut in a ScreenTip. To further help explain what a button does, many buttons in the Ribbon display **Enhanced ScreenTips**. For example, the ⬛ button in the Clipboard group of the Home tab is a two-part button. Clicking on the upper part will immediately perform an action, whereas clicking on the lower part will display additional options. You will use this feature next to see the Enhanced ScreenTips.

WWW.MHHE.COM/OLEARY

Office 2013

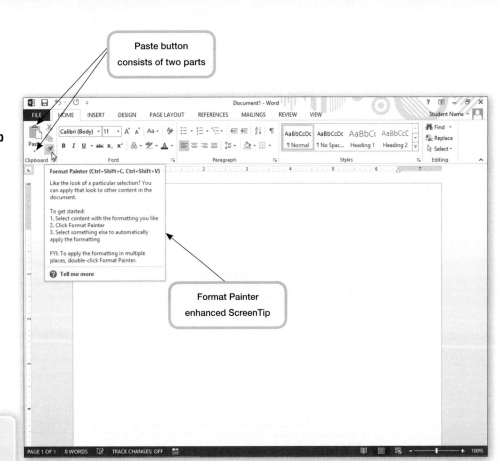

Paste button
consists of two parts

1

- **Click on the Home tab to open it.**

- **Point to the upper part of the ⬚ Paste button in the Clipboard group.**

- **Point to the lower part of the Paste button in the Clipboard group.**

- **Point to ✨ Format Painter in the Clipboard group.**

Additional Information

Depending upon your screen resolution and size, the ✨ button may appear as ✨ Format Painter.

Your screen should be similar to Figure 10

Figure 10

Additional Information

Not all commands have keyboard shortcuts.

Additional Information

You will learn about using Help shortly.

Touch Tip

On a touch device, it may be difficult to touch the arrow only. To add space between buttons, turn on Touch Mode from the Quick Access toolbar.

Because the ⬚ Paste button is divided into two parts, both parts display separate Enhanced ScreenTips containing the button name; the keyboard shortcut key combination, Ctrl + V; and a brief description of what action will be performed when you click on that part of the button. Pointing to ✨ Format Painter displays an Enhanced ScreenTip that provides more detailed information about the command including steps on how to use the feature. Enhanced ScreenTips help you find out what the feature does without having to look it up using Office Help, a built-in reference source. If a feature has a Help article, you can automatically access it by pressing F1 while the Enhanced ScreenTip is displayed or by choosing "Tell me more."

Using Command Buttons

Clicking on most command buttons immediately performs the associated action. Some command buttons, however, include an arrow as part of the button that affects how the button works. If a button includes an arrow that is separated from the graphic with a line when you point to the button (as in ⋮≡ ▾ Bullets), clicking the button performs the associated default action and clicking the arrow displays a menu of options. If a button displays an arrow that is not separated from the graphic with a line when you point to it (as in ⫟≡ ▾ Line and Paragraph Spacing), clicking the button immediately displays a menu of options. To see an example of a drop-down menu, you will open the ⋮≡ ▾ Bullets menu.

1

Click ▾ in the ▤ ▾
Bullets button.

Your screen should be similar to
Figure 11

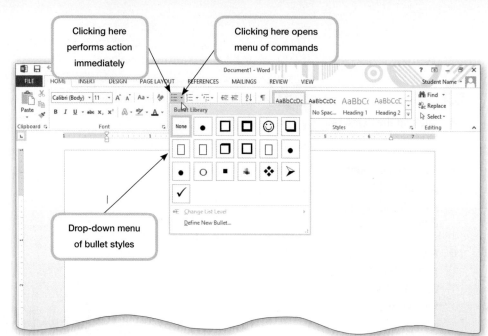

Clicking here
performs action
immediately

Clicking here opens
menu of commands

Drop-down menu
of bullet styles

Figure 11

A drop-down menu of different bullet styles is displayed. The drop-down menu
will disappear when you make a selection or click on any other area of the window.

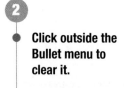

2

Click outside the
Bullet menu to
clear it.

Click ▤ ▾ Line and
Paragraph Spacing.

Your screen should be similar to
Figure 12

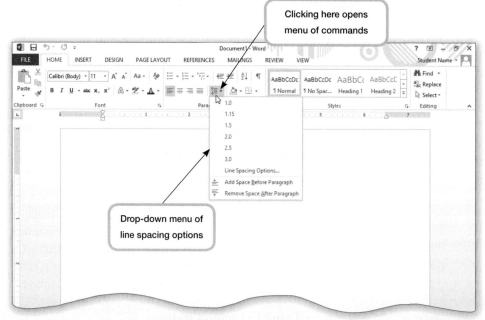

Clicking here opens
menu of commands

Drop-down menu of
line spacing options

Figure 12

Another Method

You also can open tabs and choose
Ribbon commands using the access key
shortcuts. Press Alt or F10 to display
the access key letters in KeyTips over
each available feature. Then type the
letter for the feature you want to use.

The menu of options opened automatically when you clicked ▤ ▾ Line and Paragraph Spacing.

Using the Dialog Box Launcher

Because there is not enough space, only the most used commands are displayed in the Ribbon. If more commands are available, a ⬜ button, called the **dialog box launcher**, is displayed in the lower-right corner of the group. Clicking ⬜ opens a dialog box or task pane of additional options.

1

Click outside the Line and Paragraph Spacing menu to clear it.

Point to the ⬜ of the Paragraph group to see the ScreenTip.

Click ⬜ of the Paragraph group.

Your screen should be similar to Figure 13

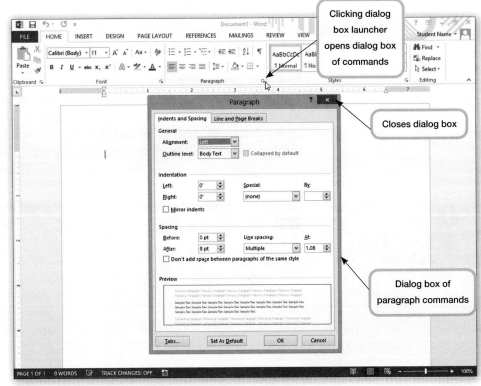

Figure 13

The Paragraph dialog box appears. It provides access to the more advanced paragraph settings options. Selecting options from the dialog box and clicking OK will close the dialog box and apply the options as specified. To cancel the dialog box, you can click Cancel or ✕ Close in the dialog box title bar.

2

Click ✕ to close the dialog box.

Click ⬜ in the Clipboard group.

Your screen should be similar to Figure 14

Figure 14

A **task pane** is open (see Figure 14) that contains features associated with the Clipboard. Unlike a dialog box, a task pane is a separate window that can be sized and moved. Generally, task panes are attached or docked to one edge of the application window. Also, task panes remain open until you close them. This allows you to make multiple selections from the task pane while continuing to work on other areas of your document.

● Click ✕ Close in the upper-right corner of the task pane to close it.

Collapse and Expand the Ribbon

Currently, the entire Ribbon is pinned in place in the application window. Sometimes you may not want to see the entire Ribbon so that more space is available in the document area. To do this, you can collapse the Ribbon to minimize it to display the tabs only by double-clicking the active tab.

● **Double-click the Home tab.**

Your screen should be similar to Figure 15

Ribbon hidden except for tabs

Figure 15

Now, the only part of the Ribbon that is visible is the tab area. Then, to access the entire Ribbon while you are working, simply single-click on any tab and the Ribbon reappears temporarily. It collapses again as you continue to work. To permanently expand the Ribbon, simply double-click on the tab you want to make active and the Ribbon is again fully displayed.

● **Click on the Insert tab.**

● **Click in the document window.**

● **Double-click the Home tab.**

● **Click in the document window.**

The full Ribbon reappears and remains fixed in place and the Home tab is active.

Using the Office Backstage

To the left of the Home tab in the Ribbon is the File tab. Unlike the other tabs that display a Ribbon of commands, the File tab opens the Office Backstage. The Office **Backstage** contains commands that allow you to work *with* your document, unlike the Ribbon that allows you to work *in* your document. The Backstage contains commands that apply to the entire document. For example, you will find commands to open, save, print, and manage your files and set your program options. The File tab is common to all the Office 2013 applications, although the options may vary slightly.

1

● **Click the File tab to open the Backstage.**

● **Click Info in the list of sidebar options.**

Your screen should be similar to Figure 16

Figure 16

The Backstage window is open and completely covers the application window. The left side of the window displays a list of options in a sidebar. Pointing to an option selects it and it appears highlighted. Clicking an option chooses it and displays related commands and features in the right side. Choosing some options opens a dialog box or immediately performs the associated action. The last two options in the sidebar are used to change account and program settings.

Another Method

You also can use the directional keys to move up, down, left, or right within Backstage and press (Enter) to choose a selected option or command.

The Info window is open and displays information about the current document. The three command buttons are used to control changes that can be made to the document, check for issues related to distribution, and manage document versions for the current document. A description of these buttons and the current document settings is shown to the right of the button. Notice that the buttons display a ⬇. This indicates that a menu of commands will be displayed when you click the button. The right side of the window displays a list of settings, called **properties**, associated with the document. The current properties displayed in the Info window show the initial or **default** properties associated with a new blank document.

Additional Information

You will learn more about document properties shortly.

● Click [Protect Document] to open the menu.

● **Point to Restrict Access.**

Your screen should be similar to Figure 17

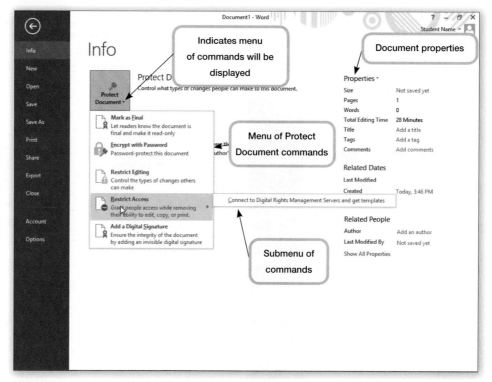

Figure 17

The highlighted command displays a submenu of additional commands. Next, you will clear the Protect Document menu and open the New window in Backstage.

New window displays options to create new documents

Template files

Figure 18

3
● Click [Protect Document] again to clear the submenu.

● Click the New option in the sidebar.

Your screen should be similar to Figure 18

The Backstage window now displays options for creating a new document. It is very similar to the Start screen that appears when you first start Word 2013.

4
● Click [←] at the top of the sidebar.

Another Method
You also can press [Esc] to close the Backstage window.

Backstage is closed and the document window is displayed again.

COMMON APPLICATION FEATURES

So far you have learned about using the Office 2013 user interface features. Next, you will learn about application features that are used to work in and modify documents and are the same or similar in all Office 2013 applications. These include how to open, close, and save files; navigate, scroll, and zoom a document; enter, select, edit, and format text; and document, preview, and print a file. To do this, you will open a Word document file and make a few changes to it. Then you will save and print the revised document. Once you have gained an understanding of the basic concepts of the common features using Word, you will be able to easily apply them in the other Office applications.

Opening a File

In all Office 2013 applications, you either need to create a new file using the blank document template or another template or open an existing file. Opening a file retrieves a file that is stored on your computer hard drive or an external storage location and places it in RAM (random-access memory) of your computer so it can be read and modified.

1

- **Click the File tab to open the Backstage.**

- **Click the Open option in the sidebar.**

Your screen should be similar to Figure 19

Figure 19

The left side of the Open window displays locations where the file you want to open is stored. The location may be the hard drive of your computer, an external storage device, a local network, or in the cloud on SkyDrive or SharePoint. The **cloud** refers to any applications and services that are hosted and run on servers connected to the Internet. The Recent Documents option is selected by default and displays a list of file names of documents that have been recently opened in Word 2013 in the Recent Documents pane. Below the file name the path location of the file is displayed. If the file you want to open appears in the Recent Documents list, clicking on the file immediately opens it.

First you need to change to the location where your data files for completing these labs are stored.

Additional Information

Microsoft SkyDrive and SharePoint are subscription file storage services that you can access anytime you are online.

WWW.MHHE.COM/OLEARY

2

● **Click on**

 ☐ Computer **in the**

locations section.

● **Click** [Browse].

Your screen should be similar to
Figure 20

Figure 20

The Open dialog box is displayed in which you specify the location where the file you want to open is stored and the file name. The location consists of identifying the hard drive of your computer or an external storage device or a remote computer followed by folders and subfolders within that location. The Address bar displays the default folder as the location to open the file. The file list displays folder names as well as the names of any Word documents in the current location. Only Word documents are listed because All Word Documents is the specified file type in the File Type list box. In Excel and PowerPoint, only files of that application's file type would be displayed.

There are several methods that can be used to locate files. One is to use the Address bar to specify another location by either typing the complete folder name or path or by opening the drop-down list of previously accessed locations and clicking a new location. Another is to use the features in the Navigation pane, to choose a link to a Favorite item or location, to search the folders and files in the Libraries or to navigate through the hierarchical structure of drives and folders on your computer. Clicking a link or folder from the list displays files at that location in the file list. Then, from the file list, you can continue to select subfolders until the file you want to open is located.

You will open the file IO_Common Features that is supplied with your student data files for this lab.

3

- Change to the location where your student data files for this lab are located.

Having Trouble?

The text assumes the location is on your computer in a folder named Introduction to Office. If your files are in a different location, your instructor will provide further directions.

Your screen should be similar to **Figure 21**

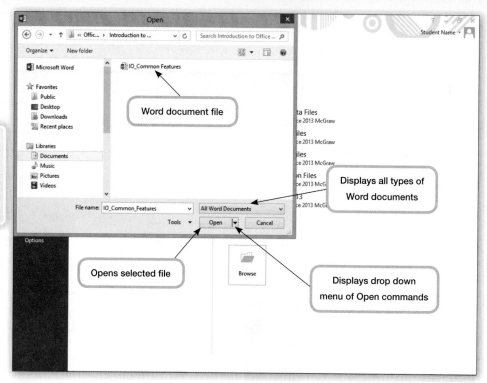

Word document file

Displays all types of Word documents

Opens selected file

Displays drop down menu of Open commands

Figure 21

Now the file list displays the names of all Word files at that location. Next, you open the file by clicking on the file name to select it and clicking the [Open ▾] button. In addition, in the Office applications you can specify how you want to open a file by choosing from the [Open ▾] drop-down menu options described in the following table.

Open Options	Description
Open	Opens with all formatting and editing features enabled. This is the default setting.
Open Read-only	Opens file so it can be read or copied only, not modified in any way.
Open as Copy	Automatically creates a copy of the file and opens the copy with complete editing capabilities.
Open in Browser	Opens HTML type files in a web browser.
Open with Transform	Opens certain types of documents and lets you change it into another type of document.
Open in Protected View	Opens files from potentially unsafe locations with editing functions disabled.
Open and Repair	Opens file and attempts to repair any damage.

Another Method

You could also press [Enter] to open a selected file or double-click on the file name.

You will open the file IO_Common Features. Clicking the [Open ▾] button opens the file using the default Open option so you can read and edit the file.

4

● **Select** IO_Common Features.

● **Click** `Open ▼`.

Your screen should be similar to Figure 22

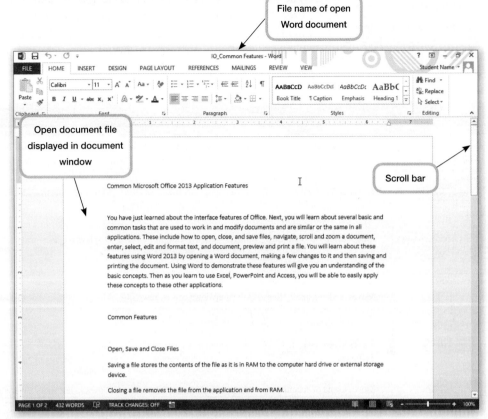

File name of open Word document

Open document file displayed in document window

Scroll bar

Figure 22

A Word document file describing the common Microsoft Office application features is displayed in the document window.

Scrolling the Document Window

As documents increase in size, they cannot be easily viewed in their entirety in the document window and much time can be spent moving to different locations in the document. All Office 2013 applications include features that make it easy to move around and view the information in a large document. The basic method is to scroll through a document using the scroll bar or keyboard. Both methods are useful, depending on what you are doing. For example, if you are entering text using the keyboard, using the keyboard method may be more efficient than using the mouse.

Additional Information

Scroll bars are also found in task panes and dialog boxes and operate similarly.

Touch Tip

With a touch device, you can touch the document and slide it up and down.

The table below explains the basic mouse and keyboard techniques that can be used to vertically scroll a document in the Office 2013 applications. There are many other methods for navigating through documents that are unique to an application. They will be discussed in the specific application text.

Mouse or Key Action	Effect in:			
	Word	Excel	PowerPoint	Access
Click ▼ Or ↓	Moves down line by line.	Moves down row by row	Moves down slide by slide	Moves down record by record
Click ▲ Or ↑	Moves up line by line.	Moves up row by row	Moves up slide by slide	Moves up record by record
Click above/below scroll box Or Page Up / Page Down	Moves up/down window by window	Moves up/down window by window	Displays previous/next slide	Moves up/down window by window
Drag Scroll Box	Moves up/down line by line	Moves up/down row by row	Moves up/down slide by slide	Moves up/down record by record
Ctrl + Home	Moves to beginning of document	Moves to first cell in worksheet or beginning of cell entry	Moves to first slide in presentation or beginning of entry in placeholder	Moves to first record in table or beginning of field entry
Ctrl + End	Moves to end of document	Moves to last-used cell in worksheet or end of cell entry	Moves to last slide in presentation or to end of placeholder entry	Moves to last record in table or end of field entry

You will use the vertical scroll bar to view the text at the bottom of the Word document. When you use the scroll bar to scroll, the actual location in the document where you can work does not change, only the area you are viewing changes. For example, in Word, the cursor does not move and in Excel the cell you can work in does not change. To move the cursor or make another cell active, you must click in a location in the window. However, when you scroll using the keyboard, the actual location as identified by the position of the cursor in the document also changes. For example, in Word the cursor attempts to maintain its position in a line as you scroll up and down through the document. In Excel the cell you can work in changes as you move through a worksheet using the keyboard.

Click [▼] **in the vertical scroll bar 10 times.**

Click at the beginning of the word Scroll in the Common Features section to move the cursor.

Press [↓] **10 times to scroll the window and move the cursor down 10 lines.**

Your screen should be similar to Figure 23

Cursor moves when scrolling using the keyboard

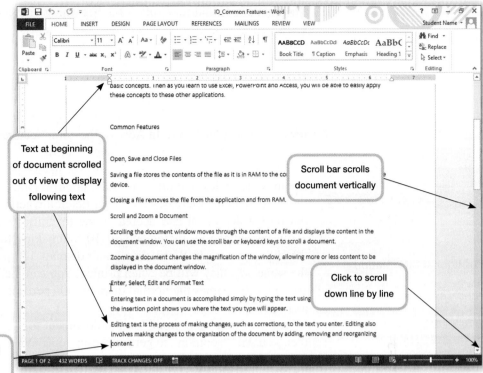

Text at beginning of document scrolled out of view to display following text

Scroll bar scrolls document vertically

Click to scroll down line by line

Figure 23

Having Trouble?

If your screen scrolls differently, this is a function of the type of monitor you are using.

The text at the beginning of the document has scrolled line by line off the top of the document window, and the following text is now displayed. In a large document, scrolling line by line can take a while. You will now try out several additional mouse and keyboard scrolling features that move by larger increments through the document.

Click below the scroll box in the scroll bar.

Press [Ctrl] + [End] **to move to the end of the last line of the document.**

Drag the scroll box to the top of the scroll bar.

Your screen should be similar to Figure 24

Cursor still on page 2 at end of document because it does not move when scrolling using the scroll bar

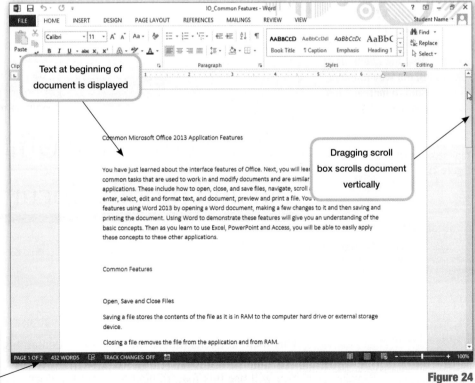

Text at beginning of document is displayed

Dragging scroll box scrolls document vertically

Figure 24

The document window displays the beginning of the document; however, the cursor is still on page 2 at the end of the document. Using these features makes scrolling a large document much more efficient.

Using the Zoom Feature

Another way to see more or less of a document is to use the zoom feature. Although this feature is available in all Office 2013 applications, Excel and PowerPoint have fewer options than Word. In Access, the zoom feature is available only when specific features are used, such as viewing reports.

The Zoom Slider in the status bar is used to change the magnification. To use the Zoom Slider, click and drag the slider control. Dragging to the right zooms in on the document and increases the magnification whereas dragging to the left zooms out on the document and decreases the magnification. You also can change the zoom percentage by increments of 10 by clicking the ➕ or ➖ on each end of the slider control. In Word, the default display, 100 percent, shows the characters the same size they will be when printed. You can increase the onscreen character size up to five times the normal display (500 percent) or reduce the character size to 10 percent.

You will first "zoom out" on the document to get an overview of the file, and then you will "zoom in" to get a close-up look. When a document is zoomed, you can work in it as usual.

Touch Tip

With a touch device, you can zoom in by stretching two fingers apart and zoom out by pinching two fingers together.

Additional Information

The degree of magnification varies with the different applications.

1

- Click ➖ in the Zoom Slider five times to decrease the zoom percentage to 50%.

- Press Ctrl + Home to move the cursor to the beginning of the document.

- Drag the Zoom Slider all the way to the right to increase the zoom to 500%.

Your screen should be similar to Figure 25

Current zoom percent enlarges characters 500%

Click to increase or decrease percent in 10% increments

Drag Zoom Slider to change percentage

Figure 25

Another Method

You can also hold down Ctrl while using the scroll wheel on your mouse to zoom a document.

Another Method

You can also click on the zoom percentage in the status bar to open the Zoom dialog box.

Another way to change the magnification is to use the 🔍 button in the View tab. This method opens the Zoom dialog box containing several preset zoom options, or an option that lets you set a precise percentage using the Percent scroll box. You will use this feature next to zoom the document. This method is available in Word only.

2

● Open the View tab.

● Click 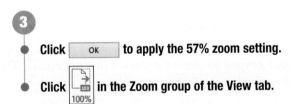 in the Zoom group.

● Click Whole Page and note that the percent value in the Percent text box and the preview area reflect the new percentage setting.

● Click the ▲ scroll button in the Percent scroll box to increase the zoom percentage to 57.

Another Method

You could also type a value in the Percent text box to specify an exact percentage.

Your screen should be similar to Figure 26

Figure 26

The Zoom dialog box preview areas show how the document will appear on your screen at the specified zoom percent. Not until you complete the command by clicking OK will the zoom percent in the document actually change. You will complete the command to apply the 57% zoom setting. Then, you will use the button in the Zoom group to quickly return to the default zoom setting.

3

● Click OK to apply the 57% zoom setting.

● Click in the Zoom group of the View tab.

The document is again at 100% magnification.

Entering and Editing Text

Touch Tip

With a touch device, a Touch keyboard appears when needed to enter text.

Now that you are familiar with the entire document, you will make a few changes to it. The keyboard is used to enter information into a document. In all applications, the location of the cursor shows you where the text will appear as you type. After text is entered into a document, you need to know how to move around within the text to edit or make changes to the text. Again, the process is similar for all Office applications.

Additional Information

The effect of pressing Enter varies in the different Office applications. For example, in Excel, it completes the entry and moves to another cell. You will learn about these differences in the individual application labs.

Currently, in this Word document, the cursor is positioned at the top of the document. You will type your name at this location. As you type, the cursor moves to the right and the characters will appear to the left of the cursor. Then you will press Enter to end the line following your name and press Enter again at the beginning of a line to insert a blank line.

● **Type your first and last name.**

● **Press** Enter **two times.**

Your screen should be similar to Figure 27

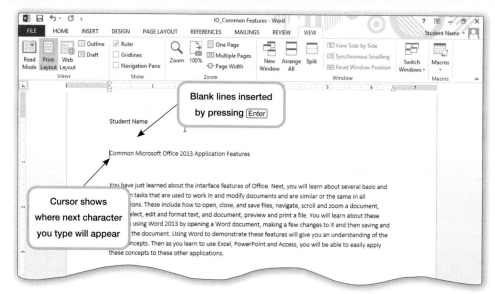

Blank lines inserted by pressing Enter

Student Name

Common Microsoft Office 2013 Application Features

Cursor shows where next character you type will appear

You have just learned about the interface features of Office. Next, you will learn about several basic and ... tasks that are used to work in and modify documents and are similar or the same in all ...ions. These include how to open, close, and save files, navigate, scroll and zoom a document, ...elect, edit and format text, and document, preview and print a file. You will learn about these ... using Word 2013 by opening a Word document, making a few changes to it and then saving and ... the document. Using Word to demonstrate these features will give you an understanding of the ...ncepts. Then as you learn to use Excel, PowerPoint and Access, you will be able to easily apply these concepts to these other applications.

Figure 27

Additional Information

You can use the directional keys on the numeric keypad or the dedicated directional keypad area. If using the numeric keypad, make sure the Num Lock feature is off; otherwise, numbers will be entered in the document. The Num Lock indicator light above the keypad is lit when on. Press Num Lock to turn it off.

Touch Tip

With a touch device, tap in the text to place the cursor.

As you typed your name, to make space for the text on the line, the existing text moved to the right. Then, when you pressed Enter the first time, all the text following your name moved down one line. A blank line was inserted after pressing Enter the second time.

Next, you want to add a word to the first line of the first paragraph. To do this, you first need to move the cursor to the location where you want to make the change. The keyboard or mouse can be used to move through the text in the document window. Depending on what you are doing, one method may be more efficient than another. For example, if your hands are already on the keyboard as you are entering text, it may be quicker to use the keyboard rather than take your hands off to use the mouse.

You use the mouse to move the cursor to a specific location in a document simply by clicking on the location. When you can use the mouse to move the cursor, the mouse pointer is shaped as an I I-beam. You use the arrow keys located on the numeric keypad or the directional keypad to move the cursor in a document. The keyboard directional keys are described in the following table.

Key	Word/PowerPoint	Excel	Access
→	Right one character	Right one cell	Right one field
←	Left one character	Left one cell	Left one field
↑	Up one line	Up one cell	Up one record
↓	Down one line	Down one cell	Down one record
Ctrl + →	Right one word	Last cell in row	One word to right in a field entry
Ctrl + ←	Left one word	First cell in row	One word to left in a field entry
Home	Beginning of line	First cell in row	First field of record
End	End of line		Last field of record

In the first line of the first paragraph, you want to add the word "basic" before the word "interface" and the year "2013" after the word "Office." You will move to the correct locations using both the keyboard and the mouse and then enter the new text.

Additional Information

Many of the keyboard keys and key combinations have other effects depending on the mode of operation at the time they are used. You will learn about these differences in the specific application labs as they are used.

- **Click at the beginning of the word You in the first paragraph.**

- **Press → four times to move to the beginning of the second word.**

- **Press Ctrl + → five times to move to the beginning of the seventh word.**

Additional Information

Holding down a directional key or key combination moves quickly in the direction indicated, saving multiple presses of the key.

- **Type basic and press Spacebar.**

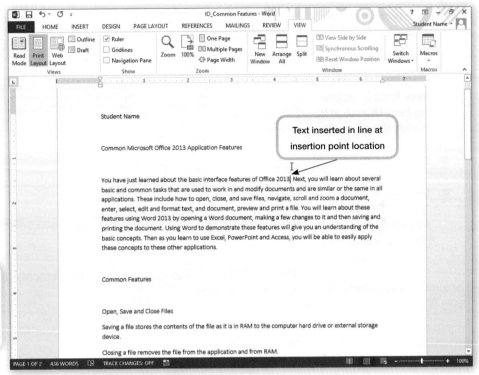

Figure 28

Having Trouble?

Do not be concerned if you make a typing error; you will learn how to correct them next.

- **Position the I-beam between the e in Office and the period at the end of the first sentence and click.**

- **Press Spacebar and type 2013**

Your screen should be similar to Figure 28

Next, you want to edit the text you just entered by changing the word "basic" to "common." Removing typing entries to change or correct them is one of the basic editing tasks. Corrections may be made in many ways. Two of the most basic editing keys that are common to the Office applications are the Backspace and Delete keys. The Backspace key removes a character or space to the left of the cursor. It is particularly useful when you are moving from right to left (backward) along a line of text. The Delete key removes the character or space to the right of the cursor and is most useful when moving from left to right along a line.

You will use these features as you make the correction.

③

- Move the cursor between the s and i in "basic" (in the first sentence).

- Press [Delete] two times to remove the two characters to the right of the insertion point.

- Press [Backspace] three times to remove the three characters to the left of the cursor.

- Type common

- Correct any other typing errors you may have made using [Backspace] or [Delete].

Your screen should be similar to Figure 29

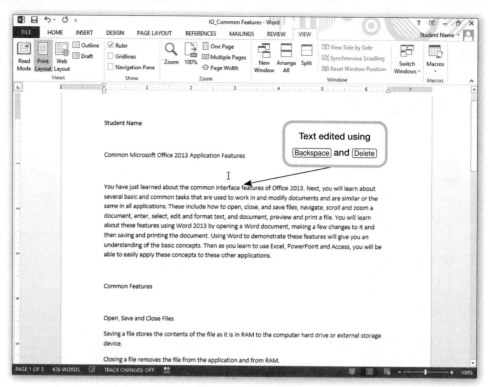

Figure 29

The word "basic" was deleted from the sentence and the word "common" was entered in its place.

Selecting Text

While editing and formatting a document, you will need to select text. Selecting highlights text and identifies the text that will be affected by your next action. To select text using the mouse, first move the cursor to the beginning or end of the text to be selected, and then drag to highlight the text you want selected. You can select as little as a single letter or as much as the entire document. You also can select text using keyboard features. The following table summarizes common mouse and keyboard techniques used to select text in Word.

To Select	Mouse	Keyboard
Next/previous space or character	Drag across space or character.	[Shift] + [→]/[Shift] + [←]
Next/previous word	Double-click in the word.	[Ctrl] + [Shift] + [→]/[Ctrl] + [Shift] + [←]
Sentence	Press [Ctrl] and click within the sentence.	
Line	Click to the left of a line when the mouse pointer is ⇗.	
Multiple lines	Drag up or down to the left of a line when the mouse pointer is ⇗.	
Text going backward to beginning of paragraph	Drag left and up to the beginning of the paragraph when the mouse pointer is ⇗.	[Ctrl] + [Shift] + [↑]
Text going forward to end of paragraph	Drag right and down to the end of the paragraph when the mouse pointer is ⇗.	[Ctrl] + [Shift] + [↓]
Paragraph	Triple-click on the paragraph or double-click to the left of the paragraph when the mouse pointer is ⇗.	
Multiple paragraphs	Drag to the left of the paragraphs when the mouse pointer is ⇗.	
Document	Triple-click or press [Ctrl] and click to the left of the text when the mouse pointer is ⇗.	[Ctrl] + A

Having Trouble?

If you accidentally select the incorrect text, simply click anywhere in the document or press any directional key to clear the selection and try again.

You want to change the word "tasks" in the next sentence to "application features". Although you could use Delete and Backspace to remove the unneeded text character by character, it will be faster to select and delete the word. First you will try out several of the keyboard techniques to select text. Then you will use several mouse features to select text and finally you will edit the sentence.

1

- Move the cursor to the beginning of the word "basic" in the second sentence.

- Press Shift + → five times to select the word basic.

- Press Shift + Ctrl + → to extend the selection word by word until the entire line is selected.

- Press Shift + Ctrl + ↓ to extend the selection to the end of the paragraph.

Your screen should be similar to Figure 30

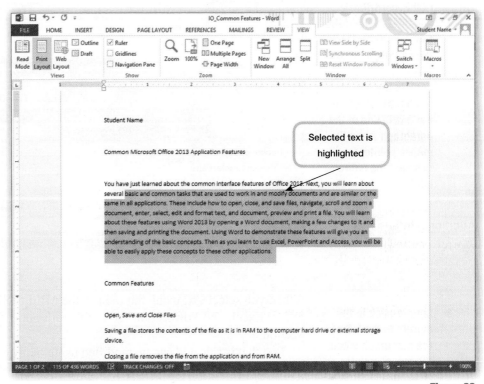

Figure 30

The text from the cursor to the end of the paragraph is selected. Next, you will clear this selection and then use the mouse to select text.

2

- Click anywhere in the paragraph to clear the selection.

- Click at the beginning of the word "basic" and drag to the right to select the text to the end of the line.

- Click in the left margin to the left of the fourth line of the paragraph when the mouse pointer is 𝒜 to select the entire line.

Additional Information

When positioned in the left margin, the mouse pointer shape changes to 𝒜, indicating it is ready to select text.

- Double-click in the margin to the left of the paragraph when the mouse pointer is 𝒜 to select the paragraph.

Your screen should be similar to Figure 31

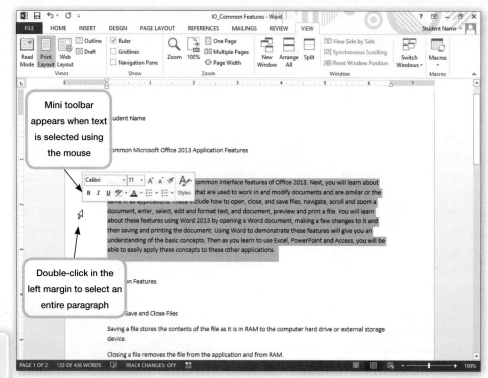

Figure 31

When you select text using the mouse, the **Mini toolbar** appears automatically in Word, Excel, and PowerPoint. You will learn about using this feature in the next section.

Text that is selected can be modified using many different features. In this case, you want to replace the word "tasks" in the second sentence with "application features".

3

- Double-click on the word "tasks" in the second sentence.

- Type **application features**

Your screen should be similar to Figure 32

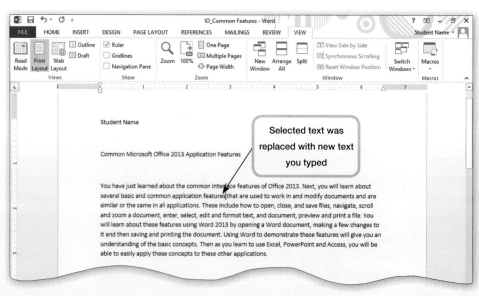

Figure 32

As soon as you began typing, the selected text was automatically deleted. The new text was inserted in the line by pushing the existing text to the right. Any text that could not fit on the line moved to the beginning of the next line. This is the **word wrap** feature. Although this feature is used mostly in Word, it is also used in the other applications.

Formatting Text

An important aspect of all documents you create using Office 2013 is the appearance of the document. To improve the appearance you can apply many different formatting effects. The most common formatting features are font and character effects. A **font**, also commonly referred to as a **typeface**, is a set of characters with a specific design. The designs have names such as Times New Roman and Courier. Each font has one or more sizes. **Font size** is the height and width of the character and is commonly measured in points, abbreviated "pt." One point equals about 1/72 inch. **Character effects** are enhancements such as bold, italic, and color that are applied to selected text. Using font and character effects as design elements can add interest to your document and give readers visual cues to help them find information quickly.

First you want to change the font and increase the font size of the title of this document.

1

- **Click in the left margin next to the title line when the mouse pointer is** ⇗ **to select it.**

- **Open the Home tab.**

- **Open the** Calibri **Font drop-down menu in the Font group.**

- **Point to the Arial Black font option in the menu.**

Your screen should be similar to Figure 33

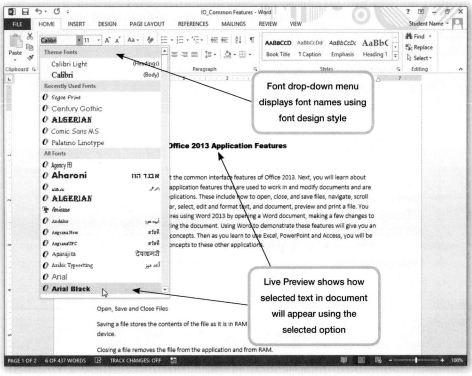

Figure 33

As you point to the font options, the **Live Preview** feature shows you how the selected text in the document will appear if this option is chosen.

2

- Point to several different fonts in the menu to see the Live Preview.

- Scroll the menu and click Segoe Print to choose it.

Additional Information

Font names are listed in alphabetical order.

Having Trouble?

If this font is not available on your computer, choose a similar font.

Figure 34

Your screen should be similar to
Figure 34

The title appears in the selected font and the name of the font used in the selection is displayed in the Segoe Print ▾ Font button. Next you want to increase the font size. The current (default) font size of 11 is displayed in the 11 ▾ Font Size button. You will increase the font size to 16 points.

3

- Open the 11 ▾ Font Size drop-down menu in the Font group of the Home tab.

- Point to several different font sizes to see the Live Preview.

- Click 16 to choose it.

Another Method

The keyboard shortcut is
Ctrl + Shift + P.

Figure 35

Your screen should be similar to
Figure 35

Touch Tip

With a touch device, tap on the selected text, then tap on the formatting option.

Now the title stands out much more from the other text in the document. Next you will use the Mini toolbar to add formatting to other areas of the document. As you saw earlier, the Mini toolbar appears automatically when you select text. Initially the Mini toolbar appears dimmed (semi-transparent) so that it does not interfere with what you are doing, but it changes to solid when you point at it. It displays command buttons for often-used commands from the Font and Paragraph groups that are used to format a document.

4

- Select the line "Common Features" and point to the Mini toolbar.

- Click [11 ▼] Font Size and choose 14.

- Click **B** Bold.

- Click *I* Italic.

- Click U Underline.

Your screen should be similar to Figure 36

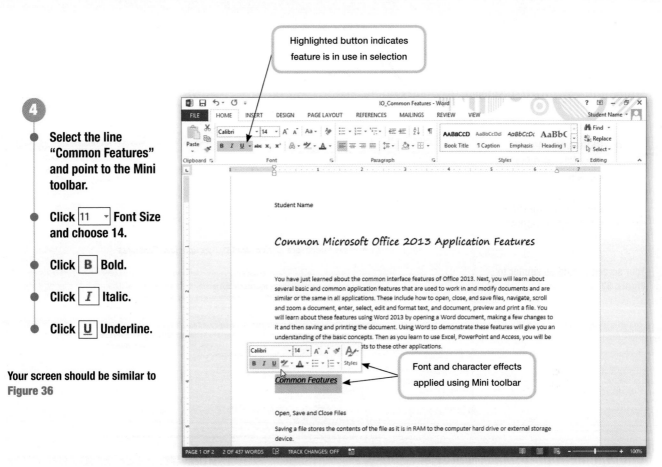

Highlighted button indicates feature is in use in selection

Font and character effects applied using Mini toolbar

Figure 36

The increase in font size as well as the text effects makes this topic heading much more prominent. Notice the command button for each selected effect is highlighted, indicating the feature is in use in the selection.

Using the Mini toolbar is particularly useful when the Home tab is closed because you do not need to reopen the Home tab to access the commands. It remains available until you clear the selection or press [Esc]. If you do nothing with a selection for a while, the Mini toolbar will disappear. To redisplay it simply right-click on the selection again. This will also open the context menu.

You will remove the underline effect from the selection next.

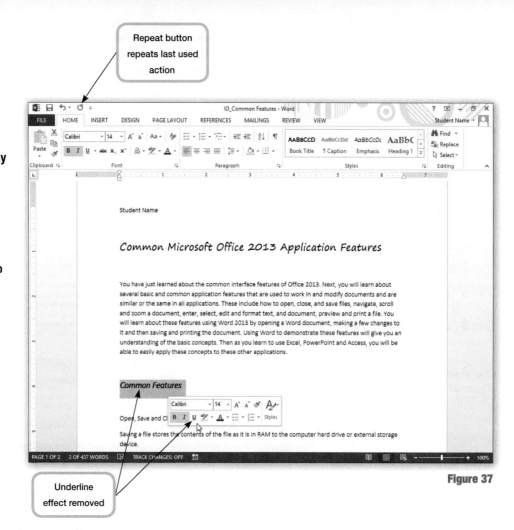

Repeat button repeats last used action

5

● Right-click on the selection to redisplay the Mini toolbar.

● Click U Underline on the Mini toolbar.

Your screen should be similar to Figure 37

Underline effect removed

Figure 37

The context menu and Mini toolbar appeared when you right-clicked the selection. The context menu displayed a variety of commands that are quicker to access than locating the command on the Ribbon. The commands that appear on this menu change depending on what you are doing at the time. The context menu disappeared after you made a selection from the Mini toolbar. Both the Mini toolbar and context menus are designed to make it more efficient to execute commands.

Also notice that the ⟳ Redo button in the Quick Access Toolbar has changed to a ⟲ Repeat button. This feature allows you to quickly repeat the last-used command at another location in the document.

Undoing and Redoing Editing Changes

Instead of reselecting the U Underline command to remove the underline effect, you could have used ↩ Undo to reverse your last action or command. You will use this feature to restore the underline (your last action).

● Click 🔄 ▾ Undo in
the Quick Access
Toolbar.

Another Method

The keyboard shortcut is Ctrl + Z.

**Your screen should be similar to
Figure 38**

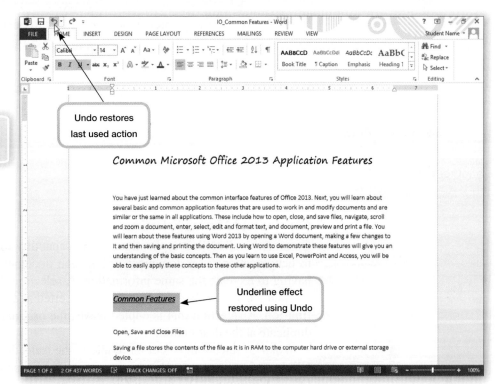

Undo restores
last used action

Common Microsoft Office 2013 Application Features

You have just learned about the common interface features of Office 2013. Next, you will learn about several basic and common application features that are used to work in and modify documents and are similar or the same in all applications. These include how to open, close, and save files, navigate, scroll and zoom a document, enter, select, edit and format text, and document, preview and print a file. You will learn about these features using Word 2013 by opening a Word document, making a few changes to it and then saving and printing the document. Using Word to demonstrate these features will give you an understanding of the basic concepts. Then as you learn to use Excel, PowerPoint and Access, you will be able to easily apply these concepts to these other applications.

Common Features

Underline effect
restored using Undo

Open, Save and Close Files

Saving a file stores the contents of the file as it is in RAM to the computer hard drive or external storage device.

Figure 38

Undo reversed the last action and the underline formatting effect was restored. Notice that the 🔄 ▾ button includes a drop-down menu button. Clicking this button displays a menu of the most recent actions that can be reversed, with the most-recent action at the top of the menu. When you select an action from the drop-down menu, you also undo all actions above it in the menu.

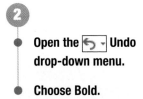

● Open the 🔄 ▾ Undo
drop-down menu.

● Choose Bold.

**Your screen should be similar to
Figure 39**

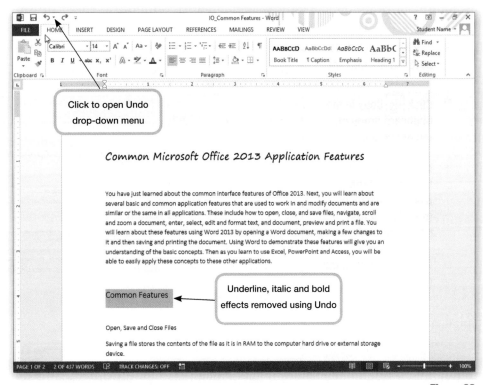

Click to open Undo
drop-down menu

Common Microsoft Office 2013 Application Features

You have just learned about the common interface features of Office 2013. Next, you will learn about several basic and common application features that are used to work in and modify documents and are similar or the same in all applications. These include how to open, close, and save files, navigate, scroll and zoom a document, enter, select, edit and format text, and document, preview and print a file. You will learn about these features using Word 2013 by opening a Word document, making a few changes to it and then saving and printing the document. Using Word to demonstrate these features will give you an understanding of the basic concepts. Then as you learn to use Excel, PowerPoint and Access, you will be able to easily apply these concepts to these other applications.

Common Features

Underline, italic and bold
effects removed using Undo

Open, Save and Close Files

Saving a file stores the contents of the file as it is in RAM to the computer hard drive or external storage device.

Figure 39

The underline, italic, and bold effects were all removed.

Immediately after you undo an action, the Repeat button changes to the Redo button and is available so you can restore the action you just undid. You will restore the last-removed format, bold.

3

● Click Redo.

Another Method

The keyboard shortcut is Ctrl + Y.

Copying and Moving Selections

Common to all Office applications is the capability to **copy** and **move** selections to new locations in a document or between documents, saving you time by not having to recreate the same information. A selection that is moved is cut from its original location, called the **source**, and inserted at a new location, called the **destination**. A selection that is copied leaves the original in the source and inserts a duplicate at the destination.

When a selection is cut or copied, the selection is stored in the system **Clipboard**, a temporary Windows storage area in memory. It is also stored in the **Office Clipboard**. The system Clipboard holds only the last cut or copied item, whereas the Office Clipboard can store up to 24 items that have been cut or copied. This feature allows you to insert multiple items from various Office documents and paste all or part of the collection of items into another document.

First, you will copy the text "Office 2013" to two other locations in the first paragraph.

Additional Information

You will learn about using the Office Clipboard in the individual application texts.

1

● Select the text "Office 2013" in the title line.

● Click Copy in the Clipboard group of the Home tab.

● Move to the beginning of the word "applications" (third line of first paragraph).

● Click Paste in the Clipboard group.

Another Method

The Copy keyboard shortcut is Ctrl + C.
The Paste keyboard shortcut is Ctrl + V.

Your screen should be similar to Figure 40

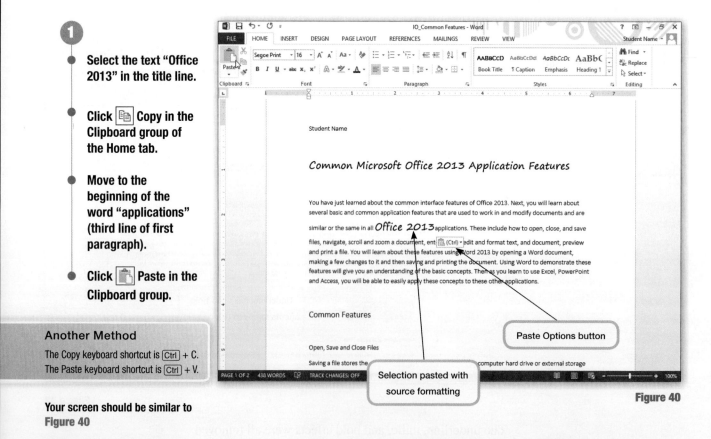

Paste Options button

Selection pasted with source formatting

Figure 40

The copied selection is inserted at the location you specified with the same formatting as it has in the title. The 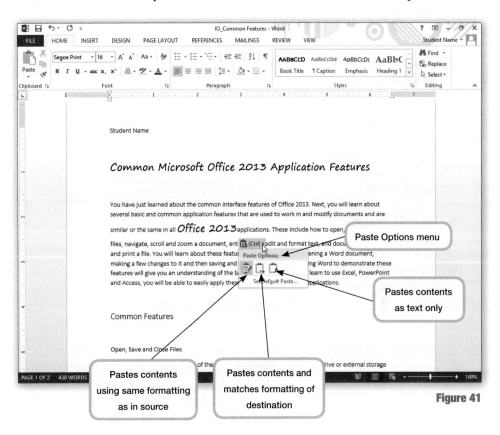 (Ctrl) ▼ Paste Options button appears automatically whenever a selection is pasted. It is used to control the format of the pasted item.

2

● **Click the ☐ (Ctrl) ▼**
Paste Options button.

● **If necessary, insert a**
blank space after the
year.

Your screen should be similar to
Figure 41

Figure 41

The Paste Options are used to specify whether to insert the item with the same formatting that it had in the source, to change it to the formatting of the surrounding destination text, or to insert text only (from a selection that is a combination of text and graphics). The default as you have seen is to keep the formatting from the source. You want to change it to the formatting of the surrounding text. As you point to a Paste Options button, a **Paste Preview** will show how that option will affect the selection. Then you will copy it again to a second location.

3

- Click 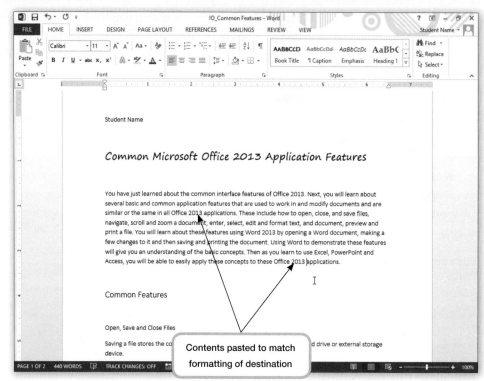 Merge Formatting.

- Select "other" in the last line of the first paragraph.

- Right-click on the selection and point to each of the Paste Options in the context menu to see the Paste Preview.

- Click Merge Formatting.

- If necessary, insert a blank space after the year.

Your screen should be similar to Figure 42

Figure 42

The selected text was deleted and replaced with the contents of the system Clipboard. The system Clipboard contents remain in the Clipboard until another item is copied or cut, allowing you to paste the same item multiple times.

Now you will learn how to move a selection by rearranging several lines of text in the description of common features. You want to move the last sentence in the document, beginning with "Opening a file", to the top of the list. The Cut and Paste commands in the Clipboard group of the Home tab are used to move selections.

4

● Scroll to see the end of the document.

● Double-click in the left margin next to the last sentence in the document to select it.

● Click Cut in the Clipboard group.

Another Method

The Cut keyboard shortcut is [Ctrl] + X. You also can choose Cut from the context menu.

Your screen should be similar to Figure 43

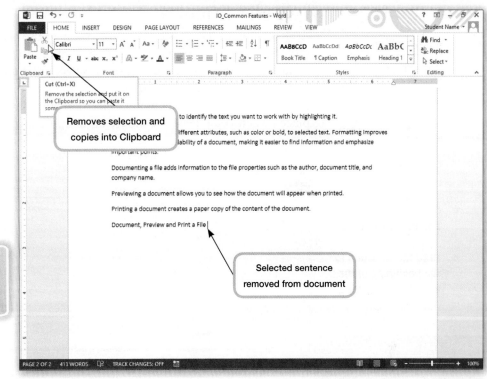

Figure 43

The selected paragraph is removed from the source and copied to the Clipboard. Next, you need to move the cursor to the location where the text will be inserted and paste the text into the document from the Clipboard.

5

● Move to the beginning of the word "Saving" at the top of the Common Features list.

● Press [Ctrl] + V.

Your screen should be similar to Figure 44

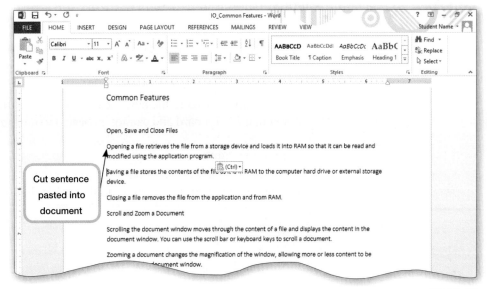

Figure 44

The cut sentence is reentered into the document at the cursor location. That was much quicker than retyping the whole sentence! Because the source has the same formatting as the text at the destination, the default setting to keep the source formatting is appropriate.

Additional Information

You also can move or copy by clicking the right mouse button in your highlighted selection. A context menu appears with the available move and copy options.

Using Drag and Drop

Another way to move or copy selections is to use the drag-and-drop editing feature. This feature is most useful for copying or moving short distances in a document. To use drag and drop to move a selection, point to the selection and drag it to the location where you want the selection inserted. The mouse pointer appears as as you drag, and a temporary insertion point shows you where the text will be placed when you release the mouse button.

Additional Information

You also can use drag and drop to copy and paste a selection by holding down ⌃Ctrl while dragging. The mouse pointer shape is ⯬.

1

- Select the last line of text in the document.

- Drag the selection to the beginning of the word "Documenting" (four lines up).

Touch Tip

With a touch device, tap in the selection and then slide or drag the selection to move it.

Your screen should be similar to Figure 45

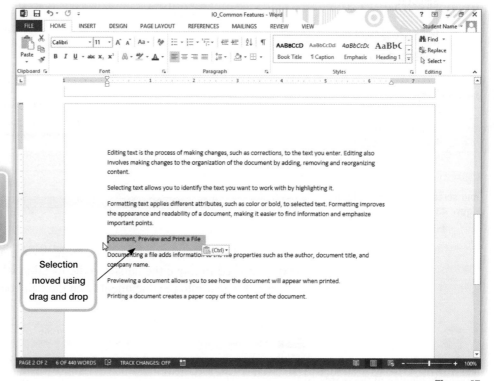

Figure 45

The selection moved to the new location. However, the selection is not copied and stored in the Clipboard and cannot be pasted to multiple locations in the document.

Copying Formats

Many times, you will find you want to copy the formats associated with a selection, but not the text. It is easy to do this using the **Format Painter** tool.

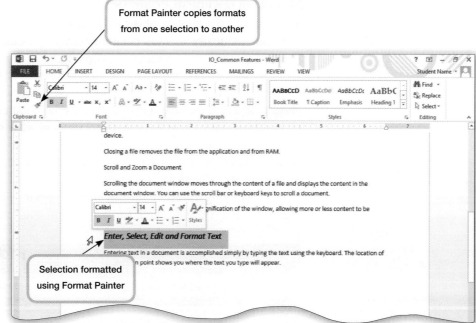

Format Painter copies formats from one selection to another

1

- Apply bold and italic effects and increase the font size to 14 for the currently selected text.

- Click Format Painter in the Clipboard group.

- Scroll the document up and select the topic line of text "Enter, Select, Edit and Format text".

Selection formatted using Format Painter

Figure 46

Additional Information

The mouse pointer appears as 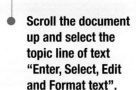 when this feature is on.

Your screen should be similar to Figure 46

The text you selected is formatted using the same formats. This feature is especially helpful when you want to copy multiple formats at one time. Next, you want to format the other topic heads in the Common Features list using the same formats. To do this, you can make the Format Painter "sticky" so that it can be used to copy the format multiple times in succession.

2

- Double-click Format Painter in the Clipboard group.

- Select the remaining two topic heads in the Common Features list:

  Scroll and Zoom a Document

  Open, Save and Close Files

- Click Format Painter to turn off this feature.

- Clear the selection.

Your screen should be similar to Figure 47

Multiple selections formatted using Format Painter

Figure 47

Specifying Document Properties

In addition to the content of the document that you create, all Office 2013 applications automatically include details about the document that describe or identify it called **metadata** or document **properties**. Document properties include details such as title, author name, subject, and keywords that identify the document's topic or contents (described below). Some of these properties are automatically generated. These include statistics such as the number of words in the file and general information such as the date the document was created and last modified. Others such as author name and tags or keywords are properties that you can specify. A **tag** or **keyword** is a descriptive word that is associated with the file and can be used to locate a file using a search.

By specifying relevant information as document properties, you can easily organize, identify, and search for your documents later.

Property	Action
Title	Enter the document title. This title can be longer and more descriptive than the file name.
Tags	Enter words that you associate with the presentation to make it easier to find using search tools.
Comments	Enter comments that you want others to see about the content of the document.
Categories	Enter the name of a higher-level category under which you can group similar types of presentations.
Author	Enter the name of the presentation's author. By default this is the name entered when the application was installed.

You will look at the document properties that are automatically included and add documentation to identify you as the author, and specify a document title and keywords to describe the document.

- **Open the File tab.**

- **Click the "Show all properties" link at the bottom of the Properties panel in the Info window to display all properties.**

Your screen should be similar to Figure 48

Figure 48

The Properties panel in the right section of the Info tab is divided into four groups and displays the properties associated with the document. Properties such as the document size, number of words, and number of pages are automatically maintained. Others such as the title and tag properties are blank waiting for you to specify your own information.

You will add a title, a tag, and your name as the author name.

2

- Click in the Title text box and type **Common Office Features**

- In the same manner, enter common, features, interface as the tags.

- Click in the Add an Author text box and enter your name.

- If necessary, click outside the search results box to clear it.

Your screen should be similar to Figure 49

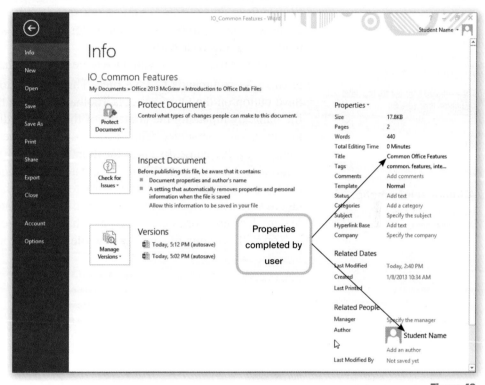

Figure 49

Once the document properties are specified, you can use them to identify and locate documents. You also can use the automatically updated properties for the same purpose. For example, you can search for all files created by a specified user or on a certain date.

Saving a File

As you enter and edit text to create a document in Word, Excel, and PowerPoint, the changes you make are immediately displayed onscreen and are stored in your computer's memory. However, they are not permanently stored until you save your work to a file on a disk. After a document has been saved as a file, it can be closed and opened again at a later time to be edited further. Unlike Word, Excel, and PowerPoint, where you start work on a new document and then save your changes, Access requires that you name the new database file first and create a table for your data. Then, it saves your changes to the data automatically as you work. This allows multiple users to have access to the most up-to-date data at all times.

Additional Information

You can specify different AutoRecover settings by choosing Options/Save in the Backstage and specifying the AutoRecover settings of your choice.

As a backup against the accidental loss of work from power failure or other mishap, Word, Excel, and PowerPoint include an AutoRecover feature. When this feature is on, as you work you may see a pulsing disk icon briefly appear in the status bar. This icon indicates that the program is saving your work to a temporary recovery file. The time interval between automatic saving can be set to any period you specify; the default is every 10 minutes. After a problem has occurred, when you restart the program, the recovery file is automatically opened containing all changes you made up to the last time it was saved by AutoRecover. You then need to save the recovery file. If you do not save it, it is deleted when closed. AutoRecover is a great feature for recovering lost work but should not be used in place of regularly saving your work.

You will save the work you have done so far on the document. You use the Save or Save As commands to save files. The Save option on the File tab or the 💾 Save button on the Quick Access Toolbar will save the active file using the same file name by replacing the contents of the existing disk file with the document as it appears on your screen. The Save As option on the File tab is used to save a file using a new file name, to a new location, or as a different file type. This leaves the original file unchanged. When you create a new document, you can use either of the Save commands to save your work to a file on the disk. It is especially important to save a new document very soon after you create it because the AutoRecover feature does not work until a file name has been specified.

Additional Information

Saving a file is the same in all Office 2013 applications, except Access.

You will save this file using a new file name to your solution file location.

1

Click Save As in the sidebar of the Backstage.

Your screen should be similar to Figure 50

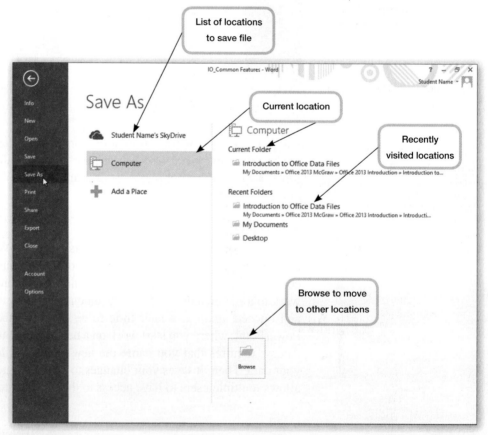

Figure 50

The Save As window is displayed in which you select the location where you want to save the file. Just as in the Open window, the location may be the hard drive of your computer, an external storage device, a local network, or in the cloud on SkyDrive or SharePoint. The location where the file was opened is the current location in the list. A list of current and recent folders is displayed in the right section. If the current folder location is where you want to save the file, clicking on the folder immediately opens it. If you need to open a different folder, click on it in the Recent Folders list or click [Browse] to locate the folder.

2

● **If necessary, select a different location from the list of locations.**

● **Select the folder from the Current Folder or Recent Folders list or click [Browse].**

Your screen should be similar to Figure 51

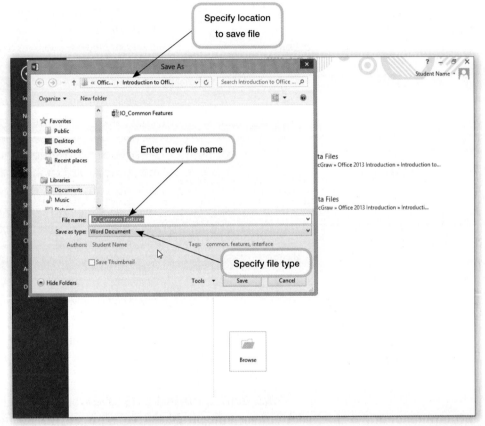

Figure 51

Having Trouble?

Do not be concerned if your Save As dialog box Save location and file details such as the size, type, and date modified are different. These features are determined by the Folder and dialog box settings on your computer.

Additional Information

You can set a default location to save a file by choosing Options/Save in the Backstage and specifying the default save location.

The Save As dialog box is used to specify the location where you will save the file and the file name. The Address bar displays the current folder location and the File name text box displays the name of the open file. The file name is highlighted, ready for you to enter a new file name. The Save as type box displays "Word Document" as the default format in which the file will be saved. Word 2013 documents are automatically saved using the file extension .docx. The file type you select determines the file extension that will be automatically added to the file name when the file is saved. The file types and extensions for the four Office 2013 applications are described in the following table.

Extensions	File Type
Word 2013	
.docx	Word 2007–2013 document without macros or code
.dotx	Word 2007–2013 template without macros or code
.docm	Word 2007–2013 document that could contain macros or code
.xps	Word 2007–2013 shared document (see Note)
.doc	Word 95–2003 document
Excel 2013	
.xlsx	Excel 2007–2013 default workbook without macros or code
.xlsm	Excel 2007–2013 default workbook that could contain macros
.xltx	Excel 2007–2013 template without macros
.xltm	Excel 2007–2013 template that could contain macros
.xps	Excel 2007–2013 shared workbook (see Note)
.xls	Excel 97–2003 workbook
PowerPoint 2013	
.pptx	PowerPoint 2007–2013 default presentation format
.pptm	PowerPoint 2007–2013 presentation with macros
.potx	PowerPoint 2007–2013 template without macros
.potm	PowerPoint 2007–2013 template that may contain macros
.ppam	PowerPoint 2007–2013 add-in that contains macros
.ppsx	PowerPoint 2007–2013 slide show without macros
.ppsm	PowerPoint 2007–2013 slide show that may contain macros
.thmx	PowerPoint 2007–2013 theme
.ppt	PowerPoint 2003 or earlier presentation
Access 2013	
.accdb	Access 2007–2013 database
.mdb	Access 2003 or earlier database

NOTE XPS file format is a fixed-layout electronic file format that preserves document formatting and ensures that when the file is viewed online or printed, it retains exactly the format that you intended. It also makes it difficult to change the data in the file. To save as an XPS file format, you must have installed the free add-in.

Office 2007, 2010, and 2013 save Word, Excel, and PowerPoint files using the XML format (Extensible Markup Language) and a four-letter file extension. This format makes your documents safer by separating files that contain macros (small programs in a document that automate tasks) to make it easier for a virus checker to identify and block unwanted code or macros that could be dangerous to your computer. It also makes file sizes smaller by compressing the content upon saving and makes files less susceptible to damage. In addition, XML format makes it easier to open documents created with an Office application using another application.

Previous versions of Word, Excel, and PowerPoint did not use XML and had a three-letter file extension. If you plan to share a file with someone using an Office 2003 or earlier version, you can save the document using the three-letter file type; however, some features may be lost. Otherwise, if you save it as a four-letter file type, the recipient may not be able to view all features. There also may be loss of features for users of Office 2007 (even though it has an XML file type) because the older version does not support several of the new features in Office 2013. Office 2013 includes a feature that checks for compatibility with previous versions and advises you what features in the document may be lost if opened by an Office 2007 user or if the document is saved in the 2003 format.

If you have an Office Access 2007 (.accdb) database that you want to save in an earlier Access file format (.mdb), you can do so as long as your .accdb database does not contain any multivalued lookup fields, offline data, or attachments. This is because older versions of Access do not support these new features. If you try to convert an .accdb database containing any of these elements to an .mdb file format, Access displays an error message.

First you may need to change the location to the location where the file will be saved. The same procedures you used to specify a location to open a file are used to specify the location to save a file. Then, you will change the file name to Common Features using the default Word document type (.docx).

3
- If necessary, select the location where you save your solution files.

- If necessary, drag in the File Name text box to highlight the existing file name.

- Type **Common Features**

- Click [Save].

Your screen should be similar to Figure 52

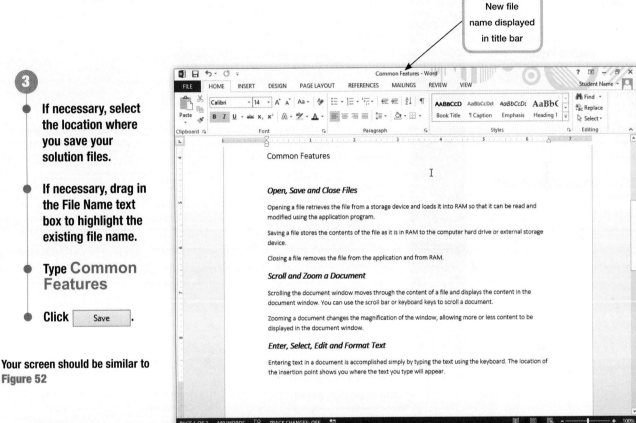

Figure 52

Additional Information

Windows file names can contain letters, numbers, and spaces; however, the symbols \, /, ?, :, *, ", <, and > cannot be used. The file name can be entered in either uppercase or lowercase letters and will appear exactly as you type it.

The document is saved as Common Features.docx at the location you selected, and the new file name is displayed in the Word application window title bar. Depending upon your Windows setup, the file extension also may be displayed in the title bar.

Printing a Document

Once a document appears how you want, you may want to print a hard copy for your own reference or to give to others. All Office 2013 applications include the capability to print and have similar options. You will print this document next.

Open the File tab and choose Print.

Another Method

The keyboard shortcut for the Print command is Ctrl + P.

Your screen should be similar to Figure 53

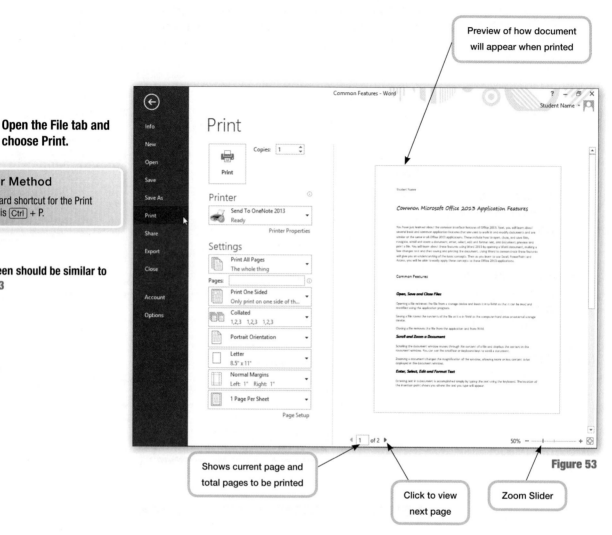

Preview of how document will appear when printed

Shows current page and total pages to be printed

Click to view next page

Zoom Slider

Figure 53

The right section of the Print page displays a preview of the current page of your document. To save time and unnecessary printing and paper waste, it is always a good idea to preview each page of your document before printing. Notice below the preview, the page scroll box shows the page number of the page you are currently viewing and the total number of pages. The scroll buttons on either side are used to scroll to the next and previous pages. Additionally, a Zoom Slider is available to adjust the size of the preview.

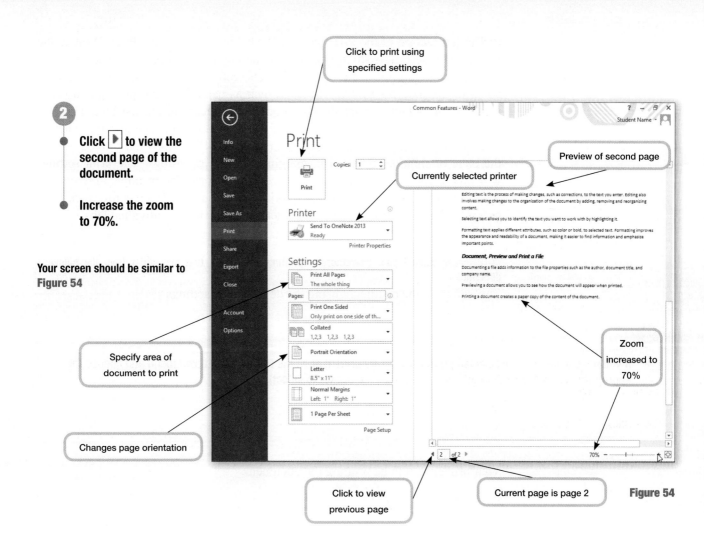

2

Click ▶ to view the second page of the document.

Increase the zoom to 70%.

Your screen should be similar to Figure 54

Click to print using specified settings

Preview of second page

Currently selected printer

Specify area of document to print

Changes page orientation

Zoom increased to 70%

Click to view previous page

Current page is page 2

Figure 54

If you see any changes you want to make to the document, you would need to close the File tab and make the changes. If the document looks good, you are ready to print.

The left section of the Print page is divided into three areas: Print, Printer, and Settings. In the Print section you specify the number of copies you want printed. The default is to print one copy. The Printer section is used to specify the printer you will use and the printer properties such as paper size and print quality. The name of the default printer on your computer appears in the list box. The Settings area is used to specify what part of the document you want to print, whether to print on one or both sides of the paper or to collate (sort) the printed output, the page orientation, paper size, margins, and sheet settings. The print settings will vary slightly with the different Office applications. For example, in Excel, the options to specify what to print are to print the entire worksheet, entire workbook, or a selection. The differences will be demonstrated in the individual labs.

NOTE Please consult your instructor for printing procedures that may differ from the following directions.

You will print the document using the default print settings.

3

● If you need to change the selected printer to another printer, open the Printer drop-down menu and choose the appropriate printer (your instructor will tell you which printer to select).

● Click [Print] .

Your printer should be printing the document.

Closing a File

Finally, you want to close the document.

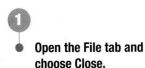

Open the File tab and choose Close.

Another Method

The keyboard shortcut is Ctrl + F4.

Your screen should be similar to Figure 55

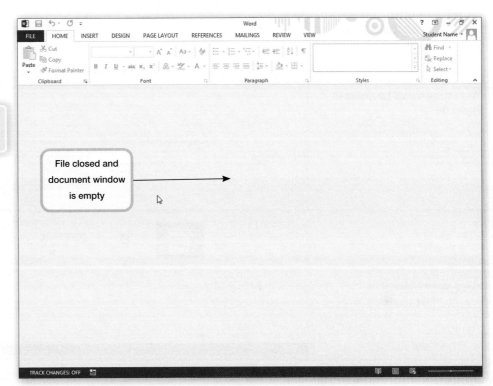

File closed and document window is empty

Figure 55

Additional Information

Do not click ✕ Close in the window title bar as this closes the application.

Now the Word window displays an empty document window. Because you did not make any changes to the document since saving it, the document window closed immediately. If you had made additional changes, the program would display a dialog box asking whether you wanted to save the file before closing it, to close the file without saving the changes or to cancel the action. This prevents the accidental closing of a file that has not been saved first.

USING OFFICE HELP

Another Method

You also can press F1 to access Help.

The ? in the upper-right corner of the Ribbon is used to access the Microsoft Help system. This button is always visible even when the Ribbon is hidden. Because you are using the Microsoft Word 2013 application, Microsoft Word Help will be accessed.

Click ? Microsoft Word Help.

Your screen should be similar to Figure 56

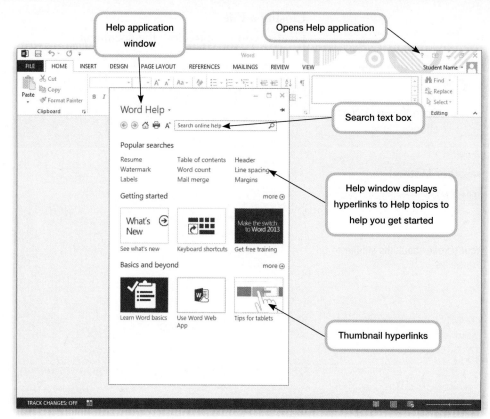

Help application window

Opens Help application

Search text box

Help window displays hyperlinks to Help topics to help you get started

Thumbnail hyperlinks

Figure 56

The Word Help feature is a separate application and is opened and displayed in a separate window. If you are connected to the Internet, the Microsoft Office Online website, Office.com, is accessed and help information from this site is displayed in the window. If you are not connected, the offline help information that is provided with the application and stored on your computer is located and displayed. Generally, the listing of topics is similar but fewer in number.

Selecting Help Topics

The Home window is displayed and provides several ways you can get help. The first is to type in the Search text box a word or phrase about a topic you want help on. A second is to select a topic from the Popular searches list. Each topic is a **hyperlink** or connection to the information located on the Office.com website or in Help on your computer. When you point to a hyperlink, it appears underlined and the mouse pointer appears as ⟨🖑⟩. Clicking the hyperlink accesses and displays the information associated with the hyperlink. A third method is to click one of the thumbnail hyperlinks in the Getting Started or Basics and beyond sections to access information about these topics.

1

● **Click the "Learn Word basics" thumbnail.**

● **Scroll the Help window to see the "Choose a template" topic.**

Your screen should be similar to Figure 57

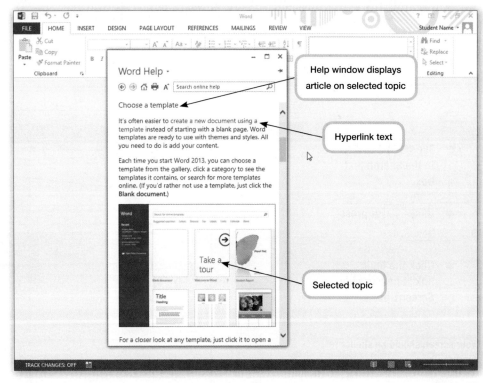

Figure 57

An article containing information about basic features of Word 2013 is displayed. Notice the colored text "create a new document using a template." This indicates the text is a hyperlink to more information about this topic.

2

● **Click "create a new document using a template."**

● **Scroll the window and read the information about this topic.**

● **Scroll back to the top of the window.**

Your screen should be similar to Figure 58

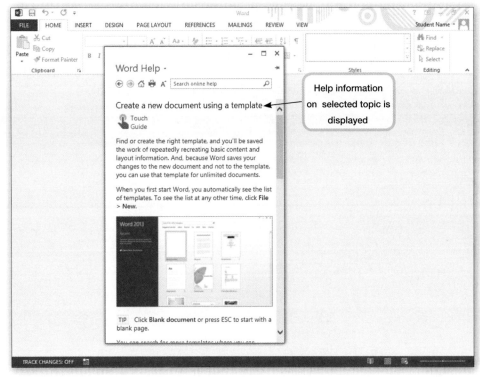

Figure 58

Common Office 2013 Features **IO.65**

The information on the selected topic is displayed in the window. Next, you will use the Search text box to find information about ScreenTips.

3

● **Type screentips in the Search text box.**

● **Click 🔍 or press [Enter].**

● **Click the topic link "Show or hide ScreenTips."**

Your screen should be similar to Figure 59

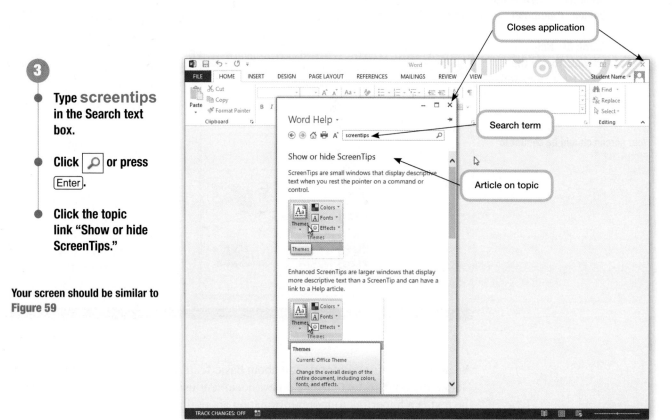

Figure 59

Now information about ScreenTips is displayed in the Help window. To move through previously viewed Help topics, you can use the ⊙ Back and ⊙ Forward buttons in the Help toolbar. You can quickly redisplay the opening Help window using 🏠 Home on the Help toolbar.

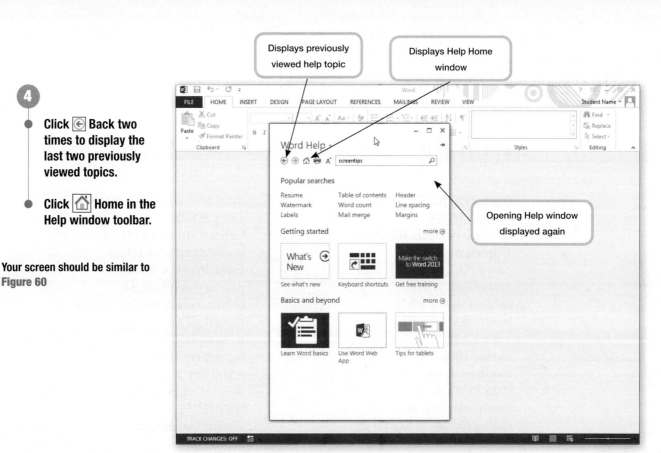

Displays previously viewed help topic

Displays Help Home window

Opening Help window displayed again

Figure 60

4

● Click ⬅ Back two times to display the last two previously viewed topics.

● Click 🏠 Home in the Help window toolbar.

Your screen should be similar to Figure 60

The Help Home window is displayed again.

EXITING AN OFFICE 2013 APPLICATION

Now you are ready to close the Help window and exit the Word program. The ☒ Close button located on the right end of the window title bar can be used to exit most application windows. If you attempt to close an application without first saving your document, a dialog box appears asking if you want to save your work before exiting the application, not to save your latest changes to the document or to cancel the action. If you do not save your work and you exit the application, any changes you made since last saving it are lost.

1

● Click ☒ Close in the Help window title bar to close the Help window.

● Click ☒ Close in the Word window title bar to exit Word.

Another Method

The keyboard shortcut for the Exit command is Alt + F4.

The program window is closed and the Windows desktop is visible again.

KEY TERMS

Backstage IO.27
buttons IO.16
character effects IO.43
Clipboard IO.48
cloud IO.3, 30
commands IO.20
context menu IO.19
contextual tabs IO.22
copy IO.48
cursor IO.17
database IO.8
default IO.28
destination IO.48
dialog box launcher IO.25
document window IO.17
edit IO.3
Enhanced ScreenTips IO.22
fields IO.8
font IO.43
font size IO.43
format IO.4
Format Painter IO.52
groups IO.20
hyperlink IO.64
insertion point IO.17
keyboard shortcut IO.18
keyword IO.54
Live Preview IO.43
metadata IO.54

Mini toolbar IO.42, IO.44
move IO.48
Office Clipboard IO.48
on-demand tabs IO.22
Paste Preview IO.49
properties IO.28, 54
Quick Access Toolbar IO.16
records IO.8
Ribbon IO.17
ScreenTip IO.18
scroll bar IO.17
shortcut menu IO.19
slide IO.11
slide shows IO.11
source IO.48
status bar IO.17
tables IO.8
tabs IO.20
tag IO.54
task pane IO.26
template IO.15
tooltip IO.18
typeface IO.43
user interface IO.14
View buttons IO.17
word wrap IO.43
worksheet IO.6
Zoom Slider IO.17

COMMAND SUMMARY

Command/Button	Shortcut	Action
Quick Access Toolbar		
↺ ▾ Undo	Ctrl + Z	Restores last change
↻ ▾ Redo	Ctrl + Y	Restores last Undo action
↺ Repeat	Ctrl + Y	Repeats last action

COMMAND SUMMARY (CONTINUED)

Command/Button	Shortcut	Action
[W]		Displays a menu of commands to open, close, and size the application window.
[?] Microsoft Word Help	F1	Opens Microsoft Help
File tab		
Info		Displays document properties
New		Starts a new document file
Open	Ctrl + O	Opens existing file
Save	Ctrl + S or [💾]	Saves document using same file name
Save As	F12	Saves document using a new file name, type, and/or location
Print	Ctrl + P	Prints document using specified settings
Close	Ctrl + F4 or [✕]	Closes document
View tab		
Zoom group [🔍 Zoom]		Changes magnification of document
Home tab		
Clipboard group [📋 Paste] Paste	Ctrl + V	Inserts copy of Clipboard at location of cursor
[✂] Cut	Ctrl + X	Removes selection and copies to Clipboard
[📄] Copy	Ctrl + C	Copies selection to Clipboard
[🖌] Format Painter		Duplicates formats of selection to other locations
Font group [Calibri ▾] Font	Ctrl + Shift + F	Changes typeface
[11 ▾] Font Size	Ctrl + Shift + P	Changes font size
[B] Bold	Ctrl + B	Adds/removes bold effect
[I] Italic	Ctrl + I	Adds/removes italic effect
[U] Underline	Ctrl + U	Adds/removes underline effect

STEP-BY-STEP

EXPLORING EXCEL 2013

1. In this exercise you will explore the Excel 2013 application and use many of the same features you learned about while using Word 2013 in this lab.

   a. Start Office Excel 2013 and choose Blank workbook.

   b. What shape is the mouse pointer when positioned in the document window area? _____

   c. Excel has _____ tabs. Which tabs are not the same as in Word? _____

   d. Open the Formulas tab. How many groups are in the Formulas tab? _____

   e. Which tab contains the group to work with charts? _____

   f. From the Home tab, click the Number group dialog box launcher. What is the name of the dialog box that opens? _____ How many number categories are there? _____ Close the dialog box.

   g. Display ScreenTips for the following buttons located in the Alignment group of the Home tab and identify what action they perform.

   _____

   _____

   _____

   h. Open the Excel Help window. From the Help window choose "Learn Excel Basics" and then choose "Enter data manually in worksheet cells" and answer the following:

   • What is the definition of worksheet? Hint: Click on the hyperlinked term "worksheet" to view a definition.

   _____

   • What four types of data can be entered in a worksheet? _____, _____, _____, _____

   i. Read the topic "Quick Start: Edit and enter data in a worksheet." If you have an Internet connection, click the Watch the video link and view the video. Close your browser window.

   j. Enter the term "formula" in the Search text box. Look at several articles and answer the following question: All formula entries begin with what symbol? _____

   k. Redisplay the "Enter data manually in worksheet cells" topic. Return to the Home page.

   l. Close the Help window. Exit Excel.

EXPLORING POWERPOINT 2013

2. In this exercise you will explore the PowerPoint 2013 application and use many of the same features you learned about while using Word 2013 in this lab.

   a. Start PowerPoint 2013 and choose Blank presentation.
   b. PowerPoint has _____ tabs. Which tabs are not the same as in Word?
      _____

   c. Open the Animations tab. How many groups are in this tab? _____
   d. Which tab contains the group to work with themes? _____
   e. Click on the text "Click to add title." Type your name. Select this text and change the font size to 72; add italic and bold. Cut this text. Click in the box containing "Click to add subtitle" and paste the cut selection. Use the Paste Options to keep the source formatting.
   f. Click on the text "Click to add title" and type the name of your school. Select the text and apply a font of your choice.
   g. Open the PowerPoint Help window. From the Help window, choose "Learn PowerPoint Basics." Read the information in this article:

      • In the "Insert a new slide" topic, click the link to "Add, rearrange, and delete slides."

      • What is a layout?
      _____

   h. Enter the term "menus" in the Search text box. What do the commands in the Animations tab do?
      _____

   i. Display the Help Home window again. Close the Help window. Exit PowerPoint and do not save the changes you made to the presentation.

LAB EXERCISES

EXPLORING ACCESS 2013

3. As noted in this Introduction to Microsoft Office 2013, when you start Access 2013 you need to either open an existing database file or create and name a new database. Therefore, in this exercise, you will simply explore the Access 2013 Help information without opening or creating a database file.

   a. Use the Start menu to start Office Access 2013.

   b. Click [?] Help in the Access Start window.

   c. Choose the topic "Basic tasks for an Access 2013 desktop database."

   - In the first paragraph, what are three examples of kinds of information that can be stored in a database?

     _____, _____, and _____.

   d. In the Search box enter "table." Choose the topic "Introduction to tables" and from the Overview answer the following questions:

   - What is a database?

     _____

   - What are the three parts of a table?

     _____, _____, and _____.

   - A field is also commonly called a _____.

   - Each row in a table is also called a _____.

   e. Close the Help window. Exit Access.

ON YOUR OWN

USING TOUCH IN OFFICE

1. In addition to the Help information you used in this lab, Office 2013 Help also includes online tutorials. Selecting a Help topic that starts a tutorial will open the browser program on your computer. You will use one of these tutorials to learn more about using touch features.

   Start Word 2013. Open Help and choose "Learn Word basics" from the Help Home window. Click on the Touch Guide. The Office Touch Guide web page is opened in your browser. Read the information in this article. When you are done, close the browser window, close Help, and exit Word 2013.

Objectives

After completing this lab, you will know how to:

1. Create new worksheets.

2. Enter and edit data.

3. Modify column widths and row heights.

4. Use proofing tools.

5. Copy and paste cell contents.

6. Create formulas.

7. Insert and delete rows and columns.

8. Format cells and cell content.

9. Hide and unhide rows and columns.

10. Create a basic chart.

11. Format values as a date.

12. Preview and print a worksheet.

13. Display and print formulas.

14. Change worksheet orientation and scale content.

CASE STUDY

Downtown Internet Café

You are excited about your new position as manager and financial planner for a local coffeehouse. Evan, the owner, has hired you as part of a larger effort to increase business at the former Downtown Café. Evan began this effort by completely renovating his coffeehouse and installing a wireless network. He plans to offer free WiFi service for customers to use with their own laptop computers. In addition, he has set up several computer kiosks for customers to use who do not have laptops and has provided a printer and copier for all customers to use. He also has decided to rent an MP3 download kiosk for customers who may want to update the music on 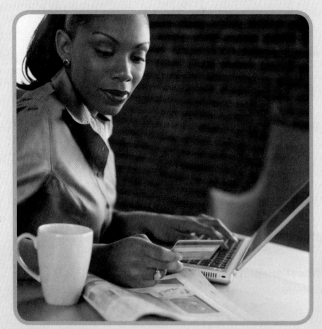 their iPods or PDAs. Finally, to reflect the new emphasis of the café, he has changed its name to the Downtown Internet Café.

You and Evan expect to increase sales by attracting techno-savvy café-goers, who you hope will use the Downtown Internet Café as a place to meet, study, work, or download music for their iPods and PDAs. You also believe the rental computers will be a draw for vacationers who want to check e-mail during their travels.

Evan wants to create a forecast estimating sales and expenses for the first quarter. As part of a good business plan, you and Evan need a realistic set of financial estimates and goals.

In this lab, you will help with the first quarter forecast by using Microsoft Office Excel 2013, a spreadsheet application that can store, manipulate, and display numeric data. You will learn to enter numbers, perform calculations, copy data, and label rows and columns as you create the basic structure of a worksheet for the Downtown Internet Café. You will then learn how to enhance the worksheet using formatting features and by adding color as shown here.

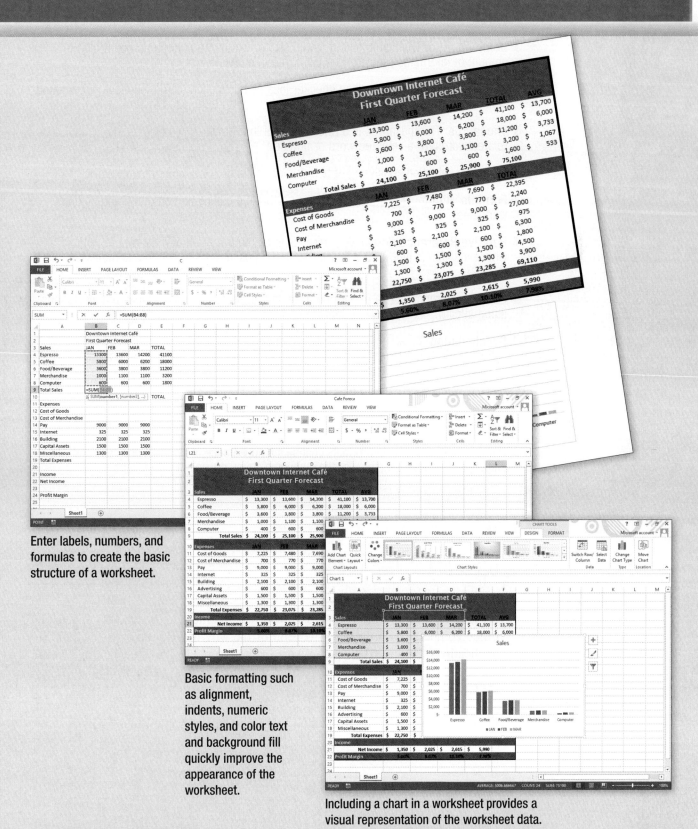

Enter labels, numbers, and formulas to create the basic structure of a worksheet.

Basic formatting such as alignment, indents, numeric styles, and color text and background fill quickly improve the appearance of the worksheet.

Including a chart in a worksheet provides a visual representation of the worksheet data.

The following concepts will be introduced in this lab:

1 **Data** The basic information or data you enter in a cell can be text or numbers.

2 **AutoCorrect** The AutoCorrect feature makes some basic assumptions about the text you are typing and, based on these assumptions, automatically corrects the entry.

3 **Column Width** The column width is the size or width of a column and controls the amount of information that can be displayed in a cell.

4 **Spelling Checker** The spelling checker locates misspelled words, duplicate words, and capitalization irregularities in the active worksheet and proposes the correct spelling.

5 **Thesaurus** The thesaurus is a reference tool that provides synonyms, antonyms, and related words for a selected word or phrase.

6 **Range** A selection consisting of two or more cells on a worksheet is a range.

7 **Formula** A formula is an equation that performs a calculation on data contained in a worksheet.

8 **Relative Reference** A relative reference is a cell or range reference in a formula whose location is interpreted in relation to the position of the cell that contains the formula.

9 **Function** A function is a prewritten formula that performs certain types of calculations automatically.

10 **Recalculation** When a number in a referenced cell in a formula changes, Excel automatically recalculates all formulas that are dependent upon the changed value.

11 **Alignment** Alignment settings allow you to change the horizontal and vertical placement and the orientation of an entry in a cell.

12 **Row Height** The row height is the size or height of a row measured in points.

13 **Number Formats** Number formats change the appearance of numbers onscreen and when printed, without changing the way the number is stored or used in calculations.

Creating a Workbook

As part of the renovation of the Downtown Internet Café, Evan upgraded the office computer with the latest version of the Microsoft Office System suite of applications, Office 2013. You are very excited to see how this new and powerful application can help you create professional budgets and financial forecasts for the Café.

You will use the spreadsheet application Excel 2013 included in the Microsoft Office 2013 System suite to create the first quarter forecast for the Café.

① **Start Excel 2013.**

Choose Blank workbook from the Start screen.

If necessary, maximize the Excel application window.

Having Trouble?

See "Common Office 2013 Features," page IO.14, for information on how to start the application and for a discussion of features common to all Microsoft Office 2013 applications.

Your screen should be similar to Figure 1.1

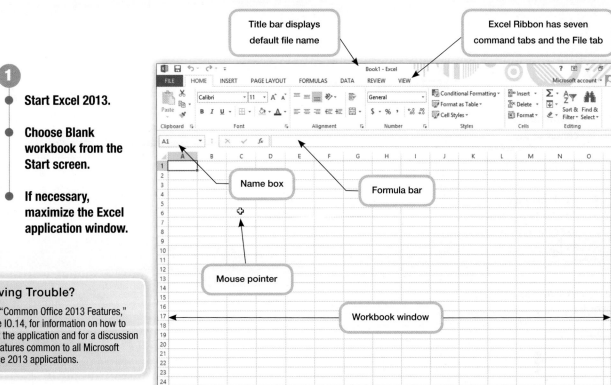

Title bar displays default file name

Excel Ribbon has seven command tabs and the File tab

Name box

Formula bar

Mouse pointer

Workbook window

Figure 1.1

Additional Information

Because the Ribbon can adapt to the screen resolution and orientation, your Ribbon may look slightly different. It also may display additional tabs if other application add-ins associated with Office 2013 are on.

After a few moments, the Excel application window is displayed. Because Excel remembers many settings that were in use when the program was last closed, your screen might look slightly different.

The Excel application window title bar displays the default file name, Book1, and program name. The Ribbon below the title bar consists of seven tabs that provide access to the commands and features you will use to create and modify a worksheet and the File tab for managing printing, saving, and sharing workbooks.

Below the Ribbon is the formula bar. The **formula bar** displays entries as they are made and edited in the workbook window. The **Name box**, located at the left end of the formula bar, provides information about the selected item.

The large center area of the program window is the **workbook window**. A **workbook** is an Excel file that stores the information you enter using the program. You will learn more about the different parts of the workbook window shortly.

The mouse pointer can appear as many different shapes. The mouse pointer changes shape depending upon the task you are performing or where the pointer is located on the window. Most commonly it appears as a ⌖ or ⊕. When it appears as a ⊕, it is used to move to different locations in the workbook window; when it appears as a ⌖, it is used to choose items, such as commands from the Ribbon.

2

• Move the mouse pointer into the center of the workbook window to see it appear as ⊕.

• Move the mouse pointer to the Ribbon to see it appear as ↖.

Your screen should be similar to Figure 1.2

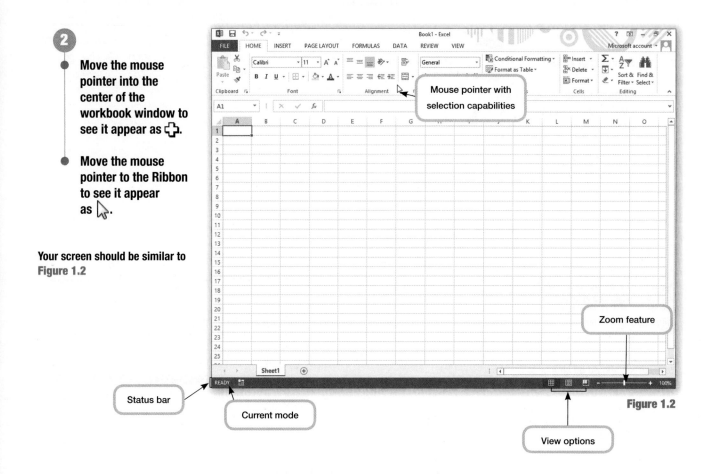

Mouse pointer with selection capabilities

Zoom feature

Status bar

Current mode

View options

Figure 1.2

The status bar at the bottom of the Excel window displays information about various Excel settings. The left side of the status bar displays the current mode or state of operation of the program, in this case, Ready. When Ready is displayed, you can move around the workbook, enter data, use the function keys, or choose a command. As you use the program, the status bar displays the current mode. The right side of the status bar contains buttons to change the view and a zoom feature.

Exploring the Workbook Window

When you open a blank workbook from the Start screen, the new workbook includes basic default settings. These settings include font style and size, column width and row height, and a single blank worksheet. A **worksheet,** also called a **sheet,** is used to store and work with different types of information, such as financial data or charts. It is a rectangular grid of **rows** and **columns** used to enter data. It is always part of a workbook and is the primary type of sheet you will use in Excel. The worksheet is much larger than the part you are viewing in the window. The worksheet actually extends 16,384 columns to the right and 1,048,576 rows down.

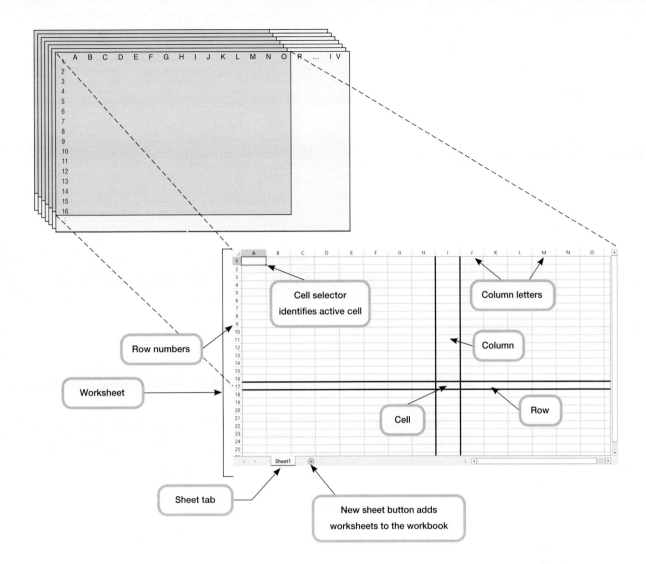

The **row numbers** along the left side and the **column letters** across the top of the workbook window identify each worksheet row and column. The intersection of a row and column creates a **cell**. Notice the green border, called the **cell selector**, surrounding the cell located at the intersection of column A and row 1. This identifies the **active cell**, which is the cell your next entry or procedure affects. Additionally, the Name box in the formula bar displays the **cell reference**, consisting of the column letter and row number of the active cell. The reference of the active cell is A1.

Each sheet in a workbook is named. The first blank sheet in a workbook is named Sheet1. As additional sheets are added to the workbook they are named Sheet2, and so on. The sheet names are displayed on **sheet tabs** at the bottom of the workbook window. The name of the **active sheet**, which is the sheet you can work in, appears bold green. The currently displayed worksheet in the workbook window, Sheet1, is the active sheet. You will use the ⊕ New Sheet button to add a second sheet to the workbook.

1   Click ⊕ **New sheet in the sheet tab area.**

Your screen should be similar to Figure 1.3

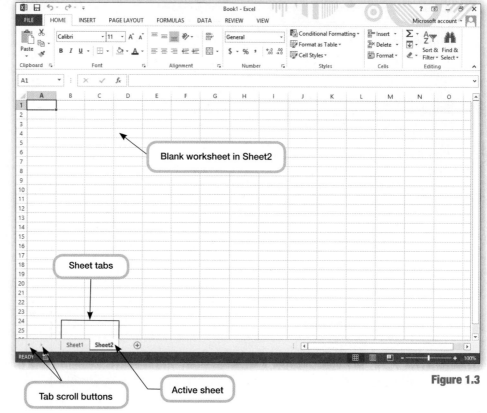

Blank worksheet in Sheet2

Sheet tabs

Tab scroll buttons

Active sheet

Figure 1.3

An identical blank worksheet is displayed in the window. The Sheet2 tab letters are green, and it appears in front of the other sheet tabs to show it is the active sheet.

The sheet tab area also contains **tab scroll buttons**, which are used to scroll tabs right or left when there are more sheet tabs than can be seen. You will learn about these features throughout the labs.

MOVING AROUND THE WORKSHEET

The mouse or keyboard commands can be used to move the cell selector from one cell to another in the worksheet. To move using a mouse, simply point to the cell you want to move to and click the mouse button. Depending upon what you are doing, using the mouse to move may not be as convenient as using the keyboard, in which case the directional keys can be used. You will make Sheet1 active again and use the mouse, then the keyboard, to move in the worksheet.

1

Click the Sheet1 tab to make it the active sheet again.

Another Method

You also can press [Ctrl] + [Page Down] to move to the next sheet and [Ctrl] + [Page Up] to move to the previous sheet.

Click cell B3.

Press [→] (3 times).

Press [↓] (4 times).

Your screen should be similar to Figure 1.4

Figure 1.4

Cell E7 is outlined in green, indicating this cell is the active cell. The Name box displays the cell reference. In addition, the row number and column letter are gray to further identify the location of the active cell.

As you have learned, the worksheet is much larger than the part you are viewing in the window. To see an area of the worksheet that is not currently in view, you need to scroll the window. The keyboard procedures shown in the table that follows can be used to move around the worksheet.

Having Trouble?

Refer to the "Scrolling the Document Window" section of the Introduction to Office 2013 for more keyboard and mouse procedures.

Keyboard	Action
[Alt] + [Page Down]	Moves right one full window.
[Alt] + [Page Up]	Moves left one full window.
[Home]	Moves to beginning of row.
[Ctrl] + [Home]	Moves to upper-left corner cell of worksheet.
[Ctrl] + [End]	Moves to last-used cell of worksheet.
[End] [→]	Moves to last-used cell in row.
[End] [↓]	Moves to last-used cell in column.

Touch Tip

Another way to scroll is to touch the worksheet or scroll bar with your finger and slide it up or down.

In addition, if you hold down an arrow key, the [Alt] + [Page Up] or [Alt] + [Page Down] keys, or the [Page Up] or [Page Down] keys, you can quickly scroll through the worksheet.

You will scroll the worksheet to see the rows below your current last row and the columns to the right of your current last column.

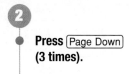

2

● Press Page Down (3 times).

● Press Alt + Page Down (3 times).

Your screen should be similar to Figure 1.5

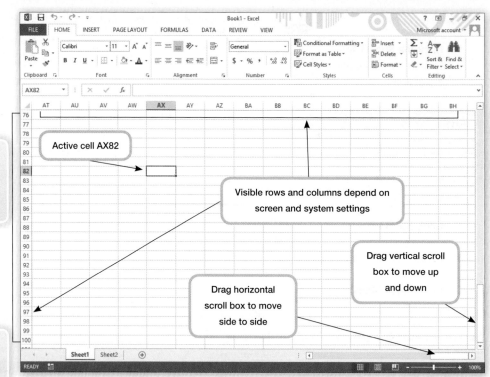

Active cell AX82

Visible rows and columns depend on screen and system settings

Drag vertical scroll box to move up and down

Drag horizontal scroll box to move side to side

Figure 1.5

The worksheet scrolled downward and left three full windows, The cell reference of your active cell depends on the screen resolution set at your computer. As you scroll the worksheet using the keyboard, the active cell also changes.

It is even more efficient to use the scroll bar to move long distances.

3

● **Slowly drag the vertical scroll box up the scroll bar until row 1 is displayed.**

● **Slowly drag the horizontal scroll box left along the scroll bar until column A is displayed.**

Your screen should be similar to Figure 1.6

 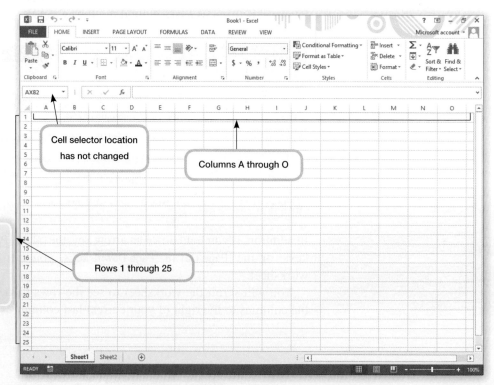

Cell selector location has not changed

Columns A through O

Rows 1 through 25

Figure 1.6

Another Method

You also can type a cell address in the Name box and press (←Enter) to move to that location.

The beginning rows and columns are displayed again. Notice that the Name box displays the same active cell location. When you use the scroll bar to scroll the worksheet, the active cell does not change until you click on a cell that is visible in the window.

- Practice moving around the worksheet using the keys presented in the table on page EX1.9.

Additional Information

The (Ctrl) + (End) key presented in the table will not change the worksheet location until the worksheet contains data.

- Press (Ctrl) + (Home) to move to cell A1.

You can use the mouse or the keyboard with most of the exercises in these labs. As you use both the mouse and the keyboard, you will find that it is more efficient to use one or the other in specific situations.

DEVELOPING A WORKSHEET

Now that you are familiar with the parts of the workbook and with moving around the worksheet, you are ready to create a worksheet showing the forecast for the first three months of operation for the Downtown Internet Café.

Worksheet development consists of four steps: planning, entering and editing, testing, and formatting. The objective is to create well-designed worksheets that produce accurate results and are clearly understood, adaptable, and efficient.

Step	Description
1. Plan	Specify the purpose of the worksheet and how it should be organized. This means clearly identifying the data that will be input, the calculations that are needed to achieve the results, and the output that is desired. As part of the planning step, it is helpful to sketch out a design of the worksheet to organize the worksheet's structure. The design should include the worksheet title and row and column headings that identify the input and output. Additionally, sample data can be used to help determine the formulas needed to produce the output.
2. Enter and edit	Create the structure of the worksheet using Excel by entering the worksheet labels, data, and formulas. As you enter information, you are likely to make errors that need to be corrected or edited, or you will need to revise the content of what you have entered to clarify it or to add or delete information.
3. Test	Test the worksheet for errors. Use several sets of real or sample data as the input, and verify the resulting output. The input data should include a full range of possible values for each data item to ensure the worksheet can function successfully under all possible conditions.
4. Format	Enhance the appearance of the worksheet to make it more readable or attractive. This step is usually performed when the worksheet is near completion. It includes many features such as boldface text, italic, and color.

As the complexity of the worksheet increases, the importance of following the design process increases. Even for simple worksheets like the one you will create in this lab, the design process is important. You will find that you will generally follow these steps in the order listed above for your first draft of a worksheet. However, you will probably retrace steps such as editing and formatting as the final worksheet is developed.

During the planning phase, you have spoken with the Café manager, Evan, regarding the purpose of the worksheet and the content in general. The primary purpose is to develop a forecast for sales and expenses for the next year. First, Evan wants you to develop a worksheet for the first quarter forecast and then extend it by quarters for the year. After reviewing past budgets and consulting with Evan, you have designed the basic layout for the first quarter forecast for the Café, as shown below.

Downtown Internet Café
First Quarter Forecast

Sales:	January	February	March	Total
Beverage	$ 13,600	$ 14,600	$ 15,600	$ 43,800
				(sum of beverage sales)
Food	xx,xxx			
Total Sales	$ xx,xxx	$ xx,xxx	$ xx,xxx	$ xxx,xxx
				(sum of total sales)
Expenses:				
Cost of Goods	$(0.25 * beverage sales + 0.50 * food sales)			$(sum of cost of goods)
Salary				
Total Expenses	$ xx,xxx	$ xx,xxx	$ xx,xxx	$ xxx,xxx
	(sum of monthly expenses)			(sum of total expenses)
Income				
Net Income	$(Total sales − Total expenses)			
Profit Margin	$(Net income/Total sales)			

Entering and Editing Data

Now that you understand the purpose of the worksheet and have a general idea of the content, you are ready to begin entering the data. Each worksheet is like a blank piece of paper that already has many predefined settings. You will use the blank Sheet1 worksheet with the default settings to create the worksheet for the Café.

As you can see, the budget you designed above contains both descriptive text entries and numeric data. These are two types of data you can enter in a worksheet.

Concept Data

Basic information or **data** you enter in a cell can be text, numbers, dates, or times. **Text** entries can contain any combination of letters, numbers, spaces, and any other special characters. **Number** entries can include only the digits 0 to 9 and any of the special characters $+ − (), ./ \$ \% ? =$. Number entries can be used in calculations.

Text and number entries generally appear in the cell exactly as they are entered. However, some entries such as formulas direct Excel to perform a calculation on values in the worksheet. In these cases, the result of the formula appears in the cell, not the formula itself. You will learn about formulas later in the lab.

Adding Text Entries

You enter data into a worksheet by moving to the cell where you want the data displayed and typing the entry using the keyboard. First, you will enter the worksheet headings. Row and column **headings** are entries that are used to create the structure of the worksheet and describe other worksheet entries. Generally, headings are text entries. The column headings in this worksheet consist of the three months (January through March) and a total (sum of entries over three months) located in columns B through E. You will begin by entering the column heading for January in cell B2.

- Click on cell B2 to move to it.

- Type **January**

Having Trouble?

Do not be concerned if you make a typing error. You will learn how to correct it shortly.

Your screen should be similar to Figure 1.7

Figure 1.7

Several changes have occurred in the window. As you type, the entry is displayed both in the active cell and in the formula bar. The cursor appears in the active cell and marks your location in the entry. Two new buttons, ☒ and ☑, appear in the formula bar. They can be used with a mouse to cancel your entry or complete it.

Notice also that the mode displayed in the status bar has changed from Ready to Enter. This notifies you that the current mode of operation in the worksheet is entering data.

Although the entry is displayed in both the active cell and the formula bar, you need to press the ⏎Enter or Tab key, click ☑, or click on any other cell to complete your entry. If you press Esc or click ☒, the entry is cleared and nothing appears in the cell. Since your hands are already on the keyboard, it is quicker to press ⏎Enter or Tab than it is to use the mouse.

2 Press ↵Enter.

Your screen should be similar to Figure 1.8

Text entry is left-aligned in cell space

Cell selector moves down to next cell after pressing ↵Enter

Figure 1.8

Additional Information

Pressing ⇧Shift + ↵Enter to complete an entry moves up a cell, and Ctrl + ↵Enter completes the entry without moving to another cell.

The entry January is displayed in cell B2, and the mode has returned to Ready. In addition, the active cell is cell B3. Whenever you use the ↵Enter key to complete an entry, the cell selector moves down one cell.

Notice that the entry is positioned to the left side of the cell space. This is one of the worksheet default settings.

CLEARING AN ENTRY

After looking at the entry, you decide you want the column headings to be in row 3 rather than in row 2. This will leave more space above the column headings for a worksheet title. The Delete key can be used to clear the contents from a cell. You will remove the entry from cell B2 and enter it in cell B3.

1 Move to B2.

Press Delete.

Another Method

You also can use ✐ ▾ Clear/Clear Contents in the Editing group of the Home tab.

Move to B3.

Type January

Click ✓ Enter.

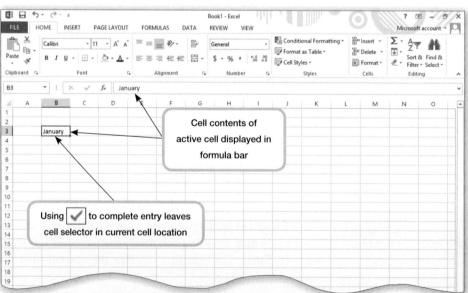

Cell contents of active cell displayed in formula bar

Using ✓ to complete entry leaves cell selector in current cell location

Figure 1.9

Your screen should be similar to Figure 1.9

The active cell does not change when you click ✓ to complete an entry. Because the active cell contains an entry, the cell content is displayed in the formula bar.

EDITING AN ENTRY

Next, you decide to change the heading from January to JAN. An entry in a cell can be entirely changed in the Ready mode or partially changed or edited in the Edit mode. To use the Ready mode, you move to the cell you want to change and retype the entry the way you want it to appear. As soon as a new character is entered, the existing entry is cleared.

Generally, however, if you need to change only part of an entry, using the Edit mode is quicker. To change to Edit mode, double-click on the cell whose contents you want to edit.

Double-click B3.

Having Trouble?

The mouse pointer must be ✛ when you double-click on the cell.

Another Method

Pressing the [F2] key also will change to Edit mode. The cursor is positioned at the end of the entry.

Your screen should be similar to Figure 1.10

Figure 1.10

The status bar shows that the new mode of operation is Edit. The cursor appears at the location you clicked in the entry, and the mouse pointer changes to an I-beam when positioned on the cell. Now you can click again or use the directional keys to move the cursor within the cell entry to the location of the text you want to change.

After the cursor is appropriately positioned, you can edit the entry by removing the incorrect characters and typing the correct characters. To do this, you can use the [Backspace] and [Delete] keys to delete text character by character and enter the new text, or you can select the text to be changed and then type the correction. You will change this entry to JAN.

Having Trouble?

Refer to the "Entering and Editing Text" and "Selecting Text" sections of the Introduction to Office 2013 to review these features.

Additional Information

You also can use [Ctrl] + [Delete] to delete everything to the right of the cursor in the active cell.

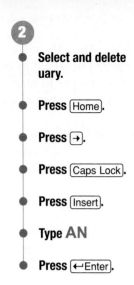

2
- Select and delete **uary.**
- Press [Home].
- Press [→].
- Press [Caps Lock].
- Press [Insert].
- Type **AN**
- Press [←Enter].

Your screen should be similar to Figure 1.11

Edited entry replaces existing entry

Figure 1.11

Additional Information

The Caps Lock indicator light on your keyboard is lit when this feature is on.

Additional Information

Overwrite is automatically turned off when you leave Edit mode or you press [Insert] again.

The four characters at the end of the entry were deleted. Turning on the Caps Lock feature produced the uppercase letters AN without having to hold down [⇧Shift]. Finally, by pressing [Insert], the program switched from inserting text to overwriting text as you typed. When overwriting text is on, the cursor changes to a highlight to show that the character will be replaced with the new text you type.

The new heading JAN is entered into cell B3, replacing January. As you can see, editing will be particularly useful with long or complicated entries.

Next, you will enter the remaining three headings in row 3. Because you want to move to the right one cell to enter the next month label, you will complete the entries using [→] or [Tab ⇥].

3

- Click on cell C3.

- Type **FEB**

- Press → or Tab ↹.

- Complete the column headings by entering **MAR** in cell D3 and **TOTAL** in cell E3.

Having Trouble?

Remember to press ←Enter, Tab ↹, or an arrow key or click in another cell to complete each entry.

- Press Caps Lock to turn off this feature.

Your screen should be similar to Figure 1.12

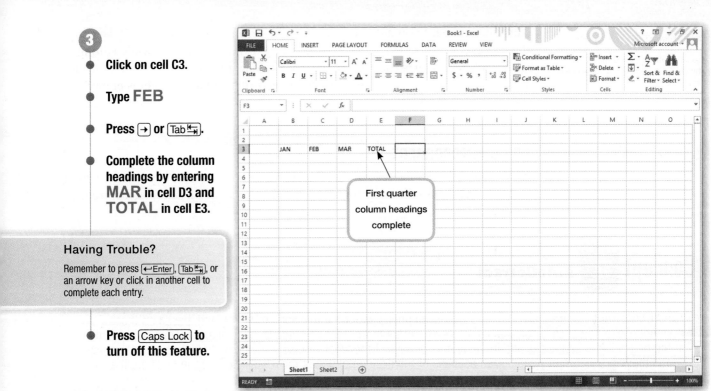

First quarter column headings complete

Figure 1.12

The column headings are now complete for the first quarter. Above the column headings, you want to enter a title for the worksheet. The first title line will be the café name, Downtown Internet Café.

4

- Move to B1.

- Type **Downtown Cafe** and click ✓ Enter.

- Double-click on cell B1 to change to Edit mode.

- Move the cursor to the beginning of the word **Café**.

- Type **Internet** followed by a space.

- Press Ctrl + ←Enter.

Your screen should be similar to Figure 1.13

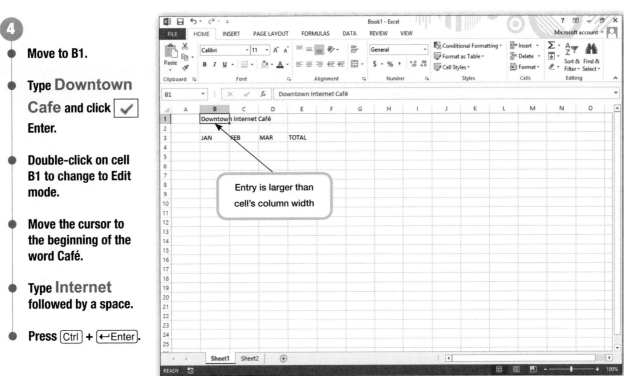

Entry is larger than cell's column width

Figure 1.13

This time, because you did not change to overwriting text as you edited the entry, the new text was inserted between the existing text. Inserting text while editing is the default setting. Also notice that the entry is longer than the cell's column width and overlaps into the cell to the right. As long as the cell to the right is empty, the whole entry will be displayed. If the cell to the right contains an entry, the overlapping part of the entry is not displayed.

USING AUTOCORRECT

Next, you will enter the second title line, First Quarter Report. As you enter text in a cell, Excel checks the entry for accuracy. This is part of the automatic correcting feature of Excel.

Concept 2 AutoCorrect

The **AutoCorrect** feature makes some basic assumptions about the text you are typing and, based on these assumptions, automatically corrects the entry. The AutoCorrect feature automatically inserts proper capitalization at the beginning of sentences and in the names of days of the week. It also will change to lowercase letters any words that were incorrectly capitalized because of the accidental use of the Caps Lock key. In addition, it also corrects many common typing and spelling errors automatically.

One way the program automatically makes corrections is by looking for certain types of errors. For example, if two capital letters appear at the beginning of a word, the second capital letter is changed to a lowercase letter. If a lowercase letter appears at the beginning of a sentence, the first letter of the first word is capitalized. If the name of a day begins with a lowercase letter, the first letter is capitalized.

Another way the program makes corrections is by checking all entries against a built-in list of words that are commonly spelled incorrectly or typed incorrectly. If it finds the entry on the list, the program automatically replaces the error with the correction. For example, the typing error "aboutthe" is automatically changed to "about the" because the error is on the AutoCorrect list. You also can add words that you want to be automatically corrected to the AutoCorrect list. Words you add are added to the list on the computer you are using and will be available to anyone who uses the machine later.

You will enter the second title line and will intentionally misspell two words to demonstrate how the AutoCorrect feature works.

● **Move to B2.**

● **Type Firts Quater Forecast**

● **Press ←Enter.**

Your screen should be similar to Figure 1.14

Figure 1.14

The two typing errors were automatically corrected as soon as you completed a word by pressing the spacebar. If the entry was a single word, it would be checked as soon as you completed the entry.

Next, the row headings need to be entered into column A of the worksheet. The row headings and what they represent are shown in the following table.

Heading	Description
Sales	
Espresso	Income from sales of espresso-based drinks
Coffee	Income from drip coffee sales
Food/Beverage	Income from sales of baked goods, sandwiches, salads, and other beverages
Merchandise	Income from sales of mugs, books, magazines, candy, etc.
Computer	Income from computer rental usage, printing, copier use, and MP3 downloads
Total Sales	Sum of all sales
Expenses	
Cost of Goods	Cost of espresso, coffee, and food items sold
Cost of Merchandise	Cost of merchandise other than food and beverage
Wages	Manager and labor costs
Internet	WiFi access, MP3 kiosk rental, etc.
Building	Lease, insurance, electricity, water, etc.
Capital Assets	Equipment leases, interest, depreciation
Miscellaneous	Maintenance, phone, office supplies, outside services, taxes, etc.
Income	
Net Income	Total sales minus total expenses
Profit Margin	Net income divided by total sales

2

Complete the row headings for the Sales portion of the worksheet by entering the following headings in the indicated cells.

Cell	Heading
A3	Sales
A4	Espresso
A5	Coffee
A6	Food/Beverage
A7	Merchandise
A8	Computer
A9	Total Sales

Your screen should be similar to Figure 1.15

Figure 1.15

ADDING NUMBER ENTRIES

Additional Information

You can use the number keys above the alphabetic keys or the numeric keypad area to enter numbers. If you use the numeric keypad, the [Num Lock] key must be on.

Next, you will enter the expected sales numbers for January into cells B4 through B8. As you learned earlier, number entries can include the digits 0 to 9 and any of these special characters: + − ( ) , . / $ % ? =. When entering numbers, it is not necessary to type the comma to separate thousands or the currency ($) symbol. You will learn about adding these symbols shortly.

- Move to B4.

- Type **13300** and press [←Enter].

- In the same manner, enter the January sales numbers for the remaining items using the values shown below.

Cell	Number
B5	5800
B6	3600
B7	1000
B8	600

Your screen should be similar to Figure 1.16

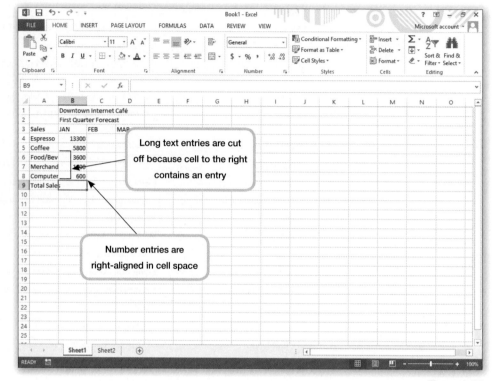

Long text entries are cut off because cell to the right contains an entry

Number entries are right-aligned in cell space

Figure 1.16

Unlike text entries, Excel displays number entries right-aligned in the cell space by default. Also notice that the entries in cells A6 and A7 are no longer completely displayed. They contain long text entries and because the cells to the right now contain an entry, the overlapping part of the entry is shortened. However, the entire entry is fully displayed in the formula bar. Only the display of the entry in the cell has been shortened.

Modifying Column Widths

To allow the long text entries in column A to be fully displayed, you can increase the column's width.

Concept Column Width

The **column width** is the size or width of a column and controls the amount of information that can be displayed in a cell. A text entry that is larger than the column width will be fully displayed only if the cells to the right are blank. If the cells to the right contain data, the text is interrupted. On the other hand, when numbers are entered in a cell, the column width is automatically increased to fully display the entry.

The default column width setting is 8.43. The number represents the average number of digits that can be displayed in a cell using the standard type style. The column width can be any number from 0 to 255. If it is set to 0, the column is hidden.

When the worksheet is printed, it appears as it does currently on the screen. Therefore, you want to increase the column width to display the largest entry. Likewise, you can decrease the column width when the entries in a column are short.

There are several ways to change the column width. Using the mouse, you can change the width by dragging the boundary of the column heading. You also can set the column width to an exact value or to automatically fit the contents of the column.

DRAGGING THE COLUMN BOUNDARY

Touch Tip

You can also slide/drag the boundary line with your fingertip.

The column width can be quickly adjusted by dragging the boundary line located to the right of the column letter. Dragging it to the left decreases the column width, while dragging it to the right increases the width. As you drag, a temporary column reference line shows where the new column will appear and a ScreenTip displays the width of the column.

1

- Point to the boundary line to the right of the column letter A, and when the mouse pointer changes to , click and drag the mouse pointer to the right.

- When the ScreenTip displays 24.00, release the mouse button.

Your screen should be similar to Figure 1.17

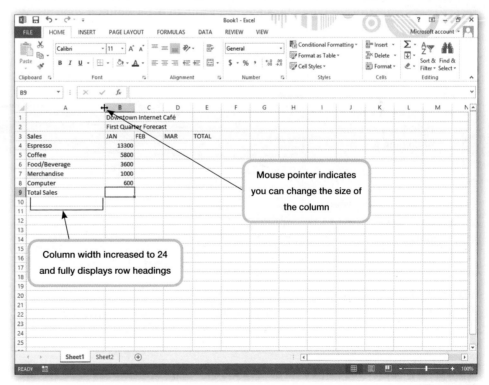

Figure 1.17

Now column A is more than wide enough to fully display all the row headings.

USING A SPECIFIED VALUE

Next, you will reduce the width of column A to 20.

● **Move to any cell in column A.**

● **Click** [Format ▾] **in the Cells group and choose Column Width.**

● **Type 20 in the Column Width text box and click** [OK] **.**

Your screen should be similar to Figure 1.18

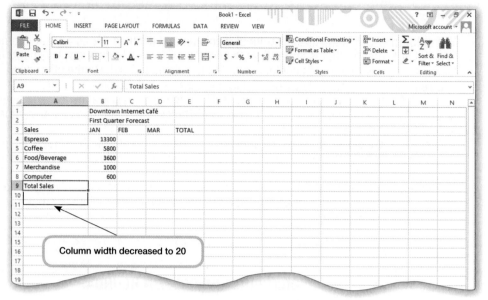

Column width decreased to 20

Figure 1.18

Although this is close, you would like to refine it a little more.

USING AUTOFIT

Another way to change the column width is to use the **AutoFit** feature to automatically adjust the width to fit the column contents. When using AutoFit, double-click the boundary to the right of the column heading of the column you want to fit to contents.

● **Double-click the right boundary line of column A.**

Having Trouble?

Make sure the mouse pointer changes to ↔ before you double-click on the column boundary line.

Your screen should be similar to Figure 1.19

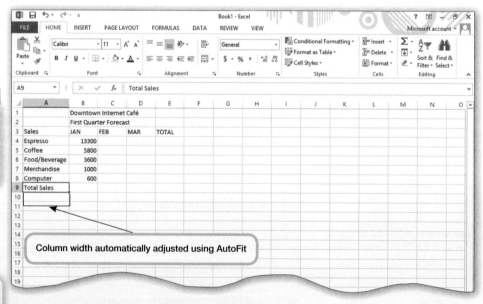

Column width automatically adjusted using AutoFit

Figure 1.19

Another Method

You also can use [Format ▾] /AutoFit Column Width.

The column width is sized to just slightly larger than the longest cell contents.

Saving, Closing, and Opening a Workbook File

Having Trouble?

Refer to the section "Saving a File" in the Introduction to Office 2013 to review this feature.

You have a meeting you need to attend shortly, so you want to save the work you have completed so far on the workbook to a file and then close the file. You will name the file Cafe Forecast and use the default file type settings of Excel Workbook (*.xlsx). The file extension .xlsx identifies the file as an Excel 2007–2013 workbook.

Excel 2003 and earlier versions used the .xls file extension. If you plan to share a file with someone using Excel 2003 or earlier, you can save the file using the .xls file type; however, some features may be lost. Otherwise, if you save it as an .xlsx file type, the recipient may not be able to view all the features.

1

- Click Save in the Quick Access Toolbar.

- Select the location where you want to save your file.

- If necessary, click in the File Name text box to highlight the proposed file name, or triple-click on the file name to select it.

- Type Cafe Forecast

- Click **Save** or press ⏎Enter.

Your screen should be similar to Figure 1.20

New file name

Figure 1.20

Additional Information

The file name in the title bar may display the workbook file extension, .xlsx, depending on your Windows Folder settings.

The new file name is displayed in the application window title bar. The worksheet data that was on your screen and in the computer's memory is now saved at the location you specified in a new file called Cafe Forecast.

You are now ready to close the workbook file.

2

- Click the File tab to open Backstage and choose Close.

Additional Information

The New option on the File tab is used to open a new blank workbook file or use a template.

Having Trouble?

Refer to the "Opening a File" section in the Introduction to Office 2013 to review this feature.

Because you did not make any changes to the workbook after saving it, the workbook file is closed immediately and the Excel window displays an empty workbook window. If you had made changes to the file before closing it, you would have been prompted to save the file to prevent the accidental loss of data.

After attending your meeting, you continued working on the Café forecast. To see what has been done so far, you will open the workbook file named ex01_CafeForecast1.

3

- **Click the File tab to open Backstage and choose Open.**

Another Method

The keyboard shortcut is Ctrl + O.

- **Select the location containing your data files.**
- **Select** ex01_Cafe Forecast1**.**
- **Click** Open ▼**.**

Another Method

You also could double-click the file name to open it.

- **If necessary, click** Enable Editing **and maximize the workbook window.**

Your screen should be similar to Figure 1.21

Figure 1.21

The workbook is opened and displayed in the workbook window. The workbook contains the additional sales values for February and March, the expense row headings, and several of the expense values for the month of January.

Using Proofing Tools

When entering information into a worksheet, you are likely to make spelling and typing errors. To help locate and correct these errors, the spelling checker feature can be used. Additionally, you may find that the descriptive headings you have entered may not be exactly the word you want. The thesaurus can suggest better words to clarify the meaning of the worksheet.

CHECKING SPELLING

In your rush to get the row headings entered you realize you misspelled a few words. For example, the Expenses label is spelled "Espenses." Just to make sure there are no other spelling errors, you will check the spelling of all text entries in this worksheet.

Concept 4 Spelling Checker

The **spelling checker** locates misspelled words, duplicate words, and capitalization irregularities in the active worksheet and proposes the correct spelling. This feature works by comparing each word to a dictionary of words, called the **main dictionary**, that is supplied with the program. You also can create a **custom dictionary** to hold words you commonly use but that are not included in the main dictionary. If the word does not appear in the main dictionary or in a custom dictionary, it is identified as misspelled.

When you check spelling, the contents of all cell entries in the entire active sheet are checked. If you are in Edit mode when you check spelling, only the contents of the text in the cell are checked. The spelling checker does not check spelling in formulas or in text that results from formulas.

Excel begins checking all worksheet entries from the active cell forward.

1

- If necessary, move to A1.

- Open the Review tab.

- Click [✓ Spelling] in the Proofing group.

Another Method

The keyboard shortcut is F7.

Your screen should be similar to Figure 1.22

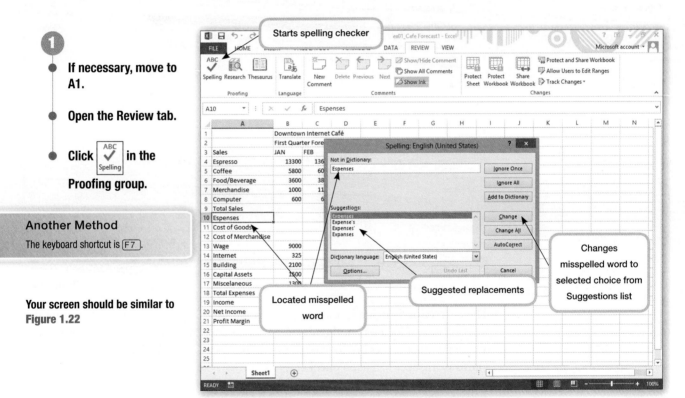

Figure 1.22

Additional Information

Spell-checking operates the same way in all Office 2013 programs. The dictionaries are shared among Office applications.

The spelling checker immediately begins checking the worksheet for words that it cannot locate in its main dictionary. The first cell containing a misspelled word, in this case Espenses, is now the active cell and the Spelling dialog box is displayed. The word it cannot locate in the dictionary is displayed in the Not in Dictionary text box. The Suggestions text box displays a list of possible replacements. If the selected replacement is not correct, you can select another choice from the suggestions list or type the correct word in the Not in Dictionary text box.

The option buttons shown in the table below have the following effects:

Option	Effect
Ignore Once	Leaves selected word unchanged.
Ignore All	Leaves this word and all identical words in worksheet unchanged.
Add to Dictionary	Adds the word in the Not in Dictionary box to a custom dictionary so Excel will not question this word during subsequent spell-checks.
Change	Changes selected word to word highlighted in Suggestions box.
Change All	Changes this word and all identical words in worksheet to word highlighted in Suggestions box.
AutoCorrect	Adds a word to the AutoCorrect list so the word will be corrected as you type.

You want to accept the suggested replacement, Expenses.

2

Click .

Your screen should be similar to Figure 1.23

Figure 1.23

The correction is made in the worksheet, and the program continues checking the worksheet and locates another error, Miscellaneous. You will make this correction. When no other errors are located, a dialog box is displayed, informing you that the entire worksheet has been checked.

3

Change this word to Miscellaneous.

Click [OK] to end spell-checking.

The worksheet is now free of spelling errors.

USING THE THESAURUS

The next text change you want to make is to find a better word for "Wage" in cell A13. To help find a similar word, you will use the thesaurus tool.

Concept Thesaurus

The **thesaurus** is a reference tool that provides synonyms, antonyms, and related words for a selected word or phrase. **Synonyms** are words with a similar meaning, such as "cheerful" and "happy." **Antonyms** are words with an opposite meaning, such as "cheerful" and "sad." Related words are words that are variations of the same word, such as "cheerful" and "cheer." The thesaurus can help to liven up your documents by adding interest and variety to your text.

To use the thesaurus, first move to the cell containing the word you want to change. If a cell contains multiple words, you need to select the individual word in the cell.

1

Move to A13.

Click in the Proofing group.

Another Method

You also can hold down Alt while clicking on the cell containing the word you want looked up to access the thesaurus in the Research task pane.

Your screen should be similar to Figure 1.24

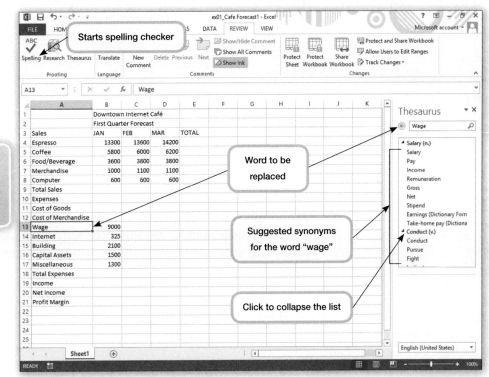

Figure 1.24

The Thesaurus task pane opens. The word in the active cell, Wage, is entered in the text box and the list box displays words in the thesaurus that have similar meanings for this word. The list contains synonyms for "wage" used as a noun or as a verb. The first word at the top of each group is the group heading and is closest in meaning. It is preceded by a ⊿ collapse symbol, and the word is bold. The ⊿ indicates the list of synonyms is displayed. Clicking this button will hide or collapse the list of synonyms. After collapsing a list the ◢ collapse symbol changes to an ▷ expand symbol. Clicking this symbol redisplays the list.

When you point to a word in the list, a drop-down list of two menu options, Insert and Copy, becomes available. The Insert option inserts the word into the active cell. The Copy option is used to copy and then paste the word into any worksheet cell. Clicking a word in the list looks up that word in the thesaurus. You decide to use the word "Pay" and will insert the word into cell A13 in place of "Wage."

2

● Point to "Pay" and click ▼ to display the menu.

● Choose Insert.

● Click ✕ in the title bar of the Thesaurus task pane to close it.

Your screen should be similar to Figure 1.25

Figure 1.25

The word "Wage" is replaced with the selected word from the thesaurus. Notice the replacement word is capitalized correctly. This is because the replacement text follows the same capitalization as the word it replaces.

Copying and Pasting Cell Contents

Having Trouble?

Refer to the section "Copying and Moving Selections" in the Introduction to Microsoft Office 2013 to review this feature.

Next, you want to enter the estimated expenses for pay, Internet, building, and miscellaneous for February and March. They are the same as the January expense numbers. Because these values are the same, instead of entering the same number repeatedly into each cell you can quickly copy the contents of one cell to another. You also want to move information from one location in the worksheet to another.

COPYING AND PASTING DATA

To use the Copy command, you first select the cell or cells in the source containing the data to be copied. This is called the **copy area**. You will copy the Pay value in cell B13 into cells C13 and D13.

1
● **Move to B13.**

● **Open the Home tab.**

● **Click** 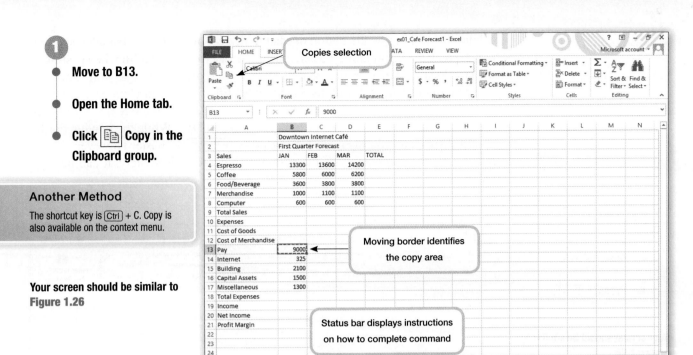 **Copy in the Clipboard group.**

Another Method

The shortcut key is Ctrl + C. Copy is also available on the context menu.

Your screen should be similar to Figure 1.26

Figure 1.26

A moving border identifies the copy area and indicates that the contents have been copied to the system Clipboard. The instructions displayed in the status bar tell you to select the destination, called the **paste area**, where you want the contents copied. You will copy them to cell C13.

2
● **Move to C13.**

● **Click the top part of the** 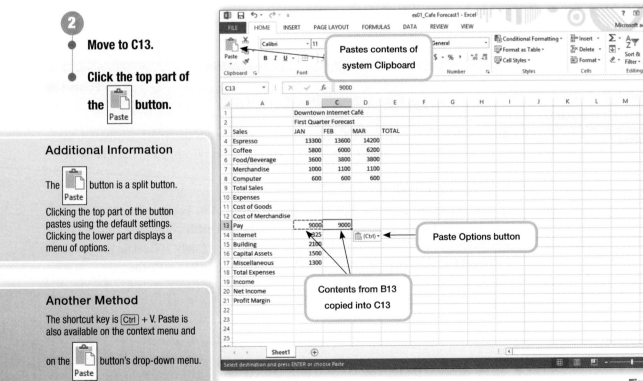 **button.**

Additional Information

The ![Paste] button is a split button. Clicking the top part of the button pastes using the default settings. Clicking the lower part displays a menu of options.

Another Method

The shortcut key is Ctrl + V. Paste is also available on the context menu and on the ![Paste] button's drop-down menu.

Your screen should be similar to Figure 1.27

Figure 1.27

The contents of the system Clipboard are inserted at the specified destination location. Each time the Paste command is used, the ![Ctrl] Paste Options button is

Copying and Pasting Cell Contents   **EX1.29**

available. Clicking on the button opens the Paste Options menu that allows you to control how the information you are pasting is inserted. Be careful when pasting to the new location because any existing entries are replaced.

The moving border is still displayed, indicating the system Clipboard still contains the copied entry. Now you can complete the data for the Pay row by pasting the value again from the system Clipboard into cell D13. While the moving border is still displayed, you also can simply press ⏎Enter to paste. However, as this method clears the contents of the system Clipboard immediately, it can be used only once.

Additional Information

You will learn about the different Excel paste options in later labs.

3

● **Move to D13.**

● **Press** ⏎Enter.

Your screen should be similar to Figure 1.28

Figure 1.28

Additional Information

You also can cancel a moving border and clear the system Clipboard contents by pressing Esc.

The contents of the system Clipboard are inserted at the specified destination location and the moving border is cleared, indicating the system Clipboard is empty.

SELECTING A RANGE

Now you need to copy the Internet value in cell B14 to February and March. You could copy and paste the contents individually into each cell as you did with the Pay values. A quicker method, however, is to select a range and paste the contents to all cells in the range at once.

Concept 6 Range

A selection consisting of two or more cells on a worksheet is a **range**. The cells in a range can be adjacent or nonadjacent. An **adjacent range** is a rectangular block of adjoining cells. A **nonadjacent range** consists of two or more selected cells or ranges that are not adjoining. In the example shown below, the shaded areas show valid adjacent and nonadjacent ranges. A **range reference** identifies the cells in a range. A colon is used to separate the first and last cells of an adjacent range reference. For example, A2:C4 indicates the range consists of cells A2 through C4. Commas separate the cell references of a nonadjacent range. For example, A10, B12, C14 indicates the range consists of cells A10, B12, and C14 of a nonadjacent range.

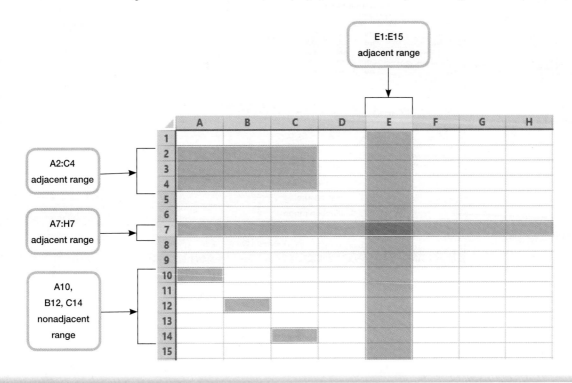

Additional Information

Selecting a range identifies the cells to be included in the selection, rather than the specific text within the cells.

You can select a range using the mouse procedures shown in the following table. You also can select using the keyboard by moving to the first cell of the range, holding down ⇧Shift or pressing F8 and using the navigational keys to expand the highlight. Using the F8 key turns on and off Extend mode. When this mode is on, Extend Selection appears in the status bar.

Touch Tip

To select a range on a touch screen, tap a cell and drag the selection handle to the extent of the range you want.

To Select	Mouse
A range	Click first cell of range and drag to the last cell.
A large range	Click first cell of range, hold down ⇧Shift, and click last cell of range.
All cells on worksheet	Click the ▨ All button located at the intersection of the row and column headings.
Nonadjacent cells or ranges	Select first cell or range, hold down Ctrl while selecting the other cell or range.
Entire row or column	Click the row number or column letter heading.
Adjacent rows or columns	Drag across the row number or column letter headings.
Nonadjacent rows or columns	Select first row or column, hold down Ctrl, and select the other rows or columns.

To complete the data for the Internet row, you want to copy the value in cell B14 to the system Clipboard and then copy the system Clipboard contents to the adjacent range of cells C14 through D14.

- **Move to B14.**

- **Click ▦ Copy.**

- **Drag to select the range of cells C14 through D14.**

- **Click ▦ Paste.**

Your screen should be similar to Figure 1.29

Figure 1.29

Quick Analysis button

Entry in copy area is copied into destination range

Information about contents of selected range

Additional Information

The paste area does not have to be adjacent to the copy area.

The destination range is highlighted and identified by a dark border surrounding the selected cells. The source entry was copied from cell B14 and pasted into the selected destination range. In addition to the ▼ Paste Options button, the ▦ Quick Analysis button is displayed. This button appears whenever a range is selected that contains data that can be formatted or analyzed. You will learn about this feature shortly. Also notice the status bar now displays the average, count, and sum of values in the selected range.

USING THE FILL HANDLE

Next, you will copy the January Building expenses to cells C15 through D15, the Capital Assets expenses to cells C16 through D16, and the Miscellaneous expenses to cells C17 through D17. You can copy all values at the same time across the row by first specifying a range as the source. Another way to copy is to select the cells that contain the data you want to copy and drag the **fill handle**, the green box in the lower-right corner of a selection across or down the cells you want to fill.

1

- Press `Esc` to clear the moving border.

- Drag to select cells B15 through B17.

- Point to the fill handle and when the mouse pointer is a **+**, drag the mouse to extend the selection to cells D15 through D17.

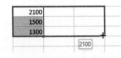

- Release the mouse button.

Another Method

You also can select the range B15:D17, click ⬇ Fill in the Editing group, and choose Right. The shortcut key is `Ctrl` + R.

Your screen should be similar to Figure 1.30

Additional Information

You will learn more about the AutoFill feature in later labs.

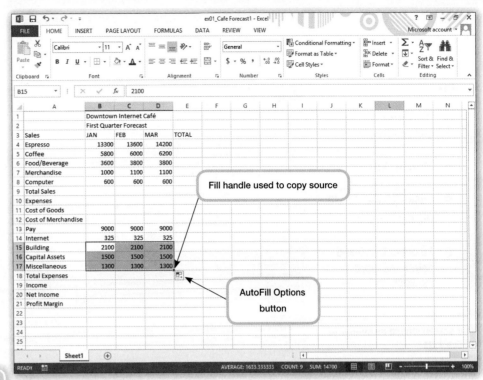

Figure 1.30

The range of cells to the right of the source is filled with the same values as in the source range. Using this method does not copy the source to the system Clipboard and therefore you cannot paste the source multiple times. When you copy by dragging the fill handle, the ⬛ ▾ AutoFill Options button appears. Its menu commands are used to modify how the fill operation was performed. It will disappear as soon as you make an entry in the worksheet.

INSERTING COPIED CELL CONTENT

You also decide to include another row of month headings above the expenses to make the worksheet data easier to read. To do this quickly, you can insert copied data between existing data. To indicate where to place the copied content, you move the cell selector to the upper-left cell of the area where you want the selection inserted.

The column headings you want to copy are in cells B3 through E3. You will also copy cell A3, and clear the text in column A of the new row when you paste the contents.

1

- Copy the contents of cells A3 through E3.

- Move to A10.

- Click in the Cells group.

- Select cell A10 and delete the word "Sales".

Your screen should be similar to Figure 1.31

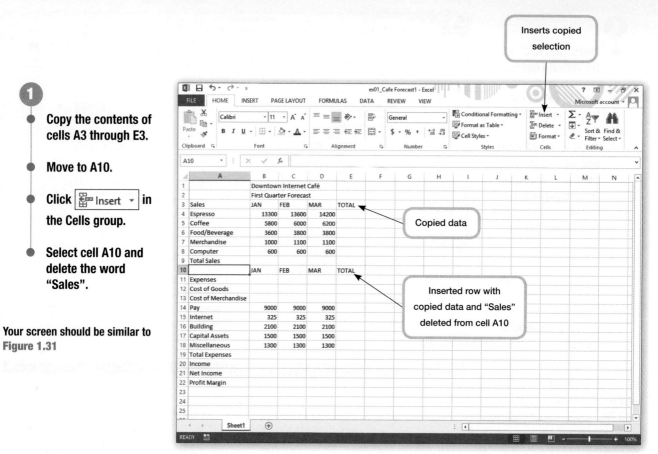

Figure 1.31

The copied data is inserted into the existing row (10) and all entries below are moved down one row.

CUTTING AND PASTING DATA

Next, you decide the Income, Net Income, and Profit Margin rows of data would stand out more if a blank row separated them from the expenses. Also, the Profit Margin row of data would be better separated from the Net Income row by a blank row. You will first remove the cell contents of the three cells using ✂ Cut and then paste the contents from the system Clipboard into the new location. The pasted content will copy over any existing content. You will use the keyboard shortcuts for these commands to complete this process.

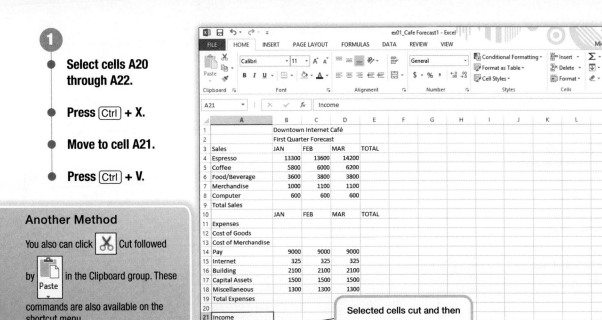

1

- Select cells A20 through A22.
- Press Ctrl + X.
- Move to cell A21.
- Press Ctrl + V.

Another Method

You also can click ✂ Cut followed by 📋 Paste in the Clipboard group. These commands are also available on the shortcut menu.

Your screen should be similar to Figure 1.32

Figure 1.32

The contents of the three selected cells are copied to the system Clipboard. Then, when you paste, the cell contents are removed and inserted at the new location, copying over any existing content.

Another way you can cut and paste is to use drag and drop to move the cell contents. This method is quickest and most useful when the distance between cells is short and they are visible within the window, whereas cut and paste is best for long-distance moves. You will use this method to move the Profit Margin entry down one cell.

Additional Information

You also can hold down Ctrl and drag a selection to copy it to a new location. The mouse pointer appears as ▷⁺ as you drag when copying.

Move to cell A23.

Point to the border of the selection and when the mouse pointer shape is ⬆̶̲̥ , drag the selection down one row to cell A24 and release the mouse button.

Additional Information

As you drag, an outline of the cell selection appears and the mouse pointer displays the cell reference to show its new location in the worksheet.

Open the File tab and choose Save As.

Save the changes you have made to the workbook as Cafe Forecast1 **to your solution file location.**

Your screen should be similar to Figure 1.33

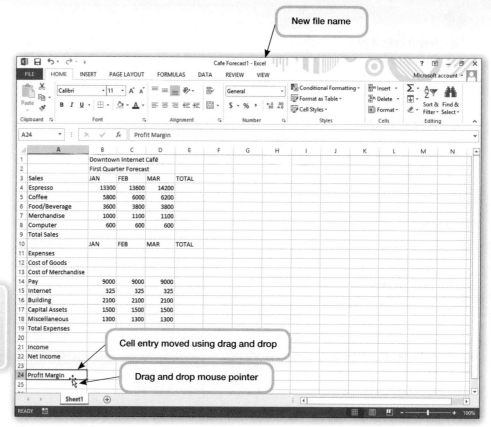

Figure 1.33

The cell contents were moved into cell A24 and cleared from the original cell.

When you use the Copy and Cut commands, the contents are copied to the system Clipboard and can be copied to any location in the worksheet, another workbook, or a document in another application multiple times. When you use ⬇ Fill or drag the fill handle, the destination must be in the same row or column as the source, and the source is not copied to the system Clipboard. Dragging the cell border to move or copy also does not copy the source to the system Clipboard.

NOTE If you are running short on lab time, this is an appropriate place to end your session. When you begin again, open the file Cafe Forecast1.

Working with Formulas

The remaining entries that need to be made in the worksheet are formula entries.

Concept 7 Formula

A **formula** is an equation that performs a calculation on data contained in a worksheet. A formula always begins with an equal sign (=) and uses arithmetic operators. An **operator** is a symbol that specifies the type of numeric operation to perform. Excel includes the following operators: + (addition), − (subtraction), / (division), * (multiplication), % (percent), and ^ (exponentiation). The calculated result from a formula is a **variable** value because it can change if the data it depends on changes. In contrast, a number entry is a **constant** value. It does not begin with an equal sign and does not change unless you change it directly by typing in another entry.

In a formula that contains more than one operator, Excel calculates the formula from left to right and performs the calculation in the following order: percent, exponentiation, multiplication and division, and addition and subtraction (see Example A). This is the **order of operations, that determines which operations take precedence before other operations**. If a formula contains operators with the same precedence (for example, addition and subtraction), they are again evaluated from left to right. The order of precedence can be overridden by enclosing the operation you want performed first in parentheses (see Example B). When there are multiple sets of parentheses, Excel evaluates them working from the innermost set of parentheses out.

Example A: =5*4−3   Result is 17 (5 times 4 to get 20, and then subtract 3 for a total of 17)
Example B: =5*(4−3)   Result is 5 (4 minus 3 to get 1, and then 1 times 5 for a total of 5)

The values on which a numeric formula performs a calculation are called **operands**. Numbers or cell references can be operands in a formula. Usually cell references are used, and when the numeric entries in the referenced cell(s) change, the result of the formula is automatically recalculated.

ENTERING FORMULAS

The first formula you will enter will calculate the total Espresso sales for January through March (cell E4) by summing the numbers in cells B4 through D4. You will use cell references in the formula as the operands and the + arithmetic operator to specify addition. A formula is entered in the cell where you want the calculated value to be displayed. As you enter the formula, Excel helps you keep track of the cell references by identifying the referenced cell with a colored border and using the same color for the cell reference in the formula.

Move to E4.

Type =b

Your screen should be similar to Figure 1.34

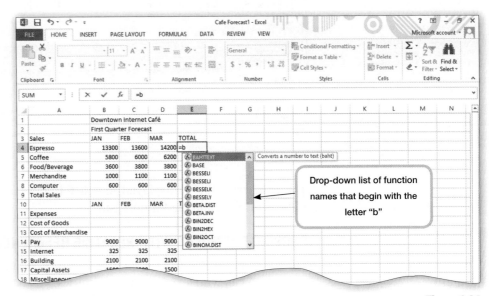

Figure 1.34

A drop-down list of function names that begin with the letter "b" is displayed. Functions are a type of formula entry that you will learn about shortly.

2 • Type 4+c4+d4

Additional Information

Cell references can be typed in either uppercase or lowercase letters. Spaces between parts of the formula are optional.

Your screen should be similar to Figure 1.35

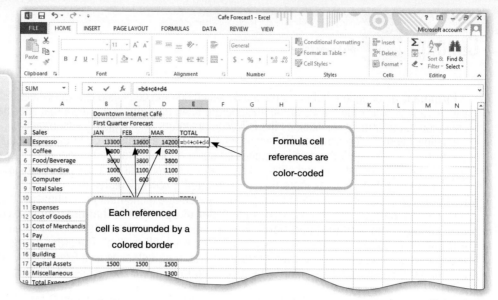

Figure 1.35

As you enter the formula, each cell that is referenced in the formula is surrounded by a colored box that matches the color of the cell reference in the formula.

3 • Press Ctrl + ←Enter or click ✓ Enter in the formula bar.

Your screen should be similar to Figure 1.36

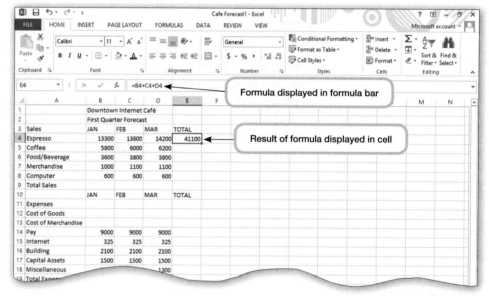

Figure 1.36

The number 41100 is displayed in cell E4, and the formula that calculates this value is displayed in the formula bar.

COPYING FORMULAS WITH RELATIVE REFERENCES

The formulas to calculate the total sales for rows 5 through 8 can be entered next. Just as you can with text and numeric entries, you can copy formulas from one cell to another.

1

Copy the formula in cell E4 to cells E5 through E8 using any of the copying methods.

Move to E5.

If necessary, press [Esc] to clear the moving border.

Your screen should be similar to Figure 1.37

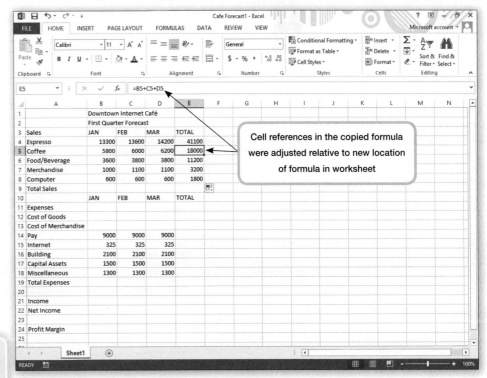

Figure 1.37

Additional Information

The AutoFill Options button may appear, depending on the method you use for copying the formula.

The calculated result, 18000, is displayed in the cell. The formula displayed in the formula bar is =B5+C5+D5. The formula to calculate the Coffee total sales is not an exact duplicate of the formula used to calculate the Espresso total sales (=B4+C4+D4). Instead, the cells referenced in the formula have been changed to reflect the new location of the formula in row 5. This is because the references in the formula are relative references.

Concept ⑧ Relative Reference

A **relative reference** is a cell or range reference in a formula whose location is interpreted by Excel in relation to the position of the cell that contains the formula. When a formula is copied, the referenced cells in the formula automatically adjust to reflect the new worksheet location. The relative relationship between the referenced cell and the new location is maintained. Because relative references automatically adjust for the new location, the relative references in a copied formula refer to different cells than the references in the original formula. The relationship between cells in both the copied and the pasted formulas is the same although the cell references are different.

For example, in the figure here, cell A1 references the value in cell A4 (in this case, 10). If the formula in A1 is copied to B2, the reference for B2 is adjusted to the value in cell B5 (in this case, 20).

2

● Move to cell E6, E7, and then to cell E8.

Your screen should be similar to Figure 1.38

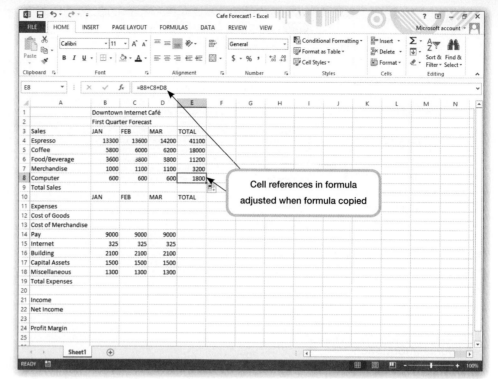

Cell references in formula adjusted when formula copied

Figure 1.38

The formulas in these cells also have changed to reflect the new row location and to appropriately calculate the total based on the sales.

SUMMARIZING DATA

Next, you will calculate the monthly total sales. The formula to calculate the total sales for January needs to be entered in cell B9 and copied across the row. You could use a formula similar to the formula used to calculate the category sales in column E. The formula would be =B4+B5+B6+B7+B8. However, it is faster and more accurate to use a function.

Concept Function

A **function** is a prewritten formula that performs certain types of calculations automatically. The **syntax,** or rules of structure for entering all functions, is as follows:

=Function name (argument1, argument2, . . .)

The function name identifies the type of calculation to be performed. Most functions require that you enter one or more arguments following the function name. An **argument** is the data the function uses to perform the calculation. The type of data the function requires depends upon the type of calculation being performed. Most commonly, the argument consists of numbers or references to cells that contain numbers. The argument is enclosed in parentheses, and commas separate multiple arguments. The beginning and ending cells of a range are separated with a colon.

Some functions, such as several of the date and time functions, do not require an argument. However, you still need to enter the opening and closing parentheses; for example, =NOW(). If a function starts the formula, enter an equal sign before the function name; for example, =SUM(D5:F5)/25.

Excel includes several hundred functions divided into 11 categories. Some common functions from each category and the results they calculate are shown in the following table.

Category	Function	Calculates
Financial	PMT	Calculates the payment for a loan based on constant payments and a constant interest rate.
	PV	Returns the present value of an investment—the total amount that a series of future payments is worth now.
	FV	Returns the future value of an investment—the total amount that a series of payments will be worth.
Date & Time	TODAY	Returns the serial number that represents today's date.
	DATE	Returns the serial number of a particular date.
	NOW	Returns the serial number of the current date and time.
Math & Trig	SUM	Adds all the numbers in a range of cells.
	ABS	Returns the absolute value of a number (a number without its sign).
Statistical	AVERAGE	Returns the average (arithmetic mean) of its arguments.
	MAX	Returns the largest value in a set of values; ignores logical values and text.
	MIN	Returns the smallest value in a set of values; ignores logical values and text.
	COUNT	Counts the number of cells in a range that contain numbers.
	COUNTA	Counts the number of cells in a range that are not empty.
Lookup & Reference	COLUMNS	Returns the number of columns in an array or reference.
	HLOOKUP	Looks for a value in the top row of a table and returns the value in the same column from a row you specify.
	VLOOKUP	Looks for a value in the leftmost column of a table and returns the value in the same row from a column you specify.
Database	DSUM	Adds the numbers in the field (column) or records in the database that match the conditions you specify.
	DAVERAGE	Averages the values in a column in a list or database that match conditions you specify.
Text	PROPER	Converts text to proper case in which the first letter of each word is capitalized.
	UPPER	Converts text to uppercase.
	LOWER	Converts text to lowercase.
	SUBSTITUTE	Replaces existing text with new text in a text string.
Logical	IF	Returns one value if a condition you specify evaluates to TRUE and another value if it evaluates to FALSE.
	AND	Returns TRUE if all its arguments are TRUE; returns FALSE if any arguments are FALSE.
	OR	Returns TRUE if any arguments are TRUE; returns FALSE if all arguments are FALSE.
	NOT	Changes FALSE to TRUE or TRUE to FALSE.
	IFERROR	Returns value-if-error if expression is an error and the value of the expression itself otherwise.
Information	ISLOGICAL	Returns TRUE if value is a logical value, either TRUE or FALSE.
	ISREF	Returns TRUE if value is a reference.
Engineering	BIN2DEC	Converts a binary number to decimal.
	CONVERT	Converts a number from one measurement system to another.
Cube	CUBESETCOUNT	Returns the number of items in a set.

You will use the SUM function to calculate the total sales for January. Because the SUM function is the most commonly used function, it has its own command button.

1

● Move to **B9**.

● Click ∑ ▾ **Sum** in the Editing group.

Another Method

Pressing Alt + = is the keyboard shortcut for Sum. This function is also available on the Formulas tab.

Your screen should be similar to Figure 1.39

Additional Information

The ∑ ▾ Sum button also can calculate a grand total if the worksheet contains subtotals. Select a cell below or to the right of a cell that contains a subtotal and then click ∑ ▾ Sum.

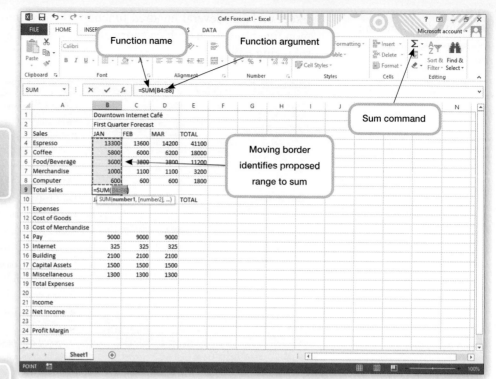

Figure 1.39

Excel automatically proposes a range based upon the data above or to the left of the active cell. The formula bar displays the name of the function followed by the range argument enclosed in parentheses. You will accept the proposed range and enter the function.

2

● Click **Enter**.

Your screen should be similar to Figure 1.40

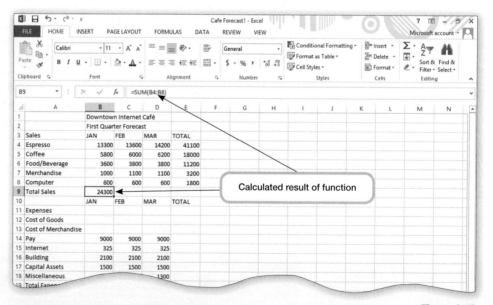

Figure 1.40

The result, 24300, calculated by the SUM function is displayed in cell B9.

USING THE QUICK ANALYSIS TOOL

Next, you need to calculate the total sales for February and March and the Total column. You will use the **Quick Analysis tool** to insert the SUM function for this range. The Quick Analysis button appears in the bottom-right corner of the selection when you select a range of cells for which there are several likely actions.

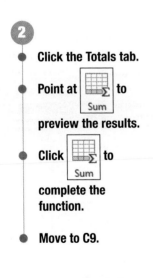

- Select the range C4 through E8.

- Click Quick Analysis.

Your screen should be similar to Figure 1.41

Figure 1.41

The Quick Analysis gallery displays five tabs. Each tab contains several options for the most likely action suited to the selected data. Pointing to an option displays a preview of the results in the worksheet.

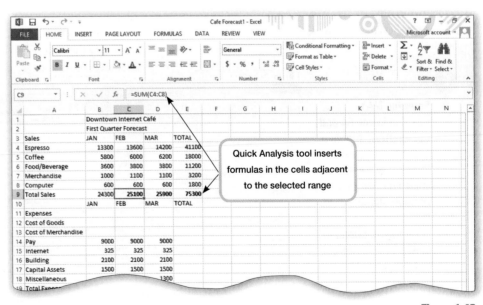

- Click the Totals tab.

- Point at [Sum] to preview the results.

- Click [Sum] to complete the function.

- Move to C9.

Your screen should be similar to Figure 1.42

Figure 1.42

The results calculated by the SUM function are displayed in bold in the blank row (9) below the range. You will adjust the display of these values shortly. The Totals functions in the Quick Analysis tool can be used only when the range to be calculated is adjacent to the range where the function will be entered.

USING THE MIN, MAX, AND AVERAGE FUNCTIONS

You also decide to calculate the minimum, maximum, and average sales for each sales category. You will add appropriate column headings and enter the functions in columns F, G, and H. The Σ Sum button also includes a drop-down menu from which you can select several other common functions. As you enter these functions, the proposed range will include the Total cell. Simply select another range to replace the proposed range.

- Enter MIN in cell F3, MAX in cell G3, and AVG in cell H3.

- Move to F4.

- Open the Σ Sum drop-down menu and choose Min.

Having Trouble?
Click ▾ to the right of the button to open the drop-down menu.

- Select the range B4 through D4 to specify the January through March sales values and click ✓ Enter.

Your screen should be similar to Figure 1.43

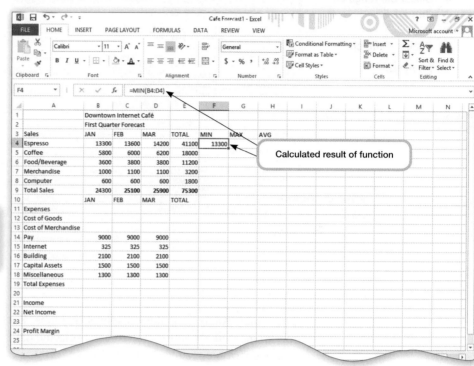

Calculated result of function

Figure 1.43

The MIN function correctly displays 13300, the smallest value in the range.

Next, you will enter the functions to calculate the maximum and average values for the Espresso sales. Then you will copy the functions down the column through row 8.

- Enter the MAX function in cell G4 and the AVERAGE function in cell H4 to calculate the Espresso sales values for January through March.

- Copy the functions in cells F4 through H4 to F5 through H8.

- Move to H8.

Your screen should be similar to Figure 1.44

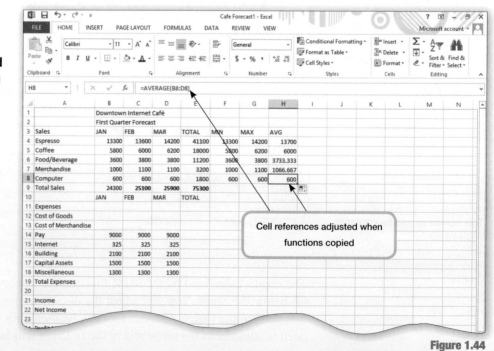

Cell references adjusted when functions copied

Figure 1.44

EX1.44   Lab 1: Creating and Editing a Worksheet   WWW.MHHE.COM/OLEARY

Excel 2013

The minimum, maximum, and average values for the five sales categories have been calculated. The Average column displays as many decimal places as cell space allows.

USING POINTING TO ENTER A FORMULA

Next, you will enter the formula to calculate the cost of goods for espresso, coffee, and food and beverages sold. These numbers are estimated by using a formula to calculate the number as a percentage of sales. Evan suggested using estimated percents for this worksheet so he could get an idea of what to expect from the first three months after the remodel. He wants you to calculate espresso expenses at 25 percent of espresso sales, coffee expenses at 30 percent of coffee sales, and food and beverage expenses at 60 percent of food sales.

Rather than typing in the cell references for the formula, you will enter them by selecting the worksheet cells. In addition, to simplify the process of entering and copying entries, you can enter data into the first cell of a range and have it copied to all other cells in the range at the same time by using Ctrl + ←Enter to complete the entry. You will use this feature to enter the formulas to calculate the beverage expenses for January through March. This formula needs to calculate the beverage cost of goods at 25 percent first and add it to the food cost of goods calculated at 50 percent.

Additional Information

The Quick Analysis tool does not include the MIN or MAX functions.

1

- Select B12 through D12.
- Type =
- Click cell B4.

Additional Information

Even when a range is selected, you can still point to specify cells in the formula. You also can use the direction keys to move to the cell.

Your screen should be similar to Figure 1.45

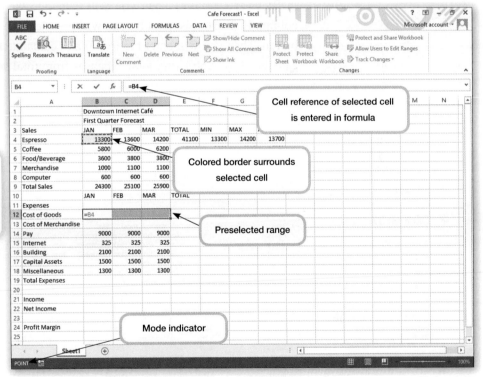

Figure 1.45

Additional Information

While entering the formula in Point mode, if you make an error, edit the entry like any other error and then continue entering the remainder of the formula.

Notice that the status bar displays the current mode as Point. This tells you that the program is allowing you to select cells by highlighting them. The cell reference, B4, is entered following the equal sign. You will complete the formula by entering the percentage value to multiply by and adding the Food percentage to the formula.

2

- Type *25%+
- Click on B5.
- Type *30%+
- Click on B6.
- Type *60%
- Press Ctrl + ←Enter.

Your screen should be similar to Figure 1.46

Figure 1.46

Having Trouble?

If you made an error in the formula, edit the entry in the formula bar and then press Ctrl + ←Enter again to copy it to the selected range.

The formula to calculate the January Cost of Goods expenses was entered in cell B12 and copied to all cells of the selected range.

Now you will enter the Cost of Merchandise expenses by multiplying the value in B8 by 70 percent. Then you will calculate the total expenses in row 19 and column E. To do this quickly, you will preselect the range and use the Σ ▾ Sum button. Then you will enter the formula to calculate the net income. Net income is calculated by subtracting total expenses from total sales.

3

- Select cells B13 through D13.
- Type =
- Click on B7.
- Type *70%
- Press Ctrl + ←Enter.
- Select B12 through E19.
- Click Σ ▾ Sum.
- Select B22 through E22.
- Enter the formula =B9-B19 and press Ctrl + ←Enter.

Your screen should be similar to Figure 1.47

Figure 1.47

The formulas were quickly entered into all cells of the specified ranges.

WWW.MHHE.COM/OLEARY

Finally, you will enter the formula to calculate the profit margin. Profit margin is calculated by dividing net income by total sales.

Select B24 through E24.

Enter the formula =B22/B9 and press Ctrl + ←Enter.

Your screen should be similar to Figure 1.48

	A	B	C	D	E	F	G	H
1		Downtown Internet Café						
2		First Quarter Forecast						
3	Sales	JAN	FEB	MAR	TOTAL	MIN	MAX	AVG
4	Espresso	13300	13600	14200	41100	13300	14200	13700
5	Coffee	5800	6000	6200	18000	5800	6200	6000
6	Food/Beverage	3600	3800	3800	11200	3600	3800	3733.333
7	Merchandise	1000	1100	1100	3200	1000	1100	1066.667
8	Computer	600	600	600	1800	600	600	600
9	Total Sales	24300	25100	25900	75300			
10		JAN	FEB	MAR	TOTAL			
11	Expenses							
12	Cost of Goods	7225	7480	7690	22395			
13	Cost of Merchandise	700	770	770	2240			
14	Pay	9000	9000	9000	27000			
15	Internet	325	325	325	975			
16	Building	2100	2100	2100	6300			
17	Capital Assets	1500	1500	1500	4500			
18	Miscellaneous	1300	1300	1300	3900			
19	Total Expenses	22150	22475	22685	67310			
20								
21	Income							
22	Net Income	2150	2625	3215	7990			
23								
24	Profit Margin	0.088477	0.104582	0.124131	0.106109			
25								

Profit margin calculated for all cells of range

Figure 1.48

The net income and profit margins are calculated and displayed in the worksheet.

RECALCULATING THE WORKSHEET

Now that you have created the worksheet structure and entered some sample data for the forecasted sales for the first quarter, you want to test the formulas to verify that they are operating correctly. A simple way to do this is to use a calculator to verify that the correct result is displayed. You can then further test the worksheet by changing values and verifying that all cells containing formulas that reference the value are appropriately recalculated.

Concept 10 Recalculation

When a number in a referenced cell in a formula changes, Excel automatically **recalculates** all formulas that are dependent upon the changed value. Because only those formulas directly affected by a change in the data are recalculated, the time it takes to recalculate the workbook is reduced. Without this feature, in large worksheets it could take several minutes to recalculate all formulas each time a number is changed in the worksheet. Recalculation is one of the most powerful features of electronic worksheets.

After considering the sales estimates for the three months, you decide that the estimated sales generated from Computer usage for January are too high and you want to decrease this number from 600 to 400.

1

- Change the entry in cell B8 to **400**

- Click [💾] Save to save the workbook using the same file name.

Your screen should be similar to Figure 1.49

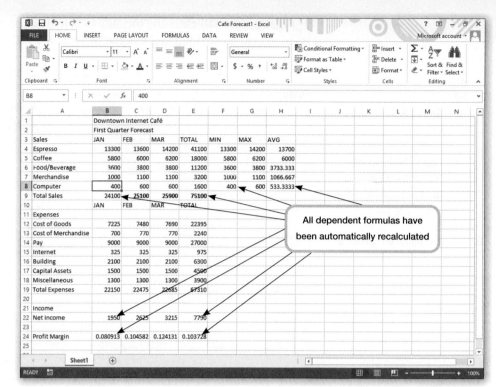

Figure 1.49

The Computer total in cell E8 has been automatically recalculated. The number displayed is now 1600. The MIN and AVG values in cells F8 and H8 have been recalculated to 400 and 533.3333, respectively. Likewise, the January total in cell B9 of 24100 and the grand total in cell E9 of 75100 each decreased by 200 from the previous totals to reflect the change in cell B8. Finally, the Net Income and Profit Margin values also have adjusted appropriately.

The formulas in the worksheet are correctly calculating the desired result. The Sales portion of the worksheet is now complete.

Inserting and Deleting Rows and Columns

As you are developing a worksheet, you may realize you forgot to include information or decide that other information is not needed. To quickly add and remove entire rows and columns of information, you can insert and delete rows and columns. A new blank row is inserted above the active cell location and all rows below it shift down a row. Similarly, you can insert blank cells and columns in a worksheet. Blank cells are inserted above or to the left of the active cell, and blank columns are inserted to the left of the active cell. Likewise, you can quickly delete selected cells, rows, and columns, and all information in surrounding cells, rows, or columns automatically shifts appropriately to fill in the space.

Additionally, whenever you insert or delete cells, rows, or columns, all formula references to any affected cells adjust accordingly.

INSERTING ROWS

You realize that you forgot to include a row for the Advertising expenses. To add this data, you will insert a blank row above the Capital Assets row.

- Move to A17.

- Open the [Insert ▾] drop-down menu in the Cells group and choose Insert Sheet Rows.

Another Method

You also can choose Insert from the active cell's context menu.

- Enter the heading **Advertising** in cell A17 and the value **600** in cells B17 through D17.

- If necessary, copy the function from cell E16 to E17 to calculate the total advertising expense.

- Move to cell B20.

Your screen should be similar to Figure 1.50

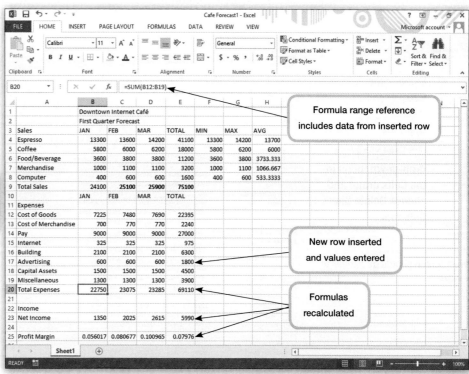

Figure 1.50

A blank row was inserted in the worksheet and the cell references in all formulas and functions below the inserted row adjusted appropriately. The range in the formula to calculate monthly total expenses in row 20 has been adjusted to include the data in the inserted row, and the total expense for the first quarter is 69110. Additionally, the net income in row 23 and the profit margin in row 25 have been recalculated to reflect the change in data.

Additional Information

Click [Insert ▾] to insert blank cells, shifting existing cells down, and [Insert ▾] /Sheet Columns to insert blank columns, shifting existing columns right.

DELETING COLUMNS

As you look at the worksheet data, you decide the minimum and maximum values are not very useful since this data is so easy to see in this small worksheet. You will delete these two columns from the worksheet to remove this information. To specify which column to delete, select any cell in the column.

Another Method

You could also click on the column heading to select the entire worksheet column and choose Delete from the shortcut menu.

- Select cells F20 and G20.

- Open the drop-down menu in the Cells group and choose Delete Sheet Columns.

Your screen should be similar to Figure 1.51

Additional Information

Select a cell or row and choose Delete /Delete Cells or Delete Sheet Rows to delete it and shift the other cells or rows up or to the left.

	A	B	C	D	E	F	G
1		Downtown Internet Café					
2		First Quarter Forecast					
3	Sales	JAN	FEB	MAR	TOTAL	AVG	
4	Espresso	13300	13600	14200	41100	13700	
5	Coffee	5800	6000	6200	18000	6000	
6	Food/Beverage	3600	3800	3800	11200	3733.333	
7	Merchandise	1000	1100	1100	3200	1066.667	
8	Computer	400	600	600	1600	533.3333	
9	Total Sales	24100	25100	25900	75100		
10		JAN	FEB	MAR	TOTAL		
11	Expenses						
12	Cost of Goods	7225	7480	7690	22395		
13	Cost of Merchandise	700	770	770	2240		
14	Pay	9000	9000	9000	27000		
15	Internet	325	325	325	975		
16	Building	2100	2100	2100	6300		
17	Advertising	600	600	600	1800		
18	Capital Assets	1500	1500	1500	4500		
19	Miscellaneous	1300	1300	1300	3900		
20	Total Expenses	22750	23075	23285	69110		
21							
22	Income						
23	Net Income	1350	2025	2615	5990		
24							
25	Profit Margin	0.056017	0.080677	0.100965	0.07976		

MIN and MAX columns deleted

Figure 1.51

The two columns have been removed and the columns to the right of the deleted columns automatically shifted to the left.

Formatting Cells and Cell Content

Now that the worksheet data is complete, you want to improve the appearance of the worksheet. Applying different formatting to text and numbers can greatly enhance the appearance of the document. In Excel, formats control how entries are displayed in a cell and include such features as the position of data in a cell, character font and color, and number formats such as commas and dollar signs.

You want to change the appearance of the row and column headings and apply formatting to the numbers. Applying different formats greatly improves both the appearance and the readability of the data in a worksheet.

CHANGING CELL ALIGNMENT

You decide the column headings would look better if they were right-aligned in their cell spaces, so that they would appear over the numbers in the column. Alignment is a basic format setting that is used in most worksheets.

Concept Alignment

Alignment settings allow you to change the horizontal and vertical placement and the orientation of an entry in a cell.

Horizontal placement allows you to left-, right-, or center-align text and number entries in the cell space. Entries also can be indented within the cell space, centered across a selection, or justified. You also can fill a cell horizontally with a repeated entry.

Vertical placement allows you to specify whether the cell contents are displayed at the top, the bottom, or the center of the vertical cell space or justified vertically.

You also can change the orientation or angle of text in a cell by varying the degrees of rotation.

The default workbook horizontal alignment settings left-align text entries and right-align number entries. The vertical alignment is set to Bottom for both types of entries, and the orientation is set to zero degrees rotation from the horizontal position. You want to change the horizontal alignment of the month headings in rows 3 and 10 to right-aligned.

The Alignment group contains commands to control the horizontal and vertical placement of entries in a cell. You can quickly apply formatting to a range of cells by selecting the range first. A quick way to select a range of filled cells is to hold down ⇧Shift and double-click on the edge of the active cell in the direction in which you want the range expanded. For example, to select the range to the right of the active cell, you would double-click the right border. You will use this method to select and right-align these entries.

Additional Information

If you do not hold down ⇧Shift while double-clicking on a cell border, the active cell moves to the last-used cell in the direction indicated.

1

- Move to B3.

- Hold down ⇧Shift and double-click the right cell border of cell B3.

Having Trouble?
The mouse pointer must be ⬍ when you click the cell border.

- Click ☰ Align Right from the Alignment group.

- Select B10 through E10.

- Click ☰ Align Right.

Your screen should be similar to Figure 1.52

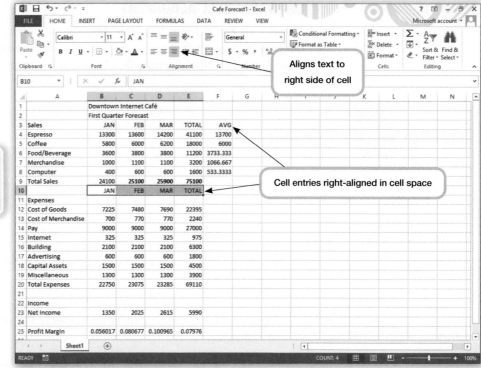

Figure 1.52

The entries in the selected ranges are right-aligned in their cell spaces. You notice the month labels do not stand out well and decide to try rotating them.

2

- Select cells B3 through F3.

- Click 🗘 ▾ Orientation and choose Angle Counterclockwise.

Your screen should be similar to Figure 1.53

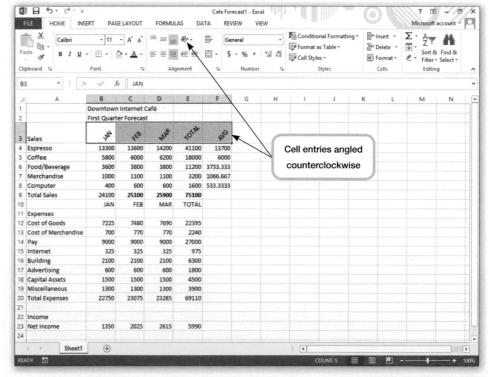

Figure 1.53

Notice how the row height increased automatically to accommodate the change in size.

CHANGING ROW HEIGHT

You do not like the way it looks rotated and decide to undo the change, add height to the row manually to help identify the month label row better, and center-align the labels. You also decide to move the month labels in row 10 down a row to match the first row of month labels.

Concept 12 Row Height

The **row height** is the size or height of a row measured in points. The default row height is 15.00 points which is larger than the default font point size of 11. The row height can be any number from 0 to 409. If it is set to 0, the row is hidden. The row height automatically adjusts to changes in the character size, style, and orientation.

The row height can also be changed manually using methods that are similar to those used to change the column width. The difference is that you drag or click the boundary below the row heading to adjust the row height.

● Click ↺ Undo.

● Move the entries in cells B10 through E10 into the same columns in row 11.

● Drag the bottom boundary of rows 3 and 11 to increase the row height to 22.50.

● Select cells B3 through F3 and click ☰ Center.

● Center-align the labels in cells B11 through E11.

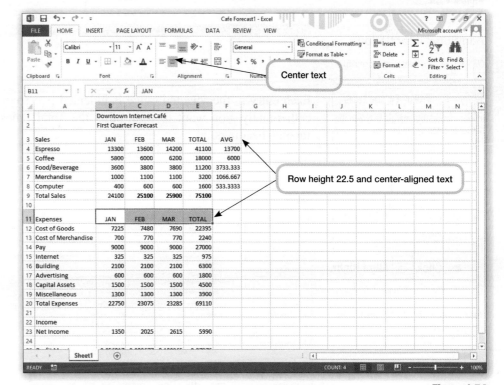

Figure 1.54

Your screen should be similar to Figure 1.54

Additional Information

You also can select entire nonadjacent rows or columns by holding down Ctrl while selecting the rows or columns.

Increasing the row height of the month labels visually separates the labels from other worksheet entries.

INDENTING CELL CONTENT

Next, you would like to indent the row headings in cells A4 through A8 and A12 through A19 to show that the entries are subtopics below the Sales and Expenses headings. You want to indent the headings in both ranges at the same time. To select nonadjacent cells or cell ranges, after selecting the first cell or range, hold down Ctrl while selecting each additional cell or range.

- Select A4 through A8.

- Hold down Ctrl.

- Select A12 through A19.

- Release Ctrl.

- Click ⊒ Increase Indent in the Alignment group.

- AutoFit the width of column A.

Your screen should be similar to Figure 1.55

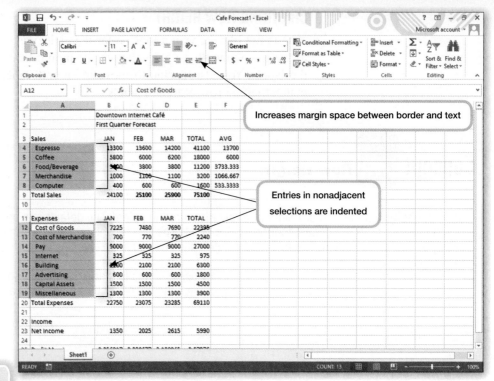

Increases margin space between border and text

Entries in nonadjacent selections are indented

Figure 1.55

Each entry in the selected range is indented two spaces from the left edge of the cell. Finally, you want to right-align the Total Sales, Total Expenses, and Net Income headings.

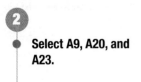

- Select A9, A20, and A23.

- Click ☰ Align Right.

Your screen should be similar to Figure 1.56

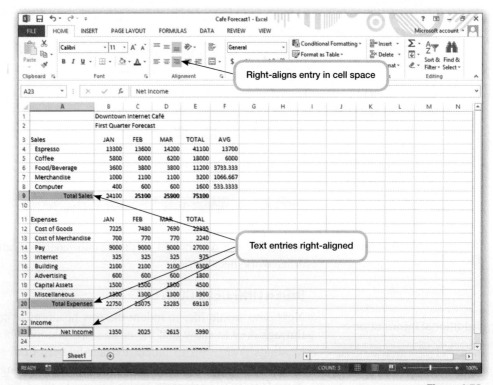

Right-aligns entry in cell space

Text entries right-aligned

Figure 1.56

MERGING CELLS

Next, you want to center the worksheet titles across columns A through F so they are centered over the worksheet data. To do this, you will merge or combine the cells in the range over the worksheet data (A1 through F1) into a single large **merged cell** and then center the contents of the range in the merged cell.

Select A1 through F1.

Click ⊞ ▾ **Merge & Center in the Alignment group.**

Your screen should be similar to Figure 1.57

Figure 1.57

The six cells in the selection have been combined into a single large cell, and the entry that was in cell B1 is centered within the merged cell space. Only the contents of the first cell containing an entry in the upper-leftmost section of the selected range are centered in the merged cell. If other cells to the right of that cell contain data, they will be deleted. The cell reference for a merged cell is the upper-left cell in the original selected range, in this case A1.

②

Merge and center the second title line across columns A through F.

Your screen should be similar to Figure 1.58

Figure 1.58

You also can use the commands in the 〔⊞ ▾〕 Merge & Center drop-down menu shown in the following table to control a merge. You can merge cells horizontally and vertically.

Merge Menu	Action
⊞ ▾ Merge & Center	Merges cells and centers entry
⊞ Merge Across	Merges cells horizontally
⊞ Merge Cells	Merges cells horizontally and vertically
⊞ Unmerge Cells	Splits cells that have been merged back into individual cells

CHANGING FONTS AND FONT SIZES

Having Trouble?

Refer to the section "Formatting Text" in the Introduction to Microsoft Office 2013 to review fonts.

Finally, you want to improve the worksheet appearance by enhancing the appearance of the title. One way to do this is to change the font and font size used in the title. There are two basic types of fonts: serif and sans serif. **Serif** fonts have a flare at the base of each letter that visually leads the reader to the next letter. Two common serif fonts are Roman and Times New Roman. Serif fonts generally are used in paragraphs. **Sans serif** fonts do not have a flare at the base of each letter. Arial and Helvetica are two common sans serif fonts. Because sans serif fonts have a clean look, they are often used for headings in documents. It is good practice to use only two types of fonts in a worksheet, one for text and one for headings. Too many styles can make your document look cluttered and unprofessional.

Here are several examples of the same text in various fonts and sizes.

Typeface	Font Size (12 pt/18 pt)
Calibri (Sans Serif)	This is 12 pt. This is 18 pt.
Comic Sans MS (Sans Serif)	This is 12 pt. This is 18 pt.
Book Antiqua (Serif)	This is 12 pt. This is 18 pt.

Using fonts as a design element can add interest to your document and give readers visual cues to help them find information quickly. First you will try a different font for the title and a larger font size.

1

● Select A1 and A2.

● Open the

Calibri   ▼

Font drop-down list box in the Font group.

Your screen should be similar to Figure 1.59

Selected font

Font names appear in font style

Open Type fonts are cross-platform

Figure 1.59

The Font drop-down list displays examples of the available fonts on your system in alphabetical order. The default worksheet font, Calibri, is highlighted. Notice the O preceding the font name. This indicates the font is an Open Type font, a standard font format developed by Adobe Systems and Microsoft. Open Type fonts can be used by almost any application and can display many more characters than previous font formats. Other font names are preceded with a T. This indicates the font is a TrueType font. TrueType fonts appear onscreen as they will appear when printed. They are installed when Windows is installed. You will change the font and increase the font size to 14. As you point to the font options, Live Preview will show how it will appear if chosen.

2

Scroll the list and choose Lucida Sans.

Having Trouble?

You will not be able to see the Fonts Live Preview because the drop-down menu covers the selection to be formatted.

Open the `11 ▾` **Font Size drop-down list box.**

Point to several different font sizes in the list to see the Live Preview.

Choose 14.

Your screen should be similar to Figure 1.60

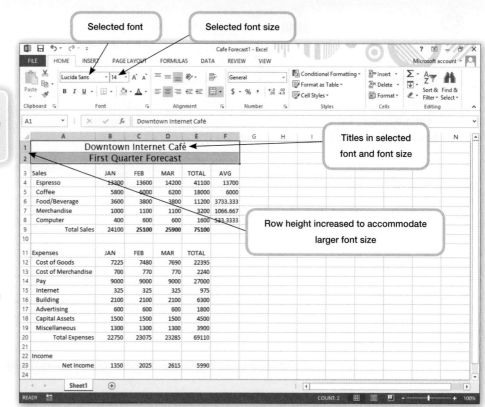

Figure 1.60

Another Method

The Font and Font Size commands are also available on the Mini toolbar.

The title appears in the selected typeface and size, and the Font and Font Size buttons display the name of the font and the size used in the active cell. Notice that the height of the row has increased to accommodate the larger font size of the heading.

APPLYING TEXT EFFECTS

Having Trouble?

Refer to the section "Formatting Text" in the Introduction to Microsoft Office 2013 to review text effects.

In addition to changing font and font size, you can apply different text effects to enhance the appearance of text. The table below describes some of the text effects and their uses.

Format	Example	Use
Bold	**Bold**	Adds emphasis.
Italic	*Italic*	Adds emphasis.
Underline	<u>Underline</u>	Adds emphasis.
Strikethrough	~~Strikethrough~~	Indicates words to be deleted.
Superscript	"To be or not to be."[1]	Used in footnotes and formulas.
Subscript	H_2O	Used in formulas.
Color	Color Color Color	Adds interest.

First you want to enhance the appearance of the column headings by increasing the font size and adding bold, italic, and underlines.

1
- Select B3 through F3.

- Increase the font size to 12.

- Click **B** Bold.

- Click **U** ▾ Underline.

Your screen should be similar to **Figure 1.61**

Figure 1.61

Having Trouble?

Refer to the section "Formatting Text" in the Introduction to Microsoft Office 2013 to review using the Mini toolbar.

Many of the formatting commands are also available on the Mini toolbar. In Excel, you must right-click on a cell to display the Mini toolbar and the shortcut menu. The selected formatting is applied to the entire cell contents. If you select text in a cell, the Mini toolbar appears automatically and the formatting is applied to the selected text only.

2
- Select A4 through A8.

- Right-click on the selection to display the Mini toolbar.

- Click **B** Bold.

- Click **I** Italic.

Another Method

The keyboard shortcut for bold is [Ctrl] + B; for italic, it is [Ctrl] + I; and for underline, it is [Ctrl] + U.

Your screen should be similar to **Figure 1.62**

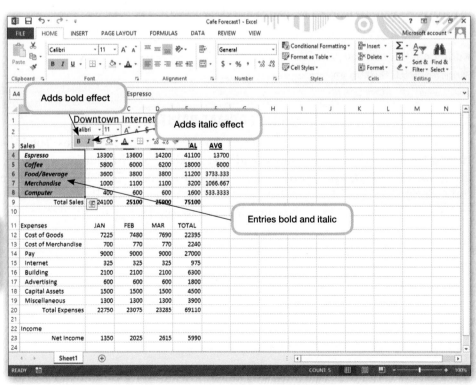

Figure 1.62

Formatting Cells and Cell Content   **EX1.59**

CLEARING FORMATS

Sometimes formatting changes you make do not have the expected result. In this case, you feel that the sales category names would look better without the formatting. One way to remove the format from cells is to use ![eraser icon] Clear in the Editing group and choose Clear Formats. Because this will remove all formatting in the selected cells, you will need to redo the indenting in those cells.

1

- With cells A4 through A8 still selected, open the ![eraser icon] Clear drop-down list in the Editing group.

- Choose Clear Formats.

- Click ![indent icon] Increase Indent.

Another Method

You could also use ![undo icon] Undo to remove the formats by reversing your last actions.

Your screen should be similar to Figure 1.63

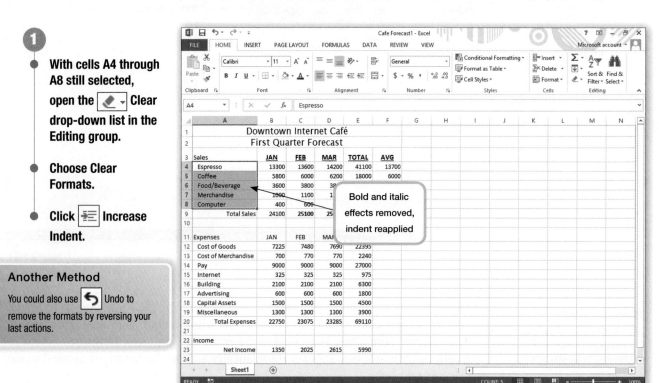

Figure 1.63

Additional Information

You can remove both formatting and content using ![eraser icon] Clear/Clear All.

USING FORMAT PAINTER

You do think, however, that the Total Sales, Total Expenses, and Net Income headings would look good in bold. In addition, you want to bold the total values in cell B9 and row 20. You will bold the entry in cell A9 and then copy the format from A9 to the other cells using Format Painter. You also will copy the format from the headings in row 3 to row 11.

Having Trouble?

Refer to the section "Copying Formats" in the Introduction to Microsoft Office 2013 to review the Format Painter.

1

- Apply bold to cell A9.

- With cell A9 selected, double-click 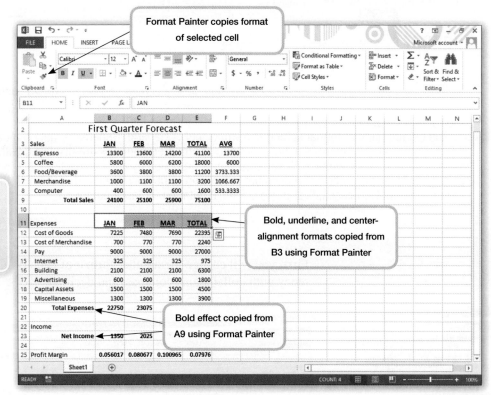 Format Painter in the Clipboard group.

Additional Information

When Format Painter is on, the mouse pointer appears as ⊕🖌 and the cell whose format will be copied appears with a moving border.

- Click B9.

- Select A20:E20.

- Select A23:E23.

- Select B25:E25

- Click 🖌 Format Painter to turn it off.

Another Method

You also can press Esc to turn off Format Painter.

- Use Format Painter to copy the format from cell B3 to cells B11 through E11.

Your screen should be similar to Figure 1.64

Figure 1.64

The formatting was quickly added to each cell or range as it was selected.

FORMATTING NUMBERS

You also want to improve the appearance of the numbers in the worksheet by changing their format.

Concept 13 Number Formats

Number formats change the appearance of numbers onscreen and when printed, without changing the way the number is stored or used in calculations. When a number is formatted, the formatting appears in the cell, while the value without the formatting is displayed in the formula bar.

The default number format setting in a worksheet is General. General format, in most cases, displays numbers just as you enter them, unformatted. Unformatted numbers are displayed without a thousands separator such as a comma, with negative values preceded by a − (minus sign), and with as many decimal place settings as cell space allows. If a number is too long to be fully displayed in the cell, the General format will round numbers with decimals and use scientific notation for large numbers.

First, you will change the number format of cells B4 through F9 to display as currency with dollar signs, commas, and decimal places.

1

- Select cells B4 through F9.

- Open the

  General ▼

  Number Format drop-down list in the Number group.

- Choose Currency.

Your screen should be similar to
Figure 1.65

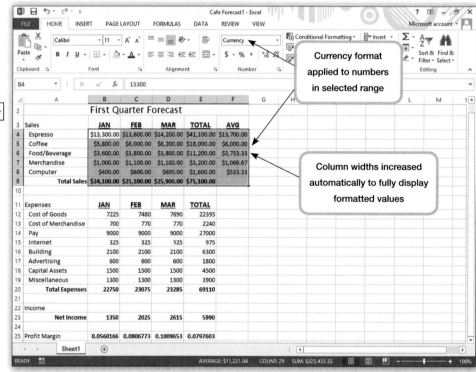

Figure 1.65

Another Method

Excel will also automatically apply a format to a cell based on the symbols you use when entering the number. For example, entering 10,000 in a cell formats the cell to Comma format, and entering $102.20 formats the cell to Currency with two decimal places.

The number entries in the selected range appear with a currency symbol, comma, and two decimal places. The column widths increased automatically to fully display the formatted values.

A second format category that displays numbers as currency is Accounting. You will try this format next on the same range. Additionally, you will specify zero as the number of decimal places because most of the values are whole values. To specify settings that are different than the default setting for a format, you can use the Format Cells dialog box.

②

Make sure you still have cells B4 through F9 selected.

Click ⬚ in the Number group to open the Format Cells: Number dialog box.

Another Method
The keyboard shortcut to open the Format Cells dialog box is Ctrl + 1.

From the Category list box, choose Accounting.

Reduce the decimal places to 0.

Click   OK   .

Your screen should be similar to Figure 1.66

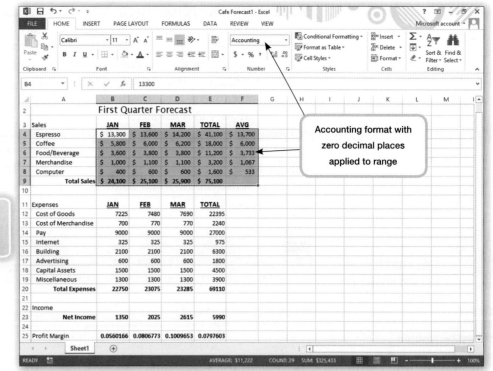

Figure 1.66

The numbers now appear in Accounting format. The primary difference between the Accounting and the Currency formats is that the Accounting format aligns numbers at the decimal place and places the dollar sign in a column at the left edge of the cell space. In addition, it does not allow you to select different ways of displaying negative numbers but displays them in black in parentheses.

You decide the Accounting format will make it easier to read the numbers in a column and you will use this format for the rest of the worksheet. An easier way to apply the Accounting format with 0 decimals is to use the commands in the Number group.

③

Select the range B12 through E20.

Click $ ▾ Accounting Number Format in the Number group.

Click .00→.0 Decrease Decimal twice.

Your screen should be similar to Figure 1.67

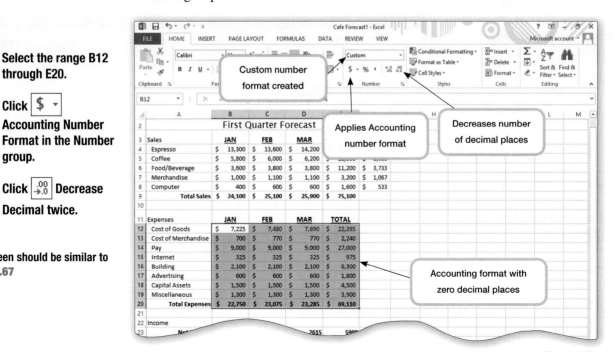

Figure 1.67

Formatting Cells and Cell Content **EX1.63**

Notice the Number Format box displays Custom because you modified a copy of the existing Accounting number format code. The custom number format is added to the list of number format codes. Between 200 and 250 custom formats can be added depending on the language version of Excel you are using. You can then reapply the custom format by selecting it from the Custom category of the Format Cells: Number dialog box. This is useful for complicated formats, but not for formats that are easy to re-create.

Finally, you will format the Net Income values as Accounting with zero decimal places and the Profit Margin values as percentages with two decimal places. You will do this using the Mini toolbar. This feature is particularly helpful when working at the bottom of the worksheet window.

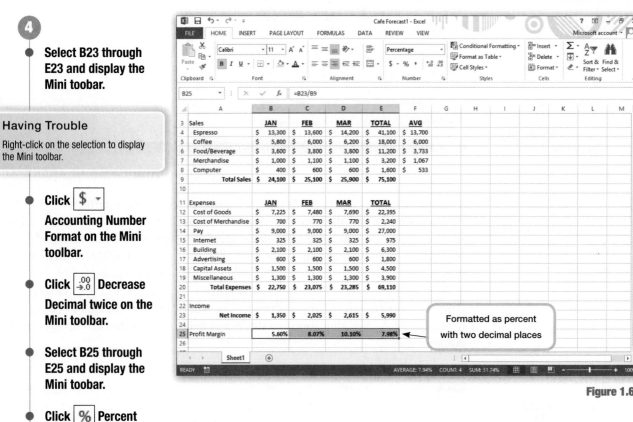

Figure 1.68

- Select B23 through E23 and display the Mini toolbar.

Having Trouble

Right-click on the selection to display the Mini toolbar.

- Click $ ▾ Accounting Number Format on the Mini toolbar.

- Click .00 →.0 Decrease Decimal twice on the Mini toolbar.

- Select B25 through E25 and display the Mini toolbar.

- Click % Percent Style on the Mini toolbar.

- Click ←.0 .00 Increase Decimal twice on the Mini toolbar.

Your screen should be similar to Figure 1.68

ADDING FONT COLOR

The last formatting change you would like to make to the worksheet is to add color to the text of selected cells. Font color can be applied to all the text in a selected cell or range or to selected words or characters in a cell.

1

- Select A1 through A2.

- Open the ▼ Font Color drop-down menu in the Font group.

Another Method

▲ ▼ Font Color is also available on the Mini toolbar.

Your screen should be similar to Figure 1.69

Figure 1.69

Additional Information

You will learn about using themes in Lab 2.

A palette of colors is displayed. Automatic is the default text color setting. This setting automatically determines when to use black or white text. Black text is used on a light background and white text on a dark background. The center area of the palette displays the theme colors. Theme colors are a set of colors that are associated with a **theme**, a predefined set of fonts, colors, and effects that can be applied to an entire worksheet. If you change the theme, the theme colors change. The Standard Colors bar displays 10 colors that are always the same.

As you point to a color, the entry in the selected cell changes color so you can preview how the selection would look. A ScreenTip displays the name of the standard color or the description of the theme color as you point to it.

2

- Choose Yellow from the Standard Colors bar.

- Click **B** Bold.

Your screen should be similar to Figure 1.70

Figure 1.70

The font color of all the text in cells A1 and A2 has changed to the selected color and bold. The selected color appears in the button and can be applied again simply by clicking the button.

ADDING FILL COLOR

Next, you will change the cell background color, also called the fill color, behind the titles and in several other areas of the worksheet. Generally, when adding color to a worksheet, use a dark font color with a light fill color or a light font color with a dark fill color.

1

- Select cells A1 through F3.

- Open the ⬚ ▾ Fill Color drop-down color palette.

- Point to several colors to see a Live Preview.

- Select Red Accent 2 (from the Theme Colors bar).

- Select cells A11 through F11 and click ⬚ ▾ Fill Color to apply the last selected fill color.

- Apply the same fill color to A22 through F22 and A25 through F25.

Your screen should be similar to Figure 1.71

Figure 1.71

The color highlight helps distinguish the different areas of the worksheet.

ADDING AND REMOVING CELL BORDERS

Finally, you decide to add a border around the entire worksheet area. Excel includes many predefined border styles that can be added to a single cell or to a range of cells. Then you will make several additional formatting changes to improve the appearance and readability of the worksheet.

1

- Select the range A1 through F25.

- Open the Borders drop-down menu in the Font group and choose the Thick Box Border style.

- Click outside the range to see the border.

Your screen should be similar to Figure 1.72

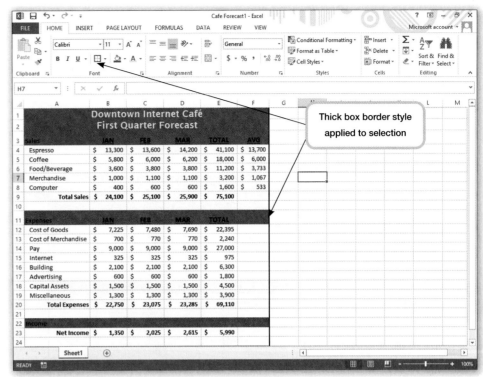

Figure 1.72

The range is considered a single block of cells, and the box border surrounds the entire worksheet selection.

When adding borders, the border also is applied to adjacent cells that share a bordered cell boundary. In this case, cells G1 through G25 acquired a left border and cells A26 through F26 acquired a top border. When pasting a cell that includes a cell border, the border is included unless you specify that the paste does not include the border. To see how this works, you will first copy a cell and its border, and then you will copy it again without the border.

2

- Copy cell A1 and paste it in cell G2.

- Move to G4, open the drop-down menu, and choose No Borders.

- Move to G6 to see the changes.

Your screen should be similar to Figure 1.73

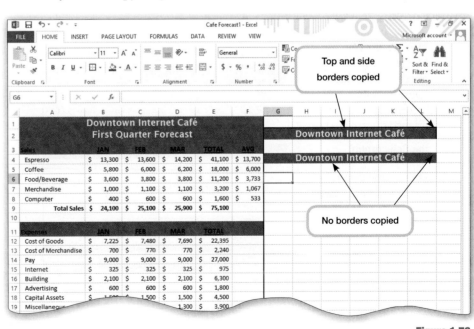

Figure 1.73

If you want to add additional borders or replace an existing border with another, select the range and then add the border. However, if you want to remove a border

Formatting Cells and Cell Content   **EX1.67**

style from one area of a selection and add a border to another area, you need to remove all borders first and then apply the new border styles. You will try these features next on the entry in cell G2.

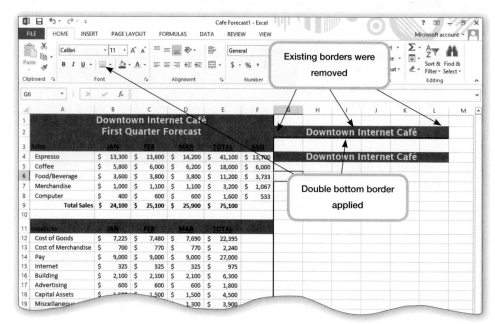

3

- Move to G2 and choose No Border from the [icon] Borders drop-down menu.

- Apply a Bottom Double Border to the selection.

- Move to G6 to see the changes.

Your screen should be similar to Figure 1.74

Figure 1.74

All existing borders were removed, including those that share a cell boundary, and the new double bottom border is applied to the selection. You will restore the worksheet to how it was prior to copying the title using Undo and then make some final adjustments to the worksheet.

4

- Undo your last four actions to remove the copied data.

- Move to any cell in row 10 and choose Delete Sheet Rows from the [icon] Delete ▼ drop-down menu in the Cells group.

- In the same manner, delete the blank rows 20 and 22.

- Add bold and yellow font color to cells A3, A10, A20, and A22.

- Click [icon] Save to save the worksheet changes.

Your screen should be similar to Figure 1.75

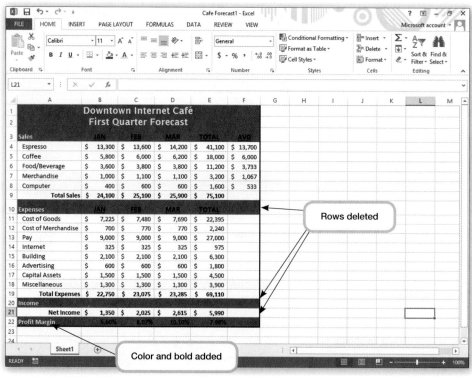

Figure 1.75

Hide and Unhide Rows and Columns

Now that the worksheet is nicely formatted, you want to focus on the data. One way to do this is to hide areas of data that you do not want to see in order to emphasize others. You will use this method to emphasize the total data.

1

Select columns B through D.

Additional Information

Any range of cells within the area you want to hide can be selected.

Open the

Format ▾

drop-down menu in the Cells group and select Hide & Unhide.

Choose Hide Columns.

Your screen should be similar to Figure 1.76

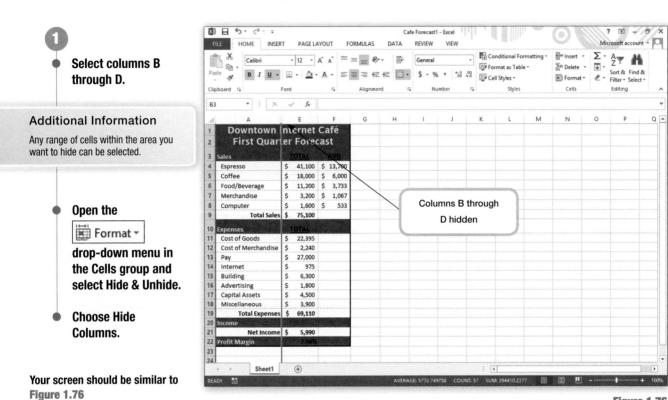

Figure 1.76

Now the worksheet focus is on the monthly total values, not the monthly values. The columns were hidden by reducing their column width to zero. Instead, you want to hide the rows.

2

● Click on column A heading and drag to select columns A and E.

● Right-click either column heading and choose Unhide from the context menu.

● Select any range of cells within rows 4 through 8.

● Open the

drop-down menu, select Hide & Unhide, and then choose Hide Rows.

● Repeat to hide rows 11 through 18.

Figure 1.77

Notice how hiding the rows emphasizes the monthly totals by category.

Your screen should be similar to Figure 1.77

3

● Click Undo twice to unhide the rows.

Creating a Simple Chart

Another way to better understand the data in a worksheet is to create a chart. A **chart** is a visual representation of data that is used to convey information in an easy-to-understand and attractive manner. You decide to create a chart of the sales data for the three months.

SPECIFYING DATA TO CHART

To tell Excel what data to chart, you need to select the range containing the data you want to appear in the chart plus any row or column headings you want used in the chart.

1

- **Select cells A3 through D8.**

- **Click the 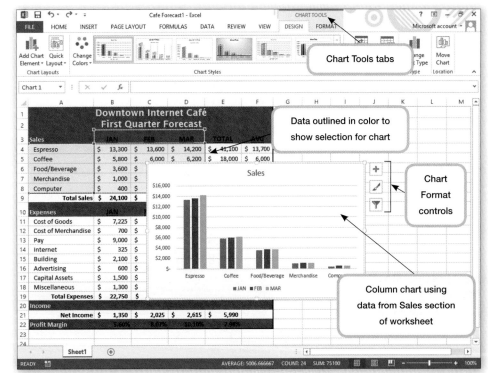 Quick Analysis button.**

- **Click the Charts tab.**

- **Point to the five chart options to see a preview of each.**

- **Click Clustered Column.**

- **Click on Chart Title in the chart.**

- **With the mouse pointer as an I-beam, drag to select the text in the box.**

- **Type Sales**

Your screen should be similar to
Figure 1.78

Figure 1.78

A column chart showing the sales for the five items over three months was quickly created.

2

- **Click on the edge of the chart object and drag to move it below the worksheet to cover rows 24 to 38.**

- **Click outside the chart object to deselect it.**

Formatting Values as a Date

Now that the worksheet is complete, you want to include your name and the date in the worksheet as documentation. There are many ways to enter the date. For example, you could type the date using the format mm/dd/yy or as month dd, yyyy. When a date is entered as text, Excel converts the entry to a numeric entry that allows dates to be used in calculations. Excel stores all dates as **serial values** with each day numbered from the beginning of the 20th century. The date serial values are consecutively assigned beginning with 1, which corresponds to the date January 1, 1900, and ending with 2958465, which is December 31, 9999.

1

Enter your first and last name in cell A40.

Type the current date as mm/dd/yy in cell A41.

Another Method

You also could use the Today function, =Today(), to display the current date in the default date format, or you could use the keyboard shortcut Ctrl + ;.

Your screen should be similar to Figure 1.79

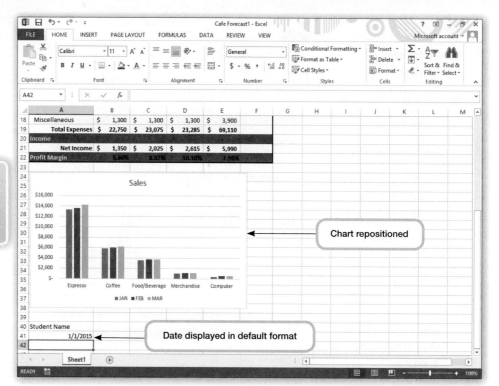

Figure 1.79

The date is displayed using the default date format, which is based on the settings in Windows. It is right-aligned in the cell because it is a numeric entry. You can change the date format in the worksheet without changing the Windows settings using the Format Cells: Number dialog box.

2

If necessary, move to cell A41.

Click 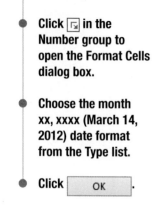 in the Number group to open the Format Cells dialog box.

Choose the month xx, xxxx (March 14, 2012) date format from the Type list.

Click ⬚ OK ⬚.

Your screen should be similar to Figure 1.80

Figure 1.80

The date appears in the specified format.

Documenting a Workbook

Having Trouble?

Refer to the section "Specifying Document Properties" in the Introduction to Microsoft Office 2013 to review this feature.

You are finished working on the worksheet for now and want to save the changes you have made to the file. In addition, you want to update the file properties to include your name as the author, a title, and keywords.

1

● Press Ctrl + Home.

● Open the File tab.

● In the Backstage Info window, enter the following information in the appropriate boxes.

Title	Downtown Internet Cafe
Tags	Sales Projections
Author	Your Name

Additional Information

The Author text box may be blank or may show your school or some other name. Clear the existing contents first if necessary.

Figure 1.81

Your screen should be similar to Figure 1.81

Previewing and Printing a Worksheet

Although you still plan to make more changes to the worksheet, you want to print a copy of the estimated first quarter forecast for the owner to get feedback regarding the content and layout.

1

Choose Print and view the preview in the right pane.

Your screen should be similar to Figure 1.82

Figure 1.82

Another Method

You also can use the keyboard shortcut Ctrl + P from the worksheet window to open the Print tab of Backstage view.

Additional Information

You can change printer-specific settings, such as color, by clicking Printer Properties and specifying the settings you want in the Printer Properties dialog box.

The preview displays the worksheet as it will appear on the printed page. Notice that the row and column gridlines are not displayed and will not print. This is one of the default worksheet print settings.

The preview of your worksheet may appear slightly different from that shown in Figure 1.82. This is because the way pages appear in the preview depends on the available fonts, the resolution of the printer, and the available colors. If your printer is configured to print in black and white, the preview will not display in color.

The Excel print settings let you specify how much of the worksheet you want printed. The options are described in the following table.

Option	Action
Print Active Sheets	Prints the active worksheet (default).
Print Entire Workbook	Prints all worksheets in the workbook.
Print Selection	Prints selected range only.
Pages	Prints pages you specify by typing page numbers in the text box.

The worksheet looks good and does not appear to need any further modifications immediately. Now you are ready to print the worksheet using the default print settings.

NOTE Please consult your instructor for printing procedures that may differ from the following directions.

Having Trouble?

Refer to the section "Printing a Document" in the Introduction to Microsoft Office 2013 to review this feature.

2

● If necessary, make sure your printer is on and ready to print.

● If you need to change the selected printer to another printer, open the Printer drop-down list box and select the appropriate printer.

● Click .

The printed copy should be similar to the document shown in the preview area.

When printing is complete, Backstage view is automatically closed. A dotted line may appear between columns G and H. This is the automatic page break line that shows where one printed page ends and the next begins.

DISPLAYING AND PRINTING FORMULAS

Often, when verifying the accuracy of the data in a worksheet, it is helpful to display all the formulas in a worksheet rather than the resulting values. This way you can quickly verify that the formulas are referencing the correct cells and ranges.

1

● Open the Formulas tab.

● Click [icon] Show Formulas in the Formula Auditing group.

Another Method

You also can use Ctrl + ` (accent grave is located to the left of the number 1 key) to toggle between values and formulas.

● Move to E8.

Your screen should be similar to Figure 1.83

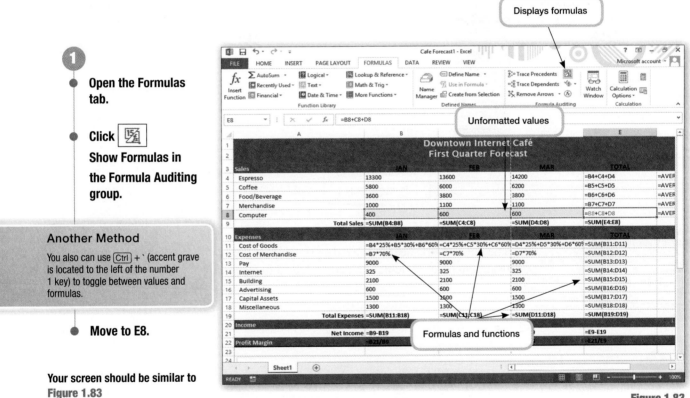

Figure 1.83

The display of the worksheet has changed to display unformatted values and the formulas and functions. It has automatically increased the column widths so the formulas and text do not overflow into the adjacent cells.

CHANGING WORKSHEET ORIENTATION AND SCALING CONTENT

Next, you will print the worksheet with formulas. Because the worksheet is so much wider, you will need to change the orientation to landscape, which prints across the length of the paper. Then you will reduce the scale of the worksheet so it fits on one page. The **scaling** feature will reduce or enlarge the worksheet contents by a percentage or fit them to a specific number of pages by height and width. You want to scale the worksheet to fit on one page.

1

- Open the File tab and choose Print.

- Change the orientation setting to Landscape Orientation.

- Open the

drop-down menu and choose Fit Sheet on One Page.

Your screen should be similar to Figure 1.84

Figure 1.84

Another Method
You also can scale the worksheet using Scale: in the Scale to Fit group of the Page Layout tab and setting the scale percentage.

The entire worksheet will easily print across the length of the page when printed using landscape orientation and scaled to fit a single page.

2

- Print the worksheet.

- Press Ctrl + ` (accent grave is located to the left of the number 1 key) to return the display to values.

Another Method
You could also click [icon] Show Formulas again to display the values.

Having Trouble?

Refer to the "Closing a File" and "Exiting an Office 2013 Application" sections in the Introduction to Microsoft Office 2013 to review these features.

You are now ready to exit the Excel application. If you attempt to close the application without first saving the workbook, Excel displays a warning asking whether you want to save your work. If you do not save your work and you exit the application, all changes you made from the last time you saved will be lost.

1

• **Move to cell A1.**

• **Click** ☒ **Close (in the application window title bar).**

• **Click** [Save] **to resave the worksheet.**

Additional Information

Excel saves the file with the cell selector in the same cell location it is in at the time it is saved.

Because you made several edits since last saving the worksheet, you were prompted to save it again before closing it.

FOCUS ON CAREERS

EXPLORE YOUR CAREER OPTIONS

Event Marketing Representative

Did you know that 40 percent of the advertised positions in sports are for marketing and promotion? A marketing graduate hired as a basketball event marketing representative would use Excel to keep track of the income and expenses for coordinated halftime activities at professional sporting events. These worksheets would provide valuable information for promoting sponsors' products and services at games. An event marketing representative might start out as an unpaid intern, but after graduation could expect to earn from $40,000 to $50,000.

Data (EX1.12)

Basic information or data you enter in a cell can be text, numbers, dates, or times.

AutoCorrect (EX1.18)

The AutoCorrect feature makes some basic assumptions about the text you are typing and, based on these assumptions, automatically corrects the entry.

Column Width (EX1.21)

The column width is the size or width of a column and controls the amount of information that can be displayed in a cell.

Spelling Checker (EX1.25)

The spelling checker locates misspelled words, duplicate words, and capitalization irregularities in the active worksheet and proposes the correct spelling.

Thesaurus (EX1.27)

The thesaurus is a reference tool that provides synonyms, antonyms, and related words for a selected word or phrase.

Range (EX1.31)

A selection consisting of two or more cells on a worksheet is a range.

Formula (EX1.37)

A formula is an equation that performs a calculation on data contained in a worksheet.

Relative Reference (EX1.39)

A relative reference is a cell or range reference in a formula whose location is interpreted by Excel in relation to the position of the cell that contains the formula.

Function (EX1.40)

A function is a prewritten formula that performs certain types of calculations automatically.

Recalculation (EX1.47)

When a number in a referenced cell in a formula changes, Excel automatically recalculates all formulas that are dependent upon the changed value.

Alignment (EX1.51)

Alignment settings allow you to change the horizontal and vertical placement and the orientation of an entry in a cell.

Row Height (EX1.53)

The row height is the size or height of a row measured in points.

Number Formats (EX1.62)

Number formats change the appearance of numbers onscreen and when printed, without changing the way the number is stored or used in calculations.

KEY TERMS

active cell EX1.7
active sheet EX1.7
adjacent range EX1.31
alignment EX1.51
antonym EX1.27
argument EX1.40
AutoCorrect EX1.18
AutoFit EX1.22
cell EX1.7
cell reference EX1.7
cell selector EX1.7
chart EX1.70
column EX1.6
column letter EX1.7
column width EX1.21
constant EX1.37
copy area EX1.28
custom dictionary EX1.25
data EX1.12
fill handle EX1.32
formula EX1.37
formula bar EX1.5
function EX1.40
heading EX1.12
main dictionary EX1.25
merged cell EX1.55
Name box EX1.5
nonadjacent range EX1.31
number EX1.12
number formats EX1.62

operand EX1.37
operator EX1.37
order of operations EX1.37
paste area EX1.29
Quick Analysis tool EX1.42
range EX1.31
range reference EX1.31
recalculation EX1.47
relative reference EX1.39
row EX1.6
row height EX1.53
row number EX1.7
sans serif EX1.56
scaling EX1.76
serial value EX1.71
serif EX1.56
sheet EX1.6
sheet tab EX1.7
spelling checker EX1.25
spreadsheet EX1.6
synonym EX1.27
syntax EX1.40
tab scroll buttons EX1.8
text EX1.12
theme EX1.65
thesaurus EX1.27
variable EX1.37
workbook EX1.5
workbook window EX1.5
worksheet EX1.6

COMMAND SUMMARY

Command	Shortcut	Action
File tab		
Open	Ctrl + O	Opens an existing workbook file
Save	Ctrl + S	Saves file using same file name
Save As	F12	Saves file using a new file name
Close	Ctrl + F4	Closes open workbook file
New	Ctrl + N	Opens a new blank workbook
Print / [Print icon]	Ctrl + P	Prints a worksheet
Print / [No Scaling — Print sheets at their actual size] / Fit sheet on one page		Scales worksheet to fit on a single page
Quick Access Toolbar		
[Save icon] Save	Ctrl + S	Saves document using same file name
[Undo icon] Undo	Ctrl + Z	Reverses last editing or formatting change
[Redo icon] Redo	Ctrl + Y	Restores changes after using Undo
Home tab		
Clipboard group		
[Paste icon] Paste	Ctrl + V	Pastes selections stored in system Clipboard
[Cut icon] Cut	Ctrl + X	Cuts selected data from the worksheet
[Copy icon] Copy	Ctrl + C	Copies selected data to system Clipboard
[Format Painter icon] Format Painter		Copies formatting from one place and applies it to another
Font group		
[Calibri] Font		Changes text font
[11] Font Size		Changes text size
B Bold	Ctrl + B	Bolds selected text
I Italic	Ctrl + I	Italicizes selected text

COMMAND SUMMARY (CONTINUED)

Command	Shortcut	Action
U ▾ Underline	Ctrl +U	Underlines selected text
Borders		Adds border to specified area of cell or range
Fill Color		Adds color to cell background
A ▾ Font Color		Adds color to text
Alignment group		
Align Left		Left-aligns entry in cell space
Center		Center-aligns entry in cell space
Align Right		Right-aligns entry in cell space
Increase Indent		Indents cell entry
Decrease Indent		Reduces the margin between the left cell border and cell entry
Merge & Center		Combines selected cells into one cell and centers cell contents in new cell
Number group		
General ▾ Number Format		Applies selected number formatting to selection
$ ▾ Accounting Number Format		Applies Accounting number format to selection
% Percent Style		Applies Percent Style format to selection
Increase Decimal		Increases number of decimal places
Decrease Decimal		Decreases number of decimal places
Cells group		
Insert ▾ /Insert Cells		Inserts blank cells, shifting existing cells down
Insert ▾ /Insert Cut Cells		Inserts cut row of data into new worksheet row, shifting existing rows down
Insert ▾ /Insert Copied Cells		Inserts copied row into new worksheet row, shifting existing rows down
Insert ▾ /Insert Sheet Rows		Inserts blank rows, shifting existing rows down
Insert ▾ /Insert Sheet Columns		Inserts blank columns, shifting existing columns right
Insert ▾ /Insert Sheet		Inserts a new blank worksheet in workbook

COMMAND SUMMARY (CONTINUED)

Command	Shortcut	Action
⊞ Delete ▾ /Delete Sheet Rows		Deletes selected rows, shifting existing rows up
⊞ Delete ▾ /Delete Sheet Columns		Deletes selected columns, shifting existing columns left
⊞ Delete ▾ /Delete Sheet		Deletes the active worksheet
⊞ Format ▾ /Row Height		Changes height of selected row
⊞ Format ▾ /AutoFit Row Height		Changes row height to match the tallest cell entry
⊞ Format ▾ /Column Width		Changes width of selected column
⊞ Format ▾ /AutoFit Column Width		Changes column width to match widest cell entry
⊞ Format ▾ /Default Width		Returns column width to default width
Editing group		
Σ ▾ Sum		Calculates the sum of the values in the selected cells
Σ ▾ Sum/Average		Calculates the average of the values in the selected range
Σ ▾ Sum/Min		Returns the smallest of the values in the selected range
Σ ▾ Sum/Max		Returns the largest of the values in the selected range
↓ ▾ Fill/Right	Ctrl + R	Continues a pattern to adjacent cells to the right
◆ ▾ Clear		Removes both formats and contents from selected cells
◆ ▾ Clear/Clear Formats		Clears formats only from selected cells
◆ ▾ Clear/Clear Contents	Delete	Clears contents only from selected cells
Formulas tab		
Formula Auditing group		
Show Formulas	Ctrl + `	Displays and hides worksheet formulas
Review tab		
Proofing group		
ABC ✓ Spelling	F7	Spell-checks worksheet
Thesaurus		Opens the thesaurus for the selected word in the Research task pane

LAB EXERCISES

SCREEN IDENTIFICATION

1. In the following Excel 2013 screen, letters identify important elements. Enter the correct term for each screen element in the space provided.

Possible answers for the screen identification are:

Active sheet	Name box	**A.** _____	**I.** _____
Align Right	New sheet	**B.** _____	**J.** _____
Chart title	Quick Analysis	**C.** _____	**K.** _____
Column label	Range	**D.** _____	**L.** _____
Fill color	Ribbon	**E.** _____	**M.** _____
Font	Row	**F.** _____	**N.** _____
Font color	Scroll bar	**G.** _____	**O.** _____
Format Painter	Status bar	**H.** _____	**P.** _____
Formula bar	Text label		
Increase Decimal	View buttons		

MATCHING

Match the lettered item on the right with the numbered item on the left.

1. ▦ ▾   _____ a. an arithmetic operator
2. .xlsx   _____ b. pointer shape for AutoFit
3. ▦   _____ c. a graphic representation of data
4. chart   _____ d. Excel workbook file name extension
5. /   _____ e. two or more worksheet cells
6. ▤   _____ f. enters a SUM function
7. =C19*A21   _____ g. increases decimal places shown in a cell
8. D11   _____ h. merges cells and centers entry
9. range   _____ i. a formula multiplying the values in two cells
10. Σ ▾   _____ j. a cell reference
11. ↔   _____ k. Quick Analysis

TRUE/FALSE

Circle the correct answer to the following questions.

1.	A function is a preset formula that performs a calculation.	True	False
2.	When a formula containing relative references is copied the cell references in the copied formula are adjusted based on their new location in the worksheet.	True	False
3.	The Quick Analysis tool appears when you select data for a chart.	True	False
4.	An Excel chart is a visual display of data in a worksheet.	True	False
5.	Number formats affect the way in which those values are used in calculations.	True	False
6.	When a value in a referenced formula cell is edited, Excel recalculates the formula.	True	False
7.	You can hide columns or rows in a worksheet to prohibit the data from being used in calculations.	True	False
8.	Excel's spelling checker identifies a word as misspelled if that word is not in the main dictionary.	True	False
9.	Cell alignment allows you to change the horizontal and vertical placement and the orientation of an entry in a cell.	True	False
10.	A date is a value.	True	False

LAB EXERCISES

FILL-IN

Complete the following statements by filling in the blanks with the correct key terms.

1. In a worksheet, _____ entries are right-aligned and text entries are _____-aligned.
2. Selected cells are combined into a single cell when you use the _____ command.
3. A new Excel workbook includes _____ worksheet(s).
4. When you double-click a cell with an entry, Excel changes to _____ mode.
5. Excel includes several categories of prewritten _____ to perform various arithmetic, financial, or statistical calculations.
6. In Excel, dates are stored as integers known as _____ values so that they can be used in calculations.
7. To perform an arithmetic calculation, key your own _____ in the cell.
8. When you click the File command tab, Excel changes to _____ view.
9. The values in a range of cells can be added by using the _____ function.
10. To display values with a monetary symbol and decimal places, you can use the Currency or the _____ format.

MULTIPLE CHOICE

Circle the correct response to the questions below.

1. The Excel file that stores data is a _____ .
   a. worksheet
   b. workbook
   c. workspace
   d. spreadsheet

2. To display more or less information in a cell, you can adjust the _____ .
   a. column letter
   b. row depth
   c. column width
   d. row number

3. A _____ entry can contain a combination of letters, numbers, spaces, and other special characters.
   a. number
   b. variable
   c. constant
   d. text

4. The small green square located in the lower-right corner of a cell or a selection is the _____.
   a. sheet tab
   b. fill handle
   c. scroll box
   d. sizing handle

5. Which of the following is a properly entered Excel formula as it is shown here?
   a. =(5 + 8)(2 + 1)
   b. {5 + 8*2 + 1}
   c. [5 + 8(2 + 1)]
   d. =(5 + 8)*(2 + 1)

6. Referenced cells are automatically adjusted in a copied formula if those references are _____.
   a. absolute
   b. fixed
   c. relative
   d. variable

7. Excel's _____ feature automatically inserts proper capitalization in the names of months and weekdays.
   a. AutoName
   b. AutoCorrect
   c. CorrectWords
   d. Word Wrap

8. If a worksheet does not fit on a single printed page, you can _____ it to fit.
   a. rearrange
   b. scale
   c. merge
   d. wrap

9. When a value in a cell is changed, existing formulas that refer to that cell are _____ .
   a. recalculated
   b. reformatted
   c. relooped
   d. rescaled

10. Before creating a chart, you must first _____ the data that is to be illustrated in the chart.
    a. style
    b. calculate
    c. select
    d. hide

LAB EXERCISES | Hands-On Exercises

RATING SYSTEM

★	Easy
★★	Moderate
★★★	Difficult

STEP-BY-STEP

SMARTPHONE ACTIVITIES ANALYSIS ★

1. Mary Collins works for a wireless service provider. She is analyzing data gathered in a survey of 1,200 smartphone users from ages 14 to 19 for use in marketing campaigns. After you follow the directions to complete the worksheet, your solution should look similar to that shown here.

a. Open a new blank Excel 2013 workbook.

b. Enter the data shown here into the worksheet. Save the workbook as Smartphone Activities to your solution file location.

Row	Column A	Column B	Column C	Column D
1	Activity	A Lot	Sometimes	Never
2	Check news and sports	200	550	450
3	Download or listen to music	450	400	350
4	Receive/make calls	850	200	150
5	Shop online	120	375	705
6	View/send text message	1000	100	100
7	Visit social media sites	900	180	120

c. AutoFit the widths of columns A and C. Insert a row above row 1.

d. In cell A1, enter the title **Smartphone Activities, Ages 14 through 19**.

e. Merge and center this title across columns A through D. Set the font to 16 points.

f. Bold the column labels in row 2, and center them. Apply bold to the labels in column A.

g. Add all borders to cells A2 through D8. Add an outside border to cell A1. AutoFit columns as needed.

h. Apply the Comma number format with no decimal places to the values.

i. Create a clustered column chart using the worksheet data. Move the chart to row 10, and size it to reach cell G30. Edit the chart title to **Smartphone Activities**.

j. Add a light fill color of your choice that complements the chart to row 2. Apply the same fill to every other row up to and including row 8.

k. Enter your name in cell A32 and the date in cell A33.

l. Move to cell A1. Save the workbook again. Preview and print the worksheet.

LAB EXERCISES

ANIMAL RESCUE FOUNDATION HOUSING COST ANALYSIS ★

2. Edward Corwin, an employee at the Animal Rescue Foundation, analyzes data about major shelters in the metropolitan area. He is currently working on costs for the past two years and estimating two additional years. After you follow the directions to complete the worksheet, your solution should look similar to that shown here.

   a. Open ex01_Animal Housing.

   b. Widen column A to display the longest shelter name. Spell-check the worksheet.

   c. Edit the titles in cells A2 and A3 so that the first letter of each word except "to" is capitalized. Increase the font size to 16 points for both titles. Merge and center each title across columns A through E.

   d. Bold and center the labels in row 5.

   e. In row 16, enter a function to total the values. Format the values in rows 6 and 16 with the Accounting number format and no decimal places. Format the values in rows 7 through 15 with Comma style, no decimal places.

   f. Select cells B5 and C5, and use the Fill handle to enter the following two years in cells D5 and E5.

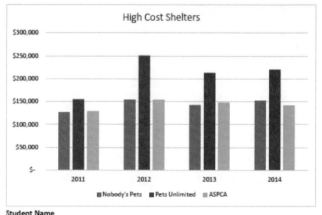

Shelter Name	2011	2012	2013	2014
Nobody's Pets	$ 127,000	$ 154,200	$ 142,600	$ 152,800
Pets Unlimited	154,500	251,000	213,500	220,300
ASPCA	129,100	154,300	148,500	142,400
FOCAS	14,500	19,200	12,500	14,700
Wood Green Animal Shelter	2,300	2,500	2,200	4,200
Pet Where Shelter	1,200	1,500	1,400	1,600
New River Animal Shelter	11,200	1,530	11,700	10,500
New Pet Shelter	19,300	19,900	18,900	25,300
City of Dogs Shelter	10,200	11,500	14,200	13,500
Humane World	29,100	12,500	26,700	29,900
Total	$ 500,411	$ 630,142	$ 594,213	$ 617,214

g. Enter the data shown here for the following two years into the worksheet. Save the workbook as Animal Housing Analysis to your solution file location.

Row	Column D	Column E
6	142600	152800
7	213500	220300
8	12500	14700
9	2200	4200
10	1400	1600
11	148500	142400
12	11700	10500
13	18900	25300
14	14200	13500
15	26700	29900

h. Copy the formula in row 16.

i. Move the ASPCA row/data so that it is above the "FOCAS" data.

j. Edit the label in cell A5 to show "Shelter Name."

k. Add all borders to cells A5 through E16. Add an outside border to cells A1 through E4.

l. Create a clustered column chart for the three shelters with the highest costs. Move the chart to cell A18, and size it to reach cell E35. Edit the chart title to High Cost Shelters.

m. In cells A1 through E4, apply a fill color of your choice to complement the chart. Then apply the same fill to row 16.

n. Enter your name in cell A36 and the current date in cell A37. Format the date to display the month spelled out, the date, and a four-digit year (March 14, 2012).

o. Move to cell A1. Save the workbook. Preview and print the worksheet.

p. Display formulas, and change to landscape orientation. Print the worksheet so that it fits on one page.

q. Remove the formula display.

LAB EXERCISES

WORK MILEAGE ANALYSIS ★★

3. Mary Ellen works for an insurance agency and is reviewing average miles driven to work. This data is available in a recent national study and is used to categorize drivers and rates. After you follow the directions to complete the worksheet, your solution should look similar to that shown here.

   a. Open ex01_Work_Mileage.

   b. Widen column A to display the longest mileage item. Spell-check the worksheet, and correct any words not found by the speller.

   c. For cells A1:A2, increase the font size to 16 points. Enter the label **Number** in cell B3. Bold and center the labels in row 3.

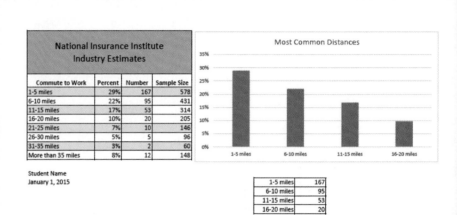

   d. Insert a column at column B. Enter the label **Percent** in cell B3.

   e. Insert a row above row 1, and insert a row above row 4. Make row 4 the same height as row 1.

   f. In cell B6, enter the formula **=c6/d6**. Format the result as Percent with zero decimal places. Copy the formula to cells B7 through B13. AutoFit column B. Save the workbook as Work Mileage Analysis to your solution file location.

   g. Merge and center the labels in cells A2 and A3 across columns A through D. Add all borders to cells A5 through D13. Add an outside border to cells A1 through D4. Make row 5 slightly taller than row 6.

   h. Create a clustered column chart for the four mileage categories with the highest percentages. Move the chart to cell E1. Edit the chart title to **Most Common Distances**.

   i. Copy cells A6 through A9 to cells G16 through G19. Then copy cells C6 through C9 to cells H16 through H19. Right-align the categories in cells G16 through G19, and make column G wide enough to show the border on the left edge.

   j. In cells A1 through D4, add a fill color of your choice to complement the chart. Then apply the same or a lighter fill to every other row of the data in columns A through D.

   k. Enter your name in cell A15 and the current date in cell A16. Format the date to display the month spelled out, the date, and a four-digit year (March 14, 2012). Left-align the date.

   l. Move to cell A1 and save the workbook.

   m. Preview the worksheet. Change to landscape orientation, and set the scaling so that the worksheet fits on one page. Print the worksheet.

4. Terrence Lewis works for an employment agency and is researching information about household income in various states. He has used data from the U.S. Census to build a worksheet. After you follow the directions to complete the worksheet, your solution should look similar to that shown here.

a. Open ex01_Household Income.

b. Edit the title in cell A1 to capitalize each word except "by." Delete the comma. Increase the font size to 20 points.

c. Widen column A to show the longest state or district. Make the labels in row 2 bold.

d. Enter the labels $ Change in cell E2, % Change in cell F2, and Average in cell G2. Bold and center these labels. Save the workbook as Household Income to your solution file location.

Median Household Income by State

Current Dollars	2011	2010	2009	$ Change	% Change	Average		2011	2010	2009	$ Change	% Change	Average
United States	50,054	49,445	49,777	277	0.56%	49,759	Nebraska	55,616	52,728	49,595	6,021	12.14%	52,646
Alabama	42,590	40,976	39,980	2,610	6.53%	41,182	Nevada	47,043	51,525	51,434	(4,391)	-8.54%	50,001
Alaska	57,431	58,198	61,604	(4,173)	-6.77%	59,078	New Hampshire	65,880	66,707	64,131	1,749	2.73%	65,573
Arizona	48,621	47,279	45,739	2,882	6.30%	47,213	New Jersey	62,338	63,540	64,777	(2,439)	-3.77%	63,552
Arkansas	41,302	38,571	36,538	4,764	13.04%	38,804	New Mexico	41,982	45,098	43,542	(1,560)	-3.58%	43,541
California	53,367	54,459	56,134	(2,767)	-4.93%	54,653	New York	50,636	49,826	50,216	420	0.84%	50,226
Colorado	58,629	60,442	55,930	2,699	4.83%	58,334	North Carolina	45,206	43,753	41,906	3,300	7.87%	43,622
Connecticut	65,415	66,452	64,851	564	0.87%	65,573	North Dakota	56,361	51,380	50,075	6,286	12.55%	52,605
Delaware	54,660	55,269	52,114	2,546	4.89%	54,014	Ohio	44,648	46,093	45,879	(1,231)	-2.68%	45,540
District of Columbia	55,251	55,528	53,141	2,110	3.97%	54,640	Oklahoma	48,455	43,400	45,878	2,577	5.62%	45,911
Florida	45,105	44,243	45,631	(526)	-1.15%	44,993	Oregon	51,526	50,526	49,098	2,428	4.95%	50,383
Georgia	45,973	44,108	43,340	2,633	6.08%	44,474	Pennsylvania	49,910	48,460	48,172	1,738	3.61%	48,847
Hawaii	59,047	58,507	55,649	3,398	6.11%	57,734	Rhode Island	49,033	51,914	51,634	(2,601)	-5.04%	50,860
Idaho	47,459	47,014	46,778	681	1.46%	47,084	South Carolina	40,084	41,709	41,101	(1,017)	-2.47%	40,965
Illinois	50,637	50,761	52,870	(2,233)	-4.22%	51,423	South Dakota	47,223	45,669	45,826	1,397	3.05%	46,239
Indiana	44,445	46,322	44,305	140	0.32%	45,024	Tennessee	42,279	38,686	40,517	1,762	4.35%	40,494
Iowa	50,219	49,177	50,721	(502)	-0.99%	50,039	Texas	49,047	47,464	47,475	1,572	3.31%	47,995
Kansas	46,147	46,229	44,717	1,430	3.20%	45,698	Utah	55,493	56,787	58,491	(2,998)	-5.13%	56,924
Kentucky	39,856	41,236	42,664	(2,808)	-6.58%	41,252	Vermont	51,862	55,942	52,318	(456)	-0.87%	53,374
Louisiana	40,658	39,443	45,433	(4,775)	-10.51%	41,845	Virginia	62,616	60,363	60,501	2,115	3.50%	61,160
Maine	49,693	48,133	47,502	2,191	4.61%	48,445	Washington	56,850	56,253	60,392	(3,542)	-5.87%	57,832
Maryland	68,876	64,025	64,186	4,690	7.31%	65,696	West Virginia	41,821	42,839	40,490	1,331	3.29%	41,717
Massachusetts	63,313	61,333	59,373	3,940	6.64%	61,340	Wisconsin	52,058	50,522	51,237	821	1.60%	51,272
Michigan	48,879	46,441	45,994	2,885	6.27%	47,105	Wyoming	54,509	52,359	52,470	2,039	3.89%	53,113
Minnesota	57,820	52,554	56,090	1,730	3.08%	55,488							
Mississippi	41,090	37,985	35,078	6,012	17.14%	38,051							
Missouri	45,774	46,184	48,769	(2,995)	-6.14%	46,909							
Montana	40,277	41,467	40,437	(160)	-0.40%	40,727							

U.S. Department of Commerce, Census Bureau

Student Name
January 1, 2015

e. In cell E3, enter the formula =b3-d3. In cell F3, enter the formula =(b3-d3)/d3 to calculate the percentage of change from 2009 to 2011.

f. Format the results in cell F3 as Percent with two decimal places. Format cells B3 through E54 as Comma style with zero decimal places.

g. In cell G3, calculate an average income for the three years using the formula =average(b3:d3).

h. Copy the three formulas in row 3 down to row 54. AutoFit columns B through G.

i. Add all borders to cells A2 through G54.

j. Cut cells A31 through G54 and paste them in cell I3. Copy cells B2 through G2 to cells J2 through O2. Widen column I to show the longest state name. Set the width of column H to 3. AutoFit columns J through O.

k. Find the state with the highest positive change, and apply a light green fill color to the data. Apply a light red fill color to the state data that shows the worst negative change.

l. Move the data in cell A56 to cell A32.

m. Enter your name in cell A34 and the current date in cell A35. Format the date to display the month spelled out, the date, and a four-digit year (March 14, 2012). Left-align the date.

n. Insert a row above row 1. Insert a row above row 3. Merge and center the label in cell A2 across columns A through O. Add an outside border to cells A1 through O3.

o. Move to cell A1 and save the workbook.

LAB EXERCISES

p. Preview the worksheet. Change to landscape orientation, and set the scaling so that the worksheet fits on one page. Print the worksheet.

q. Display the formulas, and print the worksheet. Hide the formulas.

r. Save the workbook with the same file name.

PECAN GROVES HOMEOWNERS ASSOCIATION ★★★

5. The Pecan Groves Homeowners Association has several building projects coming up for next year, and it must analyze the amount of cash available in its budget for the work. Using last year's budget data, you can prepare estimates for next year. After you follow the directions to complete the worksheet, your solution should look similar to that shown here.

a. Open ex01_Pecan Groves. Spell-check the worksheet, and check for consistent use of uppercase where needed. Save the workbook as Pecan Groves Budget to your solution file location.

b. Widen column A to show the longest income or expenditure. Center the labels in cells A6 and A11. Right-align and bold the labels in cells A10 and A23.

c. Increase the indent one time for cells A17 through A20. Delete row 21.

d. In cell C10, sum the income items. In cell C22, sum all expenditures.

e. Insert a row at row 23. In cell A23, key **Net Income** and left-align it.

f. In cell C23, enter a formula to determine net income (income – expenditures). In cell C26, enter a formula to calculate the ending cash balance (net income + cash on hand + reserves).

g. Format cell B7 as Accounting number format with zero decimal places. Apply the same format to each value in column C. Then format the remaining values as Comma style with zero decimal places.

h. Add a bottom border to cells B9, B21, and B25. Add a bottom double border to cells C10, C22, and C26.

i. Each of the income items for next year is projected to increase by 6 percent for next year. Enter a formula in cell D7 to calculate 106 percent of this year's assessment fees. Then copy the formula for the other income items. Apply the same number formats and bottom border.

Pecan Groves Homeowners Association
Projected Budget

	This Year	Next Year
Income		
Assessment Fees	$ 219,500	$ 232,670
Rentals	1,700	1,802
Earned Interest	1,200	1,272
Total Income	$ 222,400	$ 235,744
Expenditures		
Administration	120,000	129,600
Insurance	16,000	17,280
Audit & Tax Preparation	12,000	12,960
Attorney and Legal Fees	14,000	15,120
Maintenance		
Street Repair	2,700	2,916
Street Cleaning	1,582	1,709
Snow Removal	550	594
Property Signage	4,985	5,384
Miscellaneous	3,000	3,240
Total Expenditures	$ 174,817	$ 188,802
Net Income	$ 47,583	$ 46,942
Cash on Hand	16,701	16,701
Reserves	23,000	23,000
Ending Cash Balance	$ 87,284	$ 86,643

Student Name
January 1, 2015

j. In cell E10, enter a formula to calculate the total income for next year. Apply the same formatting as that used for this year.

k. Each of the expenditure items is expected to increase by 8 percent for next year. Enter the formula in cell D12, and copy it as needed. Delete a copied formula in cell D16. In cell E22, sum the expenditures for next year. Make sure the formatting matches that used for this year.

l. In cell E23, calculate net income for next year. In cells D24 and D25, enter the same values as those for this year. In cell E26, calculate the ending cash balance for next year.

m. Review and adjust number and border formatting as necessary.

n. Merge and center the contents of cell B5 across columns B through C. Make the label bold, and add a bottom border.

o. Insert a blank column at column D, and make it 3 spaces wide. Then merge and center the contents of cell E5 across columns E through F; add bold and a bottom border.

p. Increase the font size for cells A1:A2 to 16 points. Then merge and center these labels across the worksheet data.

q. Add a bottom border to cells A3 through F3. Apply a fill color to cells D6 through D26. Apply the same or complementary fill color to cells A5 through F5 and cells A27 through F27.

r. Insert a new row at row 1, and apply a fill color to cells A1 through F1. Delete row 5.

s. Widen column A to 26. Widen columns B through C and E through F so that the worksheet data appears centered on the page. Make sure, though, that these four columns are the same width.

t. Enter your name in cell A30 and the current date in cell A31. Format the date to display the month spelled out, the date, and a four-digit year. Left-align the date.

u. Move to cell A1. Save the workbook using the same file name. Print the worksheet.

v. Display the formulas, and print the worksheet using landscape orientation, fit to a single page. Hide the formulas.

ON YOUR OWN

TRACKING YOUR CALORIES ★

1. A worksheet can be used to track your calories for the day. Design and create a worksheet to record the food you consume and the exercise you do on a daily basis. The worksheet should include your food consumption for all meals and snacks and the activities you performed for a week. Use the Web as a resource to find out the caloric values for the items you consumed (or refer to the calorie information on the product packaging) and to find out the caloric expenditure for the exercises you do. Include an appropriate title, row and column headings, and formulas to calculate your total calorie intake and expenditure on a daily basis. Include a formula to calculate the percent deviation from your recommended daily calorie intake. Format the worksheet appropriately using features presented in this lab. Enter real or sample data. Include your name and date above the worksheet. Spell-check the worksheet. Save the workbook as Calorie Tracking and print the worksheet.

LAB EXERCISES

CREATING A PERSONAL BUDGET ★

2. In a blank Excel 2013 workbook, create a personal three-month budget. Enter an appropriate title and use descriptive labels for your monthly expenses (food, rent, car payments, insurance, credit card payments, etc.). Spell-check your worksheet. Enter your monthly expenses (or, if you prefer, any reasonable sample data). Use formulas to calculate total expenses for each month and the average monthly expenditures for each expense item. Add a column for projection for the next year showing a 2.5 percent increase in the cost of living. Enhance the worksheet using features you learned in this lab. Enter your name and the current date on separate rows just below the worksheet. Save the workbook as Personal Budget. Preview and print the worksheet.

TRACKING PROJECT HOURS ★★

3. Samantha Johnson is the project manager for a small publishing company. She has four part-time employees (Melanie, Bob, Vanessa, and Rudy). Using the steps in the planning process, plan and create a worksheet for Samantha that can be used to record and analyze the hours each employee works per day during the month on two projects: magazine and brochure. Hours-worked data for each employee will be entered into the worksheet. Using that data, the worksheet will calculate the total number of hours for each person per project. Additionally, it will calculate the total weekly hours for each project. Write a short paragraph describing how you used each of the planning steps. Enter sample data in a worksheet. Include your name and the current date on separate rows just below the worksheet. Spell-check the worksheet. Save the workbook as Project Hours. Preview and print the worksheet.

MUSIC ANALYSIS ★★★

4. Use the library and/or the Web to locate information on trends in CD sales versus music downloads on the Internet. Create a worksheet to display information relating to the increasing usage by country, age group, or any other trend you locate. Calculate totals or averages based on your data. Enhance the worksheet using features you learned in this lab. Enter your name and the current date on separate rows just below the worksheet. Spell-check the worksheet. Save the workbook as Music Analysis. Preview and print the worksheet.

HOME ELECTRONICS ANALYSIS ★★★

5. A national electronics retailer wants to analyze the trend in home electronics sales and usage for the past three years. Design and create a worksheet to record the number of households (one-person, two-person, and four-person) that have computers, Internet access, televisions, and cable and satellite TV access. Include an appropriate title, row and column headings, and formulas to calculate average by category and by year. Include a formula to calculate the percentage of growth over the three years. Format the worksheet appropriately using features presented in this tutorial. Enter sample data for the three years. Include your name and date above the worksheet. Spell-check the worksheet. Save the workbook as Home Electronics Analysis and print the worksheet.

Enhancing the Worksheet with Graphics and Charts

Objectives

After completing this lab, you will know how to:

1. Insert and size a graphic.

2. Use cell styles.

3. Apply and customize themes.

4. Create a column chart.

5. Move, size, and format a chart.

6. Change the type of chart.

7. Create a combo chart.

8. Create, explode, and rotate a pie chart.

9. Apply patterns and color to a chart.

10. Size and align a sheet on a page.

11. Add predefined headers and footers.

Downtown Internet Café

Evan is impressed with how quickly you were able to create the first quarter sales forecast for the Downtown Internet Café. He made several suggestions to improve the appearance of the worksheet, including applying different formats and adding a graphic. Evan also expressed concern that the sales values seem a little low and has asked you to contact several other Internet cafés to inquire about their start-up experiences.

While speaking with other Internet café managers, you heard many exciting success stories. Internet connections attract more customers, and the typical customer stays longer at an Internet café than at a regular café. As a result, the customers spend more money.

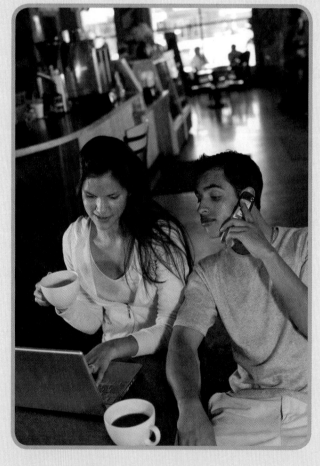

You would like to launch an aggressive advertising campaign to promote the new Internet aspect of the Café. The new Café features include free WiFi connection, computer rentals, and printing and copying services. You believe that the campaign will lead to an increase in customers and subsequently to an increase in sales. To convince Evan, you need an effective way to illustrate the sales growth you are forecasting. You will use Excel 2013's chart-creating and formatting features to produce several different charts of your sales estimates, as shown on the following page.

Use of graphics and themes adds visual interest to a worksheet.

Many different types of charts can be created and modified to visually represent worksheet data.

Features such as data labels, fill colors, textures, and shadows add a professional appearance to your charts.

The following concepts will be introduced in this lab:

1 Graphics A graphic is a nontext element or object such as a drawing or picture that can be added to a document.

2 Quick Style A quick style is a named group of formatting characteristics that allows you to quickly apply a whole group of formats to a selected object in one simple step.

3 Theme A theme is a set of formatting choices that can be applied to an entire worksheet in one simple step. A theme consists of a set of theme colors, a set of theme fonts (including heading and body text fonts), and a set of theme effects (including line and fill effects).

4 Chart Elements Chart elements are the different parts of a chart that are used to graphically display the worksheet data.

5 Chart Types Different chart types are used to represent data in different ways. The type of chart you create depends on the type of data you are charting and the emphasis you want the chart to impart.

6 Chart Object A chart object is a graphic object that is created using charting features. A chart object can be inserted into a worksheet or into a special chart sheet.

7 Group A group is two or more objects that behave as a single object when moved or sized. A chart is a group that consists of many separate objects.

8 Data Labels Data labels provide additional information about a data point in the data series. They can consist of the value of the point, the name of the data series or category, a percentage value, or a bubble size.

9 Headers and Footers Headers and footers provide information that typically appears at the top and bottom of each page and commonly include information such as the date and page number.

Inserting and Formatting Illustrations

To focus Evan's attention solely on the sales values for the Downtown Internet Café, you created a new worksheet containing only those values. Although you have added some formatting to the worksheet already, you still want to improve its appearance by adding a graphic, changing the theme, and applying different cell styles. Then you will create the charts to help Evan visualize the sales trends better.

INSERTING A PICTURE FROM A COMPUTER

You saved the sales portion of the worksheet in a new workbook file.

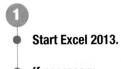

Start Excel 2013.

If necessary, maximize the Excel application window.

Open the file ex02_ Cafe Sales.

If necessary, click

| Enable Editing |

in the message bar.

Your screen should be similar to Figure 2.1

Figure 2.1

First you want to add a graphic next to the worksheet title to add interest.

Concept 1 Graphics

A **graphic** is a nontext element or object such as a drawing or picture that can be added to a document. An **object** is an item that can be sized, moved, and manipulated.

A graphic can be a simple **drawing object** consisting of shapes, such as lines and boxes, that can be created using the Shapes tool. A drawing object is part of the Excel workbook. A **picture** is an illustration such as a graphic illustration or a scanned photograph. Pictures are graphics that were created from another program and are inserted in the worksheet as embedded objects. An **embedded object** becomes part of the Excel workbook and can be opened and edited using the **source program**, the program in which it was created. Any changes made to the embedded object are not made to the original picture file because they are independent. Several examples of drawing objects and pictures are shown below.

Drawing object

Graphic illustration

Photograph

Add graphics to your worksheets to help the reader understand concepts, to add interest, and to make your worksheet stand out from others.

Digital images created using a digital camera are one of the most common types of graphic files. You also can create graphic files using a scanner to convert any printed document, including photographs, to an electronic format. **Clip art** graphics, simple drawings created using a graphics program, are another common type of graphic file. The most common graphic file formats are JPG, TIF, PNG, GIF, and BMP.

Graphic files can be obtained from a variety of sources, including files stored on your computer or a computer network and from Internet websites. All types of graphics, including clip art, photographs, and other types of images, can be found on Microsoft's Office.com Clip Art website, which offers royalty-free graphics. Graphics that you locate on other websites may be protected by copyright and should be used only with permission. You also can purchase CDs containing graphics.

You will insert a picture you have stored on your computer to the left of the title in the worksheet.

- **Open the Insert tab.**

- **Click** [Pictures] **in the Illustrations group.**

Having Trouble?

If necessary, first click [Illustrations] to open the Illustrations group.

- **Change to the location of your data files.**

- **Select** ex02_Cafe **.png.**

Having Trouble?

Depending on your Windows setup, the file extension may or may not be displayed.

- **If a thumbnail image of the selected graphic is not displayed, open the** [▼] **View drop-down menu and choose Large Icons.**

Your screen should be similar to Figure 2.2

Figure 2.2

Only files that have a graphic file type are displayed in the file list. You think the selected picture illustrates the concept of a café and that it will look good in the worksheet.

2 Click [Insert ▼].

Your screen should be similar to Figure 2.3

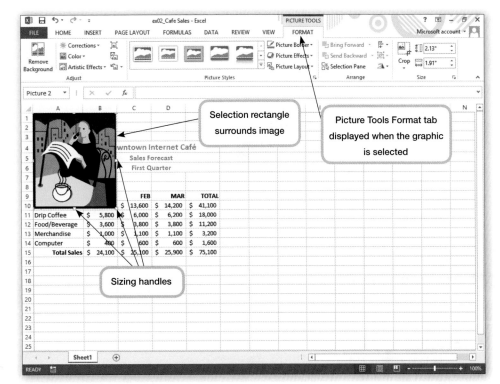

Selection rectangle surrounds image

Picture Tools Format tab displayed when the graphic is selected

Sizing handles

Figure 2.3

The picture is inserted in the worksheet at the location of the cell selector. It is inserted in a separate drawing layer and covers some of the worksheet data. The picture is surrounded by a **selection rectangle** and eight squares called **sizing handles**, indicating it is a selected object and can now be deleted, sized, moved, or modified. The Picture Tools Format tab is automatically displayed and can be used to modify the selected picture object.

SIZING AND MOVING A GRAPHIC

Usually, when a graphic is inserted, its size will need to be adjusted. To size a graphic, you select it and drag a sizing handle to increase or decrease the size of the object. The mouse pointer changes to ⬊ when pointing to a corner handle and ⬌ or ⬍ when pointing to a side handle. The direction of the arrow indicates the direction in which you can drag to size the graphic. Dragging a corner handle maintains the scale of the picture by increasing both the width and length of the graphic equally. You also can move a graphic object by pointing to the graphic and dragging it to the new location. The mouse pointer changes to ✛ when you can move the graphic.

1

- Point to the lower-right corner sizing handle.

- With the pointer as a ↖, drag the mouse inward to reduce the size of the graphic until the bottom of the graphic is even with row 6.

Additional Information

When you drag to size the graphic, the mouse pointer shape changes to a ✛.

- Point to the center of the graphic and, when the mouse pointer is ✛↖, drag the graphic to position it as in Figure 2.4.

Your screen should be similar to Figure 2.4

Having Trouble?

If you do not have an Internet connection, you cannot complete this section. Insert the picture ex02_Laptop from your data file location. Skip to the next section, "Deleting a Graphic."

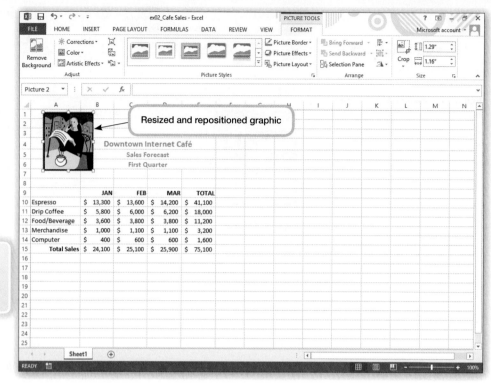

Resized and repositioned graphic

Figure 2.4

The graphic is smaller and moved to the left of the title as you want it.

INSERTING A PICTURE FROM ONLINE SOURCES

Although you like the graphic, you decide to search the online sources for pictures that show the use of a computer in a café environment.

1

- Move to cell F1 to deselect the graphic and choose the location where you want a new picture inserted.

- Open the Insert tab.

- Click [Online Pictures] in the Illustrations group.

Your screen should be similar to Figure 2.5

Figure 2.5

The Insert Pictures dialog box provides several methods to locate online graphics. The first is to use Microsoft's Office.com Clip Art website. The second is to use Microsoft's search engine, Bing, to search the web. A third is to access your Sky-Drive account to locate pictures you have stored at that location. Finally, you can access Flickr, an online photo management and sharing website, for pictures you have uploaded to an account with the website.

You will use the Office.com website to search for pictures by entering a word or phrase that is representative of the type of picture you want to locate. You can search files at Office.com or use the Bing search tool. You want to find pictures of laptop computers and coffee.

2

● Click in the Office
.com Clip Art text box
and type laptop,
coffee in the
text box.

● Click [🔍] Search.

Your screen should be similar to
Figure 2.6

Figure 2.6

Having Trouble?

Your results may display different
pictures than those shown in
Figure 2.6.

The program searches the Office.com Clip Art website for clip art and graphics
that match your search terms and displays **thumbnails**, miniature representations
of pictures, of all located graphics. Pointing to a thumbnail displays a ScreenTip
containing the description or **keywords** associated with the picture and the [🔍]
View Larger button. The bottom of the dialog box shows keywords and the size of
the picture in pixels.

3

- Scroll the list to view additional pictures.

- Point to the thumbnail shown in Figure 2.7 to see a ScreenTip.

- Click on 🔍 View Larger.

Having Trouble?

If this graphic is not available, point to another of your choice.

Your screen should be similar to Figure 2.7

Figure 2.7

The selected graphic is displayed larger so it is easier to see. The ScreenTip displays the description of the selected picture. You think this looks like a good choice and will insert it into the worksheet.

4

- Double-click on the graphic to insert it into the worksheet.

Another Method

You also could click .

Your screen should be similar to Figure 2.8

Figure 2.8

The picture is downloaded and inserted in the worksheet at the location of the cell selector. It is the selected object. You now have two graphic objects in the worksheet, a drawing and a photograph.

DELETING A GRAPHIC

You decide to use the drawing graphic and need to remove the photograph. To do this, you select the graphic and delete it.

- **If necessary, click on the photograph to select it.**

- **Press** Delete.

Your screen should be similar to Figure 2.9

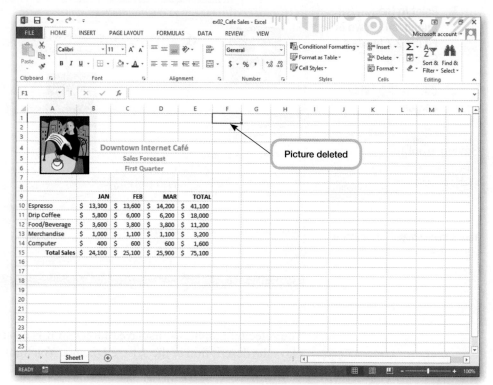

Picture deleted

Figure 2.9

The photograph is deleted from the worksheet.

APPLYING AND MODIFYING A PICTURE QUICK STYLE

Next, you want to enhance the graphic by applying a quick style to it.

Concept 2 Quick Style

A **quick style** is a named group of formatting characteristics that allows you to quickly apply a whole group of formats to a selected object in one simple step. The formatting options associated with the different quick styles vary depending upon the type of object. For example, a line quick style may consist of a combination of color, shadows, gradients, and three-dimensional (3-D) perspectives options, whereas a shape quick style may consist of a combination of fill color, line color, and line weight options.

Many quick styles are automatically applied when certain features, such as charts, are used. Others must be applied manually to the selected object. You also can create your own custom styles.

Quick styles are available for cell selections as well as many different types of objects. Some of the most common are described in the following table.

Type of Quick Style	Description
Cell style	Affects selected cells by applying effects such as fill color, text and number formatting, and bold and underline formats.
Shape style	Affects all aspects of a shape object's appearance, including fill color, outline color, and other effects.
Chart style	Provides a consistent look to charts by applying color, shading, line, and font effects.
Picture style	Adds a border around a graphic object that consists of combinations of line, shadow, color, and shape effects.

You will use a picture quick style to add a border around the picture to make it stand out more. You also can create your own picture style effects by selecting specific style elements such as borders and shadow individually using the Picture Border ▾, 🔲 Picture Effects ▾, and 🔲 Picture Layout ▾ commands.

1

- Select the graphic.

- Click ⟱ More in the Picture Styles group of the Format tab to open the Picture Styles gallery.

- Point to several styles to see the Live Preview.

Your screen should be similar to Figure 2.10

Figure 2.10

When you point to a style, the style name appears in a ScreenTip and the Live Preview shows how the selected picture style will look with your graphic. As you can see, many are not appropriate. However, you decide that the rotated style with a white border will enhance the graphic and the worksheet.

2

- Choose Rotated, White.

- Size and position the graphic as in Figure 2.11.

- Click outside the graphic to deselect the object.

Your screen should be similar to Figure 2.11

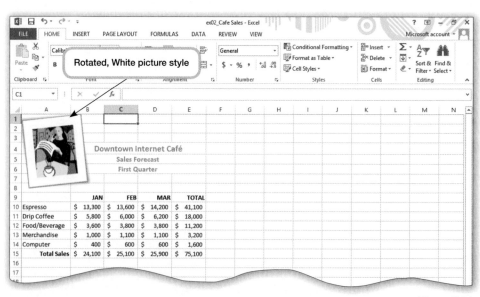

Figure 2.11

After seeing how the graphic looks with the selected picture style, you decide to modify the quick style by adding color to and changing the weight of the border.

3

- **Click on the graphic to select it again.**

- **Click** **Picture Border ▾ in the Picture Styles group of the Format tab.**

- **Choose the Orange Accent 2 color from the Theme Colors category.**

- **Click Picture Border ▾, select Weight, and choose 4½ points.**

- **Click outside the graphic to deselect the object.**

- **Document the workbook by adding your name as author and the workbook title of Sales Forecast**

- **Save the revised workbook as** Cafe Sales Forecast **to your solution file location.**

Your screen should be similar to Figure 2.12

Figure 2.12

Using Themes

The addition of a graphic adds a nice touch to the worksheet title. Now, you want to continue to improve the worksheet appearance by selecting a different theme.

Concept 3 Theme

A **theme** is a set of formatting choices that can be applied to an entire workbook in one simple step. A theme consists of a set of theme colors, a set of theme fonts (including heading and body text fonts), and a set of theme effects (including line and fill effects). Excel includes more than 20 named built-in themes. Each theme includes three subsets of themes: colors, fonts, and effects. Each color theme consists of 12 colors that are applied to specific elements in a document. Each fonts theme includes different body and heading fonts. Each effects theme includes different line and fill effects. You also can create your own custom themes by modifying an existing theme and saving it as a custom theme.

The default workbook uses the Office theme. The font and fill colors and quick style effects that are available are determined by the current theme. If you change the current theme, style choices that you've previously made will be updated to match settings in the new theme. However, colors that you've selected from the standard colors gallery will remain the same. Using themes gives your documents a professional and modern look. Because themes are shared across Office 2013 applications, all your office documents can have the same uniform appearance.

APPLYING A THEME

You decide to see how the worksheet would look using a different theme.

• **Open the Page Layout tab.**

• **Click [Themes] from the Themes group.**

Your screen should be similar to Figure 2.13

Figure 2.13

A gallery of built-in named themes is displayed. A sample shows the color and font effects included in each theme. The Office theme is highlighted because it is the default theme. Pointing to each theme will display a Live Preview of how it will appear in the worksheet.

2

● Point to several themes to preview them.

● Scroll through the selections and choose the Retrospect theme.

Your screen should be similar to Figure 2.14

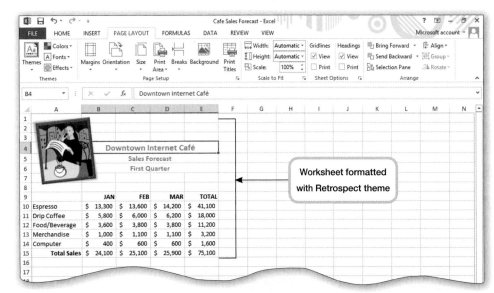

Worksheet formatted with Retrospect theme

Figure 2.14

Additional Information

If the border and font colors were colors on the Standard Colors bar, the color is updated to the new theme design.

Additional Information

Only one theme can be used in a workbook.

Additional Information

The colors you see in the

[Colors ▾] Theme Colors button

represent the current text and background colors.

The formatting settings associated with the selected theme have been applied to the worksheet. Most noticeable is the color change of the picture border and titles. This is because the colors in the theme category have been updated to the Retrospect theme colors. Consequently the available picture quick style colors and font colors have been updated to the new theme colors.

As you add other features to the worksheet, they will be formatted using the Retrospect theme colors and effects. The same theme will be applied to the other sheets in the workbook file.

CUSTOMIZING A THEME

Sometimes, you cannot find just the right combination of design elements in a built-in theme. To solve this problem, you can customize a theme by changing the color scheme, fonts, and effects. Each theme has an associated set of colors that you can change by applying a different color palette to the selected theme.

1

● Click [Colors ▾] in the Themes group.

Your screen should be similar to Figure 2.15

Opens Theme Colors gallery

Built-in color schemes

Current color scheme for Retrospect theme

Figure 2.15

A drop-down list of 23 built-in color palettes is displayed. Each palette consists of eight colors that represent the text, background, accent, and hyperlink colors. Pointing to a color palette will display a Live Preview of the selection. The Orange color scheme is selected because it is the color scheme currently in use. Notice that the fourth color from the left in the color bar is the Accent2 color that is used in the picture border. You want to see how the Red Orange color scheme would look.

2

- Point to several color schemes to preview them.

- Choose the Red Orange theme color scheme.

Your screen should be similar to Figure 2.16

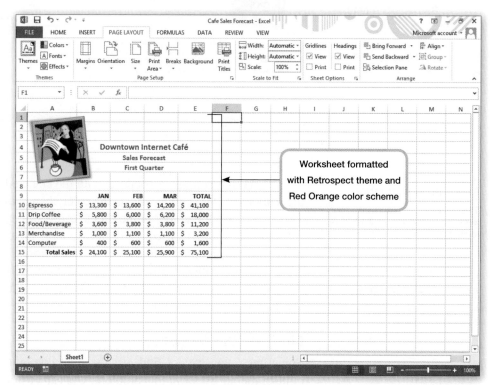

Figure 2.16

The new color scheme has been applied to the picture border and font color used in the worksheet titles. All other aspects of the Retrospect theme are unchanged.

SAVING A CUSTOM THEME

You decide to save the color change you have made to the Retrospect theme as a custom theme. This will make it easy to reapply the same settings to another workbook in the future. Custom themes are saved in the Document Themes folder by default and are available in all Office applications that use themes.

Additional Information

You can change the theme fonts and effects in a similar manner.

Additional Information

Custom themes have the .thmx file extension, which identifies the file as an Office theme template file.

1

- Click Themes.

- **Choose Save Current Theme.**

- **Enter** Retrospect1 **as the theme file name.**

- Click **Save** .

Having Trouble?

If an advisory message appears indicating this theme already exists, click **Yes** to replace it.

- Click <image>Themes</image>.

Your screen should be similar to Figure 2.17

Figure 2.17

Additional Information

To remove a custom theme, choose Delete from the theme's shortcut menu.

The custom theme you created and saved appears at the top of the Themes gallery. Now you can quickly reapply this entire theme in one step to another workbook, just like the built-in themes, or to any other Office document.

Using Cell Styles

Next, you want to enhance the worksheet more by adding background cell shading to define areas of the worksheet. You will also use a heading style for the title, and change the format of the Food/Beverage, Merchandise, and Computer values to display commas only, without dollar signs.

Although you could make these changes using individual formatting commands, a quicker way is to use a predefined **cell style** to apply several formats in one step. Excel includes 47 predefined cell styles, or you can create your own custom styles. Using cell styles helps ensure that cells have consistent formatting. Cell styles are based on the theme that is applied to the entire workbook. When you switch to another theme, the cell styles are updated to match the new theme.

APPLYING THEMED CELL STYLES

First, you want to add background shading behind the entire worksheet.

- Select the range A1 through E15.

- Open the Home tab.

- Click [Cell Styles ▾] in the Styles group.

Your screen should be similar to Figure 2.18

Figure 2.18

The Cell Styles gallery is divided into five sections. The styles in each section are designed to identify different areas of a worksheet and types of cell entries, as explained in the following table:

Section	Identifies
Good, Bad and Neutral	Data trends or outcomes; for example, selecting Bad would be used to identify a bad outcome
Data and Model	Worksheet areas; for example, calculations and warning notes
Titles and Headings	Worksheet titles and headings
Themed Cell Styles	Basic worksheet data
Number Format	Number formats

You will use a cell style in the Themed Cell Styles section. These cell styles consist of background fill colors and either white or black text color. The colors are associated with the theme colors. Pointing to a cell style displays a Live Preview of the cell style.

2

- Point to several cell styles to see the Live Preview.

- Choose 40%–Accent5 in the Themed Cell Styles section.

- Click on the worksheet to clear the selection.

Your screen should be similar to Figure 2.19

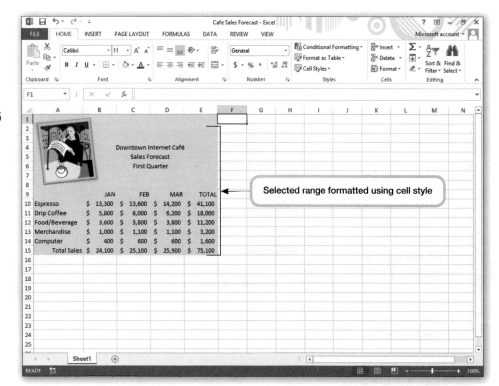

Selected range formatted using cell style

Figure 2.19

The selected range has been formatted using the selected cell style. It consists of a gold fill color for the cell background and black font color. The previous font color used in the titles was replaced with the font color associated with the cell style.

APPLYING HEADING AND TOTAL CELL STYLES

Next you will define the row headings area of the worksheet by selecting a different style from the Themed Cell Styles section. Then you will use two cell styles from the Titles and Headings section that will format the month column headings and the Total Sales row of data.

1

- Select A1 through A15.

- Click 📋 Cell Styles ▾ and choose the Accent3 style.

- Select cells A10 through A15 and make them bold.

- Select B9 through E9 and apply the Heading 3 cell style.

- Select A15 through E15 and apply the Total cell style.

- Click outside the selection to see the formatting changes.

Your screen should be similar to Figure 2.20

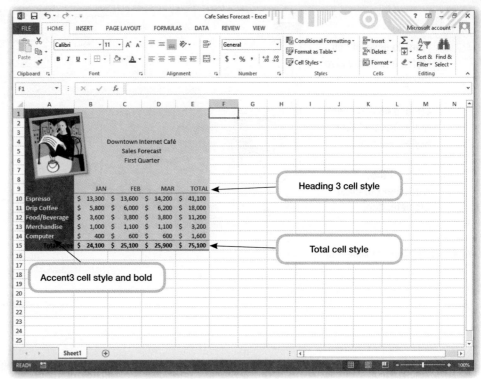

Figure 2.20

The Accent3 cell style uses a white font color with a dark red fill color. The Heading 3 style includes a dark gray font color and a bottom border. The Total cell style applies a black font color, bold text effect, and a top and bottom border.

Next, you will add formatting to the worksheet titles by applying a Title style to the first title line, a Heading 1 style to the second line, and a Heading 2 style to the third line.

2

- Apply the Title cell style to cell B4.

- Apply the Heading 1 cell style to cell B5.

- Apply the Heading 2 cell style to cell B6.

- Click outside the selection to see the formatting changes.

- Resize and reposition the graphic as needed to show the full title text.

Figure 2.21

Your screen should be similar to Figure 2.21

MODIFYING CELL STYLES

Although you like the font size change and the colored bottom border line, you feel the titles could be improved by changing the font color to a color similar to the fill color used in column A. Instead of changing the font color for each cell containing the titles, you will modify the cell styles so that the color changes to these styles will be easily available again.

1

- Click [Cell Styles ▾] and right-click on the Title cell style.

- Choose Modify from the shortcut menu.

- Click [Format...] and if necessary, open the Font tab.

- Open the Color gallery and choose Dark Red, Accent 6 from the Theme Colors category.

- Click [OK] twice.

- Modify the Heading 1 and Heading 2 cell styles in the same manner.

Your screen should be similar to Figure 2.22

Cell styles modified and font color updated

Figure 2.22

The three title lines have been updated to the new color associated with the three cell styles you modified. The changes to cell styles are saved with the current workbook file only.

APPLYING A NUMBER CELL STYLE

Additional Information

The Accounting number style with zero decimal places is the same as the Currency [0] cell style.

The final change you want to make is to change the format of some of the worksheet values. Currently all the values are formatted using the Accounting style with zero decimal places. The Cell Styles gallery also includes five predefined number format styles. Examples of the five predefined number styles are shown below.

Style	Example
Comma	89,522.00
Comma [0]	89,522
Currency	$89,522.00
Currency [0]	$89,522
Percent	89.52200%

You will use the Comma [0] style for the four rows of sales values below Espresso Sales.

1

- Select B11 through E14.

- Open the Cell Styles gallery.

- Choose Comma [0].

- Clear the selection.

- Save the file.

Your screen should be similar to Figure 2.23

Figure 2.23

The Comma [0] style applies the Comma number format with zero decimal places and does not display a currency symbol. Using a style applies many formats in one easy step, making it quicker to apply formats to cells.

Creating Charts

Although the worksheet shows the sales data for each category, it is difficult to see how the different categories change over time. To make it easier to see the sales trends, you decide to create a chart of this data.

SELECTING THE CHART DATA

As you learned in Lab 1, a **chart** is a visual representation of data in a worksheet. Because all charts are drawn from data contained in a worksheet, the first step in creating a new chart is to select the worksheet range containing the data you want displayed as a chart plus any row or column headings you want used in the chart. Excel then recommends the chart types best suited to the selected data based upon the shape and contents of the worksheet selection.

A chart consists of a number of parts or elements that are important to understand so that you can identify the appropriate data to select in the worksheet.

Concept ④ Chart Elements

Chart elements are the different parts of a chart that are used to graphically display the worksheet data. The entire chart and all its elements is called the **chart area**.

The basic elements of a two-dimensional chart are described in the following table.

Element	Description
Plot area	Area within the X- and Y-axis boundaries where the chart data series appears.
Axis	The lines bordering the chart plot area used as a frame of reference for measurement. The **Y axis**, also called the **value axis**, is usually the vertical axis and contains data. The **X axis**, also called the **category axis**, is usually the horizontal axis and contains categories.
Data series	Related data points that are distinguished by different colors or patterns, called **data markers**, and displayed in the plot area.
Data labels	Labels that correspond to the data points that are plotted along the X axis.
Chart gridlines	Lines extending from the axis line across the plot area that make it easier to read the chart data.
Legend	A box that identifies the chart data series and data markers.
Chart title	A descriptive label displayed above the charted data that explains the contents of the chart.
Category-axis title	A descriptive label displayed along the X axis.
Value-axis title	A descriptive label displayed along the Y axis.

The basic parts of a two-dimensional chart are shown in the figure below.

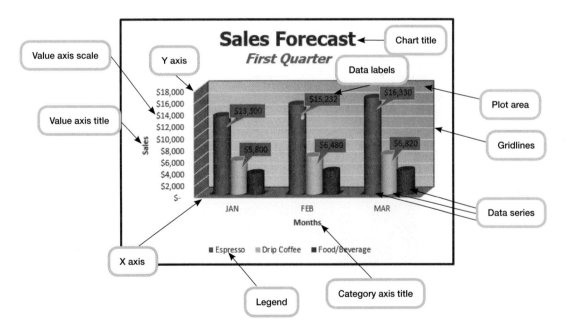

3-D column, 3-D cone, or 3-D pyramid charts have a third axis, the **depth axis** (also known as the **series axis** or **Z axis**), so that data can be plotted along the depth of a chart. Radar charts do not have horizontal (category) axes, and pie and doughnut charts do not have any axes.

The first chart you want to create will show the total sales pattern over the three months. This chart will use the month headings in cells B9 through D9 to label the X axis. The numbers to be charted are in cells B15 through D15. In addition, the heading "Total Sales" in cell A15 will be used as the chart legend, making the entire range A15 through D15.

Notice that the two ranges, B9 through D9 and A15 through D15, are not adjacent and are not the same size. When plotting nonadjacent ranges in a chart, the selections must form a rectangular shape. To do this, you will include the blank cell A9 in the selection. You will specify the range and create the chart.

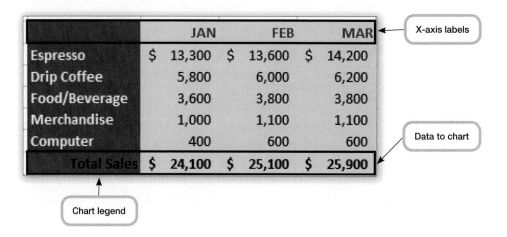

X-axis labels

Data to chart

Chart legend

- Select cells A9 through D9.

- Hold down Ctrl.

- Select cells A15 through D15.

Your screen should be similar to Figure 2.24

Selected nonadjacent ranges

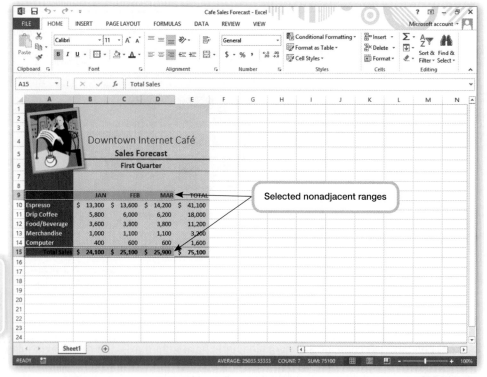

Figure 2.24

SELECTING THE CHART TYPE

The next step is to select the chart type. There are many different types of charts that can be used to convey the information in a worksheet in an attractive and easy-to-understand manner.

Concept Chart Types

Different **chart types** are used to represent data in different ways. The type of chart you create depends on the type of data you are charting and the emphasis you want the chart to impart.

Excel 2013 can produce many standard types of graphs or charts, with different subtypes for each standard type. In addition, Excel includes professionally designed, built-in custom charts that include additional formatting and chart refinements. The basic chart types and how they represent data are described in the following table.

Type	Description	Type	Description
Area Charts	**Area charts** show the magnitude of change over time by emphasizing the area under the curve created by each data series.	Pie or Doughnut Charts	**Pie charts** display data as slices of a circle or pie. They show the relationship of each value in a data series to the series as a whole. Each slice of the pie represents a single value in the series. **Doughnut charts** are similar to pie charts except that they can show more than one data series.
Bar Charts	**Bar charts** display data as evenly spaced bars. The categories are displayed along the Y axis and the values are displayed horizontally, placing more emphasis on comparisons and less on time.	Stock, Surface, or Radar Charts	**Stock charts** illustrate fluctuations in stock prices or scientific data. They require three to five data series that must be arranged in a specific order. **Surface charts** display values in a form similar to a rubber sheet stretched over a 3-D column chart. These are useful for finding the best combination between sets of data. **Radar charts** display a line or area chart wrapped around a central point. Each axis represents a set of data points.
Column Charts	**Column charts** display data as evenly spaced bars. They are similar to bar charts, except that categories are organized horizontally and values vertically to emphasize variation over time.	Scatter (X, Y) or Bubble Charts	**Scatter (X, Y) charts** are used to show the relationship between two ranges of numeric data. **Bubble charts** compare sets of three values. They are similar to a scatter chart with the third value displayed as the size of bubble markers.
Line Charts	**Line charts** display data along a line. They are used to show changes in data over time, emphasizing time and rate of change rather than the amount of change.	Combo Charts	**Combo charts** display data as two different chart types. They are used when the range of values in the chart vary widely or have mixed data types.

Each type of chart includes many variations. The Charts group in the Insert tab contains commands to create the most commonly used types of charts. In addition, it includes the 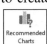 button, which lists the most likely chart types for your worksheet selection. You also can open the Charts group dialog box to have access to all the available chart types. You think a column chart may best represent this data.

1

Open the Insert tab.

Click [Recommended Charts] in the
Charts group.

Your screen should be similar to
Figure 2.25

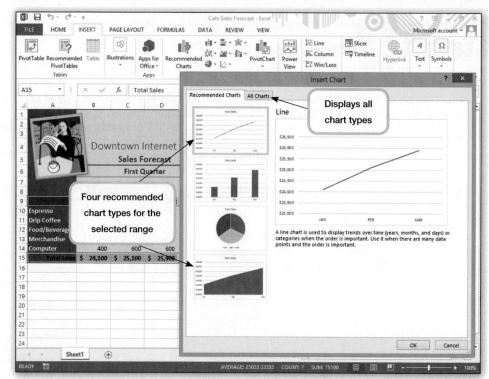

Figure 2.25

Based on the selected data, the recommended charts include a line chart, a column chart, a pie chart, and an area chart. The preview area displays a large preview of the data in the selected chart type. You can choose one of the recommended chart types, or you can click the All Charts tab to see how the selected data looks in all available chart types.

2

Click the Clustered
Column chart.

Click [OK].

Your screen should be similar to
Figure 2.26

Figure 2.26

The column chart is created using the data from the worksheet and displayed as a chart object in the worksheet.

Concept 6 Chart Object

A **chart object** is a graphic object that is created using charting features. A chart object can be inserted into a worksheet or into a special chart sheet. By default, Excel inserts the chart object into the worksheet. Charts that are inserted into a worksheet are embedded objects. An **embedded chart** becomes part of the sheet in which it is inserted and is saved as part of the worksheet when you save the workbook file. Like all graphic objects, an embedded chart object can be sized and moved in a worksheet. A worksheet can contain multiple charts.

A chart that is inserted into a separate chart sheet also is saved with the workbook file. Only one chart can be added to a chart sheet, and it cannot be sized or moved.

Excel decides which data series to plot along the X and Y axes based on the type of chart selected and the number of rows and columns defined in the series. The worksheet data range that has the greater number of rows or columns appears along the X axis, and the smaller number is charted as the Y data series. When the data series is an equal number of rows and columns as it is in this case, the default is to plot the rows. The first row defines the X-axis category labels and the second row the plotted data. The content of the first cell in the second row is used as the chart title and legend text.

MOVING AND SIZING A CHART

Notice that the new chart is on top of the worksheet data. As objects are added to the worksheet, they automatically **stack** in individual layers. The stacking order is apparent when objects overlap. Stacking allows you to create different effects by overlapping objects. Because you can rearrange the stacking order, you do not have to add or create the objects in the order in which you want them to appear.

First you want to move the chart so that it is displayed to the right of the worksheet data. In addition, you want to increase the size of the chart. A chart is moved by dragging the chart border and sized just like a graphic object. If you hold down [Alt] while dragging to move and size a chart object, the chart automatically snaps into position or aligns with the closest worksheet cell when you release the mouse button. Release the mouse button before you release [Alt].

1

Point to the chart border and drag the chart object so the upper-left corner is in cell F1.

Point to the bottom-center sizing handle, hold down Alt, and drag the chart border line down until it is even with the bottom of row 15.

Your screen should be similar to Figure 2.27

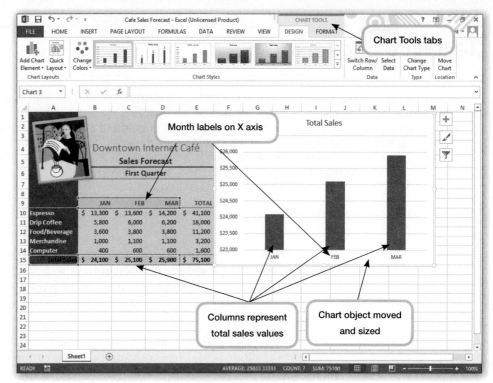

Figure 2.27

It is now easy to see how the worksheet data you selected is represented in the chart. Each column represents a value or data point in the data series (row 15) and provides a visual representation of the total sales for each month. The month labels in row 9 have been used to label the X-axis category labels. The range or scale of values along the Y axis is determined from the data in the worksheet. The upper limit is the maximum value in the worksheet rounded upward to the next highest interval. The row label in cell A15 is the chart title.

The two new Chart Tools tabs on the Ribbon contain options to modify the chart. The Design tab is used to change the layout, colors, and chart style. You can also redefine the source data, change the chart type, or move the chart to another sheet. The Format tab is used to enhance the appearance of chart elements by adding fill color, borders, and special effects. You can also add and format lines and and other shapes on the chart.

In addition, next to the upper-right corner of the chart are three buttons, ➕, 🖌, and 🔻. These buttons allow you to quickly access the most commonly used features on the Chart Tools tab.

APPLYING CHART LAYOUTS

Next, you want to improve the appearance of the chart. To help you do this quickly, Excel includes many chart layouts (also called quick layouts) and quick styles from which you can select. A **chart layout** is a predefined set of chart elements that can be quickly applied to a chart. The elements include chart titles, a legend, a data table, or data labels. These elements are displayed in a specific arrangement in the chart. Each chart type includes a variety of layouts. You can then modify or customize these layouts further to meet your needs. However, the custom layouts cannot be saved.

1

Click [Quick Layout] on the Chart Tools Design tab.

Your screen should be similar to Figure 2.28

Layout 1 is default column chart layout

Chart Tools Design tab is open

Figure 2.28

The chart layout gallery displays the 11 chart layouts for a column chart. The default chart layout is Layout 1. Pointing to a chart layout displays a Live Preview on your chart.

2

Point to several chart layouts to see the Live Preview.

Choose Layout 10.

Your screen should be similar to Figure 2.29

Default chart style

Chart Layout 10 applied

Data values displayed

Legend

Wider columns

Figure 2.29

The columns are wider and include the data values. Additionally, a legend is displayed to the right of the chart.

APPLYING CHART STYLES

Next, you want to change the visual style of the chart and the color of the columns. Although you could manually format the chart elements individually, it is quicker to use one of the predefined **chart styles** to quickly apply a combination of formats to the chart. The available chart styles are based on the document theme that has been applied. This ensures that the formats you apply to the chart will coordinate with the worksheet formatting. The chart styles use the same fonts, line, and fill effects that are defined in the theme. The chart color choices are also based on the current theme colors.

The default chart style is selected in the Chart Styles group in the Ribbon. You want to see all available choices.

- Click Chart Styles next to the upper-right corner of the chart.

Another Method

You could also click ▾ More in the Chart Styles group to open the gallery of chart styles.

Your screen should be similar to Figure 2.30

Figure 2.30

A Chart Styles pane appears next to the chart that is used to quickly preview and change the chart styles and colors. The Style tab is open and displays a gallery of chart styles. Chart styles consist of different arrangements and combinations of chart elements, background shadings, column shapes, and three-dimensional effects.

You also can change the colors used in the chart by selecting a new color palette from the Colors tab. The color pallet assigns a different color to each data series in the chart. You will change both the chart style and colors. Pointing to a chart style or color displays a Live Preview of the selection.

2

- Point to several chart styles to see the Live Preview.

- Click Style 5.

- Click the Color tab in the Chart Styles pane to open it.

- Point to several colors to see the Live Preview.

- Choose Color 3.

Your screen should be similar to Figure 2.31

Figure 2.31

The chart style selection removed the vertical axis labels, moved the legend to the bottom of the chart, and added a shaded background in the plot area. The new color palette changed the column color to gold.

ADDING AND REMOVING CHART LABELS

Finally, you want to clarify the data in the chart by displaying the vertical axis values again, adding labels along both chart axes, removing the legend, and adding a more descriptive chart title.

1

- Click Chart Elements.

- Point to Axes and click ▶ to display a submenu.

- Choose Primary Vertical.

- Click the Axis Titles check box to turn on this feature.

Another Method

You also can click [Add Chart Element ▾] in the Chart Layouts group of the Chart Tools Design tab to add and remove chart elements.

Your screen should be similar to Figure 2.32

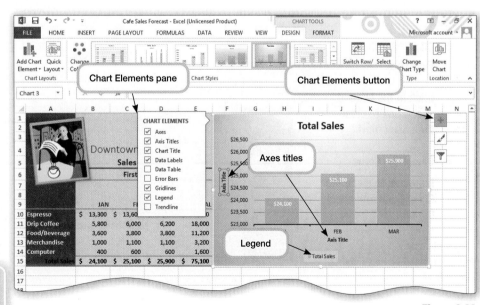

Figure 2.32

The vertical axis values are displayed again, and two axis title text boxes were inserted. The Y-axis title text box is a selected object and displays the sample text, Axis Title. A **text box** is a graphic element that is a container for specific types of information. In this case, it is designed to contain text for the axis title. You will replace the sample text with the axis title.

To replace the text in a text box, simply select the text box and type the new text. As you type, the label appears in the formula bar. After you press [Enter] it will appear in the text box. You also can edit text in a text box using the same features that are used to edit a cell entry.

2

- Type **Total Sales** and press [Enter].

- Click on the X-axis title text box to select it.

- Type **Months** and press [Enter].

Your screen should be similar to Figure 2.33

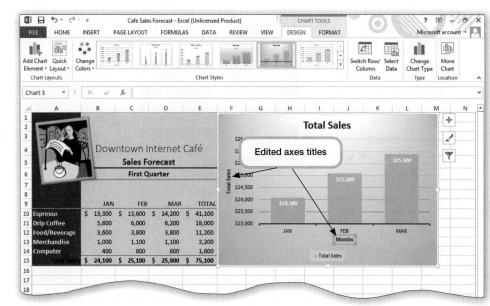

Figure 2.33

The sample text in the text boxes was replaced by the text you typed. The titles clearly describe the information displayed in the chart. Now, because there is only one data range and the horizontal category labels fully explains this data, you will remove the display of the legend.

3

- Click Chart Elements.

- Click in the Legend check box to clear the check mark.

- Click [+] Chart Elements to close the Chart Elements check list box.

Your screen should be similar to Figure 2.34

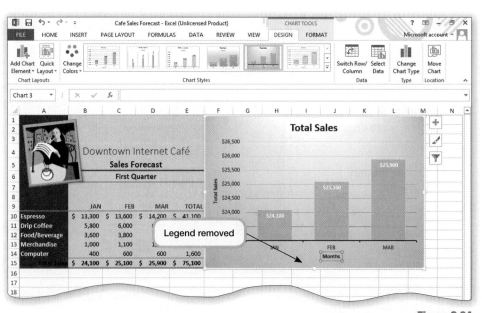

Figure 2.34

The legend is removed and the chart area resized to occupy the extra space. All chart labels can be removed in the same manner.

Finally, you want to add a more descriptive title to the chart and improve its appearance. Because this element already exists on the chart, you just need to change the text, by editing and formatting the text in the text box. When you point to different areas in the chart, a chart ScreenTip appears that identifies the chart element that will be affected by your action.

4

- Point to the chart title to see the ScreenTip.

- Click on the chart title to select it.

- Double-click on the word "Total" to select it and type **Downtown Internet Cafe**

- Select all the text in the text box and point to the Mini toolbar.

Additional Information

The Mini toolbar appears automatically when you select text and is dim until you point to it.

- Change the font color to Dark Red, Accent 6.

- Click anywhere in the chart to clear the selection.

Your screen should be similar to Figure 2.35

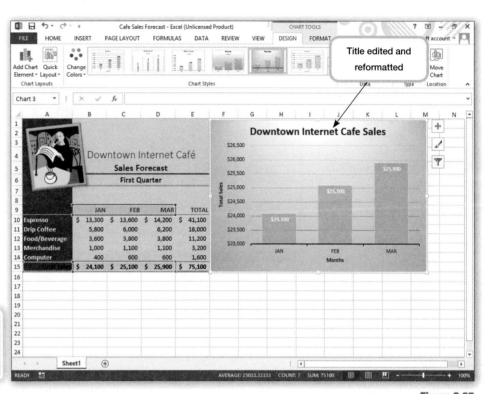

Figure 2.35

CHANGING THE CHART LOCATION

Although this chart compares the total sales for the three months, you decide you are more interested in seeing a comparison for the sales categories. You could delete this chart simply by pressing Delete while the chart area is selected. Instead, however, you will move it to a separate worksheet in case you want to refer to it again.

1

- Open the Chart Tools Design tab.

- Click 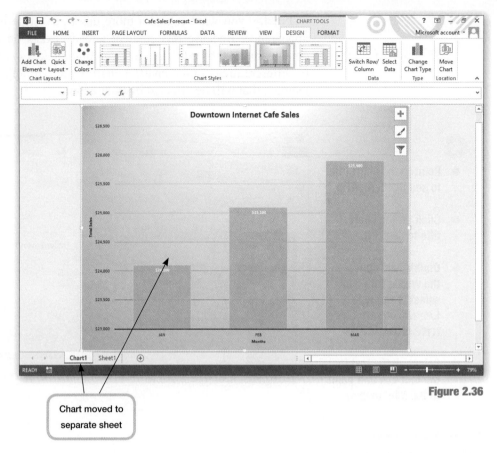 in the Location group.

- Choose New sheet.

- Click [OK].

- Save the workbook.

Your screen should be similar to Figure 2.36

Chart moved to separate sheet

Figure 2.36

The column chart is now an object displayed in a separate chart sheet. Generally, you display a chart in a chart sheet when you want the chart displayed separately from the associated worksheet data. The chart is still automatically linked to the worksheet data from which it was created. The new chart sheet, named Chart1, was inserted to the left of the worksheet, Sheet1. The chart sheet is the active sheet, or the sheet in which you are currently working.

Creating a Multiple Data Series Chart

Now you are ready to continue your analysis of sales trends. You want to create a second chart to display the sales data for each category for the three months. You could create a separate chart for each category and then compare the charts; however, to make the comparisons between the categories easier, you will display all the categories on a single chart.

The data for the three months for the four categories is in cells B10 through D14. The month headings (X-axis data series) are in cells B9 through D9, and the legend text is in the range A10 through A14.

1

- Click the Sheet1 tab.

- Select A9 through D14.

- Open the Insert tab.

- Click [Recommended Charts]

- Open the All Charts tab.

- Choose 3-D Clustered Column from the row of column chart types.

Additional Information

Pointing to a chart preview displays an enlarged image. Clicking on it selects it.

Your screen should be similar to Figure 2.37

Another Method

You also could click [Quick Analysis] and choose Charts to see the recommended chart types and to access all chart types.

Figure 2.37

The two 3-D clustered column chart variations display the total sales by category or by month.

You will insert the default chart showing the sales by category in the worksheet shown in the preview on the left.

2

Click [OK] .

Your screen should be similar to
Figure 2.38

Figure 2.38

A different column color identifies each data series, and the legend identifies the
months. When plotting the data for this chart, Excel plotted the three months as the
data series because the data range has fewer columns than rows. This time, however, you want to change the data series so that the months are along the X axis.

3

Click [Switch Row/ Column] in the
Data group of the
Chart Tools Design
tab.

Your screen should be similar to
Figure 2.39

Figure 2.39

The chart is redrawn with the new orientation. The column chart now compares
the sales by month rather than by category. The legend at the bottom of the chart
displays the names of the sales categories.

Next, you will specify the chart titles and finish the chart.

Change the chart style to Style 5.

Change the chart layout to Layout 9.

Replace the axis and title text box sample text with the titles shown below:

Title	Entry
Chart title	Sales Forecast
Horizontal Axis	Months
Vertical Axis	Sales

Move and size the chart until it covers cells F2 through L15.

Your screen should be similar to Figure 2.40

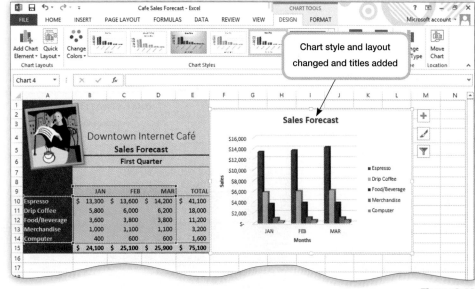

Figure 2.40

The column chart shows that sales in all categories are increasing, with the greatest increase occurring in espresso sales.

CHANGING THE DATA SOURCE

As you look at the chart, you see that the Merchandise and Computer sales values are inconsequential to the forecast because they are so small and do not change much. You will remove these data series from the chart.

Click 🔽 Chart Filters to the right of the chart.

Another Method

You can also click Select Data from the Data group of the Design tab for the same commands.

Your screen should be similar to Figure 2.41

Figure 2.41

A Chart Filters pane opens next to the chart. It is used to show or hide data series and categories and set how the series names are displayed. You will remove the Merchandise and Computer data series.

2

- **Click Merchandise to remove the check mark.**

- **Click Computer to remove the check mark.**

- **Click** Apply .

- **Click anywhere in the chart to close the Chart Filters pane.**

Your screen should be similar to Figure 2.42

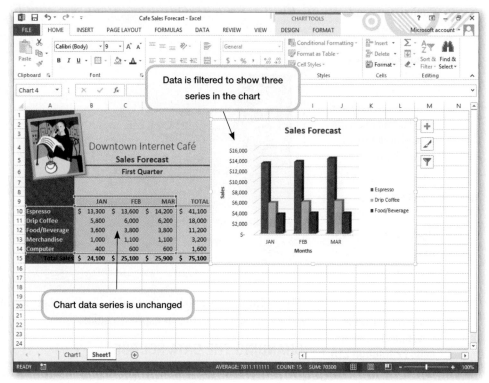

Figure 2.42

The columns representing the Merchandise and Computer series were removed from the chart along with the legend labels. The chart data series is unchanged in the worksheet because filters simply hide or display the data.

CHANGING THE CHART TYPE: LINE, BAR, AREA, STACKED

Next, you would like to see how the same data displayed in the column chart would look as a line chart. A line chart displays data as a line and is commonly used to show trends over time. You can change the chart type easily using the button on the Design tab.

1

Click [Change Chart Type] in the Type group.

Your screen should be similar to Figure 2.43

Figure 2.43

The Change Chart Type box displays all the available chart types just as in the Insert Chart dialog box. The current selection, 3-D Clustered Column, is highlighted. You want to change it to a line chart.

2

Choose Line from the chart type category list.

Choose Line with Markers.

Click OK.

Your screen should be similar to Figure 2.44

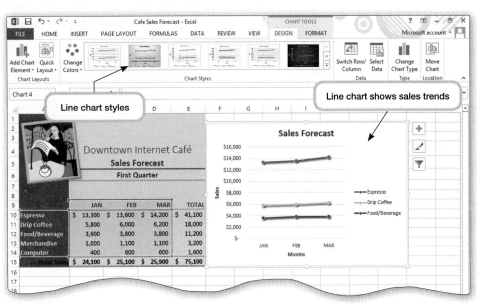

Figure 2.44

The line chart shows the sales trends from month to month. Notice the chart styles in the Ribbon reflect styles that are available for line charts.

You do not find this chart very interesting, so you will change it to a 3-D bar chart next.

3

Click [Change Chart Type] .

Choose **Bar** from the chart type category list.

Choose [img] **3-D Clustered Bar.**

Click [OK] .

Your screen should be similar to Figure 2.45

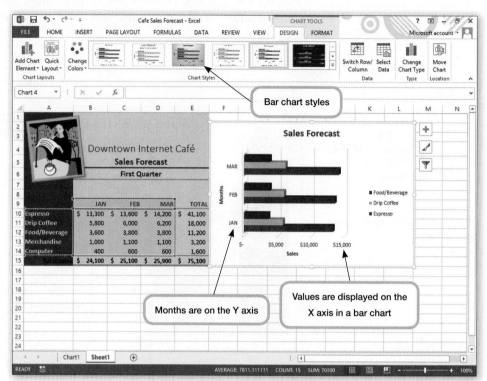

Figure 2.45

The 3-D bar chart reverses the X and Y axes and displays the data series as three-dimensional bars. As you can see, it is very easy to change the chart type and format after the data series are specified. The same data can be displayed in many different ways. Depending upon the emphasis you want the chart to make, a different chart style can be selected.

Although the 3-D bar chart shows the sales trends for the three months for the sales categories, again it does not look very interesting. You decide to look at several other chart types to see whether you can improve the appearance. First you would like to see the data represented as an area chart. An area chart represents data the same way a line chart does, but, in addition, it shades the area below each line to emphasize the degree of change.

4

● Click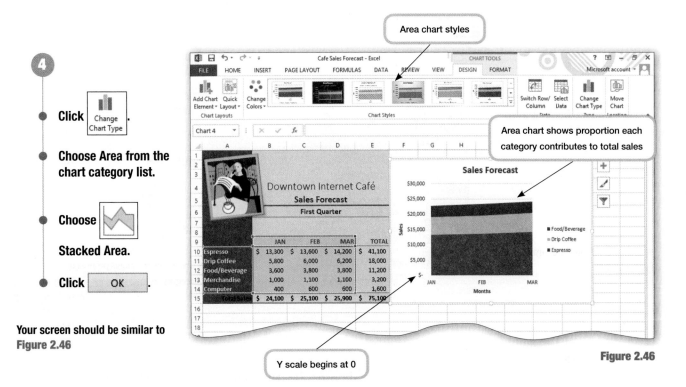

  [Change Chart Type button]

● Choose **Area** from the chart category list.

● Choose [area chart icon]

  Stacked Area.

● Click **OK**.

Your screen should be similar to Figure 2.46

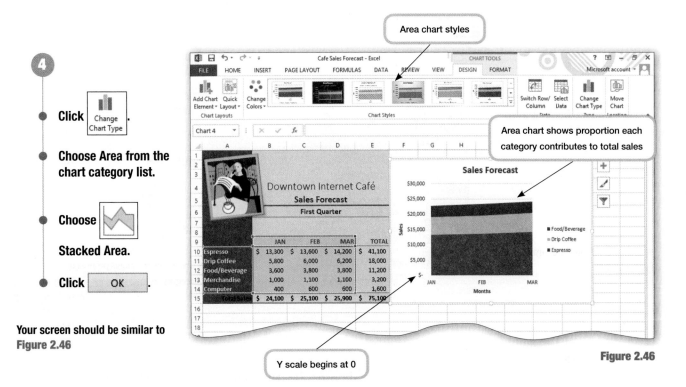

Area chart styles

Area chart shows proportion each category contributes to total sales

Y scale begins at 0

Figure 2.46

The Y-axis scale has changed to reflect the new range of data. The new Y-axis range is the sum of the four categories or the same as the total number in the worksheet. Using this chart type, you can see the magnitude of change that each category contributes to the total sales each month.

Again, you decide that this is not the emphasis you want to show and will continue looking at other types of charts. You want to see how this data will look as a stacked column chart. You also can double-click a chart type to insert it with the default selection.

5

● Click 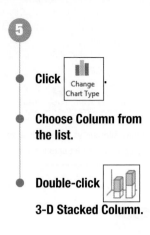 .

● Choose Column from the list.

● Double-click 3-D Stacked Column.

Your screen should be similar to Figure 2.47

Figure 2.47

The chart is redrawn showing the data as a **stacked column chart**. This type of chart also shows the proportion of each sales category to the total sales.

Although this chart is interesting, you feel that the data is difficult to read and want to see how the data will be represented in several other chart types.

6

● Choose several other chart types to see how the data appears in the chart.

● Change the chart to 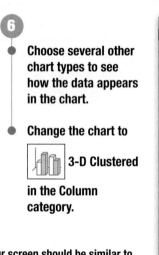 3-D Clustered in the Column category.

Your screen should be similar to Figure 2.48

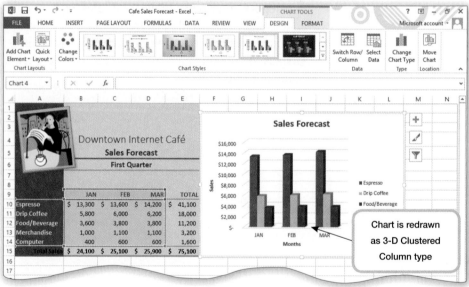

Figure 2.48

You like how the 3-D clustered columns chart represents the data best.

MOVING THE LEGEND

While looking at the chart, you decide to move the legend below the X axis.

- Click Chart Elements.

- Point to Legend and click ▶.

- Choose Bottom from the submenu.

- Close the Chart Elements pane.

Your screen should be similar to Figure 2.49

Legend displayed below chart area

Figure 2.49

The legend is displayed below the plot area of the chart.

FORMATTING CHART ELEMENTS

Next, you want to further improve the appearance of the chart by applying additional formatting to the chart titles and by changing the shape of the columns to cylinders. The chart is an object made up of many different objects or chart elements. Each element of a chart can be enhanced individually to create your own custom style chart. Because a chart consists of many separate objects, it is a group.

Concept ⑦ Group

A **group** is two or more objects that behave as a single object when moved or sized. A chart object is a group that consists of many separate objects. For example, the chart title is a single object within the chart object. Some of the objects in a chart are also groups that consist of other objects. For example, the legend is a group object consisting of separate items, each identifying a different data series.

Other objects in a chart are the axis lines, a data series, a data marker, the entire plot area, or the entire chart.

There are several methods you can use to select chart elements. One, as you have learned, is to click on the element. To help you select the correct chart element, the element name displays when you point to a chart element. Another method is to select the element from the [Chart Area   ▾] drop-down list in the Format tab. Finally, you can use the arrow keys located on the numeric keypad or the directional keypad to cycle from one element to another. The keyboard directional keys used to select chart elements are described in the following table.

Press	To
↓	Select the previous group of elements in a chart.
↑	Select the next group of elements in a chart.
→	Select the next element within a group.
←	Select the previous element within a group.
Esc	Cancel a selection.

There are also several different methods you can use to format chart elements. These methods will be demonstrated as you add formatting to the chart.

The first formatting change you want to make is to increase the font size and add color to the chart title.

1

- **Click on the chart title to select it.**

- **Triple-click on the title to select all the text.**

- **From the Mini toolbar, choose Tahoma as the font type.**

- **Change the font size to 20.**

- **Select the Gold, Accent 5, Darker 50% theme font color.**

Your screen should be similar to Figure 2.50

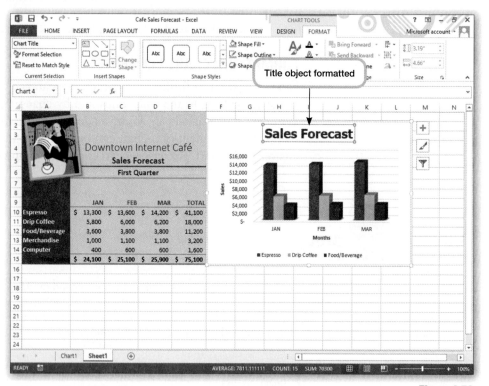

Figure 2.50

Your formatting selections were applied to all the text in the selected object.

Next, you want to add a subtitle below the main title. It will be in a smaller font size and italicized. You also can select individual sections of text in an object and apply formatting to them just as you would format any other text entry.

2

- Click at the end of the title to place the insertion point.

- Press ⏎Enter.

- Type **First Quarter**

- Triple-click on the second title line to select it.

- Use the Mini toolbar to italicize the selection.

- Change the font size to 14.

- Apply the Gold, Accent 5, Darker 25% theme color to the subtitle.

- Click anywhere in the chart to clear the selection.

Your screen should be similar to Figure 2.51

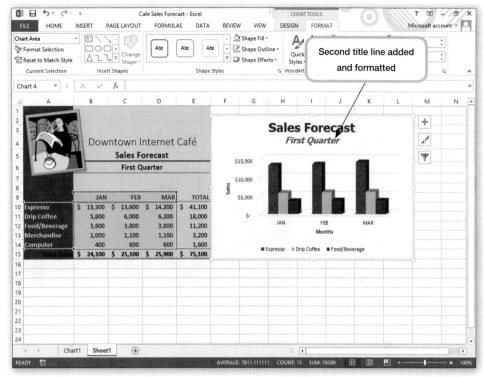

Figure 2.51

Next, you will change the shape of columns to a cylinder. From the Format Data Series pane, you can change the fill, shape, outline, and effects for each data series.

- **Right-click any Espresso column and choose Format Data Series.**

- **From the Column shape section of the Series Options list, choose Cylinder.**

- **Click the Series Options drop-down arrow ▼ and choose "Series Drip Coffee."**

- **Choose Cylinder.**

- **In a similar manner, change the Food/ Beverage series to a cylinder.**

- **Close the Format Data Series pane.**

Your screen should be similar to Figure 2.52

Figure 2.52

Next, you decide to add some formatting enhancements to the chart walls and floor.

4
- Open the
  `Chart Area` ▼
  Chart Elements drop-down list in the Current Selection group.

- **Choose Back Wall.**

- **Click**
  `Format Selection`
  in the Current Selection group.

- **If necessary, click Fill in the Format Wall task pane to expand the group.**

Your screen should be similar to Figure 2.53

Figure 2.53

Additional Information

The corners of the selected element are marked with circles.

From the Format Wall pane, you can change the wall fill colors, outside border, and style, and add shadow, 3-D format, and rotation effects. Automatic is the currently selected fill and uses the default fill color based on the current theme colors. You decide to add a gradient fill to the background and a solid line around the chart wall. A **gradient** is a gradual progression of colors and shades that can be from one color to another or from one shade to another of the same color. Excel includes several preset colors that include combinations of gradient fills.

5

- Choose Gradient Fill.

- Open the Preset gradients gallery and choose Medium Gradient - Accent 2.

- Open the Direction gallery and choose 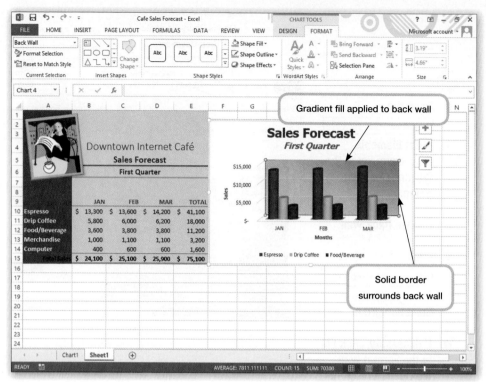 Linear Diagonal - Top Right to Bottom Left.

- Click Fill to collapse the group.

- Click Border to expand the group.

- Choose Solid line.

- Open the Color gallery and choose Gold, Accent 5, Darker 50%.

- Close the Format Wall pane.

Your screen should be similar to Figure 2.54

Figure 2.54

Next, you will format the side wall and floor using a solid fill color with a slight transparency.

6

- Press ⬅ to select the chart side wall.

- Click **Format Selection** .

- Click Fill to expand the group.

- Choose Solid Fill, and select the Dark Red, Accent 6 fill color.

- Increase the Transparency to 40%.

- Choose Floor from the Chart Elements box to select it.

- Change the chart floor to the same color and transparency as the side wall.

- Close the Format Floor pane.

Your screen should be similar to Figure 2.55

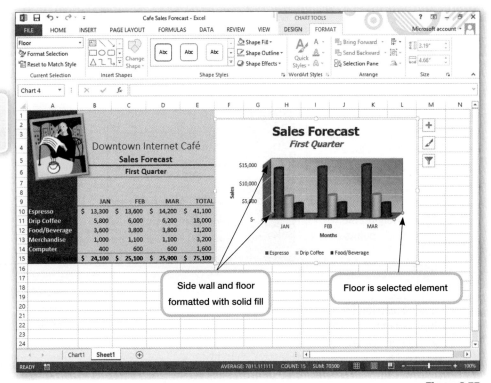

Figure 2.55

The last formatting change you will make is to modify the border line around the entire chart object.

7

- Click on the chart area (the white background) to select the entire chart.

- Click in the Shape Styles group.

- Select Weight and choose 2¼ points.

- Click 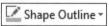 and choose the Dark Red, Accent 6, Darker 25% theme color.

- Click outside the chart to deselect it.

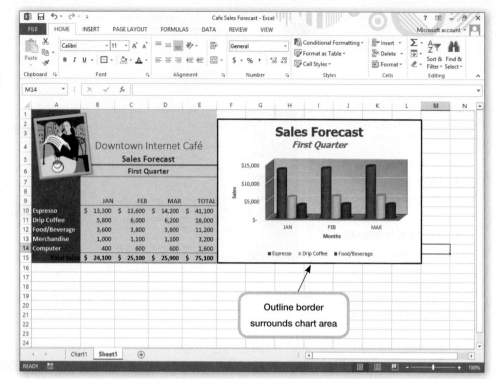

Figure 2.56

Your screen should be similar to Figure 2.56

You have modified and enhanced many of the chart elements individually, creating a unique, professional-looking chart.

ADDING AND FORMATTING DATA LABELS

Finally, to make sure that Evan sees your projected increase in espresso and coffee sales, you will include data labels containing the actual numbers plotted on the column chart.

Concept Data Labels

Data labels provide additional information about a data point in the data series. They can consist of the value of the point, the name of the data series or category, a percentage value, or a bubble size. The different types of data labels that are available depend on the type of chart and the data that is plotted.

Value data labels are helpful when the values are large and you want to know the exact value for one data series. Data labels that display a name are helpful when the size of the chart is large and when the data point does not clearly identify the value. The percentage data label is used when you want to display the percentage of each series on charts that show parts of the whole. Bubble size is used on bubble charts to help the reader quickly see how the different bubbles vary in size.

You want to display the Espresso and Drip Coffee values as data labels for the three months. By default data labels are displayed as plain text entries. To enhance their appearance, you can show data labels inside a text bubble, and add fill and text colors and other effects to make them stand out more.

1

- Click on any Espresso data column to select the series.

- Click ➕ Chart Elements and choose Data Labels to insert the default data label.

- Open the Data label submenu and choose Data Callout to display the data label in a text bubble.

- Select the Drip Coffee series and choose Data Labels.

- Choose Data Callout from the Data Labels submenu.

- Choose More Options from the Data Labels submenu.

Your screen should be similar to Figure 2.57

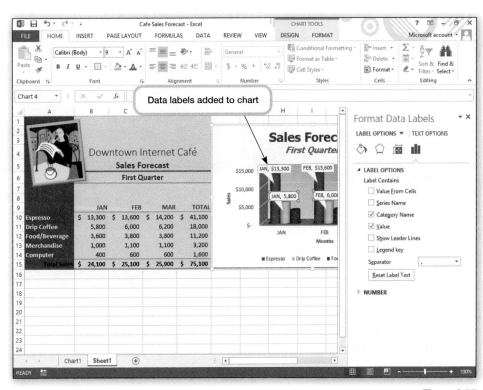

Figure 2.57

Data labels containing the category name and actual values for Espresso and Drip Coffee sales are displayed in a text bubble callout. The values use the same formatting as the values in the worksheet. You will use the Format Data Labels task pane to change the number format of the Drip Coffee data label to display the currency symbol and add color to the labels.

Another Method

You also can choose Data Labels from the data series shortcut menu.

2

- Click **Category Name** in the Label Options group to remove this label.

- Click **Number** to expand the category.

- Choose **Accounting** from the Category drop-down list and reduce the decimal places to 0.

- Click 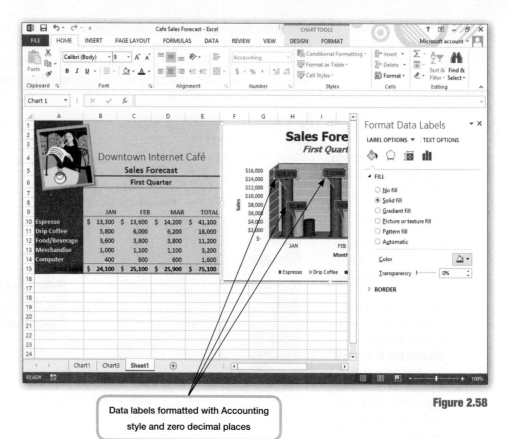 **Fill & Line**, open the Color palette and choose **Orange, Accent 4, Darker 25%**.

- Select the Espresso data label series, change the labels to the same color, and remove the category name label.

Your screen should be similar to Figure 2.58

Data labels formatted with Accounting style and zero decimal places

Figure 2.58

Next, you will reposition all the data labels so that they appear to the right of each column. Each data label needs to be selected and moved individually. Dragging the callout rectangle moves the rectangle but not the leader line. You can resize and reposition the leader line by dragging the yellow sizing square. Then rather than moving the other data labels individually, you can copy the format, including the size and location, of the selected data label to all the other data labels in the series.

3

- **Click on the January Drip Coffee data label to select it and drag to position it as in Figure 2.59.**

Having Trouble?

To select an individual data label, first click on a data label to select the entire series, and then click on the individual label.

- **Click [icon] Label Options in the task pane and click [Clone Current Label].**

- **In the same manner, select the January Espresso data label, position it as in Figure 2.59, and clone it to the other data labels in the series.**

- **Close the task pane.**

Your screen should be similar to Figure 2.59

Additional Information

You can delete individual data labels or the entire series by selecting the data label or series and pressing [Delete] or choosing Delete from the shortcut menu.

Figure 2.59

The data label callouts are positioned to the top right of each column and make it easier to see the entire chart data.

CHANGING WORKSHEET DATA

So far, the charts you have created reflect your original sales estimates for the quarter. You are planning to heavily promote the new Internet aspect of the Café and anticipate that Espresso, Drip Coffee, and Food/Beverage sales in February and March will increase dramatically and then level off in the following months. You want to change the worksheet to reflect these increases.

Increase the February and March Espresso sales by 12% and 15%, respectively.

Having Trouble?

Change the entry to a formula by inserting an = sign at the beginning of the entry and then multiply by 1 + increase; for example, a 12 percent increase in the February Espresso sales is =13600*1.12.

Increase the February and March Drip Coffee sales by 8% and 10%.

Increase the February and March Food/Beverage sales by 5% and 7%.

Move the chart to its own chart sheet.

Make Sheet1 active again.

Save the workbook.

Your screen should be similar to Figure 2.60

The worksheet has been recalculated, and the chart columns that reference those worksheet cells have been redrawn to reflect the change in the sales data. Because the chart is linked to the source data, changes to the source data are automatically reflected in the chart. Likewise, the values in the data labels reflect the revised data.

Figure 2.60

Creating a Combo Chart

Next, you want to create a chart to show how much Espresso Sales contribute toward Total sales. When you have two types of data or data whose values vary widely, as is the case with monthly sales and total sales, you can use a combo (combination) chart to illustrate how these values are related. A combo chart combines two of more chart types to make comparisons easy. A common type of combo chart uses a line chart for one of the data series and a column for the other.

①

● Select A10 through D10 and A15 through D15.

Having Trouble?

Hold down Ctrl while selecting nonadjacent ranges.

● Open the Insert tab and click

Recommended Charts.

Your screen should be similar to Figure 2.61

Suggested chart is a combination column-line type

Figure 2.61

Excel has recognized the mixed data values and proposes a Clustered Column–Line chart. The Total Sales values are plotted with the line chart and the Espresso Sales with the column chart. You want to reverse the chart types for the data series.

②

● Click **OK**.

● Click Change Chart Type on the Design tab.

● Open the Espresso series Chart Type drop-down list and choose Line with Markers.

● Open the Total Sales series Chart Type drop-down list and choose Clustered Column.

Your screen should be similar to Figure 2.62

Chart type changed for each data series

Figure 2.62

It is now easy to see how much Espresso Sales contribute to Total Sales each month.

- **3**
  - Click [OK].

  - Change the chart title to **Espresso Sales vs. Total Sales** and add a font color of your choice.

  - Move the chart to its own sheet.

  - Save the workbook.

Your screen should be similar to Figure 2.63

Figure 2.63

Creating and Formatting a Pie Chart

The last chart you will create will use the Total worksheet data in column E. You want to see what proportion each type of sales is of total sales for the quarter. The best chart for this purpose is a pie chart.

A **pie chart** compares parts to the whole in a similar manner to a stacked column chart. However, pie charts have no axes. Instead, the worksheet data that is charted is displayed as slices in a circle or pie. Each slice is displayed as a percentage of the total.

SELECTING THE PIE CHART DATA

The use of X (category) and data series settings in a pie chart is different from their use in a column or line chart. The X series labels the slices of the pie rather than the X axis. The data series is used to create the slices in the pie. Only one data series can be specified in a pie chart.

The row labels in column A will label the slices, and the total values in column E will be used as the data series.

1

- Make Sheet1 active again.

- Select A10 through A14 and E10 through E14.

- Open the Insert tab.

- Click 🥧 and choose 🥧 3-D Pie.

- Move and size the pie chart to be displayed over cells F1 through L15.

Additional Information

Hold down Alt while sizing to snap the chart to the cells.

Your screen should be similar to
Figure 2.64

Figure 2.64

A three-dimensional pie chart is drawn in the worksheet. Each value in the data series is displayed as a slice of the pie chart. The size of the slice represents the proportion of total sales that each sales category represents.

ADDING TITLES AND DATA LABELS

To clarify the meaning of the chart, you need to edit the chart title. In addition, you want to remove the legend and display data labels to label the slices of the pie instead. You will take a look at the predefined chart layouts to see if there is a layout that will accomplish all these things in one step.

1 ● Click [Quick Layout] in the

Charts Layout group of the Design tab and choose Layout 1.

Your screen should be similar to Figure 2.65

Figure 2.65

The legend has been removed and replaced with data labels that display the category name and the percentage each category is of total sales. The data labels display the category name on a separate line from the value and, if needed, include a leader line to identify the associated wedge.

Next, you will edit the title and then you will improve the appearance of the data labels by adding a gradient fill to them.

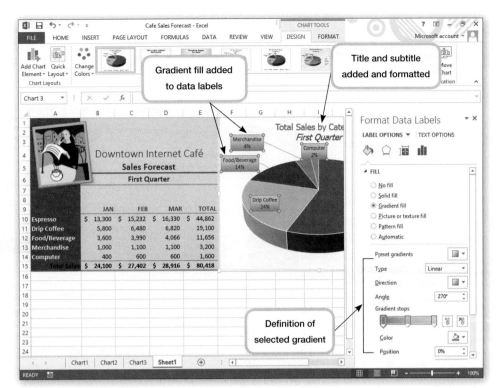

2

- Enter the chart title **Total Sales by Category**

- Add the subtitle **First Quarter**

- Change the first title line to Tahoma with the Gold, Accent 5, Darker 25% color.

- Change the subtitle line to Tahoma, with the Gold, Accent 5, Darker 50% color, and italic.

- Double-click on one of the data labels to select the data label series and open the Format Data Labels task pane.

- Click [icon] Fill & Line in the task pane, expand the Fill group if necessary, and choose Gradient Fill.

- Open the Preset gradients gallery and choose Medium Gradient - Accent 2.

Your screen should be similar to Figure 2.66

Additional Information

The maximum number of stops is 12 and the minimum is 2.

Figure 2.66

The selected gradient fill has been added to each data label. It consists of a range of dark gold fading to yellow. The Gradient stops bar shows this gradient fill is made of three "**stops**," or specific points where the blending of two adjacent colors in the gradient ends. The Stop 1 fill color is dark gold, Stop 2 is a lighter gold, and Stop 3 is yellow. You will change the Stop 1 color to orange.

3

● **Click on Stop 1 on the Gradient stops bar.**

● **Open the Color palette and choose Orange, Accent 4, Darker 25%.**

● **Click Stop 2 and drag it to the left to position 35%.**

Your screen should be similar to Figure 2.67

Figure 2.67

The data labels now include a gradient fill background that coordinates well with the chart colors. The pie chart clearly shows the percentage each category is of the total sales.

EXPLODING AND ROTATING THE PIE

Next, you want to separate slightly or **explode** the slices of the pie to emphasize the data in the categories.

1

● **Click on the pie chart to display the Format Data Series task pane.**

● **Click** 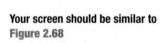 **Series Options and set the Pie Explosion to 10%.**

Your screen should be similar to Figure 2.68

Figure 2.68

All slices are exploded from the center of the pie chart. However, you do not like how this looks. Instead, you decide you want to explode only the Espresso slice to give emphasis to the increase in sales in that category.

2

- **Set the Pie Explosion back to 0%.**

- **Click on the Espresso slice to select it.**

Having Trouble?

If Format Data Point is not displayed in the task pane, the slice is not selected. Click on the slice to select it and open the Format Data Point task pane.

Your screen should be similar to Figure 2.69

Figure 2.69

Notice that the formula bar displays a **series formula**. A series formula links the chart object to the source worksheet, in this case, Sheet1. The formula contains four arguments: a reference to the cell that includes the data series name (used in the legend), references to the cells that contain the categories (X-axis numbers), references to the numbers plotted, and an integer that specifies the number of data series plotted.

The Format Data Point task pane options rotate the pie and control the amount of explosion of the slices. You want to rotate the pie approximately 330 degrees so that the Espresso slice is more to the right side of the pie. When a pie chart is created, the first data point is placed to the right of the middle at the top of the chart. The rest of the data points are placed in order to the right until the circle is complete. To change the angle of the first slice, you rotate the pie chart. Then you will explode the Espresso slice.

3

• Drag the slider to increase the Angle of first slice to 330 degrees.

• Increase the Point Explosion to 10%.

Another Method

You also can drag a slice away from the pie to explode it.

Your screen should be similar to Figure 2.70

Figure 2.70

Additional Information

Your data labels may not be positioned exactly as illustrated in the figures. Drag individual labels as needed.

Although Excel tries to determine the best position for data labels, you can try several settings. You will try another label position to see its effects, and then move individual labels.

4

• Select the data label series.

• Click Label Options in the task pane and choose Outside End from the Label Position area.

• Choose Best Fit.

• Close the task pane.

• If necessary, drag the Espresso and then the Drip Coffee label to position them as in Figure 2.71.

Figure 2.71

Your screen should be similar to Figure 2.71

The industry standard for a successful espresso café generates 60 percent of sales from espresso-based drinks. With your suggested advertising campaign, your sales forecast is very close to this standard.

APPLYING COLOR AND TEXTURE

The last change you would like to make is to change the color of the Drip Coffee slice and add a fill to the Espresso slice to make it stand out even further. First, you will enhance the Espresso slice by adding a texture.

1

- Select the Espresso slice.

- Choose Format Data Point from the context menu.

- Click Fill & Line.

- Choose Picture or texture fill from the Fill group.

- Open the Texture gallery.

Your screen should be similar to Figure 2.72

Figure 2.72

A variety of pictures and textures is displayed in the gallery. The Papyrus texture is applied by default. If none of the provided choices is suitable, you could use a picture from a file or clip art as the fill. Although you like how the Papyrus texture looks, you want to see how several other textures would look instead.

2

Choose several texture designs to see how they will look.

Having Trouble?

You will need to reopen the Texture gallery again after each selection.

Choose the Papyrus texture.

Select the Drip Coffee slice.

Choose Gradient fill from the Fill group.

Close the task pane.

Your screen should be similar to Figure 2.73

Figure 2.73

The last-used gradient fill colors are automatically applied. You decide, however, that the gradient fill does not look good and instead will try using a shape style. **Shape styles** consist of predefined combinations of fills, outlines, and effects much like chart styles. Shape styles affect only the selected element.

3

- **If necessary, select the Drip Coffee slice.**

- **Open the Chart Tools Format tab.**

- **Open the Shape Styles gallery in the Shape Styles group and point to several styles to see their effect on the slice.**

- **Choose the Subtle Effect - Red, Accent 1 Shape Style (4th row, 2nd column).**

Additional Information

If the style you want to use is displayed in the Ribbon, you can select it without opening the gallery. You also can simply scroll the gallery line by line using the Shape Style scroll buttons.

Your screen should be similar to Figure 2.74

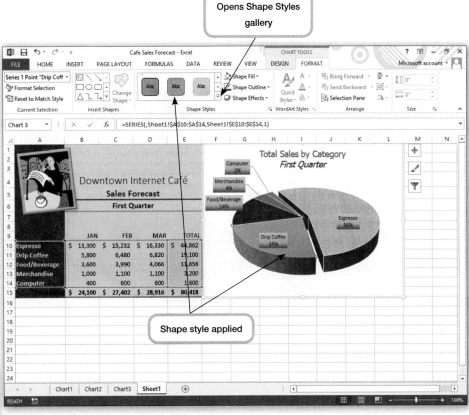

Figure 2.74

Finally, you will add a colored outline border around the entire chart, like the one you used in the column chart. Then you will move the column chart from the chart sheet back into the worksheet.

4

- Select the chart area.

- Click 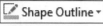 and increase the Weight to 2¼ points.

- Click and change the line color to the Gold, Accent 5, Darker 50% color.

- Make the Chart2 sheet active.

- Click [Move Chart] in the Location group of the Design tab.

- Choose Object in and choose Sheet1 from the drop-down menu.

- Click [OK].

- Move and size the column chart to fit A17 through F33.

- Move and size the pie chart to fit A35 through F50.

- Deselect the chart.

- Save the workbook.

Your screen should be similar to Figure 2.75

Figure 2.75

The column chart was moved back into the sheet as an embedded object, and the chart sheet it occupied was deleted.

Before printing a large worksheet or a worksheet that contains charts, you can quickly fine-tune it in Page Layout view. Using this view, you can change the layout and format of data just as in Normal view, but, in addition, you can adjust the layout of the data on the page by changing the page orientation, page margins, scaling, and alignment. Additionally, you can easily add headers and footers.

SCALING THE WORKSHEET

To get the worksheet ready for printing, you will first make several adjustments to the layout in Page Layout view. While in this view, you also will zoom out on the worksheet to see more information in the workbook window by adjusting the zoom percentage.

Having Trouble?

Refer to the section "Using the Zoom Feature" in the Introduction to Microsoft Office 2013 for information on using this feature.

1

- **Press** Ctrl + Home.

- **Click** 📋 **Page Layout view (in the status bar).**

Another Method

You also can use 📄 Page Layout in the View tab.

- **Click** ➖ **in the Zoom slider to reduce the zoom to 40%.**

- **Scroll the window up slightly to see the bottom of the pie chart.**

Your screen should be similar to Figure 2.76

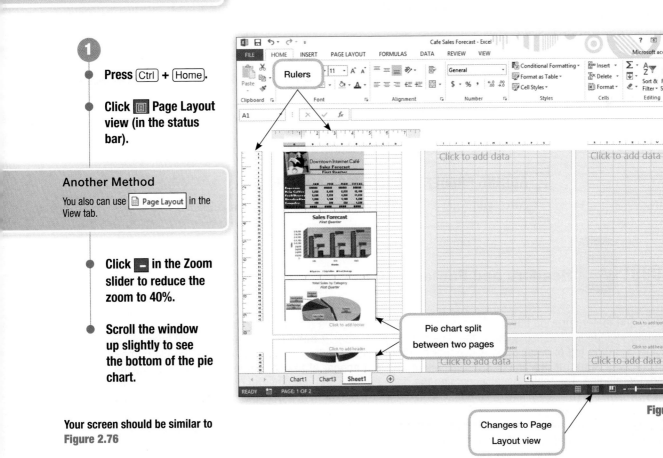

Figure 2.76

This view shows how the data and charts lay out on each page of the worksheet. Because you reduced the zoom, you can quickly see that the pie chart is divided between two pages. You also notice that the worksheet and charts are not centered on the page. In Page Layout view, horizontal and vertical rulers are displayed so you can make exact measurements of cells, ranges, and objects in the worksheet. You will make several changes to the layout of the page to correct these problems.

First you will reduce the scale of the worksheet until all the data fits on one page. Because the width is fine, you will scale only the height.

2

● Open the Page Layout tab.

● Open the
 Height: Automatic ▾
drop-down menu and choose 1 page.

Your screen should be similar to
Figure 2.77

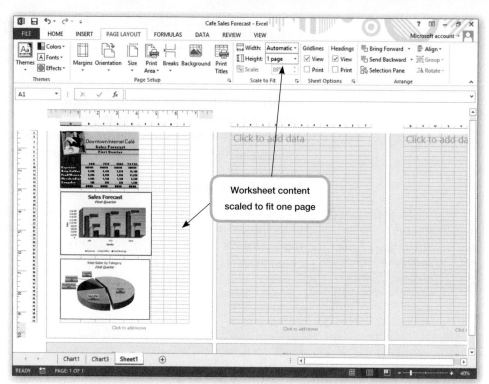

Worksheet content scaled to fit one page

Figure 2.77

The worksheet scale has been reduced to fit on a single page.

ADDING PREDEFINED HEADERS AND FOOTERS

Next, you want to include your name and the date in a header.

Concept ⑨ Headers and Footers

Headers and footers provide information that typically appears at the top and bottom of each page and commonly include information such as the date and page number. A **header** is a line or several lines of text that appear at the top of a page just above the top margin line. The header usually contains the file name or worksheet title. A **footer** is a line or several lines of text that appear at the bottom of a page just below the bottom margin line. The footer usually contains the page number and perhaps the date. Headers and footers also can contain graphics such as a company logo. Each worksheet in a workbook can have a different header and footer.

You can select from predefined header and footer text or enter your own custom text. The information contained in the predefined header and footer text is obtained from the file properties associated with the workbook and from the program and system settings.

Header and footer text can be formatted like any other text. In addition, you can control the placement of the header and footer text by specifying where it should appear: left-aligned, centered, or right-aligned in the header or footer space.

Additional Information

If the computer you are using has your name as the user name, you will not need to add your name as the author in the document properties.

You will add a predefined header to the worksheet that displays your name, the date, and page number. To have your name appear in a predefined header, you will need to first add your name as the author to the file properties.

1

- Open the File tab and in the Info window, enter your name in the Author box.

- Open the Home tab and increase the zoom to 90%.

- Click in the center section of the Header area to activate the header.

- Click [Header] in the Header and Footer group of the Header & Footer Tools Design tab.

Your screen should be similar to Figure 2.78

Figure 2.78

Activating the worksheet header displays the Header & Footer Tools Design tab. It contains commands to add elements to, format, or navigate between a header or footer. The [Header] drop-down list includes many predefined headers that can be quickly inserted into the header. Notice that several of the predefined headers include information that was entered in the document properties.

Choose the Prepared by [your name] [date], Page 1 option.

Your screen should be similar to Figure 2.79

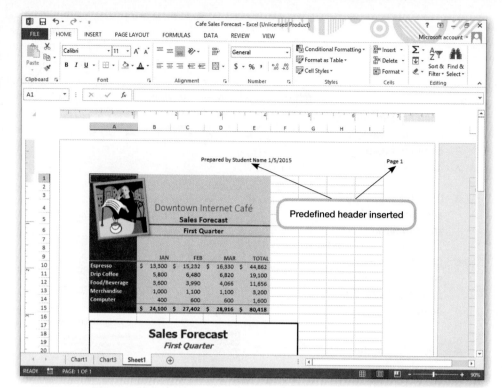

Prepared by Student Name 1/5/2015   Page 1

Downtown Internet Café
Sales Forecast
First Quarter

Predefined header inserted

	JAN	FEB	MAR	TOTAL
Espresso	$ 13,300	$ 15,232	$ 16,330	$ 44,862
Drip Coffee	5,800	6,480	6,820	19,100
Food/Beverage	3,600	3,990	4,066	11,656
Merchandise	1,000	1,100	1,100	3,200
Computer	400	600	600	1,600
	$ 24,100	$ 27,402	$ 28,916	$ 80,418

Sales Forecast
First Quarter

Chart1   Chart3   **Sheet1**

Figure 2.79

The selected header is displayed in the header area of the worksheet. It can be edited or formatted to meet your needs.

PRINTING THE ENTIRE WORKBOOK

Finally, you are ready to print the workbook. Because it includes a chart sheet and a worksheet, you first need to change the print setting to print the entire workbook.

1

- Open the File tab and choose Print.

- Click
  | Print Active Sheets |
  | Only print the active sheets |
  and choose Print Entire Workbook.

- If necessary, select the printer you will use from the Printer list box.

Your screen should be similar to Figure 2.80

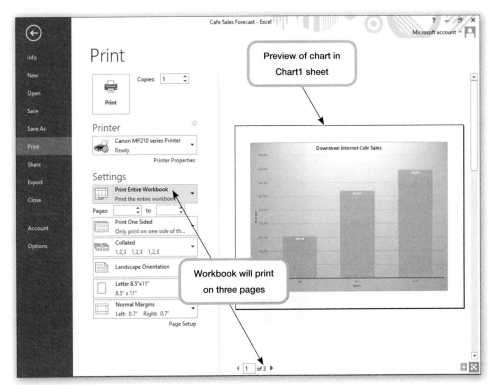

Figure 2.80

Because the Chart1 sheet containing the column chart is the first sheet in the workbook, it is displayed in the preview area. It will be printed on a separate page by itself in landscape orientation. The page indicator shows that the workbook will print on three pages. The combo chart will print on the second page and the worksheet will print on page 3. In addition, if you are not using a color printer, the preview displays the chart colors in shades of gray as they will appear when printed on a black-and-white printer.

You decide to add a footer to the column chart sheet. Each sheet can have its own header and footer definitions.

2

● Click the Page Setup link below the Print options.

● Open the Header/ Footer tab.

Your screen should be similar to Figure 2.81

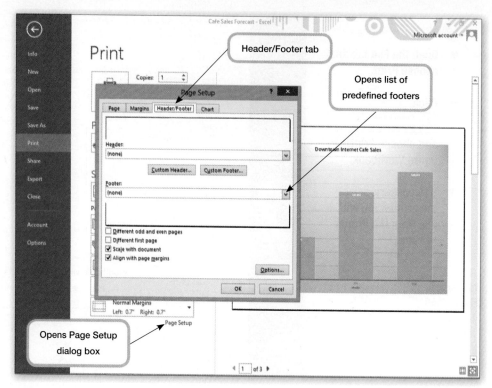

Figure 2.81

Many of the same elements that were available when adding a header in Page Layout view are available in the Page Setup dialog box. You will add a predefined footer to the chart sheet.

3

● Click ▾ More in the Footer section to open the list of predefined footers.

● Scroll the list and choose the footer that displays your name, Page 1, and date.

● Click OK.

Your screen should be similar to Figure 2.82

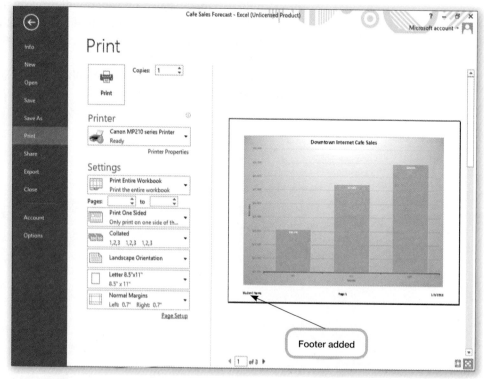

Figure 2.82

The preview shows the selected footer.

Next, you will preview the worksheet.

Worksheet will print in Portrait orientation

Selected header displayed

4

Click ▶ at the bottom of the Preview pane to see the combo chart and the worksheet and charts in Sheet1.

Your screen should be similar to Figure 2.83

Cafe Sales Forecast - Excel (Unlicensed Product)

Microsoft account

Print

Copies: 1

Print

Printer

Canon MP210 series Printer
Ready

Printer Properties

Settings

Print Entire Workbook
Print the entire workbook

Pages: ___ to ___

Print One Sided
Only print on one side of th...

Collated
1,2,3 1,2,3 1,2,3

Portrait Orientation

Letter 8.5"x11"
8.5" x 11"

Normal Margins
Left: 0.7" Right: 0.7"

Fit All Rows on One Page
Shrink the printout so that it...

Page Setup

◀ 3 of 3 ▶

Worksheet and charts are aligned with left margin

Displays next page

Figure 2.83

The preview shows the header you added to the worksheet and because the worksheet was scaled vertically, all the data fits on a single page in portrait orientation.

ALIGNING A SHEET ON A PAGE

However, in the print preview, you can see that the worksheet and charts are all aligned with the left margin. You would like to center the worksheet horizontally on the page. The default worksheet margin settings include 0.7-inch top and bottom margins and 0.75-inch right and left margins. The **margins** are the blank space outside the printing area around the edges of the paper. The worksheet contents appear in the printable area inside the margins. You want to center the worksheet data horizontally within the existing margins.

- **Click** Page Setup.

- **Open the Margins tab.**

- **Choose Horizontally.**

- **Click** OK .

Your screen should be similar to Figure 2.84

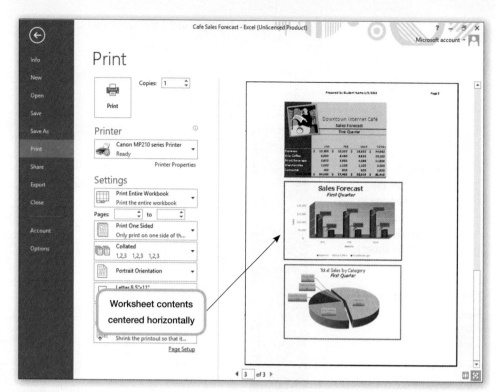

Worksheet contents centered horizontally

Figure 2.84

The preview window displays the worksheet centered horizontally between the right and left margins. It now appears the way you want it to look when printed.

Next, you will print a copy of the worksheet and chart. Then you will exit the application and save the file at the same time.

2

● Click .

● Change to Normal view and move to cell A9 of Sheet1.

> **Additional Information**
> The dotted line between columns H and I shows the page margin.

● Exit Excel, saving the workbook again.

The page layout settings you specified have been saved with the workbook file.

FOCUS ON CAREERS

EXPLORE YOUR CAREER OPTIONS

Financial Advisor
With the stock market fluctuations in the last few years, investors are demanding more from their financial advisors than ever before. An advisor needs to promote each company's potential and growth in order to persuade investors to buy stock. One way to do this is to create a worksheet of vital information and to chart that information so the investor can see why the stock is a good investment. The position of financial advisor usually requires a college degree and commands salaries from $40,000 to $60,000, depending on experience.

Graphics (EX2.5)

A graphic is a nontext element or object such as a drawing or picture that can be added to a document.

Quick Style (EX2.13)

A quick style is a named group of formatting characteristics that allows you to quickly apply a whole group of formats to a selected object in one simple step.

Theme (EX2.16)

A theme is a set of formatting choices that can be applied to an entire workbook in one simple step. A theme consists of a set of theme colors, a set of theme fonts (including heading and body text fonts), and a set of theme effects (including line and fill effects).

Chart Elements (EX2.25)

Chart elements are the different parts of a chart that are used to graphically display the worksheet data.

Chart Types (EX2.27)

Different chart types are used to represent data in different ways. The type of chart you create depends on the type of data you are charting and the emphasis you want the chart to impart.

Chart Object (EX2.29)

A chart object is a graphic object that is created using charting features. A chart object can be inserted into a worksheet or into a special chart sheet.

Group (EX2.45)

A group is two or more objects that behave as a single object when moved or sized. A chart is a group that consists of many separate objects.

Data Labels (EX2.52)

Data labels provide additional information about a data point in the data series. They can consist of the value of the point, the name of the data series or category, a percentage value, or a bubble size.

Headers and Footers (EX2.70)

Headers and footers provide information that typically appears at the top and bottom of each page and commonly include information such as the date and page number.

KEY TERMS

area chart EX2.27, EX2.43
axis EX2.25
bar chart EX2.27, EX2.42
bubble chart EX2.27
category axis EX2.25
category-axis title EX2.25
cell style EX2.13, EX2.19
chart EX2.24
chart area EX2.25
chart elements EX2.25
chart gridlines EX2.25
chart layout EX2.30
chart object EX2.29
chart style EX2.13, EX2.32
chart title EX2.25
chart type EX2.27
clip art EX2.6
column chart EX2.27
combo chart EX2.27, EX2.56
data label EX2.25, EX2.52
data marker EX2.25
data series EX2.25
depth axis EX2.25
doughnut chart EX2.27
drawing object EX2.5
embedded chart EX2.29
embedded object EX2.5
explode EX2.62
footer EX2.70
gradient EX2.49
graphic EX2.5
group EX2.45

header EX2.70
keyword EX2.10
legend EX2.25
line chart EX2.27, EX2.41
margin EX2.75
object EX2.5
picture EX2.5
picture style EX2.13
pie chart EX2.27, EX2.58
plot area EX2.25
quick style EX2.13
radar chart EX2.27
scatter (XY) chart EX2.27
selection rectangle EX2.7
series axis EX2.25
series formula EX2.63
shape style EX2.13, EX2.66
sizing handle EX2.7
source program EX2.5
stack EX2.29
stacked column chart EX2.44
stock chart EX2.27
stops (gradient stops) EX2.61
surface chart EX2.27
text box EX2.33
theme EX2.16
thumbnail EX2.10
value axis EX2.25
value-axis title EX2.25
X axis EX2.25
Y axis EX2.25
Z axis EX2.25

COMMAND SUMMARY

Command	Action
File tab	
Print/Settings/ Print Active Sheets / Only print the active sheets / Print Entire Workbook	Prints all sheets in workbook file
Page Setup	Opens Page Setup dialog box
Home tab	
Styles group	
Cell Styles ▾	Applies predefined combinations of colors, effects, and formats to selected cells
Cell Styles ▾ /Modify	Modifies existing cell style
Insert tab	
Illustrations group	
Pictures	Inserts a picture from a file on your computer or local network
Online Pictures	Inserts a graphic from online sources
Charts group	
Recommended Charts	Shows suggested charts to use with selected data
▬ ▾	Inserts a column chart
◕ ▾	Inserts a pie chart
▮ ▾	Inserts a combo chart
Text group	
Header & Footer	Adds header or footer to worksheet
Page Layout tab	
Themes group	
Themes	Applies selected theme to worksheet

LAB REVIEW

COMMAND SUMMARY (CONTINUED)

Command	Action
[Themes] /Save Current Theme	Saves modified theme settings as a custom theme
Colors ▾	Changes colors for the current theme
Scale to Fit group	
Width:	Scales worksheet width to specified number of pages
Height:	Scales worksheet height to specified number of pages
Scale:	Scales worksheet by entering a percentage
Picture Tools Format tab	
Picture Styles group	
Picture Border ▾	Specifies color, width, and line style for outline of shape
Picture Effects ▾	Adds glow, shadow, and other effects to pictures
Chart Tools Design tab	
Chart Layouts	
Add Chart Element ▾	Adds chart elements such as titles and legend
Quick Layout ▾	Changes overall layout of chart
Chart Styles	
Change Colors ▾	Changes colors associated with chart styles

COMMAND SUMMARY (CONTINUED)

Command	Action
Data group	
Switch Row/Column	Swaps the data over the axes
Select Data	Changes the data range included in chart
Type group	
Change Chart Type	Changes to a different type of chart
Location group	
Move Chart	Moves chart to another sheet in the workbook
Chart Tools Format tab	
Current Selection group	
Chart Area	Selects an element on the chart
Format Selection	Opens Format dialog box for selected element
Shape Styles group	
Shape Fill ▾	Adds selected fill to shape
Shape Outline ▾	Specifies color, weight, and type of outline
Shape Effects ▾	Adds selected effect to shape
View tab	
Zoom group	
Zoom	Changes the magnification of the worksheet

LAB EXERCISES

MATCHING

Match the lettered item on the right with the numbered item on the left.

1. category ranges   _____ a. bottom boundary line of the chart
2. chart sheet   _____ b. identifies each number represented in a data series
3. column chart   _____ c. numbered scale along the left boundary line of the chart
4. data marker   _____ d. area of chart bounded by X and Y axes
5. explode   _____ e. applies a set of colors, fonts, and effects
6. gradient   _____ f. separate location that holds only one chart
7. legend   _____ g. a chart that displays data as vertical columns
8. plot area   _____ h. identifies the chart data series and data markers
9. scaling   _____ i. to separate a slice slightly from other slices of the pie
10. theme   _____ j. identifies the data along the X axis
11. value axis   _____ k. a gradual progression of colors and shades
12. X axis   _____ l. adjusting print size to fit on the selected number of pages

TRUE/FALSE

Circle the correct answer to the following questions.

1. An object in an Excel worksheet is an element that can be sized, moved, and formatted.   **True**   **False**
2. Before selecting any chart data, click the Recommended Charts button for suggested chart types.   **True**   **False**
3. A chart style is a predefined set of colors, styles, and effects for a chart.   **True**   **False**
4. A chart title can be modified to use a larger font size.   **True**   **False**
5. A line chart is used to illustrate trends in data over a period of time.   **True**   **False**
6. The X-axis title is also referred to as the category-axis title.   **True**   **False**
7. A header is one or more lines of text at the bottom of each page above the bottom margin.   **True**   **False**
8. A combo chart is best suited for data that compares parts to the whole.   **True**   **False**
9. Worksheet data can be horizontally centered on the printed page from the Page Setup dialog box.   **True**   **False**
10. You can explode a column in a column chart or a slice in a pie chart to emphasize that data series.   **True**   **False**

FILL-IN

Complete the following statements by filling in the blanks with the correct key terms.

1. Small circles or squares that surround a selected object in a worksheet are called _____.

2. A(n) _____ is a set of colors, fonts, and effects that is applied to the entire workbook.

3. The axis of a column chart with values is known as the _____ or _____ axis.

4. A(n) _____ uses two types of charts to illustrate mixed types of data.

5. To provide an explanation of the colors used for each data series in a chart, you can display a(n) _____.

6. A large worksheet can be fit to a single page by adjusting the _____.

7. A chart is automatically redrawn when you edit its source data because the data is _____ to the chart.

8. You can use Office.com to insert royalty-free _____ in an Excel worksheet.

9. _____ are combinations of formatting styles such as font, border, shadow, and shape effects that can be applied to a graphic in a worksheet.

10. A(n) _____ is a predefined set of elements such as a title, legend, data labels, and data table that is applied to a selected chart.

LAB EXERCISES

MULTIPLE CHOICE

Circle the correct response to the questions below.

1. A graphic can be placed in an Excel worksheet from the _____ tab.
   a. Home
   b. Insert
   c. Layout
   d. Style

2. Column, bar, and line are Excel chart _____.
   a. elements
   b. groups
   c. styles
   d. types

3. A 3-D chart includes a third axis known as the _____.
   a. W axis
   b. X axis
   c. Y axis
   d. Z axis

4. A(n) _____ is the chart object that identifies each data series.
   a. X axis
   b. legend
   c. Y axis
   d. chart title

5. A company logo, the page number, or the current date might be shown in the _____ for an Excel worksheet.
   a. chart
   b. drawing
   c. footing
   d. header

6. A chart that is included in the worksheet with its data is a(n) _____ chart.
   a. attached
   b. embedded
   c. enabled
   d. inserted

7. To change the appearance of the bars in an Excel bar chart, use the _____ task pane.
   a. Format Bars
   b. Format Data Series
   c. Modify Chart
   d. Modify Data Point

8. From the _____ dialog box, you can change margins as well as the header or footer for a worksheet.
   a. Format Page
   b. File Print
   c. Page Layout
   d. Page Setup

9. An Excel _____ chart shows the relationship of each value in a data series to the series as a whole.
   a. line
   b. bar
   c. pie
   d. bubble

10. _____ are shared across Office 2013 applications so that all your documents can have a uniform style and appearance.
    a. Masks
    b. Formats
    c. Themes
    d. Styles

STEP-BY-STEP

U.S. PATENTS BY TECHNOLOGY ★

1. Max's research paper is about patents in the technology sector. He has downloaded some data from the Science and Engineering Indicators to get started. You'll be helping him chart data for the top four categories and to format the worksheet. A completed worksheet with a bar chart is shown here, but you will change the bar chart to a column chart. Your solution may look different depending upon your format choices.

   a. Open the workbook ex02_Patent Data. Save the workbook as Patent Data to your solution file location.

   b. Change to a different document theme. Use cell styles, font and fill color, alignment, row height, number formats, borders, and other formatting effects to enhance the appearance of the data.

   c. Insert a graphic of your choice. Size and position it; apply a picture style that complements the rest of your design.

   d. Select A3 through D3 and the other required cells to build a clustered bar chart, using the Recommended Charts command. Build a chart that illustrates the top four technology areas for patents. Move the chart below the worksheet data, and size it to the same width as the data.

   e. Edit the chart title to show **Top Patent Activity**. Choose a chart style, or make other formatting choices to design your chart.

   f. Change the chart type to clustered column. Display and format data labels for the 2010 values.

   g. Move to cell A1. Preview the worksheet, and scale it to fit on a single page.

USPTO[1] Patent Activity By Technology Area[2]

Area or Field	2008	2009	2010
Aerospace and defense	1434	1679	2098
Automation and control	2773	3225	3951
Biotechnology	5940	5826	8206
Computer systems	10506	11680	12654
Information processing	11672	15075	22038
Materials	3658	3582	5193
Measurement techniques and instrumentation	9478	9790	10918
Medical electronics	2439	2565	3489
Medical equipment	4582	4691	7424
Networking	4859	6921	9861
Optics	6597	6683	6875
Pharmaceuticals	3835	4275	5471
Semiconductors	11440	11974	16665
Telecommunications	10264	11138	14727
Total Activity	91485	101113	131580

[1]United States Patent and Trademark Office

[2]Technologies classified by the Patent Board™

Source: The Patent Board™, Proprietary Patent database, special tabulations (2011)
Science and Engineering Indicators 2012

h. Add a predefined footer to the worksheet to display your name, the page number, and the date. Center the worksheet horizontally.

i. Document the workbook to include your name as the author. Save the workbook. Preview and print the worksheet.

AIRLINE BAGGAGE FEES ★★

2. Larissa works for the Department of Transportation Statistics. She's preparing a report on the amount of revenue attributable to airline baggage fees. She has assembled data for four years and plans to develop the worksheet with two charts that will illustrate the trends. Your solution should resemble the sample completed worksheets, but you may make your own format choices.

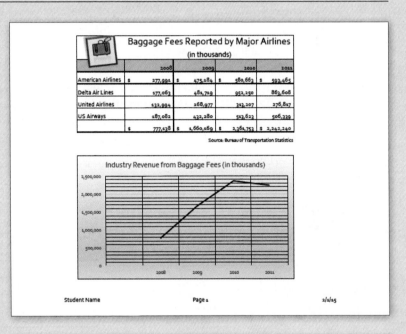

a. Open the workbook ex02_ Baggage Fees. Save the workbook as Baggage Fees to your solution file location.

b. Apply a different document theme. Change the colors associated with the theme, and save your custom theme.

c. Use cell styles, alignment, font and fill color, and other formatting features to enhance the appearance of the data.

d. Insert a graphic of your choice. Size and position it; apply a picture style, if desired, that complements the worksheet design.

e. Create a column chart for the data from the four carriers listed. Move the chart to a separate chart sheet. Enter an appropriate chart title. Choose a style, and edit individual chart elements as needed to create an attractive, easy-to-read chart.

f. Create a line chart with markers for the yearly totals. Edit and format an appropriate title. Format the chart area with a gradient fill of your choice. Show the data labels, and format and position them. Do not show a legend. Move this chart below the worksheet data.

g. Move to cell A1. Preview the worksheet, and fit the chart and data on a single page, if necessary.

h. Add a predefined footer to the worksheet and the chart sheet to display your name, the page number, and the date. Center the worksheet horizontally.

i. Document the workbook to include your name as the author. Save the workbook. Preview and print the workbook.

CUSTOMER DATA ANALYSIS ★★

3. Greenline Wheels, a bicycle and electric car rental company, has collected data about customers to help analyze future offerings. You want to graph the data to determine customer interests and purchases. The completed worksheet with charts is shown here; your worksheet may be slightly different depending on your formatting choices.

a. Open the workbook ex02_ Greenline Customers. Save the workbook as Greenline Customers Analysis to your solution file location.

b. Apply a different document theme. Use cell styles, alignment, font and fill color, or other formatting features to enhance the appearance of your worksheet.

c. Create a bar chart for the data in cells B5:D9. Move the chart below the data. Enter an appropriate chart title. Choose a style and edit individual chart elements as needed to create an attractive, easy-to-read chart.

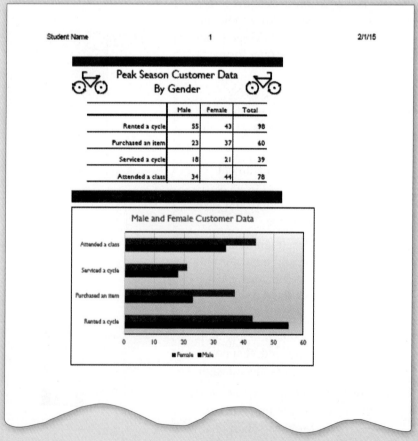

d. Insert a graphic of your choice. Size and position it; apply a picture style, if desired, that complements the worksheet design.

e. Create a column chart for the totals data. Move this chart to a separate chart sheet. Enter an appropriate chart title, and do not show a legend. Choose a style, and add and edit chart elements as needed.

f. You realize that the male and female data for the "Serviced a cycle" item is transposed. Reenter those two values.

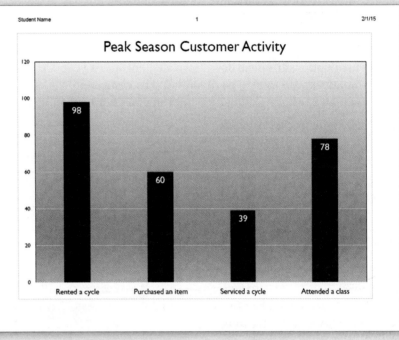

g. Move to cell A1. Preview the worksheet to determine if the data and chart fit on a single page. Scale the worksheet if necessary.

h. Add a predefined header to the worksheet to display your name, the page number, and the date. Center the worksheet horizontally. Add the same header to the chart sheet. Print both sheets.

i. Document the workbook to include your name as the author. Save the workbook.

LAB EXERCISES

ANIMAL ADOPTION ANALYSIS ★★

4. Richard Phillipe volunteers for a group that aids the Animal Rescue Foundation. He has compiled data about adoptions from the downtown shelter for last year. He plans to create charts that show adoptions by month as well as by type of animal. The completed worksheet with charts is shown here; your worksheet may be slightly different depending on your formatting choices.

    a. Open the workbook ex02_ Adoptions. Save the workbook as Animal Adoptions to your solution file location.

    b. Find and insert an image in the top-left or top-right area of the worksheet. Size and position the image. Use the Picture Tools Format tab to recolor or adjust the image if desired.

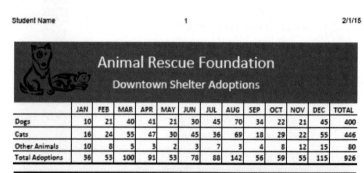

    c. Create a combo chart for the monthly data for the three categories. Show the dogs and cats categories by a clustered column chart; show the other animals category in a line chart. Edit the title to display **Adoptions by Month**.

    d. Choose a chart style; show a legend at the bottom. Move the chart below the worksheet data and size it. Add a value (Y) axis title that shows **Number of Animals**.

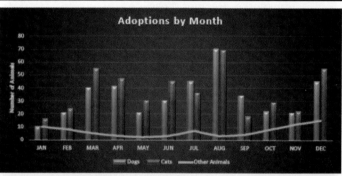

    e. Create a 3-D pie chart for the total adoptions by animal group for the year. Move this chart below the column chart. Choose a style that works well with your data and the column chart. Enter **Animal Adoptions by Category** as the chart title.

    f. Explode the Dogs slice slightly.

    g. Change the June value for Other Animals to **3**; change the October value for Dogs to **22**.

    h. Move to cell A1. Preview the worksheet. Scale it so that the data and charts fit on a single page.

    i. Add a predefined header to the worksheet to display your name, the page number, and the date. Center the worksheet horizontally.

    j. Document the workbook to include your name as the author. Save the workbook. Preview and print the worksheet.

FOOD PANTRY EXPERIENCE ★★★

5. Wendy Murray is working at the local food pantry and has been asked to assemble and analyze volunteer data gathered at a recent street fair. She plans to organize the data by task and age group. She will share this data with the organization so it can better plan food distribution events. The completed worksheet with charts is shown here; your worksheet may be slightly different depending on your formatting choices.

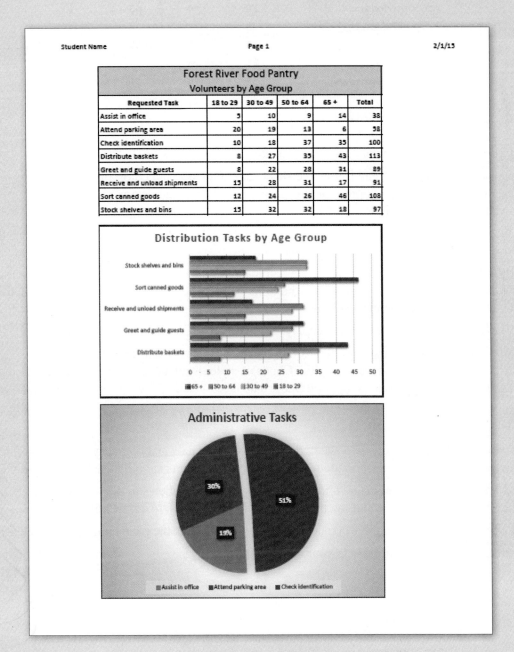

Student Name   Page 1   2/1/13

Forest River Food Pantry
Volunteers by Age Group

Requested Task	18 to 29	30 to 49	50 to 64	65 +	Total
Assist in office	5	10	9	14	38
Attend parking area	20	19	13	6	58
Check identification	10	18	37	35	100
Distribute baskets	8	27	35	43	113
Greet and guide guests	8	22	28	31	89
Receive and unload shipments	15	28	31	17	91
Sort canned goods	12	24	26	46	108
Stock shelves and bins	15	32	32	18	97

Distribution Tasks by Age Group

Administrative Tasks

LAB EXERCISES

a. Create a worksheet using the data shown here. Save the workbook as Food Pantry to your solution file location.

FOREST RIVER FOOD PANTRY				
	Volunteers by Age Group			
Requested Task	18 to 29	30 to 49	50 to 64	65+
Assist in office	5	10	9	14
Attend parking area	20	19	13	6
Check identification	10	18	37	35
Distribute baskets	8	27	35	43
Greet and guide guests	8	22	28	31
Receive and unload shipments	15	28	31	17
Sort canned goods	12	24	26	46
Stock shelves and bins	15	32	32	18

b. Add a column to total the volunteers for each task.

c. Choose a document theme, and format the sheet using font size and color, fill color, borders, cell styles, or other formatting options you have learned. Make sure all data is visible, and set the columns with values at the same width.

d. Create a bar chart for the tasks by age group; do not include the totals. Move the chart below the data. Choose a chart style to complement the data.

e. With the chart selected, use the Select Data command on the Chart Tools Design tab. In the dialog box, switch the columns and rows so that the tasks are shown in the left pane. Then remove the first three tasks. Switch the columns and rows back to the original setting.

f. Add a chart title above the chart that displays Distribution Tasks by Age Group.

g. Create a pie chart for the first three task totals. Move this chart below the bar chart. Enter Administrative Tasks as the chart title. Choose a style to balance your other choices for the worksheet. Show a legend at the bottom. Show data labels inside the slices as percentages.

h. Rotate the chart by changing the angle of the first slice until the largest slice is at the right side of the pie. Explode this slice slightly.

i. Move to cell A1. Preview the worksheet. Scale it so that the data and both charts fit on a single portrait page, and center the data horizontally. If you think the charts should have borders, add them.

j. If you would like to use an image, find and insert one that contributes to the worksheet appearance. Size and position the image, and use the Picture Tools Format tab to adjust it if desired.

k. Add a predefined header to the worksheet to display your name, the page number, and the date.

l. Document the workbook to include your name as the author. Save the workbook and print the worksheet.

ON YOUR OWN

JOB MARKET SEMINAR ★

1. Nancy Fernandez is preparing for an upcoming job market seminar she is presenting. She has collected data comparing the mean hourly pay rate for several computer and mathematical jobs in the Midwest and Northeast to the U.S. average rates. Open the workbook ex02_Job Market. Calculate the percentage difference between the Midwest states and U.S. average in column E. Calculate the percentage difference between the Northeast states and U.S. average in column F. Add appropriate fill and font colors to the worksheet. Add a graphic to the top-left corner of the worksheet. Nancy thinks the information would be much more meaningful and have greater impact if it were presented in a chart. Create an appropriate chart of the average hourly wage for computer programmers, computer support specialists, computer systems analysts, and database administrators on a separate chart sheet. Include appropriate chart titles. Add a pattern to the data series and change the plot area fill color. Enhance the chart in other ways using different font sizes and font colors. Position the legend at the bottom of the chart. Add a predefined header to the chart sheet that displays your name, page number, and date. Save the workbook as Seminar and print the chart.

GRADE TRACKING ★

2. Create a worksheet that tracks your GPA for at least four semesters or quarters. (If necessary, use fictitious data to attain four grading periods.) Create a chart that best represents your GPA trends. Use the formatting techniques you have learned to change the appearance of the worksheet and the chart. Save the workbook as Grades. Include a header or footer that displays your name and the current date in the worksheet. Print the worksheet with the chart.

STOCK MARKET WORKBOOK ★★

3. You are interested in the stock market. Use Help to learn more about the Stock chart type. Pick five related mutual funds and enter data about their performance over a period of time. Create a stock chart of the data. Save the worksheet with the chart as Mutual Funds. Include a header or footer that displays your name and the current date in the worksheet. Print the worksheet and the chart.

LAB EXERCISES

GRADUATE SCHOOL DATA ★★★

4. Andrew Romine is considering graduate school at Ohio State and has gathered some data to present to his parents to make a case for paying part of his tuition and fees. Open the file ex02_Graduate School, which has two worksheets, one that shows earnings and the other payback data if Andrew chooses Ohio State. Using what you learned in the lab, create two charts from the data on the Earnings worksheet. One chart should represent the lifetime earning potential of people based on their level of education and the other should represent median earning by level. On the Payback worksheet, create a combo chart that compares the estimated earning and salary difference amounts. Use the features you have learned to enhance the appearance of the worksheets and charts. Include a header on both worksheets that displays your name and the current date. Save the worksheet as Graduate School2. Print the worksheet with the charts.

INSURANCE COMPARISONS ★★★

5. Roberto Sanchez is thinking about purchasing a new car. However, he is concerned about the insurance rates. Before purchasing, he wants to find out the insurance rates on the cars he is evaluating. Select three different car manufacturers and models. Use the web and select three different comparable insurance companies to get the insurance premium cost information for different amounts of coverage (minimum required). Use your own personal information as the basis for the insurance quotes. Create a worksheet that contains the cost of minimum coverage, cost of optional coverage, deductibles available, and insurance premium quotes for each vehicle. Create a chart of the data that shows the coverage and premiums. Enhance the chart appropriately. Add pictures of the cars. Include a header or footer that displays your name and the current date in the worksheet. Save the workbook as Insurance. Print the worksheet and chart.

Objectives

After completing this lab, you will know how to:

1 Use absolute references.

2 Copy, move, name, and delete sheets.

3 Use AutoFill.

4 Reference multiple sheets.

5 Use Find and Replace.

6 Zoom the worksheet.

7 Split windows and freeze panes.

8 Use what-if analysis and Goal Seek.

9 Create Sparklines.

10 Control page breaks.

11 Add custom headers and footers.

12 Print selected sheets and areas.

Downtown Internet Café

You presented your new, more-optimistic, first quarter sales forecast for the Downtown Internet Café to Evan. He was impressed with the charts and the projected increase in sales if an aggressive advertising promotion is launched. However, because the Café's funds are low due to the cost of the recent renovations, he has decided to wait on launching the advertising campaign.

Evan wants you to continue working on the Café forecast using the original, more-conservative projected sales values for the first quarter. In addition, he asks you to include an average calculation and to extend the forecast for the next three quarters.

After discussing the future sales, you agree that the Café will likely make a small profit during the first quarter of operations. Then the Café should show increasing profitability. Evan stresses that the monthly profit margin should reach 20 percent in the second quarter.

As you develop the Café's financial forecast, the worksheet grows in size and complexity. You will learn about features of Office Excel 2013 that help you manage a large workbook efficiently. You also will learn how you can manipulate the data in a worksheet to reach a goal using the what-if analysis capabilities of Excel. The completed annual forecast is shown here.

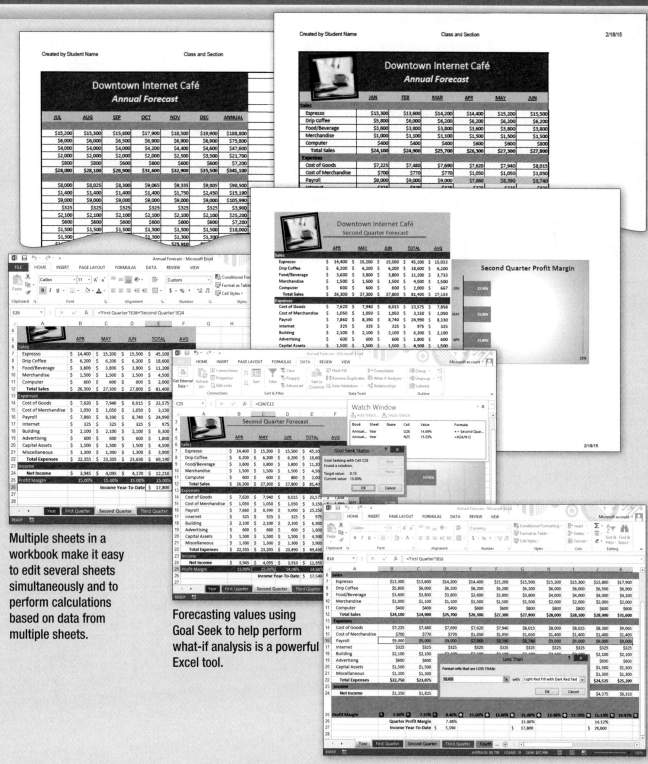

Multiple sheets in a workbook make it easy to edit several sheets simultaneously and to perform calculations based on data from multiple sheets.

Forecasting values using Goal Seek to help perform what-if analysis is a powerful Excel tool.

Conditional formatting allows you to quickly emphasize worksheet data based on specified conditions.

The following concepts will be introduced in this lab:

1 **Absolute Reference** An absolute reference is a cell or range reference in a formula whose location does not change when the formula is copied.

2 **Sheet Name** Each sheet in a workbook can be assigned a descriptive sheet name to help identify the contents of the sheet.

3 **AutoFill** The AutoFill feature makes entering a series of numbers, numbers and text combinations, dates, or time periods easier by logically repeating and extending the series. AutoFill recognizes trends and automatically extends data and alphanumeric headings as far as you specify.

4 **Sheet and 3-D References** Sheet and 3-D references in formulas are used to refer to data from multiple sheets and to calculate new values based on this data.

5 **Find and Replace** The Find and Replace feature helps you quickly find specific information and automatically replace it with new information.

6 **Split Window** The split window feature allows you to divide a worksheet window into sections, making it easier to view different parts of the worksheet at the same time.

7 **Freeze Panes** Freezing panes prevents the data in the pane from scrolling as you move to different areas in a worksheet.

8 **What-If Analysis** What-if analysis is a technique used to evaluate the effects of changing selected factors in a worksheet.

9 **Goal Seek** The Goal Seek tool is used to find the value needed in one cell to attain a result you want in another cell.

10 **Conditional Formatting** Conditional formatting changes the appearance of a range of cells based on a condition that you specify.

Correcting Formulas

After talking with Evan, the owner of the Café, about the first quarter forecast, you are ready to begin making the changes he suggested. Evan returned the workbook file to you containing several changes he made to the format of the worksheet.

1

- Start Excel 2013.

- Open the workbook ex03_First Quarter Forecast.

- If necessary, maximize the application and workbook windows.

- If necessary, scroll to see row 25.

Your screen should be similar to Figure 3.1

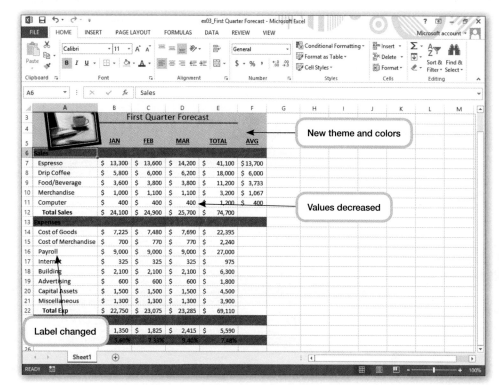

Figure 3.1

As you can see, Evan made several formatting changes to the worksheet. He added a graphic; changed the theme, fill, and text colors; and made several changes to the row headings. For example, the Pay heading has been changed to Payroll. Evan also decided to decrease the computer sales values to $400 for February and March.

IDENTIFYING FORMULA ERRORS

Now you are ready to enter the average formula for the expense values. To do this, you will copy the function down column F.

Copy the function from cell F11 into cells F12 through F24.

Move to cell F13.

Your screen should be similar to Figure 3.2

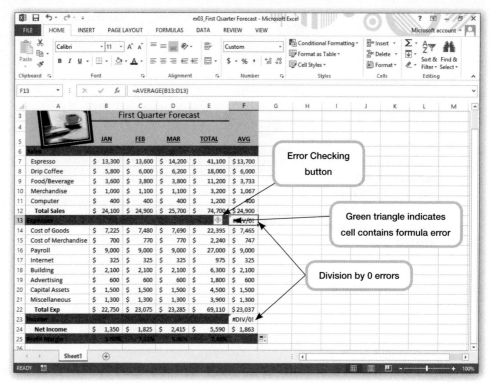

Figure 3.2

Having Trouble?

If you don't see the green triangle or the Error Checking button when you click on a cell with a formula error, you may need to turn on background error checking. To do this, open the File tab, choose Options, Formulas, and choose Enable background error checking.

The average value has been correctly calculated for each row. Notice, however, that two cells display the error value #DIV/0!, indicating the cells contain a formula error. When a formula cannot properly calculate a result, an error value may be displayed and a green triangle appears in the upper-left corner of the cell. In addition, the Error Checking button appears when you select a cell containing an error.

Each type of error value has a different cause, as described in the following table.

Error Value	Cause
#####	Column not wide enough to display result, or negative date or time is used
#VALUE!	Wrong type of argument or operand is used
#DIV/0!	Number is divided by zero
#NAME?	Text in formula not recognized
#N/A	Value not available
#REF!	Cell reference is not valid
#NUM!	Invalid number values
#NULL!	Intersection operator is not valid

Excel 2013 includes several tools to help you find and correct errors in formula entries. These tools provide the capability to display the relationships between formulas and cells and to identify and suggest corrections to potential problems in formulas.

To correct this problem, you need to find out the cause of the error. Pointing to the ⟨!⟩ Error Checking button displays a ScreenTip identifying the cause of the error. Clicking the ⟨!⟩ Error Checking button displays a list of options for error checking the worksheet. In this case, the formula is attempting to divide by zero or empty cells.

2

● Point to ⟨!⟩ Error Checking to see the ScreenTip.

● Click ⟨!⟩ Error Checking.

● Choose Edit in Formula Bar from the list of options.

Your screen should be similar to Figure 3.3

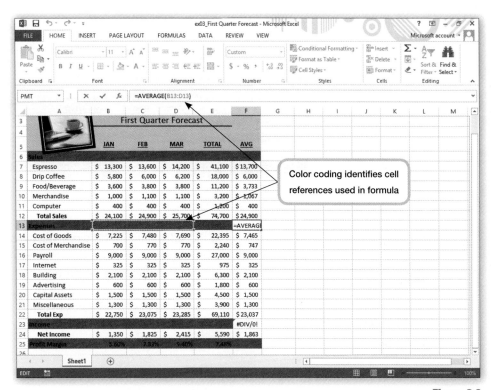

Figure 3.3

In Edit mode, the formula references are color-coded to the referenced worksheet cells and you can now easily see the error is caused by references to blank cells when the function was copied.

Since you do not need this formula, you will delete it. Likewise, you need to delete the function that was copied into cell F23.

3

- Press `Esc` to exit Edit mode.

- Press `Delete`.

- Move to cell F23.

- Delete the formula.

Your screen should be similar to Figure 3.4

Formulas deleted

Figure 3.4

While looking at the sales data in the worksheet, you decide it may be interesting to know what contribution each sales item makes to total sales. To find out, you will enter a formula to calculate the proportion of sales by each in column G. You will start by entering a new column heading in cell G5. Then you will enter the formula = Total Espresso Sales/Total Sales to calculate the proportion for Espresso sales in G7 and copy it to G8 to calculate the proportion for Drip Coffee sales.

4

- Enter the heading **Proportion** in cell G5.

- Enter the formula **=E7/E12** in cell G7.

- Drag the fill handle to copy the formula in cell G7 to G8.

Your screen should be similar to Figure 3.5

Figure 3.5

The value 0.5502008 is correctly displayed in cell G7. This shows that the Espresso sales are approximately 55 percent of Total Sales. However, a division by zero error has occurred in cell G8.

Another way to check a formula to locate errors or to confirm that the correct cell references are being used is to use the features in the Formula Auditing group of the Formulas tab.

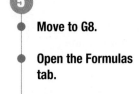

5

- Move to G8.

- Open the Formulas tab.

- Open the menu in the Formula Auditing group and choose Trace Error.

Your screen should be similar to Figure 3.6

Formula Auditing group contains features used to check formula accuracy

Arrows identify cells used in formulas

Blank cell is cause of formula error

Figure 3.6

Additional Information

You also can use

Trace Precedents or

Trace Dependents to show relationships between formulas and cells.

Excel displays arrows from each cell that affects the value in the current cell. You can now see the error occurred because the relative reference to cell E12 adjusted correctly to the new location when the formula was copied and now references cell E13, a blank cell.

USING ABSOLUTE REFERENCES

The formula in G7 needs to be entered so that the reference to the Total Sales value in cell E12 does not change when the formula is copied. To do this, you need to make the cell reference absolute.

Concept Absolute Reference

An **absolute reference** is a cell or range reference in a formula whose location does not change when the formula is copied.

To stop the relative adjustment of cell references, enter a $ (dollar sign) character before the column letter and the row number. This changes the cell reference to absolute. When a formula containing an absolute cell reference is copied to another row and column location in the worksheet, the cell reference does not change. It is an exact duplicate of the cell reference in the original formula.

A cell reference also can be a **mixed reference**. In this type of reference, either the column letter or the row number is preceded with the $. This makes only the row or the column absolute. When a formula containing a mixed cell reference is copied to another location in the worksheet, only the part of the cell reference that is not absolute changes relative to its new location in the worksheet.

The table below shows examples of relative and absolute references and the results when a reference in cell G8 to cell E8 is copied to cell H9.

Cell Contents of G8	Copied to Cell H9	Type of Reference
E8	E8	Absolute reference
E$8	F$8	Mixed reference
$E8	$E9	Mixed reference
E8	F9	Relative reference

You will change the formula in cell G7 to include an absolute reference for cell E12. Then you will copy the formula to cells G8 through G10.

You can change a cell reference to absolute or mixed by typing in the dollar signs directly or by using the ABS (Absolute) key, F4. To use the ABS key, the program must be in Edit mode and the cell reference that you want to change must be selected. If you continue to press F4, the cell reference will cycle through all possible combinations of cell reference types.

1

● Click Remove Arrows in the Formula Auditing group to remove the trace arrows.

● Move to G7.

● Click anywhere in the reference to E12 in the formula bar to enter Edit mode.

● Press F4 four times to cycle through all reference types.

● Press F4 again to display an absolute reference.

Your screen should be similar to Figure 3.7

Figure 3.7

The cell reference now displays $ characters before the column letter and row number, making this cell reference absolute. Leaving the cell reference absolute, as it is now, will stop the relative adjustment of the cell reference when you copy it again.

Click ☑ **Enter or press** ←Enter.

● **Copy the revised formula to cells G8 through G11.**

● **Move to G8 and click** 🔲 **Trace Precedents in the Formula Auditing group.**

Your screen should be similar to Figure 3.8

Identifies cells that affect value of selected cell

Absolute reference stopped the adjustment of cell references when formula was copied

Figure 3.8

The trace arrows show that when the formula was copied it correctly adjusted the relative cell reference to Drip Coffee sales in cell E8 and did not adjust the reference to E12 because it is an absolute reference.

The last change you need to make to the proportion data is to format it to the Percent style.

Correcting Formulas   **EX3.13**

3

- Click 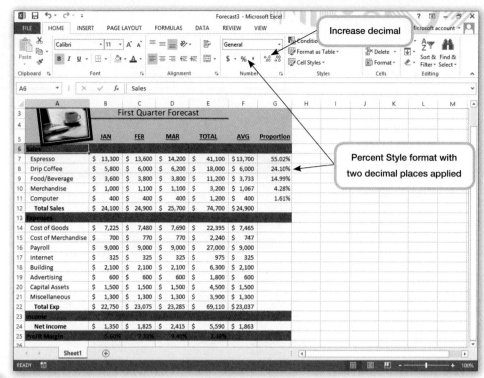 in the Formula Auditing group.

- Select G7 through G11.

- Open the Home tab.

- Click **%** Percent Style in the Number group.

- Click **Increase Decimal (twice).**

- Extend the fill in the title area to column G.

Having Trouble?

Use Format Painter or drag the fill handle to copy the fill colors.

- Extend the fill in rows 6, 13, 23, and 25 to column G.

- Move to cell A6 and save the workbook as Forecast3 to your solution file location.

Your screen should be similar to Figure 3.9

Figure 3.9

The calculated proportion shows the same values that a pie chart of this data would show.

Creating a Second-Quarter Worksheet

Next, you want to add the second-quarter forecast to the workbook. You want this data in a separate sheet in the same workbook file. To make it easier to enter the forecast for the next quarter, you will copy the contents of the first quarter forecast in Sheet1 into another sheet in the workbook. Then you will change the month headings, the title, and the number data for the second quarter. Finally, you want to include a formula to calculate a year-to-date total for the six months.

COPYING WORKSHEETS

You want to copy the worksheet data from Sheet1 to Sheet2. You can quickly make a duplicate of a worksheet including all data, objects, and formatting with the Move or Copy Sheet command.

1

- **Right-click the Sheet1 tab.**

- **Choose Move or Copy.**

- **Choose (move to end).**

- **Choose Create a copy.**

- **Click** OK **.**

Another Method

You also can use Format ▾ /Move or Copy Sheet in the Cells group of the Home tab.

Your screen should be similar to Figure 3.10

Copied sheet is active

Figure 3.10

Another Method

You also can select all the data and copy it to a new blank worksheet. With this method, you often need to resize column widths and objects.

An exact duplicate of the contents and formatting of the Sheet1 worksheet is displayed in the newly inserted sheet. It is currently named Sheet1 (2).

RENAMING SHEETS AND COLORING SHEET TABS

As more sheets are added to a workbook, remembering what information is in each sheet becomes more difficult. To help clarify the contents of the sheets, you can rename the sheets.

Concept 2 Sheet Name

Each sheet in a workbook can be assigned a descriptive **sheet name** to help identify the contents of the sheet. The following guidelines should be followed when naming a sheet. A sheet name

- Can be up to 31 characters.
- Can be entered in uppercase or lowercase letters or a combination (it will appear as entered).
- Can contain any combination of letters, numbers, and spaces.
- Cannot contain the characters : ? * / \.
- Cannot be enclosed in square brackets [ ].

Double-clicking the sheet tab makes the sheet active and highlights the existing sheet name in the tab. The existing name is cleared as soon as you begin to type the new name. You will change the name of Sheet1 to First Quarter and Sheet2 to Second Quarter.

1

- Double-click the Sheet1 tab.

- Type **First Quarter**

- Press ←Enter.

- Change the name of the Sheet1(2) tab to **Second Quarter**

Another Method

You also can use Format ▾ /
Rename Sheet in the Cells group of the Home tab.

Your screen should be similar to Figure 3.11

Figure 3.11

Sheet tabs renamed

To further differentiate the sheets, you can add color to the sheet tabs.

2

- **Right-click on the First Quarter tab.**

- **Select Tab Color from the shortcut menu.**

- **Choose the Brown, Accent 3 theme color from the color palette.**

- **In the same manner, change the color of the Second Quarter sheet tab to the Orange, Accent 1 theme color.**

Your screen should be similar to Figure 3.12

Tab colors changed

Figure 3.12

Another Method

You also can use ▦ Format ▾ /Tab Color in the Cells group.

The sheet tab name of the selected sheet is underlined in the tab color of orange and the First Quarter sheet tab is brown. When a sheet is not selected, the sheet tab is displayed with the background color.

FILLING A SERIES

Now you can change the worksheet title and data in the Second Quarter sheet. First you will change the worksheet title to identify the worksheet contents as the second-quarter forecast. Then you will change the month headings to the three months that make up the second quarter: April, May, and June.

1

● Change the title in cell B3 to Second Quarter Forecast

● Change the month heading in cell B5 to APR

Your screen should be similar to Figure 3.13

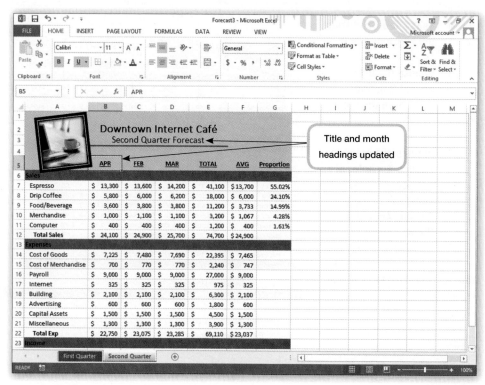

Figure 3.13

Now you need to change the remaining month headings to MAY and JUN. You will use the AutoFill feature to enter the month headings.

Concept ③ AutoFill

The **AutoFill** feature makes entering a series of numbers, numbers and text combinations, dates, or time periods easier by logically repeating and extending the series. AutoFill recognizes trends and automatically extends data and alphanumeric headings as far as you specify.

Dragging the fill handle activates the AutoFill feature if Excel recognizes the entry in the cell as an entry that can be incremented. When AutoFill extends the entries, it uses the same style as the original entry. For example, if you enter the heading for July as JUL (abbreviated with all letters uppercase), all the extended entries in the series will be abbreviated and uppercase. Dragging down or right increments in increasing order, and up or left increments in decreasing order. A linear series increases or decreases values by a constant value, and a growth series multiplies values by a constant factor. Examples of how AutoFill extends a series are shown in the table below.

Initial Selection	Extended Series
Qtr1	Qtr2, Qtr3, Qtr4
Mon	Tue, Wed, Thu
Jan, Apr	Jul, Oct, Jan

A starting value of a series may contain more than one item that can be incremented, such as JAN-15, in which both the month and year can increment. You can specify which value to increment by selecting the appropriate option from the ▦▾ AutoFill Options menu.

The entry in cell B5, APR, is the starting value of a series of months. You will drag the fill handle to the right to increment the months. The mouse pointer displays the entry that will appear in each cell as you drag.

2
● Drag the fill handle of cell B5 to extend the range from cell B5 through cell D5.

● Save the workbook.

Your screen should be similar to Figure 3.14

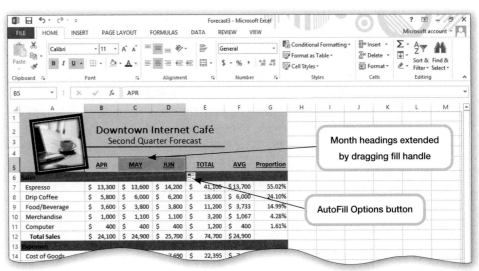

Figure 3.14

The month headings now correctly reflect the three months for the second quarter. This is because the entry in cell B5 was a month that was recognized as an entry that can be incremented. Additionally, the months appear in uppercase characters, the same as the starting month. This is because AutoFill copies formatting when extending the series.

Additional Information

If you do not want a series created when you drag the fill handle, hold down Ctrl as you drag and the entries will be copied, not incremented. Alternatively, you can choose Copy Cells from the ▦▾ AutoFill Options menu.

Creating a Second-Quarter Worksheet **EX3.19**

USING A 3-D REFERENCE

Finally, you need to update the forecast to reflect the April through June sales. You anticipate that sales will increase in all areas, except food and beverage sales, which will remain the same. Then you will enter a formula to calculate the year-to-date income total using data from both sheets.

Additional Information

To speed up the process of entering the following data, use [Tab] to move to the cell to the right. Alternatively, for each item, first select the range, then enter the first value, and press [Enter] to move to the next cell in the selection.

Enter the following values in the specified cells.

Sales	Cell	Number
Espresso	B7	14400
	C7	15200
	D7	15500
Drip Coffee	B8	6200
	C8	6200
	D8	6200
Merchandise	B10	1500
	C10	1500
	D10	1500
Computer	B11	600
	C11	600
	D11	600

Your screen should be similar to Figure 3.15

Figure 3.15

The worksheet now contains the data for the second quarter and all dependent formulas have been recalculated.

Now you can enter the formula to calculate a year-to-date income total. The formula to make this calculation will sum the total income numbers from cell E24 in the First Quarter sheet and cell E24 in the Second Quarter sheet. To reference data in another sheet in the same workbook, you enter a formula that references cells in other worksheets.

Concept 4   Sheet and 3-D References

Sheet and 3-D references in formulas are used to refer to data from multiple sheets and to calculate new values based on this data. A **sheet reference** in a formula consists of the name of the sheet, followed by an exclamation point and the cell or range reference. If the sheet name contains nonalphabetic characters, such as a space, the sheet name (or path) must be enclosed in single quotation marks.

    If you want to use the same cell or range of cells on multiple sheets, you can use a **3-D reference**. A 3-D reference consists of the names of the beginning and ending sheets enclosed in quotes and separated by a colon. This is followed by an exclamation point and the cell or range reference. The cell or range reference is the same on each sheet in the specified sheet range. If a sheet is inserted or deleted, the range is automatically updated. 3-D references make it easy to analyze data in the same cell or range of cells on multiple worksheets.

Reference	Description
=Sheet2!B17	Displays the entry in cell B17 of Sheet2 in the active cell of the current sheet
=Sheet1!A1 + Sheet2!B2	Sums the values in cell A1 of Sheet1 and B2 of Sheet2
=SUM(Sheet1:Sheet4!H6:K6)	Sums the values in cells H6 through K6 in Sheets 1, 2, 3, and 4
=SUM(Sheet1!H6:K6)	Sums the values in cells H6 through K6 in Sheet1
=SUM(Sheet1:Sheet4!H6)	Sums the values in cell H6 of Sheets 1, 2, 3, and 4

Just like a formula that references cells within a sheet, a formula that references cells in multiple sheets is automatically recalculated when data in a referenced cell changes.

    You will enter a descriptive text entry in cell D26 and then use a 3-D reference in a SUM function to calculate the year-to-date total in cell E26.

    The SUM function argument will consist of a 3-D reference to cell E24 in the First and Second Quarter sheets. Although a 3-D reference can be entered by typing it using the proper syntax, it is much easier to enter it by pointing to the cells on the sheets. To enter a 3-D reference, select the cell or range in the beginning sheet and then hold down ⇧Shift and click on the sheet tab of the last sheet in the range. This will include the indicated cell range on all sheets between and including the first and last sheets specified.

2

In cell D26, enter and right-align the entry **Income Year-to-Date**

Move to E26.

Click **Σ ▾** Sum.

Click cell E24.

Hold down ⇧Shift and click the First Quarter tab.

Release ⇧Shift.

Press ←Enter.

Move to E26.

Your screen should be similar to Figure 3.16

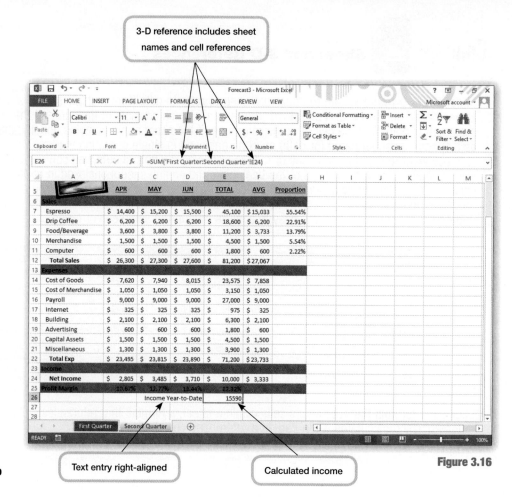

3-D reference includes sheet names and cell references

Text entry right-aligned

Calculated income

Figure 3.16

The calculated number 15590 appears in cell E26, and the function containing a 3-D reference appears in the formula bar.

HIDING GRIDLINES AND HEADINGS

Just as you completed the forecast for the first half of the year, Evan, the Café owner, stopped in and you decide to show him the forecast. To simplify the screen display while showing Evan the worksheet, you will hide the gridlines and column and row headings.

Move to cell A1 and open the View tab.

Choose ☑ Gridlines **from the Show group to clear the selection.**

Choose ☑ Headings **from the Show group to clear the selection.**

Your screen should be similar to Figure 3.17

Gridlines and Heading options not selected

Row and column gridlines hidden

Column and row headings hidden

Figure 3.17

While these features are off, you will format the year-to-date income value to Accounting with zero decimal places. Rather than opening the Home tab to access these features, you will copy the format from another cell. The Paste Special menu option, Formatting, will do this quickly for you.

Select any cell that is formatted in the Accounting format and choose Copy from the context menu.

Right-click on cell E26 and choose 🔲 **Formatting from the Paste Options section of the context menu.**

Your screen should be similar to Figure 3.18

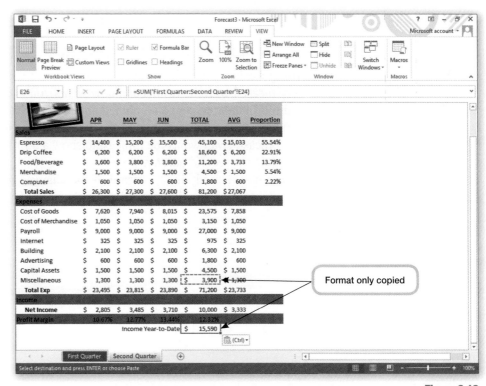

Format only copied

Figure 3.18

Hiding gridlines and headers is convenient for presenting the worksheet to others; however, it is not as easy to work in the sheet with these features off. You will turn them back on, add file documentation, and then print a copy of the workbook for Evan.

3

- Choose ☐ Gridlines from the Show group to select it.

- Choose ☐ Headings from the Show group to select it.

- Enter the following information in the workbook file properties:

Title	Downtown Internet Cafe
Subject	First and second quarter forecasts
Author	your name

Having Trouble?

If needed, click Show All Properties to display the Subject box.

- Change the Print setting to print the entire workbook.

- Preview both worksheets and scale each sheet to fit on a single page.

- Add a predefined header containing your name, page number, and the date to both worksheets.

- Print the workbook.

- Move to cell A6 in both worksheets and save the workbook.

- Close the workbook.

DELETING AND MOVING WORKSHEETS

You presented the completed first- and second-quarter forecasts to Evan. He is very pleased with the results and now wants you to create worksheets for the third and fourth quarters and a combined annual forecast. Additionally, Evan has asked you to include a column chart of the data for each quarter. Finally, after looking at the forecast, Evan wants the forecast to show a profit margin of 15 percent for each month in the second quarter.

You have already made several of the changes requested and saved them as a workbook file. You will open this file to see the revised and expanded forecast.

1

Open the workbook file ex03_Annual Forecast.

Your screen should be similar to Figure 3.19

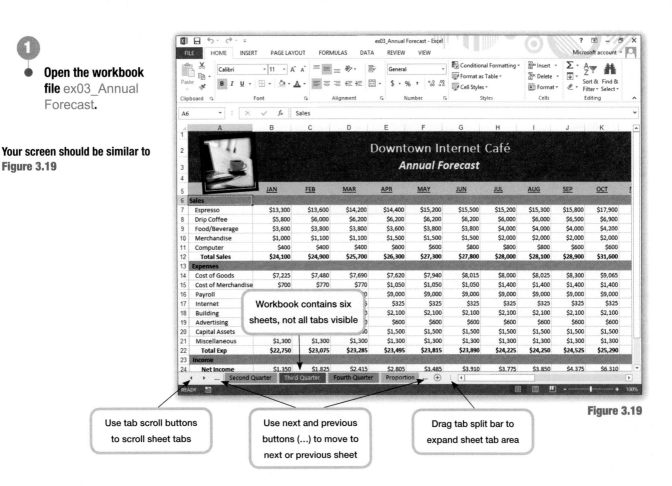

Use tab scroll buttons to scroll sheet tabs

Use next and previous buttons (...) to move to next or previous sheet

Drag tab split bar to expand sheet tab area

Figure 3.19

The workbook file now contains six sheets: First Quarter, Second Quarter, Third Quarter, Fourth Quarter, Proportion, and Year. The Proportion sheet contains the proportion of sales values from the first and second quarters. The Year sheet contains the forecast data for the entire 12 months. Each quarter sheet also includes a chart of the profit margin for that quarter.

Notice also that not all the sheet tab names are visible. This is because there is not enough space in the sheet tab area to display all the tabs. To see the tabs, you can drag the tab split bar located at the right edge of the sheet tab area to expand the area or use the sheet tab scroll buttons to scroll the tabs into view.

2

● Click ◂ once or twice to display the First Quarter tab name.

● Click on each of the Quarter sheet tabs to view the quarterly data and profit margin chart.

● Display the Proportion sheet.

Your screen should be similar to Figure 3.20

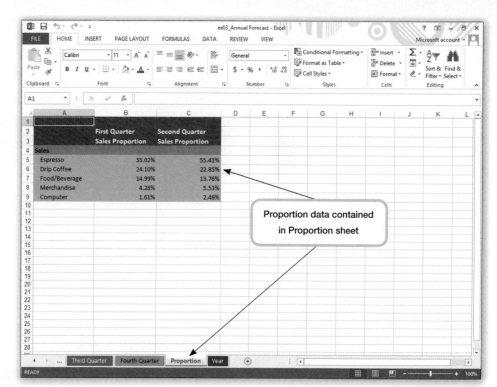

Proportion data contained in Proportion sheet

Figure 3.20

You decide this data, although interesting, is not needed in the forecast workbook and want to delete the entire sheet.

3

● In the Cells group of the Home tab, open the 🗙 Delete ▾ menu and choose Delete Sheet.

● Click Delete to confirm that you want to permanently remove the sheet.

Another Method

You also can choose Delete from the sheet tab's shortcut menu to delete a sheet.

Your screen should be similar to Figure 3.21

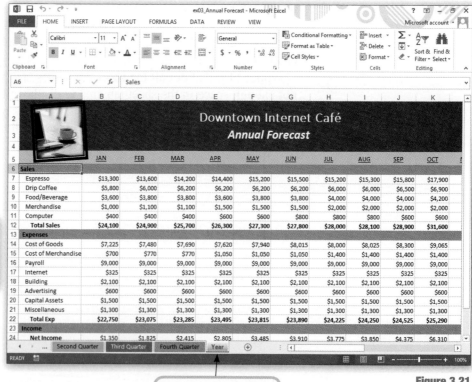

Proportion sheet deleted

Figure 3.21

The entire sheet is deleted, and the Year sheet is now the active sheet. Next you want to move the Year sheet from the last position in the workbook to the first. You can quickly rearrange the order of sheets in a workbook by dragging the selected sheet tab along the row of sheet tabs to the new location.

4 ● **Drag the Year tab to the left of the First Quarter tab.**

● **Your screen should be similar to Figure 3.22**

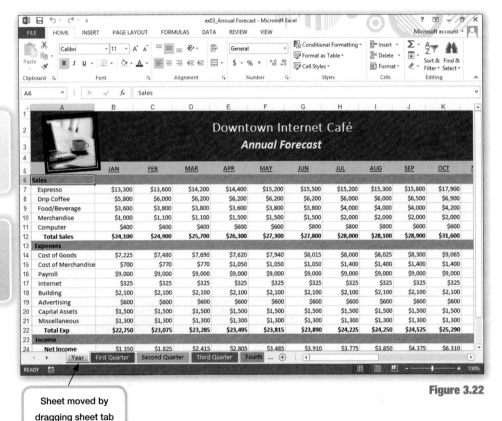

Sheet moved by dragging sheet tab

Figure 3.22

The Year sheet is now the first sheet in the workbook.

Finding and Replacing Information

As you look over the worksheets, you notice that the only abbreviation used in the entire workbook is for expenses in the Total Exp row heading. You want to change it to "Expenses" in all worksheets in the workbook.

You could change the word in each sheet by changing the text directly on the worksheet cells. However, the larger your workbook becomes, the more difficult it will be to find the data you want to modify. Therefore, you will use the Find and Replace feature to quickly locate the word and make the change.

Concept 5 Find and Replace

The **Find and Replace** feature helps you quickly find specific information and automatically replace it with new information. The Find command locates all occurrences of the text or numbers you specify. The Replace command is used with the Find command to locate the specified entries and replace the located occurrences with the replacement text you specify. You also can find cells that match a format you specify and replace the format with another. Finding and replacing data and formats is both fast and accurate, but you need to be careful when replacing that you do not replace unintended matches.

FINDING INFORMATION

First, you will locate and correct the abbreviation using the Find command. This command can be used to locate data in any type of worksheet.

- Click **Find & Select** in the **Editing group and choose Find.**

- If necessary, click **Options >>** to display the additional search options.

Another Method

The keyboard shortcut is Ctrl + F.

Your screen should be similar to Figure 3.23

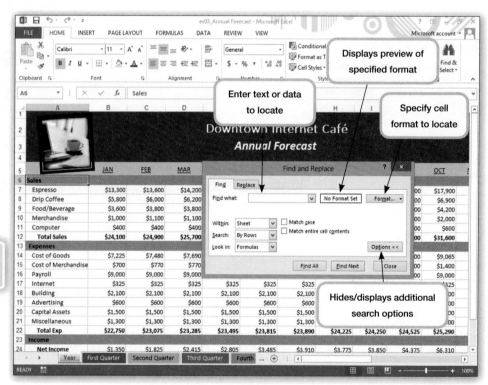

Figure 3.23

In the Find and Replace dialog box, you enter the information you want to locate in the Find what text box. It must be entered exactly as it appears in the worksheet. The additional options in the dialog box can be combined in many ways to help locate information. They are described in the table below.

Option	Effect
Within	Searches the active worksheet or workbook.
Search	Specifies the direction to search in the worksheet: By Columns searches down through columns and By Rows searches to the right across rows.
Look in	Looks for a match in the specified worksheet element: formulas, values, comments.
Match case	Finds words that have the same pattern of uppercase letters as entered in the Find what text box. Using this option makes the search case sensitive.
Match entire cell contents	Looks for an exact and complete match of the characters specified in the Find what text box.
Format	Used to specify a cell format to locate and replace. A sample of the selected format is displayed in the preview box.

You will enter the text to find, "exp," and will search using the default options.

2

• Type **exp** in the Find what box.

• Click [Options >>] to hide the additional search options.

• Click [Find Next].

Additional Information

Because the Match case option is not selected, Find looks for an exact match regardless of whether the characters are uppercase or lowercase.

Your screen should be similar to Figure 3.24

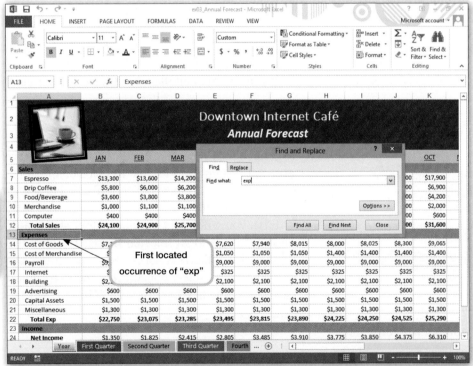

First located occurrence of "exp"

Figure 3.24

Additional Information

Clicking [Find All] displays all text or format matches in a list. Selecting an item from the list moves the cell selector to the cell containing the entry.

The cell selector jumps to the first occurrence of "exp," in cell A13, which contains the word "Expenses." It located this word because the first three letters match. However, this is not the entry you are trying to locate. You will continue the search to locate the next occurrence. Then you will edit the cell to display the word "Expenses."

3

- Click **Find Next**.

- Double-click on the selected cell.

- Change Exp to **Expenses**

- Press **←Enter**.

Your screen should be similar to Figure 3.25

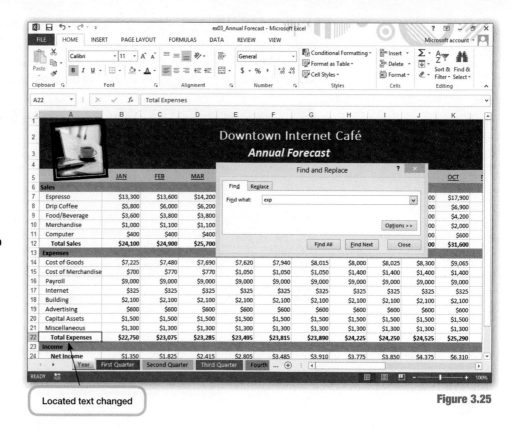

Located text changed

Figure 3.25

You manually made the correction to the label in cell A22. Next, you want to locate the word in all the other sheets and correct the entries.

REPLACING INFORMATION

You realize that "exp" will be located twice in every worksheet. Since you want to change only the Total Exp headings, you will refine your search term to locate only this heading and use the Replace command to make the correction automatically on the other sheets. The replacement text must be entered exactly as you want it to appear.

First, you will select all four quarter sheets as a group so that any changes you make are made to all selected sheets. To select two or more adjacent sheets, click on the tab for the first sheet and click on the last sheet tab while holding down **⇧Shift**. You can select nonadjacent sheets by holding down **Ctrl** while clicking on each sheet. The title bar displays "[Group]" whenever multiple sheets are selected.

Additional Information

You can select all sheets using Select All Sheets from the sheet tab shortcut menu.

Additional Information

The tabs of all sheets appear with a white top, indicating they are selected; the active sheet tab name is bold.

1

● Click on the First Quarter sheet tab, hold down ⬆Shift, and click on the Fourth Quarter tab.

● Change the entry in the Find what box to **total exp**

● Open the Replace tab.

● Type **Total Expenses** in the Replace with box.

● Click **Find Next**.

● Click **Replace All**.

Your screen should be similar to Figure 3.26

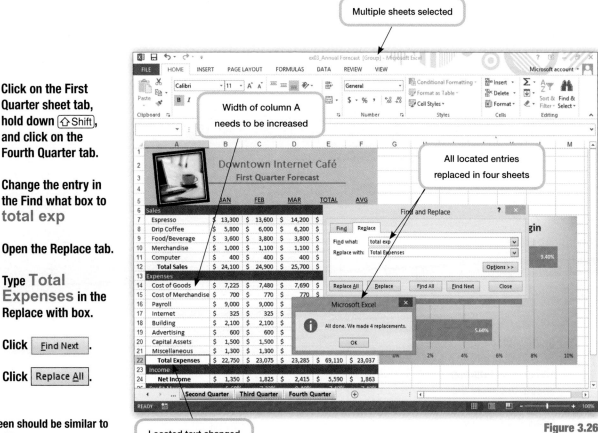

Figure 3.26

Multiple sheets selected

Width of column A needs to be increased

All located entries replaced in four sheets

Located text changed

Another Method

You also can use **Find & Select** /Replace; the keyboard shortcut is Ctrl + H.

Four replacements were made, indicating that the heading was corrected on all four sheets. It is much faster to use Replace All than to confirm each match separately. However, exercise care when using Replace All because the search text you specify might be part of another word and you may accidentally replace text you want to keep.

Now, you also notice that the labels in column A are not fully displayed, so you need to increase the column width. You will expand the group selection to include the Year sheet and adjust the width of column A on all worksheets at the same time.

2

- Click **OK**.

- Click **Close**.

- Scroll the sheet tabs and hold down Ctrl and click on the Year tab to add it to the group.

- AutoFit column A.

Having Trouble?

Double-click on the column border of column A when the mouse pointer is a ↔.

- Right-click on the Second Quarter tab and choose Ungroup Sheets to cancel the group selection and make it the active sheet.

Another Method

You also can click on any unselected sheet tab to cancel a group selection.

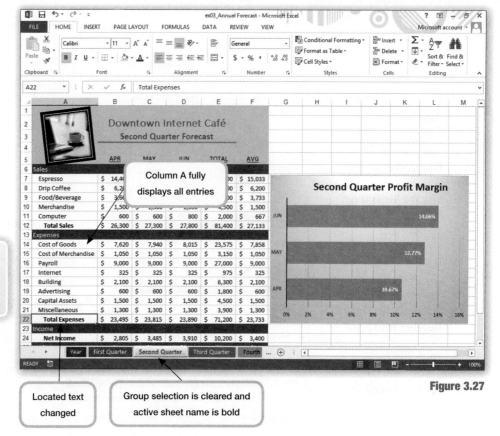

Located text changed

Group selection is cleared and active sheet name is bold

Figure 3.27

You can now see that the width of column A has been adjusted and that the Total Exp label has been replaced with Total Expenses, as it has in all other sheets. When multiple sheets are selected, be careful when making changes, as all selected sheets are affected.

Your screen should be similar to Figure 3.27

Saving to a New Folder

You have made several changes to the workbook, and before continuing, you want to save it. Since the workbook is for projected forecasts, you decide to save it in a separate folder from the rest of the Café's financial workbooks. You will save the file to a new folder named Cafe Forecasts.

1

● Display the Year sheet.

● Open the File tab and choose Save As.

● Change to the location where you save your files.

● Enter **Annual Forecast** as the file name.

● Click ⬚ New folder in the Save As dialog box.

Your screen should be similar to Figure 3.28

Figure 3.28

Having Trouble?

Your Save As dialog box may look slightly different depending upon the version of Windows you are using.

The file list displays a new folder with the default folder name, New folder. You need to replace the default folder name with a descriptive folder name. Then you will open the new folder and save the file in it.

Additional Information

You also can rename an existing folder from the Save As dialog box by choosing Rename from the folder's shortcut menu and entering the new name.

● Type **Cafe Forecasts** in place of New folder.

● Press ⬚ ←Enter to complete the folder name.

● Double-click on the Cafe Forecasts **folder to open it.**

● Click ⬚ Save .

Additional Information

If you are running short on lab time, this is an appropriate place to end this session and begin again at a later time. Open the Annual Forecast workbook and the Year sheet.

The Annual Forecast workbook is saved in the new Cafe Forecasts folder.

Managing Large Worksheets

Now that the Year worksheet is much larger and you cannot see the entire worksheet in the window, you are finding that it takes a lot of time to scroll to different areas within the worksheet. To make managing large worksheets easier, you can zoom a worksheet, split the workbook window, and freeze panes.

1

- **Reduce the zoom percentage to 80%.**

- **Move to B7.**

careful about Another Method box

Another Method

You also can use Zoom in the Zoom group on the View tab or click the zoom percentage in the status bar to open the Zoom dialog box and set the magnification.

Your screen should be similar to Figure 3.29

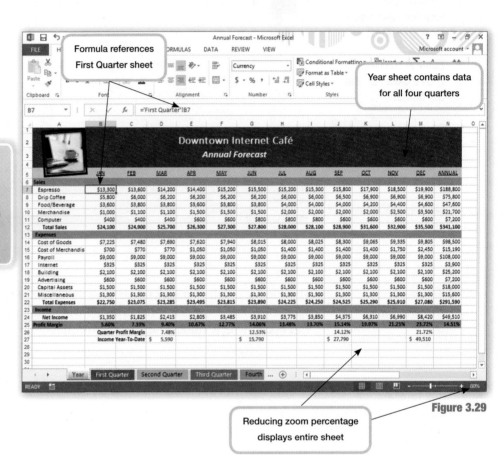

Figure 3.29

You can now see the entire worksheet. Most of the monthly values in the Year sheet, such as cell B7, contain linking formulas that reference the appropriate cells in the appropriate quarter sheets.

GOING TO A SPECIFIC CELL

The only formulas that do not reference cells outside the Year worksheet are those in the Annual column, N. Because you reduced the zoom, it is easy to see the values in column N and to move to a cell by clicking on the cell. However, when the worksheet is at 100 percent zoom, you would need to scroll the worksheet first. You will return the zoom to 100 percent and then use the Go To feature to quickly move to a cell that is not currently visible in the window.

1

● **Return the zoom to 100%.**

Additional Information

Click on the vertical line in the center of the zoom scale to jump to 100%.

● **Click in the Name box and type N16**

Having Trouble?

The Name box is located at the left end of the formula bar.

● **Press** [←Enter].

Another Method

You also can use [Find & Select ▾] and choose

Go To or the keyboard shortcut [Ctrl] + G.

Your screen should be similar to Figure 3.30

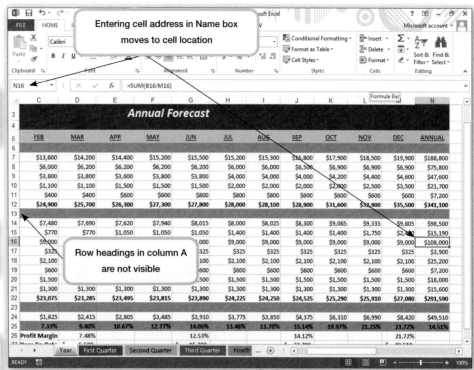

Entering cell address in Name box moves to cell location

Row headings in column A are not visible

Figure 3.30

The cell selector jumps directly to cell N16 in the Annual column. The formula in this cell calculates the total of the values in row 16 and does not reference another sheet. However, it is difficult to know what the numbers represent in this row because the row headings are not visible. For example, is this number the total for the lease expenses, advertising expenses, or miscellaneous expenses? Without scrolling back to see the row headings, it is difficult to know.

SPLITTING WINDOWS

Whenever you scroll a large worksheet, you will find that information you may need to view in one area scrolls out of view as you move to another area. Although you could reduce the zoom percentage to view more of a worksheet in the window, you still may not be able to see the entire worksheet if it is very large. And as you saw, continuing to reduce the zoom makes the worksheet difficult to read. To view different areas of the same worksheet at the same time, you can split the window.

Concept 6 Split Window

The **split window** feature allows you to divide a worksheet window into sections, making it easier to view different parts of the worksheet at the same time. The sections of the window, called **panes**, can consist of any number of columns or rows along the top or left edge of the window. You can divide the worksheet into two panes either horizontally or vertically, or into four panes if you split the window both vertically and horizontally.

Each pane can be scrolled independently to display different areas of the worksheet. When split vertically, the panes scroll together when you scroll vertically, but scroll independently when you scroll horizontally. Horizontal panes scroll together when you scroll horizontally, but independently when you scroll vertically.

Panes are most useful for viewing a worksheet that consists of different areas or sections. Creating panes allows you to display the different sections of the worksheet in separate panes and then to quickly switch between panes to access the data in the different sections without having to repeatedly scroll to the areas.

Two vertical panes

Two horizontal panes

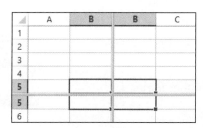

Four panes

Another Method

You also could click on a cell in row 1 of the column or in column A of the row where you want to create the split.

To split the window vertically, select a column to the right of where you want the split. To split it horizontally, select the row below the row where you want it to appear. Then use the ▭ Split command in the View tab. To create a four-way split, select a cell below and to the right of where you want the split to occur.

You will split the window into two vertical panes. This will allow you to view the headings in column A at the same time as you are viewing data in column N.

1

Position the window to display row 4 at the top of the window. Select column E.

Having Trouble?
Click the column letter to select the entire column.

Open the View tab.

Click [Split] in the Window group.

Having Trouble?
If you accidentally create a four-way split, double-click the unwanted split bar to remove it.

Click cell F16 in the right pane.

Your screen should be similar to Figure 3.31

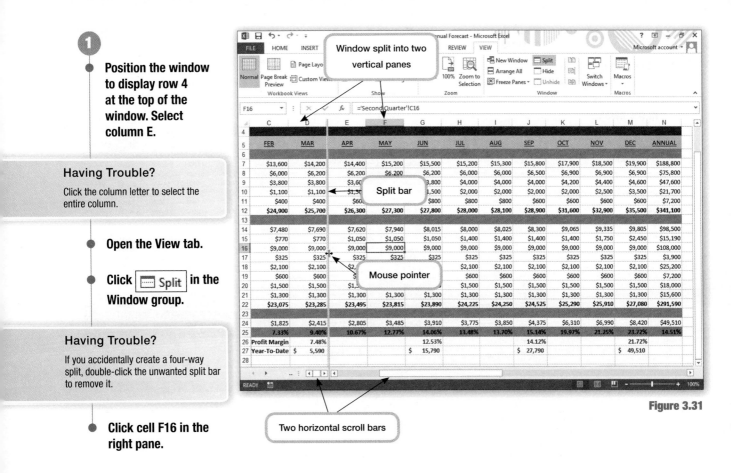

Figure 3.31

Window split into two vertical panes

Split bar

Mouse pointer

Two horizontal scroll bars

There are now two vertical panes with two separate horizontal scroll bars. The highlighted cell selector is visible in the right pane. The left pane also has a cell selector in cell F16, but it is not visible because that area of the worksheet is not displayed in the pane. When the same area of a worksheet is visible in multiple panes, the cell selector in the panes that are not active is highlighted whereas the cell selector in the active pane is clear. The active pane will be affected by your movement horizontally. The cell selector moves in both panes, but only the active pane scrolls.

You will scroll the left pane horizontally to display the month headings in column A.

2

● Click C16 in the left pane to display the active cell selector in the pane.

● Press ← twice.

Your screen should be similar to Figure 3.32

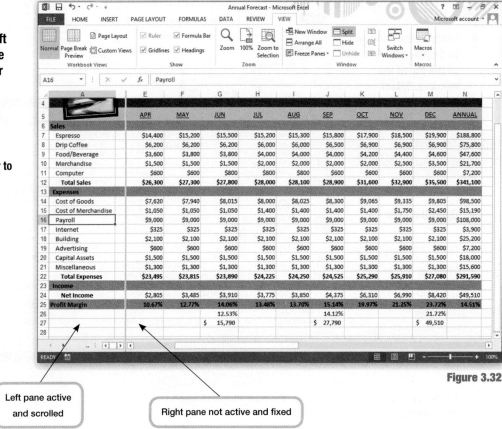

Figure 3.32

Left pane active and scrolled

Right pane not active and fixed

The right pane did not scroll when you moved horizontally through the left pane to display the row headings. The cell selector in the right pane is in the same cell location as in the left pane (A16), although it is not visible. You want to change the location of the split so that you can view an entire quarter in the left pane in order to more easily compare quarters. You can reposition a split bar by dragging it to any location in the worksheet.

3

● Drag the split bar to the right three columns.

Additional Information

The mouse pointer changes to a 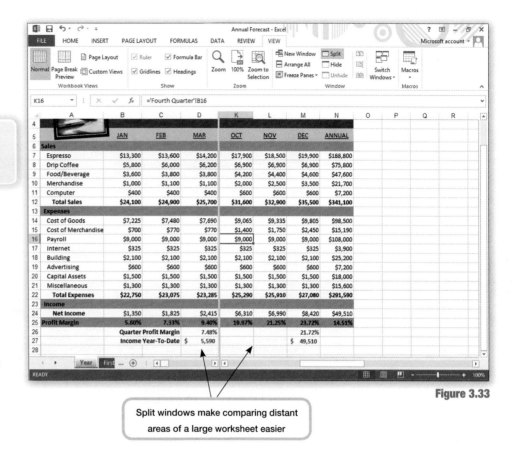 to show you can drag.

● Click cell K16 in the right pane.

● Scroll the right pane until column K appears next to the split bar.

Your screen should be similar to Figure 3.33

Split windows make comparing distant areas of a large worksheet easier

Figure 3.33

Another Method

You also can use [⊡ Split] in the Window group on the View tab to clear the split.

Now you can easily compare the first quarter data to the last-quarter data. As you can see, creating panes is helpful when you want to display and access distant areas of a worksheet quickly. After scrolling the data in the panes to display the appropriate worksheet area, you can then quickly switch between panes to make changes to the data that is visible in the pane. This saves you the time of scrolling to the area each time you want to view it or make changes to it. You will clear the vertical split from the window.

4

- Double-click anywhere on the split bar.

- Scroll to the top of the window.

Your screen should be similar to Figure 3.34

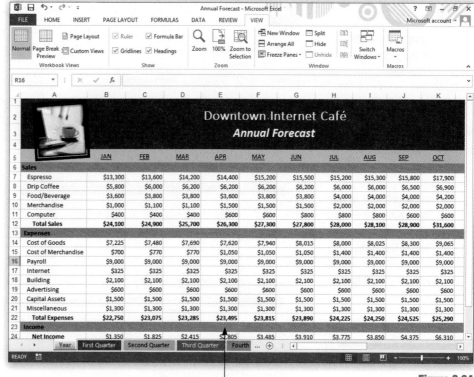

	A	B	C	D	E	F	G	H	I	J	K
5		JAN	FEB	MAR	APR	MAY	JUN	JUL	AUG	SEP	OCT
6	**Sales**										
7	Espresso	$13,300	$13,600	$14,200	$14,400	$15,200	$15,500	$15,200	$15,300	$15,800	$17,900
8	Drip Coffee	$5,800	$6,000	$6,200	$6,200	$6,200	$6,200	$6,000	$6,000	$6,500	$6,900
9	Food/Beverage	$3,600	$3,800	$3,800	$3,600	$3,800	$3,800	$4,000	$4,000	$4,000	$4,200
10	Merchandise	$1,000	$1,100	$1,100	$1,500	$1,500	$1,500	$2,000	$2,000	$2,000	$2,000
11	Computer	$400	$400	$400	$600	$600	$800	$800	$800	$600	$600
12	**Total Sales**	$24,100	$24,900	$25,700	$26,300	$27,300	$27,800	$28,000	$28,100	$28,900	$31,600
13	**Expenses**										
14	Cost of Goods	$7,225	$7,480	$7,690	$7,620	$7,940	$8,015	$8,000	$8,025	$8,300	$9,065
15	Cost of Merchandise	$700	$770	$770	$1,050	$1,050	$1,050	$1,400	$1,400	$1,400	$1,400
16	Payroll	$9,000	$9,000	$9,000	$9,000	$9,000	$9,000	$9,000	$9,000	$9,000	$9,000
17	Internet	$325	$325	$325	$325	$325	$325	$325	$325	$325	$325
18	Building	$2,100	$2,100	$2,100	$2,100	$2,100	$2,100	$2,100	$2,100	$2,100	$2,100
19	Advertising	$600	$600	$600	$600	$600	$600	$600	$600	$600	$600
20	Capital Assets	$1,500	$1,500	$1,500	$1,500	$1,500	$1,500	$1,500	$1,500	$1,500	$1,500
21	Miscellaneous	$1,300	$1,300	$1,300	$1,300	$1,300	$1,300	$1,300	$1,300	$1,300	$1,300
22	**Total Expenses**	$22,750	$23,075	$23,285	$23,495	$23,815	$23,890	$24,225	$24,250	$24,525	$25,290
23	**Income**										
24	**Net Income**	$1,350	$1,825	$2,415	$2,805	$3,485	$3,910	$3,775	$3,850	$4,375	$6,310

Figure 3.34

Double-clicking on split bar removes vertical split

FREEZING PANES

Another way to manage a large worksheet is to freeze panes.

Concept 7 Freeze Panes

Freezing panes prevents the data in the pane from scrolling as you move to different areas in a worksheet. You can freeze rows at the top and columns on the left side of the worksheet only. This feature is most useful when your worksheet is organized using row and column headings. It allows you to keep the titles on the top and left edge of your worksheet in view as you scroll horizontally and vertically through the worksheet data.

You want to keep the month headings in row 5 and the row headings in column A visible in the window at all times while looking at the Income and Profit Margin data beginning in row 22. To do this, you will create four panes with the upper and left panes frozen.

When creating frozen panes, first position the worksheet in the window to display the information you want to appear in the top and left panes. This is because data in the frozen panes cannot be scrolled like data in regular panes. Then move to the location specified in the following table before using the [Freeze Panes ▾] command in the Window group on the View tab to create and freeze panes.

To Create	Cell Selector Location	Example
Two horizontal panes with the top pane frozen	Move to the leftmost column in the window and to the row or rows that you want to keep visible when you scroll.	
		Top pane frozen
Two vertical panes with the left pane frozen	Move to the top row of the window and to the column to or columns that you want to keep visible when you scroll.	
		Left pane frozen
Four panes with the top and left panes frozen	Move to the cell below and to the right of the rows and columns that you want to keep visible when you scroll.	
		Top and left panes frozen

You want to split the window into four panes with the month column headings at the top of the window and the row headings in column A at the left side of the window.

1

Move to B6.

Click

![Freeze Panes ▾] in
the Window group
and choose Freeze
Panes.

Your screen should be similar to
Figure 3.35

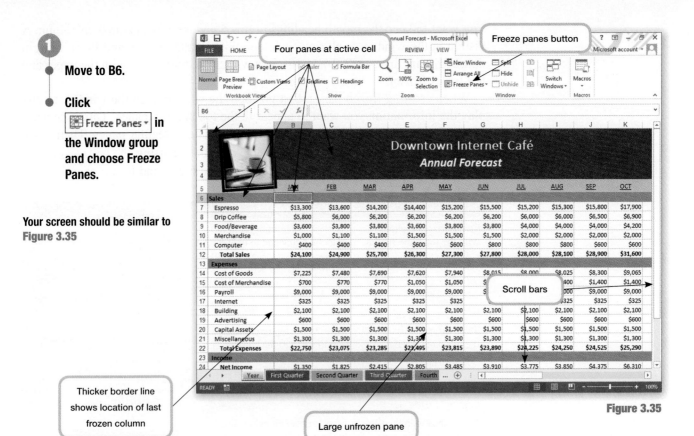

Four panes at active cell

Freeze panes button

Scroll bars

Thicker border line
shows location of last
frozen column

Large unfrozen pane

Figure 3.35

The window is divided into four panes at the cell selector location. A slightly
thicker border line appears below the last frozen row and to the right of the last
frozen column. Only one set of scroll bars is displayed because the only pane that
can be scrolled is the larger lower-right pane. You can move the cell selector into a
frozen pane, but the data in the frozen panes will not scroll. As you move the cell
selector within the worksheet it moves from one pane to another over the pane
divider, making it unnecessary to click on a pane to make it active before moving
the cell selector into that pane.

Because Evan has asked you to adjust the Profit Margin values, you want to
view this area of the worksheet only.

2

- Use the vertical scroll bar to scroll the window until row 25 is below row 5.

- Move to cell G25.

Your screen should be similar to Figure 3.36

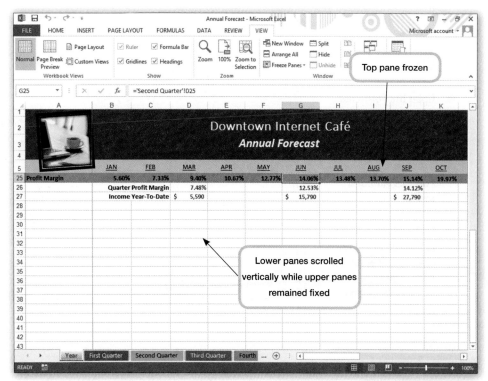

Figure 3.36

Now the Income and Profit Margin data are displayed immediately below the month headings in row 5. The data in rows 6 through 24 is no longer visible, allowing you to concentrate on this area of the worksheet.

WATCHING CELLS

While using a workbook with large worksheets and/or multiple sheets, you may want to keep an eye on how changes you make to values in one area affect cells in another. For example, if you change a value in one sheet that is referenced in a formula in another sheet, you can view the effect on the calculated value using the Watch Window toolbar.

You will be changing values in the Second Quarter sheet next and want to be able to see the effect on the second-quarter profit margin (G26) and annual profit margin (N25) in the Year sheet at the same time.

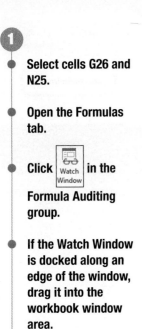

1

- Select cells G26 and N25.

- Open the Formulas tab.

- Click in the Formula Auditing group.

- If the Watch Window is docked along an edge of the window, drag it into the workbook window area.

- Click from the Watch Window toolbar.

Your screen should be similar to Figure 3.37

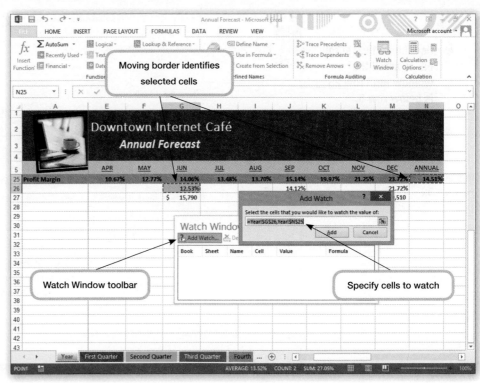

Figure 3.37

The Add Watch dialog box is used to specify the cells you want to see in the Watch Window list. The currently selected cells are identified with a moving border. You will add these cells to the Watch Window list.

2

- Click [Add].

- If necessary, move the Watch Window to the upper-right corner of the worksheet window below the column headings.

Your screen should be similar to Figure 3.38

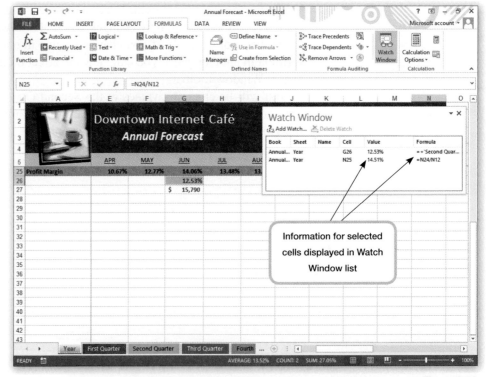

Figure 3.38

The values in the selected cells as well as the formula and location information are displayed in the Watch Window list. The Watch Window will remain open on top of the worksheet as you move from one sheet to another.

Forecasting Values

Evan has asked you to adjust the forecast for the second quarter to show a profit margin of at least 15 percent for each month. After some consideration, you decide you can most easily reduce monthly payroll expenses by carefully scheduling the hours employees work during these three months. Reducing the monthly expense will increase the profit margin for the quarter. You want to find out what the maximum payroll value you can spend during that period is for each month to accomplish this goal. The process of evaluating what effect changing the payroll expenses will have on the profit margin is called what-if analysis.

Concept 8 What-If Analysis

What-if analysis is a technique used to evaluate the effects of changing selected factors in a worksheet. This technique is a common accounting function that has been made much easier with the introduction of spreadsheet programs. By substituting different values in cells that are referenced by formulas, you can quickly see the effect of the changes when the formulas are recalculated.

You can perform what-if analysis by manually substituting values or by using one of the what-if analysis tools included with Excel.

PERFORMING WHAT-IF ANALYSIS MANUALLY

To do this, you will enter different payroll expense values for each month and see what the effect is on that month's profit margin. You will adjust the April payroll value first.

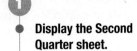

- Display the Second Quarter sheet.

- Type **7000** in cell B16.

- Press ←Enter.

- Scroll the window to see row 25.

Your screen should be similar to Figure 3.39

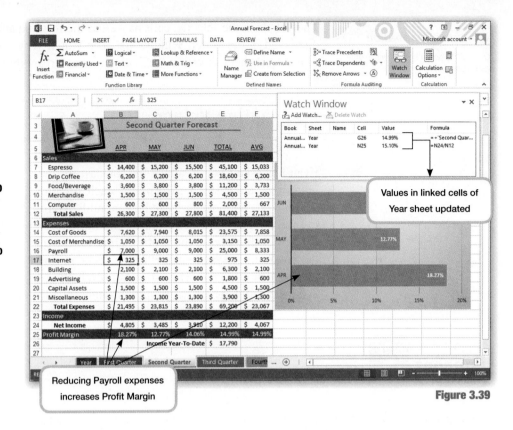

Figure 3.39

Now by looking in cell B25, you can see that decreasing the payroll expenses has increased the profit margin for the month to 18.27 percent. This is more than you need. Also notice the chart has changed to reflect the change in April's profit margin. The Watch Window shows that the values in the two linked cells in the Year sheet were updated accordingly.

You will continue to enter payroll values until the profit margin reaches the goal.

2

- Type **7900** in cell B16.

- Click ✓ Enter.

- Type **7850** in cell B16.

- Click ✓ Enter.

- Type **7860** in cell B16.

- Click ✓ Enter.

- Save the workbook.

Your screen should be similar to Figure 3.40

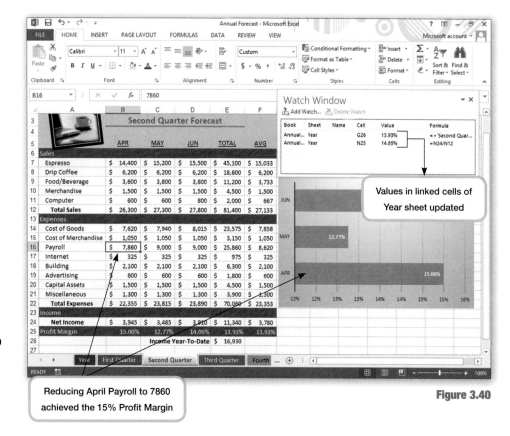

Values in linked cells of Year sheet updated

Reducing April Payroll to 7860 achieved the 15% Profit Margin

Figure 3.40

That's it! Reducing the payroll value from 9000 to 7860 will achieve the 15 percent profit margin goal for the month. Also notice that the column chart reflects the change in the April profit margin.

USING GOAL SEEK

It usually takes several tries to find the appropriate value when manually performing what-if analysis. A quicker way is to use the what-if analysis Goal Seek tool provided with Excel.

Concept ⑨ Goal Seek

The **Goal Seek** tool is used to find the value needed in one cell to attain a result you want in another cell. Goal Seek varies the value in the cell you specify until a formula that is dependent on that cell returns the desired result. The value of only one cell can be changed.

You will use this method to find the payroll value for May that will produce a 15 percent profit margin for that month. The current profit margin value is 12.77 percent in cell C25.

1

● Move to C25.

● Open the Data tab.

● Click
[⊞? What-If Analysis ▼]
in the Data Tools group.

● Choose Goal Seek.

Your screen should be similar to Figure 3.41

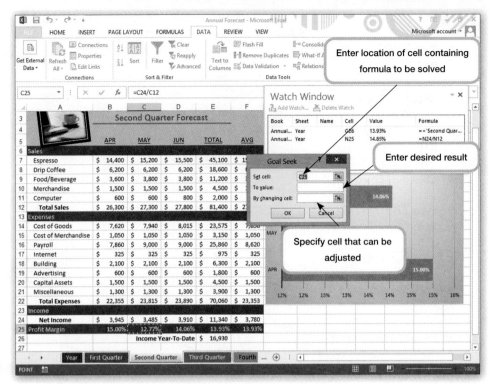

Figure 3.41

In the Goal Seek dialog box, you need to specify the location of the cell containing the formula to be solved, the desired calculated value, and the cell containing the number that can be adjusted to achieve the result. You want the formula in cell C25 to calculate a result of 15 percent by changing the payroll number in cell C16. The Set cell text box correctly displays the current cell as the location of the formula to be solved. You will enter the information needed in the Goal Seek dialog box.

2

● Click in the To value text box and enter 15.00%

● Click in the By changing cell text box and then click on cell C16 in the worksheet to enter the cell reference.

● Click [OK].

Your screen should be similar to Figure 3.42

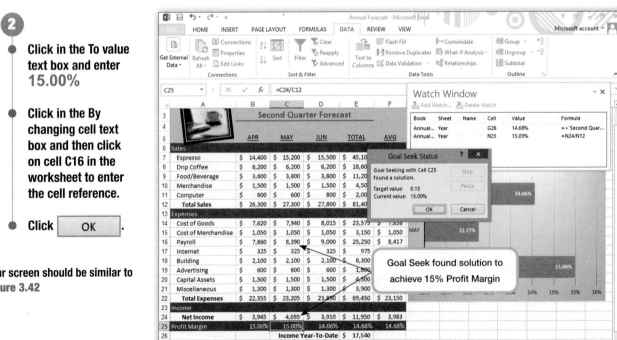

Figure 3.42

The Goal Seek dialog box tells you it found a solution that will achieve the 15 percent profit margin. The payroll value of 8390 that will achieve the desired result has been temporarily entered in the worksheet. You can reject the solution and restore the original value by choosing [Cancel]. In this case, however, you want to accept the solution.

Click [OK].

Your screen should be similar to Figure 3.43

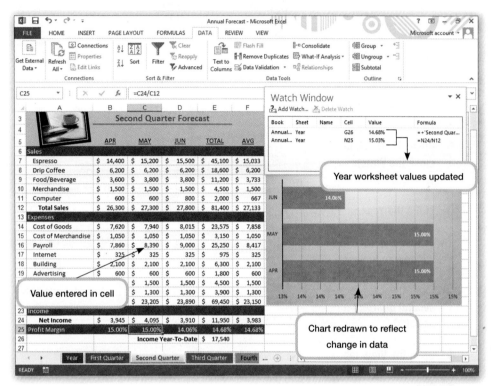

Figure 3.43

The payroll value is permanently updated and the chart redrawn to reflect the change in the May profit margin. Finally, you will adjust the June payroll value. When you are finished, you will close the Watch Window and unfreeze the Year sheet window.

4

- In a similar manner, use Goal Seek to adjust the June payroll value to achieve a 15% profit margin.

- Select both watch cell entries in the Watch Window and click ⌧ **Delete Watch**.

- Click ☒ Close to close the Watch Window.

- Make the Year sheet active and, if necessary, scroll the window to further verify that the profit margin values for the second quarter were updated.

- Open the View tab.

- Click 🔲 Freeze Panes ▾ in the Window group and choose Unfreeze Panes.

- Save the workbook file again.

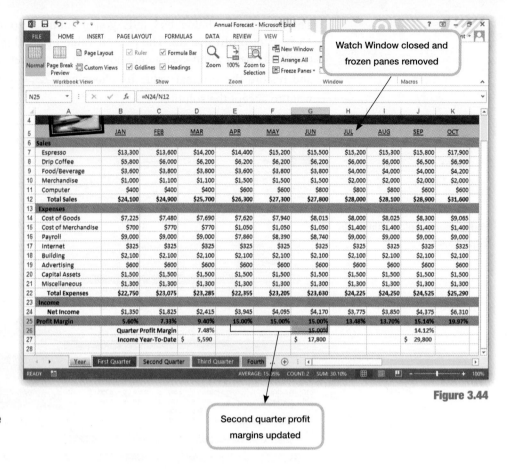

Figure 3.44

The second-quarter values are now at the 15 percent profit margin objective.

Your screen should be similar to Figure 3.44

Using Conditional Formatting

Next, you want to highlight or emphasize certain values in the worksheet to help visualize the data and quickly analyze information in a worksheet. To do this, you can use conditional formatting.

Concept 10 Conditional Formatting

Conditional formatting changes the appearance of a range of cells based on a condition that you specify. If the cells in the range meet the conditions (the condition is true), they are formatted. If they do not meet the conditions (the condition is false), they remain unformatted. There are several different ways you can apply conditional formatting as described in the following table.

Conditional Formatting	Description
Highlight Cells Rules	Highlights cells based on rules you specify, such as greater than or less than, between, or equal to. It also can highlight cells that contain certain text, dates, and duplicate values.
Top/Bottom Rules	Highlights the highest and lowest values in a range by number, percentage, or average based on a cutoff value that you specify.
Data Bars	Displays a color bar in a cell to help you see the value of a cell relative to other cells. The length of the bar represents the value in the cell. A longer bar is a higher value and a shorter bar, a lower value.
Color Scales	Applies a two- or three-color graduated scale to compare values in a range. A two-color scale uses two different colors to represent high or low values and a three-color scale uses three colors to represent high, mid, and low values.
Icon Sets	Displays different color icons in the cell to classify data into three to five categories. Each icon represents a range of values.

CREATING CELL RULES

You will use the cell rules conditional formatting to highlight the payroll values that are less than $9,000 a month.

1

- Select cells B16 through M16.

- Open the Home tab.

- Click
  Conditional Formatting ▾
  in the Styles group.

- Select Highlight Cells Rules.

- Choose Less Than.

Your screen should be similar to Figure 3.45

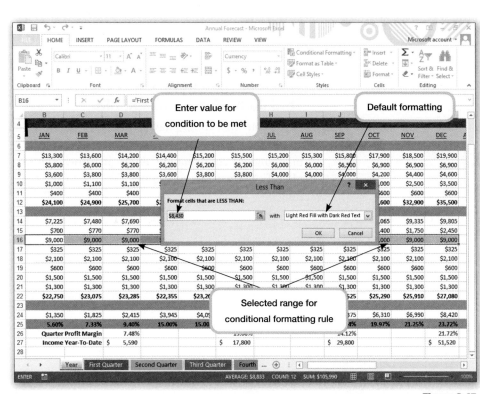

Figure 3.45

In the Less Than dialog box, you enter the value that will be used to determine which cells to highlight. In this case, you will enter the value 9000 so that all values below this amount in the selected range will be highlighted. It also lets you select the formatting to apply to those cells meeting the condition. The default formatting, a light red fill with dark red text, is acceptable.

- Type **9000** in the Less Than box.

- Click **OK**.

- Click cell H16 to clear the selection.

Your screen should be similar to Figure 3.46

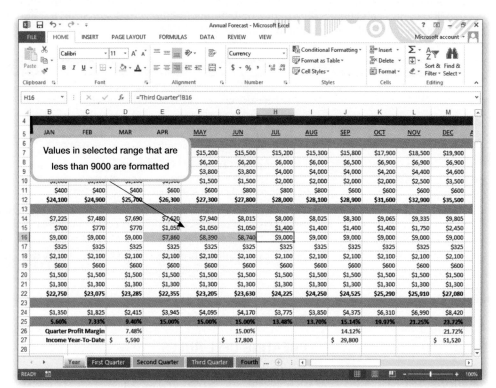

Figure 3.46

Only those cells in the Payroll row whose value is less than 9,000 are formatted using the light-red highlight and dark-red font color.

APPLYING TOP/BOTTOM RULES, DATA BARS, COLOR SCALES, AND ICON SETS CONDITIONAL FORMATTING

Next, you want to emphasize the Net Income values using the Top/Bottom Rules conditional formatting. This formatting identifies the highest and lowest values in a range of cells that are above or below a cutoff value you specify. You want to identify the net income values that are in the top 50 percent of the values in the range.

1

- Select the Net Income data in cells B24 through M24.

- Click 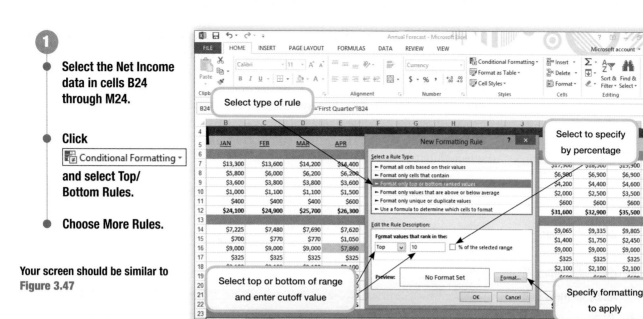 Conditional Formatting ▼ and select Top/ Bottom Rules.

- Choose More Rules.

Your screen should be similar to Figure 3.47

Figure 3.47

In the New Formatting Rule dialog box, you select the type of rule to apply and the rule conditions. The current type of rule is already correctly specified. In the Edit the Rule Description you will specify to format values that are in the top 50 percent of values in the range using red font color.

2

- Enter 50 in the value text box.

- Click in the check box for % of the selected range to select it.

- Click Format... and choose red for the font color.

- Click OK twice to exit the dialog boxes.

Your screen should be similar to Figure 3.48

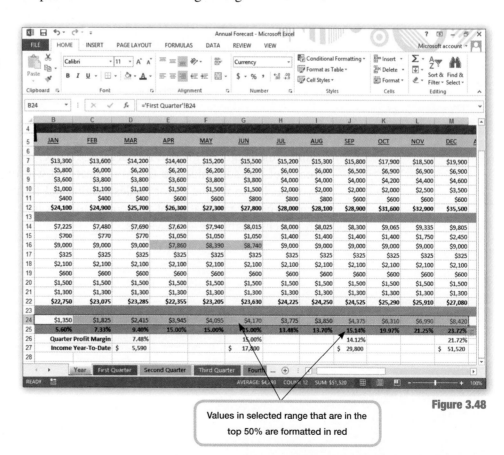

Figure 3.48

Values in selected range that are in the top 50% are formatted in red

The net income values that are in the top 50 percent of values in the selection are now formatted in red. Although this is interesting, it does not really provide much additional information. Instead, you decide to undo this formatting and see if applying data bars conditional formatting to the profit margin values is more informative. This option displays colored bars similar to a bar chart within each cell to show the relative values of the cell. This time, however, you will use the Quick Analysis tool to suggest several likely conditional formatting options for the selected data.

- Click ⟲ Undo.

- Click 📋 Quick Analysis (near cell M25).

- Choose Data Bars from the Formatting pane.

Your screen should be similar to Figure 3.49

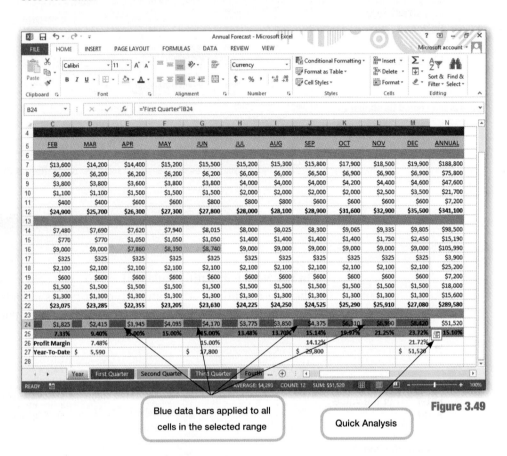

Blue data bars applied to all cells in the selected range

Quick Analysis

Figure 3.49

Color bars appear in each cell containing a number. The size of the number determines the length of the bar; the larger the value, the longer the bar. Again, you do not feel this adds much to the worksheet and will undo this formatting. Instead, you decide to try the Color Scales conditional formatting, which applies a scale consisting of a gradation of two colors to cells in a range. The shade of the color represents higher or lower values.

4 ● Click ↶ Undo.

● Click 📝 Quick Analysis and choose [Color Scale].

● Move to cell B23.

Your screen should be similar to Figure 3.50

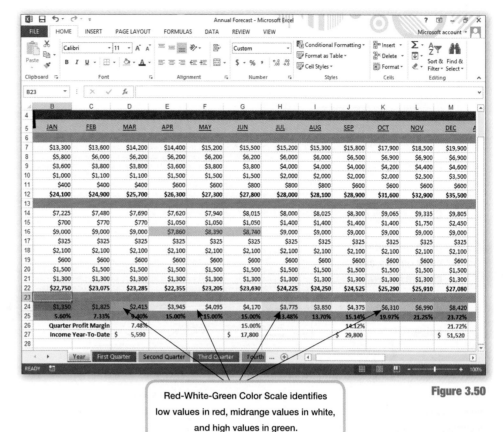

Red-White-Green Color Scale identifies low values in red, midrange values in white, and high values in green.

Figure 3.50

This formatting applies a color scale to the data in those cells, with the darkest red identifying the lowest values and the darkest green identifying the highest values. This is a red-white-green scale, so the middle values appear to be unshaded.

You will change the color scale color selection to another to show color in all cells in the range.

5

- Select B24 through M24.

- Click 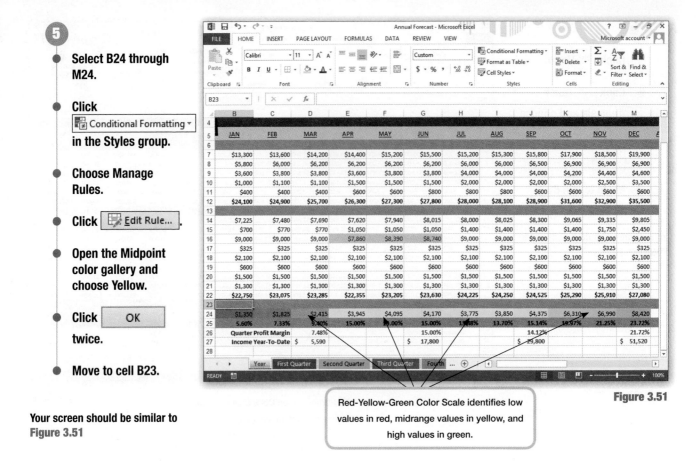 Conditional Formatting ▾ in the Styles group.

- Choose Manage Rules.

- Click Edit Rule... .

- Open the Midpoint color gallery and choose Yellow.

- Click OK twice.

- Move to cell B23.

Your screen should be similar to Figure 3.51

> Red-Yellow-Green Color Scale identifies low values in red, midrange values in yellow, and high values in green.

Figure 3.51

The color scale now shows yellow highlight identifying the middle values in the range. Next, you decide to add icons as a visual indicator to the profit margin values.

6

- Select cells B25 through M25.

- Click

  🔲 Conditional Formatting ▾.

- Select Icon Sets and point to the different icon sets to see the live preview.

- Choose 3 Traffic Lights (Rimmed) in the Shapes group.

Additional Information

The Quick Analysis tool applies the 3 Arrows (colored) icon set.

Your screen should be similar to Figure 3.52

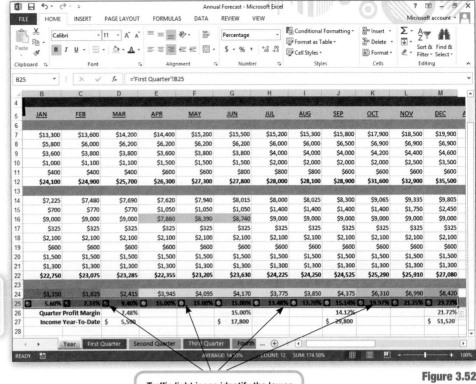

Traffic light icons identify the lower third in red, the middle third in yellow, and the upper third in green.

Figure 3.52

The icons give a better indication of which months had a higher or lower profit margin. Red shows where the profit margin value was in the lower third, yellow indicates a profit margin in the middle third, and green shows values in the upper third. These icons reflect the same trends as the color scale used in the net income row of data.

CLEARING CONDITIONAL FORMATTING

Because the icon set formatting really duplicates the information provided by the conditional formatting in the Net Income row, you decide to just keep the Profit Margin formatting. This time you cannot use Undo to remove the conditional formatting from the Net Income row because it also would remove the formatting from the Profit Margin row. To remove conditional formatting, you will need to clear the rules from the range.

● Select B24 through M24.

● Click Quick

Analysis and choose

[Clear Format]

Another Method

You also can click [Conditional Formatting ▾], select Clear Rules, and choose Clear Rules from Selected Cells.

Your screen should be similar to Figure 3.53

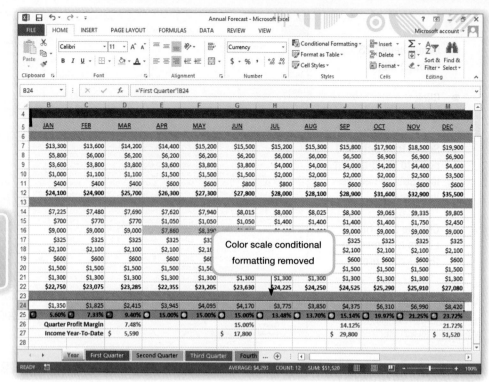

Figure 3.53

The conditional formatting rules for the specified range were cleared and the formatting removed.

Using Sparklines

Although the icon set conditional formatting in the profit margin row identifies variances in a range, the trend is not entirely obvious. To show the data trends more clearly, you decide to create a sparkline. A **sparkline** is a tiny chart of worksheet data contained in the background of a single cell. Generally, a sparkline is positioned close to the data it represents, to have the greatest impact.

CREATING A SPARKLINE

You want to display the sparkline in cell O25, to the right of the profit margin row.

1
- Select cells B25 through M25.
- Open the Insert tab.
- Click Line in the Sparklines group.
- Enter O25 as the cell location to display the chart.
- Click **OK**.
- Increase the width of column O to 30, and the height of row 25 to 50.

Your screen should be similar to Figure 3.54

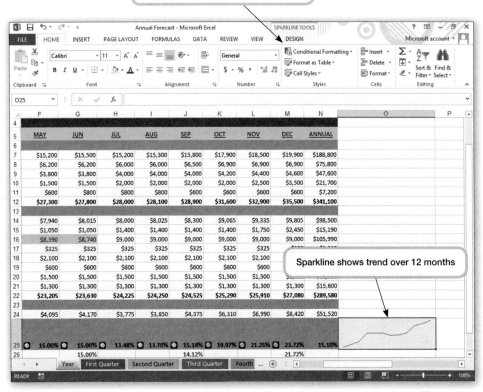

Figure 3.54

Another Method

The Quick Analysis tool will insert a sparkline chart in the cell immediately to the right of the selected range.

A simple line chart of the profit margin values clearly shows the increase in profit margin over the year.

ENHANCING A SPARKLINE

Next you want to improve the appearance of the sparkline by adding data markers and color. Then you will enter a descriptive label in the cell to clarify the meaning of the sparkline.

1

- Select cell O25 and, if necessary, open the Sparkline Tools Design tab.

- Choose Markers in the Show group.

- Open the Style gallery and choose Sparkline Style Dark #1.

- Open the Home tab, open the [icon] Fill Color gallery, and choose Brown, Accent 3, Lighter 60%.

- Type **Monthly Profit Margin** and press [⏎Enter].

Having Trouble?

The line chart will not display as you enter the text.

- Top-align the entry in cell O25.

- Save the workbook.

Your screen should be similar to Figure 3.55

Additional Information

To delete a sparkline, select the cell containing the sparkline and choose [✎ Clear ▾] in the Group group of the Sparkline Tools Design tab.

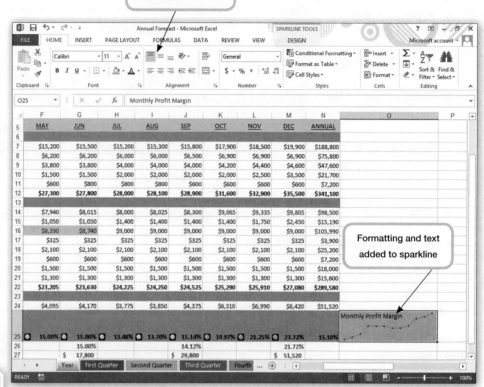

Top aligns cell entry

Formatting and text added to sparkline

Monthly Profit Margin

Figure 3.55

The addition of the sparkline helps clarify the profit margin trend for the year. Just like a chart, if the data in a referenced cell changes, the sparkline will automatically update to reflect the change.

Customizing Print Settings

Now you are ready to print the workbook. Just because your worksheet looks great on the screen, this does not mean it will look good when printed. Many times you will want to change the default print and layout settings to improve the appearance of the output. Customizing the print settings by controlling page breaks, changing the orientation of the page, centering the worksheet on the page, hiding gridlines, and adding custom header and footer information are just a few of the ways you can make your printed output look more professional.

Relative Adressing/Absolut?
*(1 + D$11) * C5*

CONTROLLING PAGE BREAKS

First you want to preview the Year sheet.

1

- Open the File tab and choose Print.

- Display page 2 of the worksheet.

Your screen should be similar to Figure 3.56

Second page displays last six months and Annual total

Displays previous page

Displays next page

Figure 3.56

The first page of the Year worksheet displays the first six months, and the second page, the remaining months and the annual total. The sparkline is by itself on a third page. Although you could change the orientation to landscape and use the Fit To feature to compress the worksheet to a single page, this would make the data small and difficult to read. Instead, you decide to fit the printout on two pages, with the sparkline on the second page.

To do this, you will change the location of the **page break**, the place where one printed page ends and another starts. Excel inserts automatic page breaks based on the paper size, margin settings, and orientation when the worksheet exceeds the width of a page. You can change the location of the automatic page break by inserting a manual page break location. To help you do this, Page Break Preview is used to adjust the location of page breaks.

2

- Close the File tab and open the View tab.

- Click in the Workbook Views group.

Another Method

You also could click 🔲 in the status bar to change to Page Break Preview.

- If a Welcome to Page Break Preview box appears, click

  [OK].

- Change the zoom to 80% and scroll the window horizontally to see the entire sheet.

Your screen should be similar to Figure 3.57

Additional Information

You can work in Page Break Preview just like in Normal view.

Another Method

You also can insert page breaks by moving to the column location in the worksheet where you want the break inserted and using /Insert Page Break in the Page Layout tab.

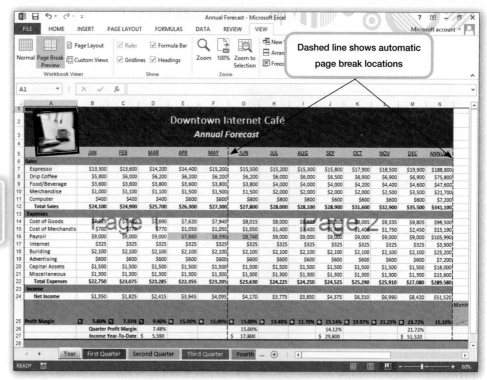

Figure 3.57

Now you can easily see the page break locations. The dashed line indicates the location of the automatic page breaks. You can change the location by dragging the page break line. When you move an automatic page break location to another location, the page break line changes to a solid line, indicating it is a manual page break. To include the sparkline on page 2, you will move the second page break to the right of column O.

Additionally, you realize that the worksheet title will be split between the two pages. You will fix the title by unmerging the cells, moving the title to the left on page 1, and copying the title to page 2.

3

- Point to the page break line after column N, and drag it to the right of column O.

- In a similar manner, drag the first page break line to after the June column.

- Select the two merged cells containing the titles.

- Open the Home tab.

- Open the 🔲 ▾ Merge & Center drop-down menu and choose Unmerge Cells.

- Copy the contents of D2 through D3 to K2 through K3.

- Press [Esc] to clear the selection and move to cell K4.

Your screen should be similar to Figure 3.58

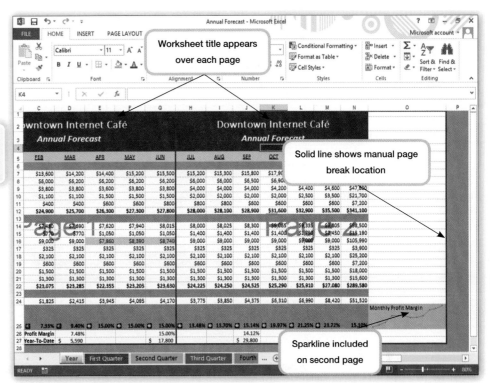

Figure 3.58

The entire worksheet will now print on two pages. Unmerging the cells split the merged cell into its original cells and moved the contents into the upper-left cell of the range of split cells. The center formatting was not removed. Now both pages of the worksheet printout will display a worksheet title.

ADDING A CUSTOM HEADER AND FOOTER

You also would like to add a custom header to this worksheet. You will do this in Page Layout view because you can add the header simply by clicking on the header area of the page and typing the header text.

1

● **Switch to Page Layout view at 70% zoom.**

● **Click on the left end of the header area of page 1.**

Your screen should be similar to Figure 3.59

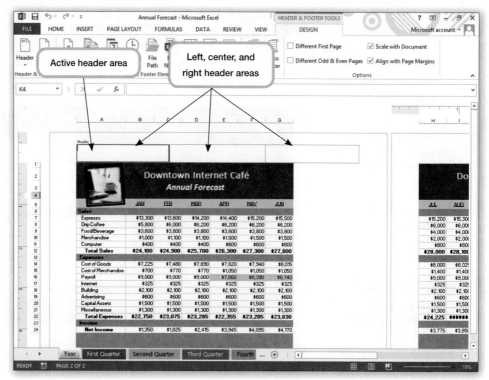

Figure 3.59

The header area is divided into three sections. The left section text box will display the text you enter aligned with the left margin; the center section will center the text; and the right section will right-align the text. You want to enter your name in the left section, class in the center, and the date in the right section. You will enter your name and class information by typing it directly in the box. You will enter the current date using the Current Date feature on the Header & Footer Tools Design tab.

2

● Type **Created by Your Name**

● Press Tab.

Another Method

You also could click on the section to move to it.

● Enter the name of your class and the section or time.

● Press Tab.

● Click [Current Date icon] in the **Header & Footer Elements group.**

Your screen should be similar to Figure 3.60

Additional Information

Be careful when making changes to multiple sheets as these changes may replace data on other sheets.

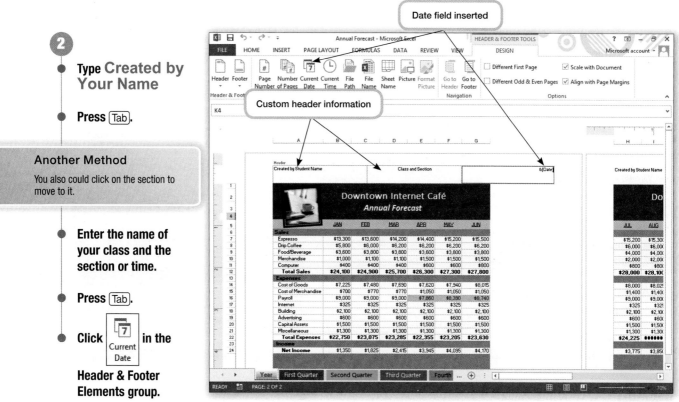

Figure 3.60

The Date field is entered in the header. It will enter the current date whenever the worksheet is opened. The actual date will display when you leave the header area.

Next, you want to add footers to the quarter sheets. It is faster to add the footer to all sheets at the same time. If you make changes to the active sheet when multiple sheets are selected, the changes are made to all sheets in the group.

- Display the First Quarter sheet.

- Select the four quarter sheets to group them.

Having Trouble?

Click the First Quarter sheet tab, hold down Ctrl and click the Fourth Quarter sheet tab.

- Open the Page Layout tab.

- Open the Page Setup dialog box.

- Open the Header/ Footer tab.

- Click **Custom Footer...**.

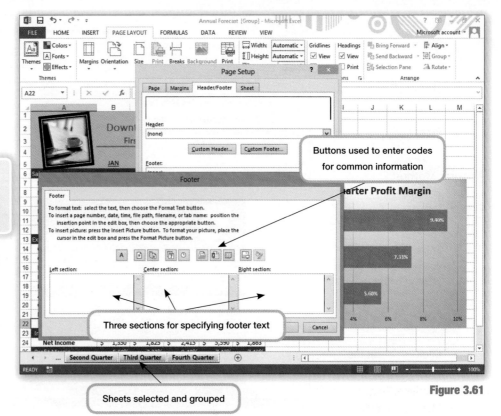

Figure 3.61

Your screen should be similar to Figure 3.61

Additional Information

The quarter sheets are displayed in Normal view. The view you are using applies only to the individual sheet.

Just like in Page Layout view, the footer area consists of three sections. The buttons above the section boxes are used to enter the codes for common header and footer information. The cursor is currently positioned in the Left section text box.

You will enter your name in the left section, the file name in the middle section, and the date in the right section.

4

● Type **your name**

● Press [Tab].

● Click **Insert File Name.**

● Press [Tab].

● Click **Insert Date.**

Your screen should be similar to Figure 3.62

Figure 3.62

Next you will change the orientation of the four sheets to landscape, change the margins to 0.5 inch, and scale the sheets to fit the page. Then you want to make one final check to see how the worksheets will look before printing the workbook.

5

- Click OK .

- **Open the Page tab and choose Landscape.**

- **Choose Fit to, to scale the sheets to one page.**

- **Open the Margins tab and reduce the left and right margins to 0.5 inch.**

Having Trouble?

Use the scroll buttons to increase or decrease the margin size.

- Click Print Preview .

- **Look at the four sheets to confirm that the footer and orientation changes were added to all the quarter sheets.**

Your screen should be similar to Figure 3.63

Additional Information

You also could drag the right or left border of the margin area in the ruler while in Page Layout view to adjust the size of the margins.

Figure 3.63

The footer as you entered it appears on all selected worksheets and the page layout changes were made as well.

PRINTING SELECTED SHEETS

You want to print the Year and Second Quarter worksheets only. Because the annual worksheet is large, you also feel the worksheet may be easier to read if the row and column gridlines were printed. Although gridlines are displayed in Page Layout view and Normal view, they do not print unless you turn on this feature.

1

● Close the File tab and open the Home tab.

● Right-click on a sheet tab and choose Ungroup Sheets.

● Make the Year sheet active.

● Open the Page Layout tab and choose Print in the Gridlines section of the Sheet Options group.

● Save the workbook again.

● Hold down ⌨Ctrl and click the Second Quarter sheet tab to add it to the selection of sheets to print.

● Open the File tab and choose Print.

● Preview the three pages and then print the worksheets.

Another Method

You also can print gridlines by choosing Gridlines from the Page Setup dialog box.

Your printed output should look like that shown in the Case Study at the beginning of the lab.

PRINTING SELECTED AREAS

You are finished printing the Year and Second Quarter sheets and you have the information Evan requested. However, you think Evan also would like a printout of the First Quarter worksheet without the chart displayed. To print a selected area, you first select the cell range that you want to print.

1

● If necessary, close the File tab.

● Make the First Quarter sheet active.

● Select cells A1 through F26.

● Open the Page Layout tab.

● Click [Print Area] in the Page Setup group and choose Set Print Area.

Your screen should be similar to Figure 3.64

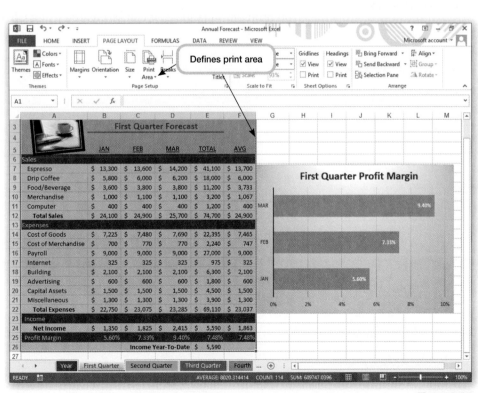

Figure 3.64

The area you selected, called the **print area**, is surrounded with a heavy line that identifies the area.

2

- **Open the File tab and choose Print.**

- **Change the orientation to Portrait Orientation.**

Your screen should be similar to Figure 3.65

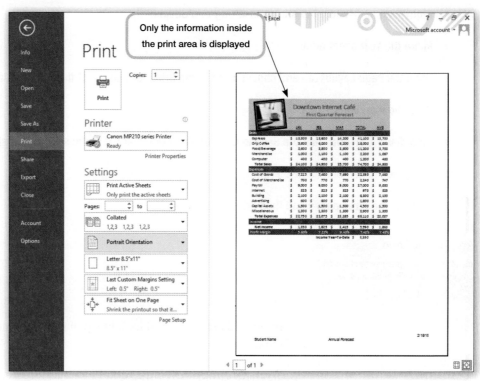

Figure 3.65

The Preview displays only the information contained in the defined print area. The print area is saved with the worksheet and will be used automatically whenever you print the worksheet. It can be cleared using Clear Print Area in the menu.

3

- If necessary, specify any printer settings.

- Print the worksheet.

- Change the Year sheet to Normal view and move to cell A6 in the First Quarter sheet.

- Close and save the workbook and exit Excel.

FOCUS ON CAREERS

EXPLORE YOUR CAREER OPTIONS

Medical Sales Account Manager

Medical sales account managers visit doctors and clinics to promote the pharmaceuticals and supplies made by the company they represent. The account managers usually specialize in a few pharmaceuticals or products so that they can help the doctor understand the benefits and risks associated with their products. Medical sales account managers must keep careful and complete records of the samples they have in inventory and what they have delivered to doctors. An Excel workbook is a useful tool to keep track of the many doctors and the deliveries made. A career as a medical sales account manager can start with a salary of $35,000 and go up to over $90,000 plus car and travel benefits.

Absolute Reference (EX3.11)

An absolute reference is a cell or range reference in a formula whose location does not change when the formula is copied.

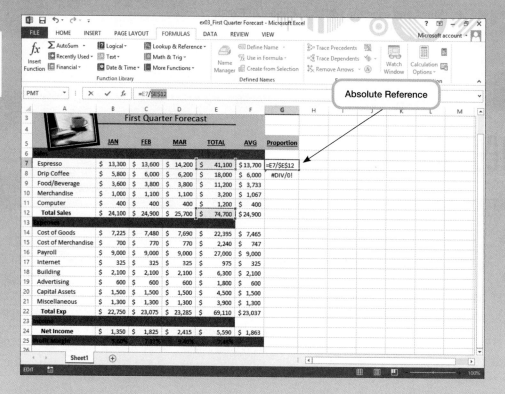

Sheet Name (EX3.16)

Each sheet in a workbook can be assigned a descriptive sheet name to help identify the contents of the sheet.

AutoFill (EX3.19)

The AutoFill feature makes entering a series of numbers, numbers and text combinations, dates, or time periods easier by logically repeating and extending the series. AutoFill recognizes trends and automatically extends data and alphanumeric headings as far as you specify.

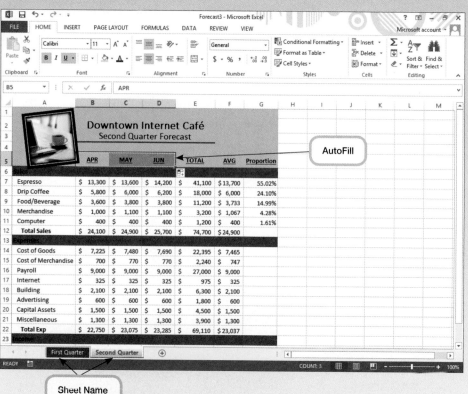

Sheet and 3-D References (EX3.21)

Sheet and 3-D references in formulas are used to refer to data from multiple sheets and to calculate new values based on this data.

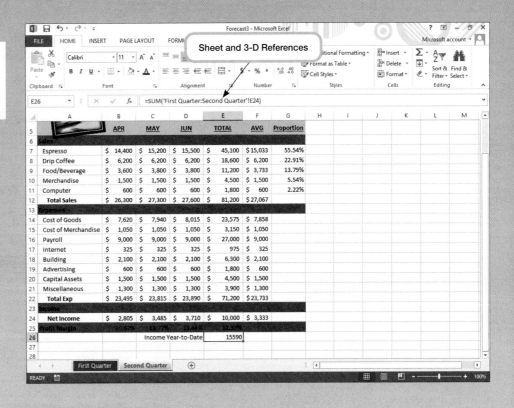

Find and Replace (EX3.28)

The Find and Replace feature helps you quickly find specific information and automatically replace it with new information.

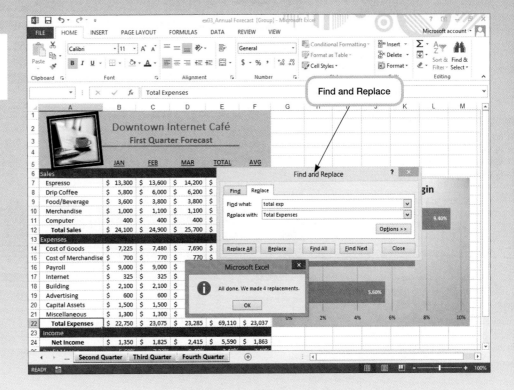

Split Window (EX3.36)

The split window feature allows you to divide a worksheet window into sections, making it easier to view different parts of the worksheet at the same time.

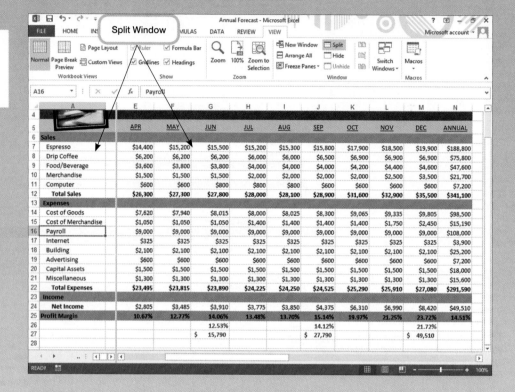

Freeze Panes (EX3.40)

Freezing panes prevents the data in the pane from scrolling as you move to different areas in a worksheet.

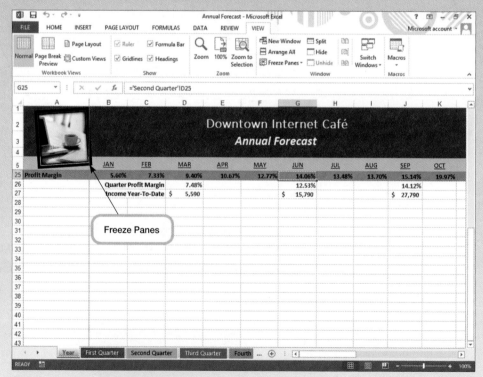

What-If Analysis (EX3.45)

What-if analysis is a technique used to evaluate the effects of changing selected factors in a worksheet.

Goal Seek (EX3.47)

The Goal Seek tool is used to find the value needed in one cell to attain a result you want in another cell.

Conditional Formatting (EX3.51)

Conditional formatting changes the appearance of a range of cells based on a condition that you specify.

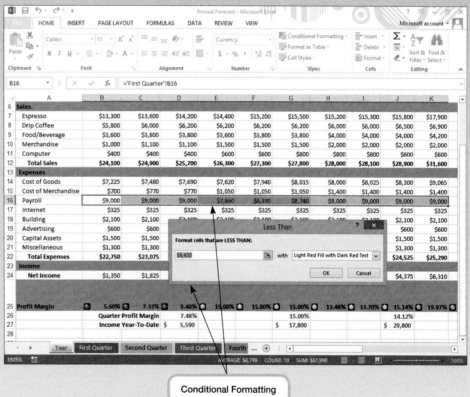

KEY TERMS

3-D reference EX3.21
absolute reference EX3.11
AutoFill EX3.19
conditional formatting EX3.51
Find and Replace EX3.28
freeze panes EX3.40
Goal Seek EX3.47
mixed reference EX3.11

page break EX3.61
pane EX3.36
print area EX3.70
sheet name EX3.16
sheet reference EX3.21
sparkline EX3.58
split window EX3.36
what-if analysis EX3.45

COMMAND SUMMARY

Command	Shortcut	Action
Home tab		
Styles group		
Conditional Formatting ▾	Quick Analysis, Conditional Formatting	Applies Highlight Cells Rules, Top/Bottom Rules, Data Bars, Color Scales, and Icons Sets to selected cells based on criteria
Cells group		
Delete ▾ /Delete Sheet		Deletes entire sheet
Format ▾ /Rename Sheet		Renames sheet
Format ▾ /Move or Copy Sheet		Moves or copies selected sheet
Format ▾ /Tab Color		Changes color of sheet tabs
Editing group		
Find & Select ▾ /Find	Ctrl + F	Locates specified text, numbers, and/or formats
Find & Select ▾ /Replace	Ctrl + H	Locates specified characters or formats and replaces them with specified replacement characters or format
Find & Select ▾ /Go To	Ctrl + G	Goes to a specified cell location in worksheet
Insert tab		
Sparklines group		
Line	Quick Analysis, Sparkline	Inserts sparkline
Sparklines Tool Design tab		
Style group		
		Applies pictured style to sparkline
Clear ▾		Removes sparkline

COMMAND SUMMARY (CONTINUED)

Command	Shortcut	Action
Page Layout tab		
Page Setup group		
Margins /Narrow		Changes margin settings
Margins /Custom Margins/Horizontally		Centers worksheet horizontally on page
Margins /Custom Margins/Vertically		Centers worksheet vertically on page
Print Area /Set Print Area		Sets print area to selected cells
Breaks /Insert Page Break		Inserts page break at cell pointer location
Breaks /Remove Page Break		Removes page break at cell pointer location
Breaks /Reset all Page Breaks		Restores automatic page breaks
Scale to Fit group		
Height: /1 page		Scales worksheet vertically to fit one page
Sheet Options group		
Print Gridlines		Displays/hides gridlines for printing
Formulas tab		
Formula Auditing group		
Error Checking		Checks worksheet for formula errors
Watch Window		Opens Watch Window

COMMAND SUMMARY (CONTINUED)

Command	Shortcut	Action
Data tab		
Data Tools group		
What-If Analysis ▾/Goal Seek		Adjusts value in specified cell until a formula dependent on that cell reaches specified result
View tab		
Workbook Views group		
Normal		Changes worksheet view to Normal
Page Layout		Displays worksheet as it will appear when printed
Page Break Preview		Displays where pages will break when a worksheet is printed
Show group		
☑ Gridlines		Turns on/off display of gridlines
☑ Headings		Turns on/off display of row and column headings
Zoom group		
Zoom		Changes magnification of window
Window group		
Freeze Panes ▾/Freeze Panes		Freezes top and/or leftmost panes
Freeze Panes ▾/Unfreeze Panes		Unfreezes window panes
Split		Divides window into four panes at active cell or removes split

LAB EXERCISES

MATCHING

Match the lettered item on the right with the numbered item on the left.

1. $B12   _____ a. technique used to evaluate the effects of changing selected factors in a worksheet
2. M34   _____ b. 3-D reference
3. #DIV/0!   _____ c. a what-if analysis tool
4. active pane   _____ d. mixed cell reference
5. conditional formatting   _____ e. applies formatting based on cell rules
6. freeze panes   _____ f. pane that contains the cell selector
7. Goal Seek   _____ g. the sections of a divided window
8. panes   _____ h. sheet reference
9. Sheet1:Sheet3!H3:K5   _____ i. absolute cell reference
10. sparkline   _____ j. indicates division by zero error
11. 'Third Quarter'!A23   _____ k. prevents data in pane from scrolling
12. what-if analysis   _____ l. a tiny chart of worksheet data contained in a single cell

TRUE/FALSE

Circle the correct answer to the following questions.

1. A relative reference is a cell or range reference in a formula whose location does not change when the formula is copied   **True**   **False**
2. A sparkline is a miniature chart contained in a single cell.   **True**   **False**
3. B$7 is an absolute reference.   **True**   **False**
4. Dragging the sizing handle activates the AutoFill feature and recognizes the cell entry as one that can be incremented.   **True**   **False**
5. Icon Sets conditional formatting applies a two- or three-color graduated scale to compare values in a range.   **True**   **False**
6. The sheet reference consists of the name of the sheet separated from the cell reference by a question mark.   **True**   **False**
7. The Trace Errors formula auditing command outlines the cells causing the error with a colored border.   **True**   **False**
8. To create two horizontal panes with the left pane frozen, move the cell selector in the top row of the window and select the column to the right of where you want the split to appear.   **True**   **False**
9. What-if analysis varies the value in the cell you specify until a formula that is dependent on that cell returns the desired result.   **True**   **False**
10. You can freeze the information in the top and right panes of a window only.   **True**   **False**

FILL-IN

Complete the following statements by filling in the blanks with the correct key terms.

1. A technique used to evaluate what effect changing one or more values in formulas has on other values in the worksheet is called _____.

2. A worksheet window can be divided into _____, either horizontal or vertical, through which different areas of the worksheet can be viewed at the same time.

3. A $ character in front of either the column or the row reference in a formula creates a(n) _____ reference.

4. A(n) _____ reference is created when the reference is to the same cell or range on multiple sheets in the same workbook.

5. _____ consist of the name of the sheet enclosed in quotes, and are separated from the cell reference by an exclamation point.

6. _____ formatting changes the appearance of a range of cells based on a set of conditions you specify.

7. The _____ feature logically repeats and extends a series.

8. The _____ tool is used to find the value needed in one cell to attain a result you want in another cell.

9. Use a(n) _____ to show the incremental change in data over time in one cell.

10. When specified rows and columns are _____, they are fixed when you scroll.

LAB EXERCISES

MULTIPLE CHOICE

Circle the correct response to the questions below.

1. A cell or range reference in a formula whose location does not change when the formula is copied is a(n) _____.
   a. absolute reference
   b. frozen cell
   c. mixed reference
   d. relative reference

2. A division of the worksheet window that allows different areas of the worksheet to be viewed at the same time is called a _____.
   a. pane
   b. part
   c. section
   d. window

3. A formula that contains references to cells in other sheets of a workbook is a(n) _____.
   a. Average formula
   b. 3-D formula
   c. Sheet formula
   d. Sparkline formula

4. _____ is used to evaluate the effects of changing selected factors in a worksheet.
   a. AutoCalculate
   b. AutoFill
   c. Value analysis
   d. What-if analysis

5. The cell reference that will adjust row 8 without adjusting column E when it is copied is _____.
   a. E8
   b. E$8
   c. $E8
   d. E8

6. The _____ error value indicates that the wrong type of argument or operand was used.
   a. #####
   b. #DIV/0
   c. #N/A
   d. #VALUE!

7. The _____ feature enters a series of numbers, numbers and text combinations, dates or time periods by logically repeating and extending the series.
   a. AutoFill
   b. AutoRepeat
   c. ExtendFill
   d. ExtendSelect

8. The _____ function key will change a selected cell reference to absolute.
   a. F3
   b. F4
   c. F7
   d. F10

9. The information in the worksheet can be _____ in the top and left panes of a window only.
   a. adjusted
   b. aligned
   c. fixed
   d. frozen

10. The number 32534 displayed with the Currency style would appear as _____ in a cell.
    a. 32,534
    b. $32534
    c. $32,534
    d. $32,534.00

11. Which of the following is NOT a valid sheet name?
    a. 3/12/12
    b. Qtr 1
    c. Second Quarter
    d. Week 8–10

12. To determine a cell value that calculates a desired result in a dependent formula, use the _____ command.
    a. Cell Rule
    b. Goal Seek
    c. Trace Dependent
    d. Trace Precedent

STEP-BY-STEP

GLOBALCOMM INCOME FORECAST ★

1. Leah Miller owns several GlobalComm franchises. She has recorded first quarter results in a worksheet and is ready to project second-quarter income. Your completed worksheet should look similar to the one shown here.

   a. Open the workbook ex03_ GlobalComm. Save the workbook as GlobalComm to your solution file location.

   b. Select the cells with values, and clear the conditional formatting.

   c. Calculate total income by location and by month.

   d. Right-click the Sheet1 tab, and make a copy of the sheet at the end. Rename Sheet1 as **First Quarter**. Rename the copied sheet as **Second Quarter**. Choose a color for each sheet tab.

   e. In the Second Quarter sheet, change the label in cell B5 to **April**. Then use AutoFill to add labels for May and June. Change the label in cell A3 to **Second Quarter**.

   f. Enter the following projected sales values for April.

Location	April
Bellevue Square	8600
Southcenter	15610
The Galleria	12030
Northgate	9580
Alderwood	6740
South Hill	8700
Pacific Place	10980

Student Name
3/1/2015

Location	January	February	March	Total
Bellevue Square	$ 6,870	$ 7,540	$ 7,990	$ 22,400
Southcenter	13,670	14,380	15,400	43,450
The Galleria	11,400	11,670	11,390	34,460
Northgate	8,560	7,650	8,700	24,910
Alderwood	5,760	6,040	6,390	18,190
South Hill	7,830	7,690	8,200	23,720
Pacific Place	9,850	10,610	10,430	30,890
Total	$ 63,940	$ 65,580	$ 68,500	$ 198,020

Student Name
3/1/2015

Location	April	May	June	Total
Bellevue Square	$ 8,600	$ 9,460	$ 10,879	$ 28,939
Southcenter	15,610	17,171	19,747	52,528
The Galleria	12,030	13,233	15,218	40,481
Northgate	9,580	10,538	12,119	32,237
Alderwood	6,740	7,414	8,526	22,680
South Hill	8,700	9,570	11,006	29,276
Pacific Place	10,980	12,078	13,890	36,948
Total	$ 72,240	$ 79,464	$ 91,384	$ 243,088
		Year-to-Date Income	$	441,108

   g. May income is estimated at 10 percent more than April income; June income is expected to be 15 percent higher than May income. Enter formulas to calculate these amounts.

h. Group the worksheets, and change the number format for cells B7:E12 to Comma Style with zero decimal places and ungroup the sheets. Set the font for the label in cell A3 to italic.

i. In the Second Quarter sheet, enter the label **Year-to-Date Income** in cell D14. Right-align the label, and match the font size to the body of the data. In cell E14, enter a formula to calculate total income for the first six months by summing cells E13 on both sheets. Apply Accounting Number format with zero decimal places, and remove fill and borders if needed.

j. Group the sheets again. In Page Layout view, add a custom header to display your name and the date on separate lines in the right section. Center the worksheets horizontally. Ungroup the sheets.

k. Document the workbook to include your name as the author. Save the workbook. Preview and print the workbook.

FORECASTING SALES ★★

2. The La Delice Cookies bakery has decided to add brownies to its offerings and wants to know the impact on sales. You are in the process of creating a worksheet of the cookie sales for the last six months. In addition, you want to add brownies to the items for sale and project how much of this item you would need to sell to increase the net income to $2,000 a month. Then, you want to set up a second sheet that you will use to enter the sales information for the second six months when it is available. When you are done, your completed worksheets should be similar to those shown here.

a. Open the workbook ex03_La Delice. Use AutoFill to complete the month headings. Save the workbook as La Delice.

b. Add a blank row below row 15 for brownies. Add the row heading **Brownies** in A16.

c. Edit the formula in B17 to include B16, and copy it across the row through column G.

Student Name
3/1/15

La Delice Cookies
Sales Analysis

	January	February	March	April	May	June	Total	Average
INCOME								
Chocolate Chip	$ 728.03	$ 678.43	$ 712.49	$ 653.51	$ 562.12	$ 622.31	$ 3,956.89	$ 659.48
Peanut Butter	$ 325.22	$ 330.13	$ 308.40	$ 440.14	$ 370.59	$ 519.08	$ 2,293.56	$ 382.26
Ginger Snaps	$ 617.07	$ 697.54	$ 655.71	$ 692.27	$ 538.59	$ 692.26	$ 3,891.54	$ 648.59
Oatmeal Raisin	$ 391.34	$ 389.67	$ 377.76	$ 324.88	$ 279.75	$ 330.00	$ 2,093.40	$ 348.90
Shortbread	$ 949.41	$ 993.50	$ 866.49	$ 893.01	$ 831.29	$ 844.02	$ 5,377.52	$ 896.25
Molasses	$ 606.33	$ 624.96	$ 619.70	$ 613.18	$ 503.40	$ 589.91	$ 3,557.48	$ 592.91
Chocolate Sandwich	$ 331.63	$ 299.84	$ 311.29	$ 408.95	$ 352.23	$ 445.76	$ 2,149.70	$ 358.28
Black & White	$ 576.82	$ 555.03	$ 560.16	$ 535.35	$ 474.15	$ 557.47	$ 3,258.98	$ 543.16

Student Name
3/1/15

La Delice Cookies
Sales Analysis

	July	August	September	October	November	December	Annual Total	Annual Average
INCOME								
Chocolate Chip							$ 3,956.89	$ 728.03
Peanut Butter							$ 2,293.56	$ 325.22
Ginger Snaps							$ 3,891.54	$ 617.07
Oatmeal Raisin							$ 2,093.40	$ 391.34
Shortbread							$ 5,377.52	$ 949.41
Molasses							$ 3,557.48	$ 606.33
Chocolate Sandwich							$ 2,149.70	$ 331.63
Black & White							$ 3,258.98	$ 576.82
Date Nut Bars							$ 4,340.96	$ 741.13
Lemon Bars							$ 1,731.78	$ 317.12
Brownies							$ 2,411.31	$ 336.88
Total Income	$ -	$ -	$ -	$ -	$ -	$ -	$ 35,063.12	$ 2,960.49
EXPENSES								
Payroll							$ 9,450.78	$ 1,589.94
Cost of Goods							$ 6,112.34	$ 1,081.04
Overhead							$ 7,500.00	$ 1,250.00
Total Expenses	$ -	$ -	$ -	$ -	$ -	$ -	$ 23,063.12	$ 1,960.49
INCOME	$ -	$ -	$ -	$ -	$ -	$ -	$ 12,000.00	$ 1,000.00

LAB EXERCISES

d. Increase the cost of goods for each month by 12 percent to account for the added goods needed to make the brownies.

e. Enter the formulas to calculate the Total Expenses in row 23.

f. Correct all the formula errors in row 25.

g. Enter the functions to calculate the Total and Average values in cells H6:I6. Copy the functions down the columns through row 25. Clear the formulas from all cells that reference blank cells, except for row 16.

h. Freeze the window with the titles in column A and above row 5 frozen so you can scroll to see the Income values in row 25 while working on the brownie sales next.

i. Assuming other cookie sales remain the same, you want to know how much brownie sales would be necessary to generate a monthly net income of $2,000. Use Goal Seek to answer these questions and calculate the brownie sales figures for all months. (*Hint:* Net income is displayed in row 25.)

j. Unfreeze the window.

k. Using conditional formatting, create a cell rule that will highlight those cookies that have total sales greater than $3,000. Use a highlight color of your choice.

l. You will soon be working on the sales figures for the second six months and want to set up a second sheet to hold this information when it is available. Make a copy of Sheet1 at the end. Change the month headings using AutoFill for the second six months (July to December).

m. Rename Sheet1 to **January-June Sales**. Rename Sheet2 to **July-December Sales**. Add tab colors of your choice.

n. In the July-December Sales sheet, delete the contents only in cells B6:G16 and B20:G22. In cell H6, enter a formula that adds the total from January through June with the monthly figures from July through December. Copy the formula down the column. Change the average formula to average the 12 months. Clear the formula from all cells that reference blank cells. Clear the conditional formatting from all cells in the July-December Sales sheet. Check the formulas by entering (and then removing) some sample data. Change the label in H4 to **Annual Total** and I4 to **Annual Average**. Best fit both columns.

o. In the January-June Sales sheet, add a line sparkline in cell J16 using the monthly sales numbers for brownies in row 16. Type **Brownie Sales** in the cell, and top-align the text. Increase the row height and column width to show the sparkline. Display markers, and choose a style of your choice. Add a thick box border to J16.

p. Use the Find and Replace command to change "bars" to "Bars" in both sheets. In Document Properties, type your name in the Author text box. Add a custom header with your name and the date left-aligned to both sheets.

q. Preview the workbook. Change the print orientation to landscape. Make the necessary adjustments to print each worksheet on a single page. Print both worksheets.

r. Save the workbook.

SPRING BREAK TOUR COST ANALYSIS ★★

3. Colleen, a travel analyst for Adventure Travel Tours, is evaluating the profitability of a proposed trip to Rome for spring break. She has determined that a cost of $5,000 is adequate and will attract a number of students and others. Colleen has started a worksheet to assess the break-even point at which the gross revenue equals the total costs (net income = 0). With that information, she can approximate how many travelers are necessary to reach certain profit levels ($5,000 and $10,000). She has set these package costs:

Air transportation	$1,400 per person
Ground transportation	$460 per person
Hotels	$1,475 per person
Included meals	$900 per person
Included admissions	$250 per person
Local tour guides	$3,000
Administrative expense	$2,000

Your completed worksheets will look similar to those shown here.

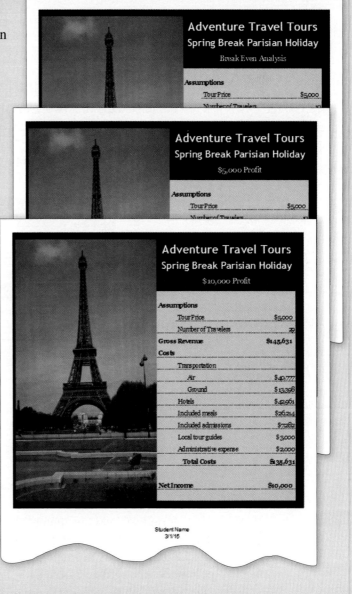

a. Open the workbook ex03_Roman Holiday. Save the workbook as Roman Holiday to your solution file location.

b. In cell E10, enter a formula to calculate revenue using the sample values. Set the result to be right-aligned, black, and bold.

c. In cell E13, enter a formula to multiple the number of travelers times $1,400. Enter similar formulas for cells E14:E17. Enter the values shown in the table above for the tour guides and administrative expense. Format these values as Currency with zero decimal places.

d. Calculate total costs in cell E20. Calculate net income in cell E22, and right-align the result. Make both cells bold.

e. Use Goal Seek to determine the number of travelers for break even, when the result for cell E22 is zero (0).

f. Make a copy of Sheet1 tab at the end. Rename Sheet1 as **BreakEven**. Rename the copied sheet as **$5,000 Profit**. Choose a color for each sheet tab.

g. Edit the label in cell C4 of the $5,000 Profit sheet to **$5,000 Profit**. Use Goal Seek again to find the number of travelers required to meet this income goal.

LAB EXERCISES

h. Make another copy of either sheet, name it **$10,000 Profit**, and use Goal Seek to find the number of travelers.

i. Group the sheets, and use Find and Replace to replace all occurrences of "Meals" with "meals." Then do the same for "Admissions."

j. With the sheets grouped, set the left and right margins at 0.5 inch and center the page horizontally. Scale it to fit one portrait page.

k. With the sheets grouped, use Page Layout view to add a footer that displays your name and the date, each on a separate line, in the center section. Ungroup the sheets.

l. Document the workbook to include your name as the author. Save the workbook. Preview and print the workbook.

GRADE POINT AVERAGE ANALYSIS ★★★

4. George Lewis has just completed the first two years of his undergraduate program in architecture. He has built a workbook that shows his grades for each semester on a separate worksheet. He has asked you to help him move all the data to a single worksheet so that he can view his two-year record on a single sheet. Your completed worksheet will look similar to the one shown here.

a. Open the workbook ex03_Grade Report. Save the workbook as Grade Report to your solution file location.

b. Clear the conditional formatting from the Fall1 worksheet. Copy cells A1:F3 to start in cell A13. Make row 13 the same height as row 1. Set row 15 to the same height as row 3. Edit the label in cell A13 to display **Spring Grades, Year 1**.

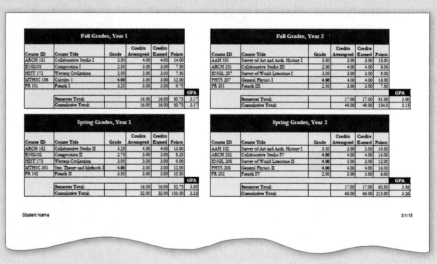

c. Select and copy cells A7:F11 on the Spring1 sheet to start in cell A16 on the Fall1 sheet. Then copy cells A9:G11 on the Fall1 sheet to cells A21:G23 on the same sheet.

d. Clear the conditional formatting from the spring data. Delete the values/formulas shown for the cumulative total for the spring data.

e. In cell D23, enter a formula to add the attempted credit hours from the spring semester to the hours from the fall semester. In cell E23, enter a formula to add the credit hours earned from the spring semester to the cumulative credits from the fall. In cell F23, enter a formula to calculate the total accumulated points after the spring semester.

f. Copy the formula in cell G22 to cell G23. Format all values to show two decimal places.

g. Copy cells A1:F3 to start in cell I1, keeping the same column widths. Edit the label in cell I1 to display **Fall Grades, Year 2**.

h. Select and copy cells A7:F11 on the Fall2 sheet to start in cell I4 on the Fall1 sheet. Clear the conditional formatting and adjust column widths to display all the data. Then copy cells A9:G15 on the Fall1 sheet to cells I9:O15 on the same sheet.

i. Delete the values in cells L11:O11. In cell L11, enter a formula to add the attempted credit hours from this semester to the cumulative hours from the previous spring semester. Enter similar formulas for the credit hours and points, and copy the formula for the GPA. Format all values to show two decimal places.

j. Complete the final section for the worksheet by copying the data from the Spring2 sheet, clearing the conditional formatting, and adjusting the formulas. Edit the title for the final semester.

k. Increase decimals where needed so that the grades, points, and GPA values all display two places. Check that all data is visible. Make column H about half its current width.

l. Select and delete the Spring1, Fall2, and Spring2 worksheets. Rename the Fall1 sheet as **Grades**.

m. Select all the grade values, and create a highlight cells rule that displays 4.0 grades in black, bold font color with yellow fill.

n. Set landscape orientation, and center the sheet horizontally. Scale the sheet to fit one page.

o. Add a footer that displays your name in the left section and the date in the right section.

p. Document the workbook to include your name as the author. Save the workbook. Preview and print the sheet.

DOGGIE DAY CARE INCOME ANALYSIS ★★★

5. Mei Liao owns Doggie Day Care Center which offers full- and half-day care for dogs as well as grooming and training services. She has prepared a worksheet with figures for January through June but still needs to complete several formulas. She will then create the worksheet for July through December and compile the year's results. Your completed worksheet will look similar to the one shown here.

LAB EXERCISES

a. Open the workbook ex03_Doggie Day Care. Save the workbook as Doggie Day Care to your solution file location.

b. Set the zoom size so that you can see all the data. Find and correct formula errors.

c. Use SUM in cells H10:H11 as well as cells H17:H30.

d. Review the formula in cell B14; it calculates the income from grooming and training using the prices shown on the Prices worksheet. Build a similar formula in cell B13 for full- and half-day care. Use absolute references so that you can copy the formula to cells B13:G13. You can key the formula or point to enter it. Enter the SUM function in column H for these rows.

e. Calculate net income in row 31.

f. Set landscape orientation, and center the sheet horizontally. Scale the sheet to fit one page.

g. Add a footer that displays your name in the right section and the date in the center section.

h. Make a copy of the Jan-June sheet that is placed before the Prices sheet. Rename the copied sheet as Jul-Dec. Choose tab colors for each sheet in the workbook.

i. On the Jul-Dec sheet, edit the label in cell B3 to show the proper month names. Then key July in cell B4, ignoring the AutoComplete suggestion. Use AutoFill to complete the other month names.

j. Delete the values in cells B7:G8 and cells B10:G11. Select cells B31:G31, and add them to the Watch Window.

k. Enter the following values to complete the data for the second half of the year.

	July	August	September	October	November	December
Full day	450	500	436	321	386	402
Half day	225	247	185	100	120	136
Grooming	130	142	116	122	156	166
Training	30	36	36	45	45	20

l. Delete the watches in the Watch Window, and then close the Watch Window.

m. Use Goal Seek to determine the number of full-day care clients needed to increase the net income for October to $10,000. Keep the solution.

n. On each sheet, apply a conditional format to the full-day client numbers that are greater than 400. Build a custom format that you think emphasizes the values.

o. Group the Jan-Jun and Jul-Dec sheets, and replace Marketing (it has one indent space) with Print and social media.

p. Document the workbook to include your name as the author. Save the workbook. Preview and print the income sheets.

ON YOUR OWN

EXPANDING BUDGET PROJECTIONS ★

1. In On Your Own exercise 2 of Lab 1, you created a Personal Budget workbook for a three-month budget. Extend the worksheet to add three more months for a total of six months. Add two additional sheets. One sheet will contain a budget for the next six months. The final sheet will present a full year's summary using 3-D references to the values in the appropriate sheets. You need to budget for a vacation. On a separate line below the total balance in the summary sheet, enter the amount you would need. Subtract this value from the total balance. If this value is negative, reevaluate your expenses and adjust them appropriately. Format the sheets using the features you have learned in the first three labs. Add your name in a custom header on all sheets. Preview, print, and save the workbook as Personal Budget2.

COMPANY EXPENSE COMPARISONS ★

2. Using the Internet or the library, obtain yearly income and expense data for three companies in a related business. In a workbook, record each company's data in a separate sheet. In a fourth sheet, calculate the total income, total expenses, and net income for each company. Also in this sheet, calculate the overall totals for income, expense, and net income. Format the sheets using the features you have learned in the first three labs. Add your name in a custom header on all sheets. Preview, print, and save the workbook as Company Expenses in a folder named Business.

HOUSE ANALYSIS ★★

3. Select three cities in which you would consider living after you graduate. Using the Internet or the library, select one price point of housing and determine each house's asking price, square footage, acreage, number of bedrooms, and number of bathrooms. In a workbook containing four sheets, record each city's housing prices and statistics in separate worksheets. In the fourth sheet, calculate the average, maximum and minimum for each city. Include a chart showing the average data for the three cities. Format the sheets using the features you have learned in the first three labs. Add your name in a custom header on all sheets. Preview, print, and save the workbook as House Analysis in a folder named Housing.

LAB EXERCISES

INVENTORY TRACKING ★★★

4. It's a good idea to have an inventory of your personal items for safe keeping. Design a worksheet that will keep track of your personal items divided by category; for example, living room, dining room, bedroom, and so forth. Each category may have as many detail lines as needed to represent the items. For example, sofa, vases, art, and so on. The worksheet should keep track of the number of items; the price paid for each item; the extended price (items * price), if applicable; and the replacement value. Determine the percentage increase in replacement value. Sum the price paid and replacement value in each category and the total value. Format the sheet using the features you have learned in the first three labs. Add your name in a custom header on all sheets. Change the worksheet orientation if necessary; preview, print, and save the workbook as Inventory Tracking.

START YOUR OWN BUSINESS ★★★

5. Owning and managing a small business is a dream of many college students. Do some research on the web or in the library, and choose a business that interests you. Create a projected worksheet for four quarters in separate worksheets. In a fifth sheet, show the total for the year. Include a year-to-date value in each quarterly sheet. In the last-quarter sheet, depending on the business you select, determine how many customers or sales you need in the last quarter to break even and to end the year with a 10 percent profit. Format the sheets using the features you have learned in the first three labs. Add your name in a custom header on all sheets. Preview, print, and save the workbook as My Business.

CASE STUDY

Downtown Internet Café

Your analysis of the sales data for the first quarter of operations for the Downtown Internet Café projects a small, steady increase in sales each month. If an advertising campaign promoting the new Internet aspect of the Café is mounted, you forecast that coffee and food sales in that quarter will increase sharply.

Evan, the cafe owner, is still trying to decide if he should advertise and has asked you to send him a report containing the worksheet data showing the expected sales without an advertising campaign and the chart showing the projected sales with an advertising

campaign. Additionally, Evan wants a copy of the second-quarter forecast showing the 15 percent profit margins for each month. He also wants a copy of the workbook file so that he can play with the sales values to see their effects on the profit margin.

You will learn how to share information between applications while you create these reports. Your completed documents will look like those shown below.

NOTE This lab assumes that you know how to use Word 2013 and that you have completed Labs 2 and 3 of Excel 2013.

Sharing Information between Applications

All Microsoft Office 2013 applications have a common user interface such as similar Ribbon commands and galleries. In addition to these obvious features, they have been designed to work together, making it easy to share and exchange information between applications. For example, the same commands and procedures to copy information within an Excel 2013 worksheet are used to copy information to other Office 2013 applications such as Word. The information can be pasted in many different formats such as a worksheet object, a bitmap, a picture, a linked object, or an embedded object. How you decide to paste the object depends on what you want to be able to do with the data once it is inserted in the Word document.

COPYING BETWEEN EXCEL AND WORD

The report to Evan about the analysis of the sales data has already been created using Word 2013 and saved as a document file.

1

- **Start Word 2013 and open the document** exwt_Sales Forecast Report.

- **Replace Student Name with your name.**

- **Save the file as** Sales Forecast Report **to your solution file location.**

Your screen should be similar to Figure 1

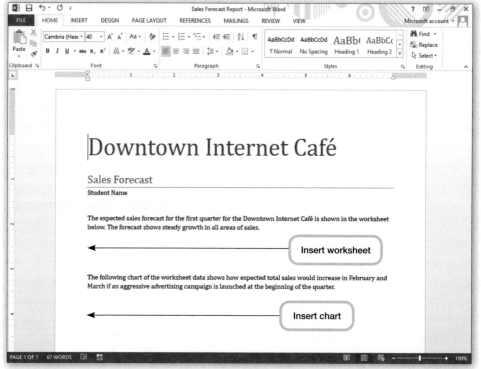

Figure 1

As you can see, you still need to add the Excel worksheet data and chart to the report. To insert the information from the Excel workbook file into the Word report, you need to open the workbook.

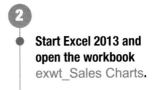

2 Start Excel 2013 and open the workbook exwt_Sales Charts.

● If necessary, enable content

Your screen should be similar to Figure 2

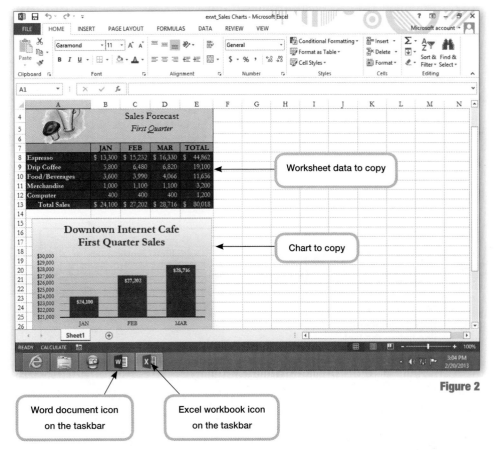

Worksheet data to copy

Chart to copy

Word document icon on the taskbar

Excel workbook icon on the taskbar

Figure 2

There are now two open applications, Word and Excel. You will insert the worksheet data of the first-quarter sales forecast below the first paragraph. Below the second paragraph, you will display the chart.

You will begin by copying the chart from Excel into the Word document. While using Excel, you have learned how to use cut, copy, and paste to move or copy information within and between worksheets. You also can perform these operations between files in the same application and between files in different Office applications. You want to insert the chart as a picture object that can be edited using the Picture Tools commands in Word.

3

● Select the column chart.

● Click Copy to copy the selected chart object to the Clipboard.

● Switch to the Word document.

Having Trouble?

Click the Word document button in the taskbar.

● Move the cursor to the second blank line below the last paragraph of the report.

● Open the Paste menu and choose Picture.

● Open the Picture Tools Format tab.

● Open the Picture Styles gallery and choose Simple Frame, Black.

● Adjust the size of the chart and position it as in Figure 3.

Your screen should be similar to Figure 3

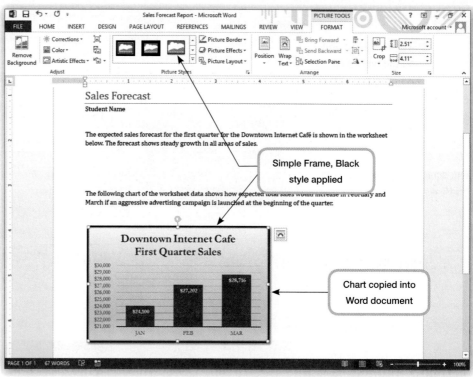

Figure 3

A copy of the chart has been inserted as a picture object into the Word document. Adding the black frame around the chart picture object makes it stand out better. It can be formatted, sized, and moved like any other picture object.

Linking between Applications

Next, you want to copy the worksheet showing the sales trends to below the first paragraph in the report. You will insert the worksheet into the report as a **linked object**. Information created in one application also can be inserted as a linked object into a document created by another application. When an object is linked, the data is stored in the **source file** (the document in which it was created). A graphic representation or picture of the data is displayed in the **destination file** (the document in which the object is inserted). A connection between the information in the destination file to the source file is established by the creation of an **external reference**, also called a **link**. The link contains references to the location of the source file and the selection within the document that is linked to the destination file.

When changes are made in the source file that affect the linked object, the changes are reflected automatically in the destination file when it is opened. This is called a **live link**. When you create linked objects, the date and time on your computer should be accurate. This is because the program refers to the date of the source file to determine whether updates are needed when you open the destination file.

You will copy the worksheet as a linked object so that it will be updated automatically if the source file is edited. To make it easier to work with the two applications, you will display the two open application windows side-by-side.

1

- Right-click on a blank area of the taskbar and choose **Show windows side by side** from the shortcut menu.

- Click in the Excel window and select cells A7 through E13.

- Click [ ] **Copy**.

- Click in the Word document and move to the center blank line between the paragraphs of the report.

- Open the [Paste] menu and choose **Paste Special**.

- Choose **Paste link** from the Paste Special dialog box.

Your screen should be similar to Figure 4

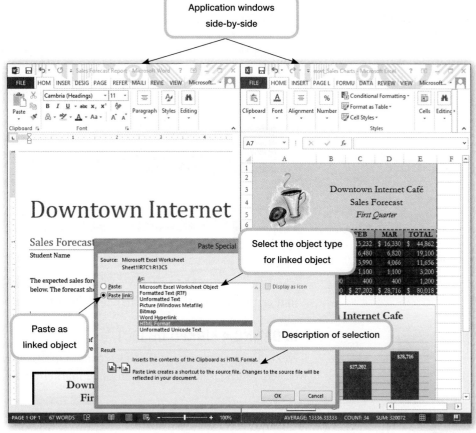

Figure 4

The Paste Special dialog box displays the type of object contained in the Clipboard and its location in the Source area. From the As list box, you select the type of format for the object you want inserted into the destination file. There are many different object types from which you can select. It is important to select the appropriate object format so that the link works correctly when inserted in the destination. In this case, you want to use the Microsoft Office Excel Worksheet Object format.

The Result area describes the effect of your selections. In this case, the object will be inserted as a picture, and a link will be created to the worksheet in the source file. Selecting the Display as Icon option changes the display of the object in the destination file from a picture to an icon. When inserted in this manner, double-clicking the icon displays the object picture.

- Choose Microsoft Office Excel Worksheet Object.

- Click OK .

Your screen should be similar to Figure 5

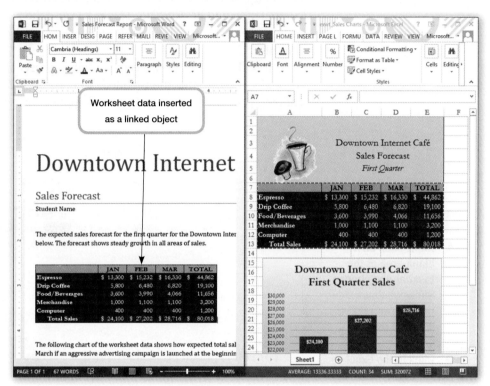

Figure 5

The worksheet data has been copied into the Word document as a linked object that can be sized and moved like any other object.

UPDATING A LINKED OBJECT

Next, you want to return the sales data in the Excel worksheet to the original forecasted values assuming an aggressive marketing campaign is not mounted.

1

- Switch to the Excel window.

- Press [Esc] to clear the selection border.

- Change the entry in C8 to **13600** (you are removing the formula).

- In the same manner, replace the formulas in the following cells with the values shown.

Cell	Value
D8	14,200
C9	6,000
D9	6,200
C10	3,800
D10	3,800

Your screen should be similar to Figure 6

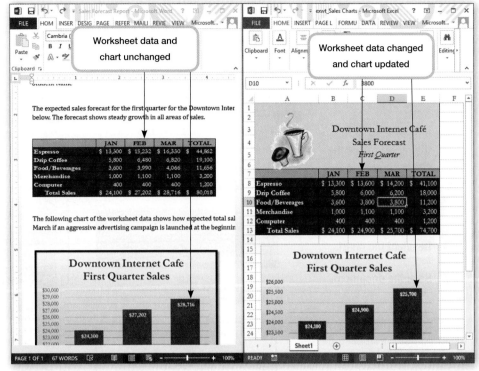

Figure 6

The Excel worksheet and chart have been updated; however, the worksheet data and chart in the Word document still reflect the original values. You will update the worksheet in the Word document next.

2

- Switch to the Word window.

- Select the worksheet object.

- Press [F9] to update the linked object.

Another Method

You also can choose Update Link from the linked object's shortcut menu.

Your screen should be similar to Figure 7

Figure 7

The linked worksheet object in the report now reflects the changes you made in Excel for the sales data. This is because any changes you make in Excel will be reflected in the linked object in the Word document. Next, you will see if the chart has been updated also.

- If necessary, scroll the report to see the entire chart.

- Click on the chart and press F9.

- Deselect the chart.

- Save the document.

Additional Information

The chart may have moved to the next page when the worksheet data was inserted. If this happened, reduce the size of the chart object.

Your screen should be similar to Figure 8

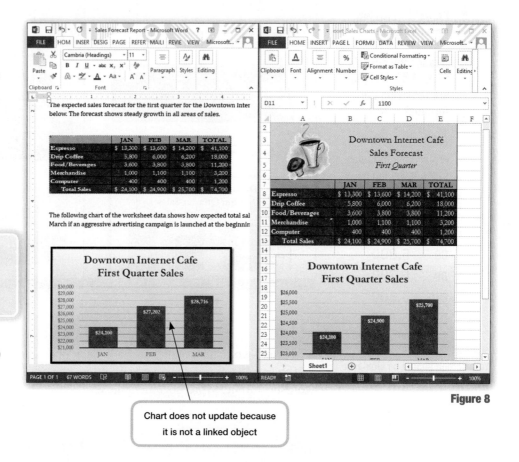

Chart does not update because it is not a linked object

Figure 8

Because the chart in the Word document is not a linked object, it does not update to reflect the changes in data that you made in Excel.

EDITING LINKS

When a document is opened that contains links, the application looks for the source file and automatically updates the linked objects. If the document contains many links, updating can take a lot of time. Additionally, if you move the source file to another location or perform other operations that may interfere with the link, your link will not work. To help with situations like these, you can edit the settings associated with links. You will look at the links to the worksheet data created in the Word document.

Working Together: Linking and Embedding
between Word 2013 and Excel 2013

WWW.MHHE.COM/OLEARY

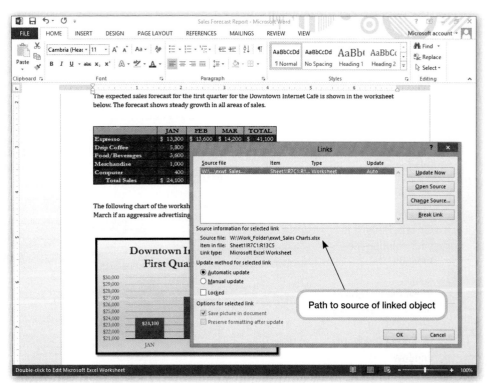

1
- Open the taskbar shortcut menu and choose Undo Show all windows side by side.

- If necessary, maximize the Word window.

- Right-click the worksheet object and select Linked Worksheet Object.

- Choose Links from the submenu.

Your screen should be similar to Figure 9

Figure 9

The Links dialog box displays the object path for all links in the document in the list box. This includes the path and name of the source file, the range of linked cells or object name, the type of file, and the update status. Below the list box, the details for the selected link are displayed.

The other options in this dialog box are described in the table below.

Option	Effect
Automatic update	Updates the linked object whenever the destination document is opened or the source file changes. This is the default.
Manual update	The destination document is not automatically updated and you must use the Update Now command button to update the link.
Locked	Prevents a linked object from being updated.
Update Now	Updates the linked object.
Open Source	Opens the source document for the selected link.
Change Source	Used to modify the path to the source document.
Break Link	Breaks the connection between the source document and the active document.

The links in the Word document are to the exwt_Sales Charts workbook file. Next, you will save the Excel workbook file using a new file name. Then you will recheck the link settings.

②

● **Click** OK .

● **Switch to the Excel window.**

● **If necessary, maximize the window.**

● **Save the Excel workbook as** Sales Charts Linked **to your solution file location.**

● **Close the workbook file (do not exit Excel).**

● **Switch to the Word window.**

Having Trouble?

Click the application taskbar button to switch between windows.

● **From the worksheet object's shortcut menu, select Linked Worksheet Object and choose Links.**

Your screen should be similar to Figure 10

The expected sales forecast for the first quarter for the Downtown Internet Cafe is shown in the worksheet below. The forecast shows steady growth in all areas of sales.

	JAN	FEB	MAR	TOTAL
Espresso	$ 13,300	$ 13,600	$ 14,200	$ 41,100
Drip Coffee	5,800			
Food/Beverages	3,600			
Merchandise	1,000			
Computer	400			
Total Sales	$ 24,100			

The following chart of the worksheet March if an aggressive advertising

Links dialog:

Source file: W\...\Sales Char... Item: Sheet1!R7C1:R1... Type: Worksheet Update: Auto.

Update Now / Open Source / Change Source... / Break Link

Source information for selected link
Source file: W:\Work_Folder\Sales Charts Linked.xlsx
Item in file: Sheet1!R7C1:R13C5
Link type: Microsoft Excel Worksheet

Update method for selected link
◉ Automatic update
○ Manual update
☐ Locked

Link updated to reflect new file name

Options for selected link
☑ Save picture in document
☐ Preserve formatting after update

OK / Cancel

Downtown I...
First Qua...

$30,000
$29,000
$28,000
$27,000
$26,000
$25,000
$24,000 $24,100
$23,000
$22,000
$21,000
JAN

Double-click to Edit Microsoft Excel Worksheet

Figure 10

You can now see that the link has been updated to reflect the new workbook file name.

③

● **Click** OK .

● **Increase the size of the worksheet object to the same width as the chart object.**

● **Open the File tab and choose Print.**

● **Check the layout of the document in the preview and if necessary return to the document and make any needed adjustments.**

● **Print and then close the Word document, saving any changes if needed.**

EMBEDDING AN OBJECT

Additional Information

The source data is stored in an Excel worksheet that is incorporated in the Word file.

The last thing you need to send Evan is a report that describes and shows the second-quarter forecast. To do this, you will open the Word document and embed the worksheet containing the second-quarter data that Evan wants in the appropriate location. An **embedded object** is stored in the destination file and becomes part of that document. The entire file, not just the selection that is displayed in the destination file, becomes part of the document. This means that you can modify it without affecting the source document where the original object resides.

1

- Open the Word document exwt_ Second Quarter Report **and enable content if necessary.**

- **Replace Student Name with your name in the last line of the document.**

- **Save the document as** Second Quarter Report **to your solution file location.**

- **Switch to Excel and open the workbook file** exwt_Second Quarter **and enable content if necessary.**

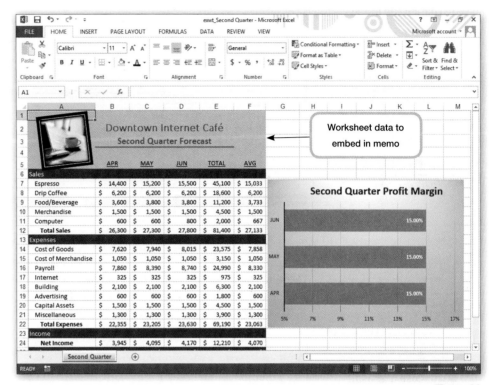

Figure 11

Your screen should be similar to Figure 11

This workbook file contains a copy of the second-quarter worksheet from the Annual Forecast workbook. You will embed the second-quarter forecast worksheet in the Word document.

2

• Copy the range A1 through F25.

• Switch to the Word window.

• Move to the blank line below the first paragraph of the report.

• Open the ▢ Paste ▾ menu and choose Paste Special.

Your screen should be similar to Figure 12

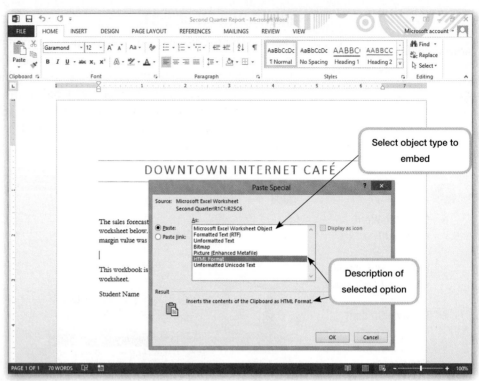

Figure 12

The Paste option inserts or embeds the Clipboard contents in the format you specify from the As list box. The default is to insert the Clipboard contents in HTML format. You want to embed the contents of the Clipboard into the document so it can be edited using the source program. To do this, you select the option that displays the source name, in this case Excel.

3

• Choose Microsoft Excel Worksheet Object.

• Click OK .

Your screen should be similar to Figure 13

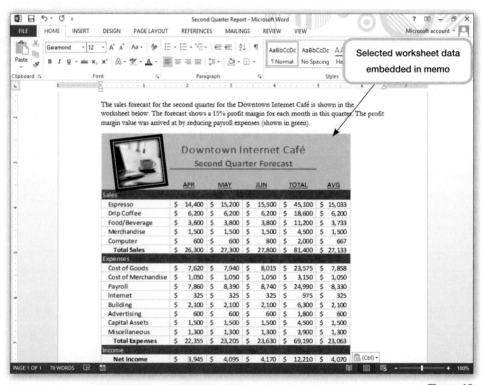

Figure 13

The selected portion of the worksheet is displayed in the report at the location of the insertion point.

UPDATING AN EMBEDDED OBJECT

You want to add color to the payroll range of cells you adjusted to arrive at the 15 percent profit margin. Because the worksheet is embedded, you can do this from within the Word document. The source program is used to edit data in an embedded object. To open the source program and edit the worksheet, you double-click the embedded object.

● **Double-click the worksheet object in Word.**

Having Trouble?

If the worksheet does not fully display the numbers, click outside the worksheet to return to the document, make the worksheet object larger, and then open the source program again.

Your screen should be similar to Figure 14

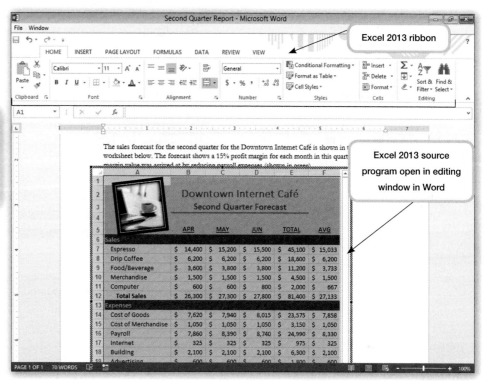

Figure 14

Additional Information

The source program must be installed on the computer system to be able to open and edit the embedded object.

The source program, in this case Excel 2013, is opened. The Excel Ribbon replaces the Word Ribbon, and the embedded object is displayed in an editing worksheet window. Now you can use the source program commands to edit the object.

2

- Change the font color of cells B16 through D16 to Green on the Standard colors bar color.

- Close the source program by clicking anywhere outside the object.

- Save the document.

Your screen should be similar to Figure 15

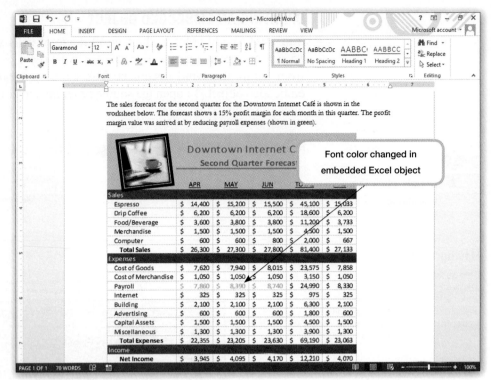

Font color changed in embedded Excel object

Figure 15

The embedded object in the document is updated to reflect the changes you made. However, the Excel worksheet is unchanged.

3

- If necessary reduce the size of the worksheet object to fit the entire report on a single page.

- Preview and print the report.

- Exit Word.

- Look at the Excel worksheet to confirm that the worksheet has not changed.

- Exit Excel.

Deciding When to Link or Embed Objects

Linking documents is a very handy feature, particularly in documents whose information is updated frequently. If you include a linked object in a document that you are giving to another person, make sure the user has access to the source file and application. Otherwise the links will not operate correctly.

Keep the following in mind when deciding whether to link or embed objects.

Use linking when:	Use embedding when:
File size is important.	File size is not important.
Users have access to the source file and application.	Users have access to the application but not to the source file.
The information is updated frequently.	The data changes infrequently.
	You do not want the source data to change.

KEY TERMS

destination file EXWT.4
embedded object EXWT.11
external reference EXWT.5
link EXWT.5

linked object EXWT.4
live link EXWT.5
source file EXWT.4

COMMAND SUMMARY

Command	Shortcut	Action
Home tab		
Clipboard group		
Paste /Paste Special/Paste		Inserts object as an embedded object
Paste /Paste Special/Paste Link		Inserts object as a linked object
Linked Object shortcut menu (Word)		
Update Link	F9	Updates linked object
Linked Worksheet Object/Links		Modifies selected link

STEP-BY-STEP

RESCUE FOUNDATION INCOME REPORT ★★

1. The Animal Rescue Foundation's agency director has asked you to provide her with information about income for 2015. She is particularly interested in the two pet show fund-raising and membership drive events that are held in April and October. You will create a report that will include a copy of the worksheet analysis of this data. Your completed report will be similar to that shown here.

   a. Start Word and open the document exwt_ Rescue Report.docx.

   b. Replace Student Name with your name at the bottom of the document.

   c. Start Excel and open the workbook exwt_ Contributions.

   d. Insert both worksheets as Microsoft Excel Worksheet Object links below the first paragraph in the Word report. Reduce the size of the worksheets until the report fits on one page.

   e. You notice the April raffle ticket sales value looks low, and after checking your records, you see it was entered incorrectly. In Excel, change the April raffle ticket sales income to $3,120.

   f. In the report, update the linked worksheet.

   g. Save the Excel workbook as Contributions. Exit Excel.

   h. Save the Word document as Rescue Report Linked. Preview and print the document.

Animal Rescue Foundation

Income Analysis

Below is the completed income analysis for 2015. As you can see, the income for Fall/Winter is much higher due to corporate donations.

Animal Rescue Foundation

	March	April	May	June	July	August	Total
Annual Memberships	$ 9,200	$ 18,783	$ 8,595	$ 9,934	$ 5,684	$ 5,781	$ 57,977
Private Donations	625	1,400		1,225			3,250
Corporate Donations		17,000	15,000		4,000	9,000	45,000
Raffle Tickets		3,120					3,120
Pet Show		8,000					8,000
Other	3,000	3,000	3,000	3,000	3,000	3,000	18,000
Total	$ 12,825	$ 51,303	$ 26,595	$ 14,159	$ 12,684	$ 17,781	$ 135,347

Animal Rescue Foundation

	September	October	November	December	January	February	Total	Annual Total
Annual Memberships	$ 6,740	$ 23,723	$ 10,595	$ 22,134	$ 11,584	$ 10,781	$ 85,557	$ 143,534
Private Donations	800	2,200	5,600	79,900	1,900	3,000	93,400	96,650
Corporate Donations		15,000		312,000		10,000	337,000	382,000
Raffle Tickets		3,294					3,294	6,414
Pet Show		11,000					11,000	19,000
Other	3,000	3,000	3,000	3,000	3,000	3,000	18,000	36,000
Total	$ 10,540	$ 58,217	$ 19,195	$ 417,034	$ 16,484	$ 26,781	$ 548,251	$ 683,598

Also, the pet show fundraising events have been very successful in boosting income during the slow periods of each year.

Student Name

1

LAB EXERCISES

STUDENT RETENTION REPORT ★★

2. As part of your job at the State College, you keep track of the number of students who return each year and how many of those students graduate in four or five years. You record this data in a worksheet and are preparing to include the results for the class of 2014 in a report. Your completed report will be similar to that shown here.

a. Start Word and open the exwt_ Student Retention.docx document. Replace Student Name with your name at the end of the report.

b. Start Excel and open the exwt_ College Student Retention workbook.

c. Copy the worksheet as a linked object to below the paragraph of the report.

d. In Excel, enter the fourth-year graduation data for 2014 of **1495** in cell E10 and the fifth-year graduation rate for 2014 of **67** in E12.

e. In Word, update the linked worksheet object.

f. Save the workbook as Student Retention to your solution file location. Exit Excel.

g. Save the Word document as Student Retention Rates to your solution file location. Print the report.

State College

Student Retention Analysis

The rate of student retention for four years is displayed in the worksheet below. The number of students who return to State College every year and finish their degrees in four years is laudable, but there is growing concern at the increasing number of students who either do not return for the fourth year, or don't graduate after four years. There is a meeting scheduled for next week to discuss this issue and possible ways to decrease the rate of change. Please review this information prior to the meeting.

State College
Student Retention Rates

	2011	2012	2013	2014	Average
Enrolled First Year Students	1537	1579	1670	1700	1622
Returning Second Year Students	1397	1433	1571	1598	1500
Returning Third Year Students	1285	1398	1520	1562	1441
Returning Fourth Year Students	1221	1324	1484	1555	1396
Graduating Fourth Year Students	1211	1312	1461	1495	1370
Percent Graduate in Four Years	79%	83%	87%	88%	84%
Graduating Fifth Year Students	44	55	62	67	57
Percent Graduate in Five Years	82%	87%	91%	92%	88%

Student Name

HOME SALE PRICE REPORT ★★

3. Jennifer works in the marketing department for a local real estate company. She has recently researched the median home prices and number of days on the market over the last three years for existing homes in the local market area. She has created a worksheet and column charts of the data. Now Jennifer wants to send a report containing the information to her supervisor. The completed report will be similar to that shown here.

a. Start Word and open the document exwt_Home Price Report.docx.

b. Replace Student Name with your name.

c. Start Excel and open the workbook exwt_Real Estate Prices. Copy the worksheet and each chart as embedded objects below the first paragraph in the Word document. Size the charts so that everything fits on one page.

d. Open the embedded worksheet object in Word, and change the chart title from Average Price to Median Price.

e. Change the Days on Market chart to a 3-D clustered bar.

f. Click within the paragraph text to close the embedded object.

g. Save the Word document as Home Price Report to your solution file location. Preview and print the document.

MEDIAN EXISTING HOME PRICES

Below is a chart showing the median existing home prices over the past three years. As you can see, existing home sale prices increased slightly in 2013 and also in 2014. Another dramatic change has been the decrease in the number of days on the market for homes since 2012 which shows a marked upturn in real estate market demand. This workbook is embedded in this memo and can be viewed in its entirety by double-clicking on the object.

Median Price Existing Single Family Homes 2012 - 2014			
	2012	2013	2014
Average Price	$ 135,000	$ 158,000	$ 166,000
Days on Market	45	32	28

Student Name

1

EXCEL 2013 COMMAND SUMMARY

COMMAND	SHORTCUT	ACTION
Quick Access Toolbar		
🖫 Save	Ctrl + **S**	Saves document using same file name
↰ Undo	Ctrl + **Z**	Reverses last editing or formatting change
↱ Redo	Ctrl + **Y**	Restores changes after using Undo
File Tab		
Save	Ctrl + **S**	Saves file using same file name
Save As	F12	Saves file using a new file name
Open	Ctrl + **O**	Opens an existing workbook file
Close	Ctrl + F4	Closes open workbook file
New	Ctrl + **N**	Opens a new blank workbook
Print	Ctrl + **P**	Opens Print dialog box
Print/ 🔲 Scale: /Fit To		Scales the worksheet to fit a specified number of pages
Options		Displays and changes program settings
Home Tab		
Clipboard Group		
📋 Paste	Ctrl + **V**	Pastes selections stored in system Clipboard
📋 Paste Special/Paste		Inserts object as an embedded object
📋 Paste Special/Paste Link		Inserts object as a linked object
✂ Cut	Ctrl + **X**	Cuts selected data from the worksheet
📋 Copy	Ctrl + **C**	Copies selected data to system Clipboard
🖌 Format Painter		Copies formatting from one place and applies it to another
Font Group		
Calibri ▾ Font		Changes text font
11 ▾ Font Size		Changes text size
B Bold	Ctrl + **B**	Bolds selected text
I Italic	Ctrl + **I**	Italicizes selected text

EXCEL 2013 COMMAND SUMMARY

COMMAND	SHORTCUT	ACTION
U ▼ Underline	Ctrl + U	Underlines selected text
⊡ ▼ Borders		Adds border to specified area of cell or range
⬧ ▼ Fill Color		Adds color to cell background
A ▼ Font Color		Adds color to text
Alignment Group		
≡ Align Left		Left-aligns entry in cell space
≡ Center		Center-aligns entry in cell space
≡ Align Right		Right-aligns entry in cell space
⇤ Decrease Indent		Reduces the margin between the left cell border and cell entry
⇥ Increase Indent		Indents cell entry
⊞ ▼ Merge & Center		Combines selected cells into one cell and centers cell contents in new cell
Number Group		
General ▼ Number Format		Applies selected number formatting to selection
$ ▼ Accounting Number Format		Applies Accounting number format to selection
% Percent Style		Applies Percent Style format to selection
' Comma Style		Applies Comma Style format with two decimals to selection
←.0/.00 Increase Decimal		Increases number of decimal places
.00/→.0 Decrease Decimal		Decreases number of decimal places
Styles group		
Cell Styles ▼		Applies predefined combinations of colors, effects, and formats to selected cells
Cell Styles ▼ /Modify		Modifies existing cell style
Conditional Formatting ▼		Applies Highlight Cells Rules, Top/Bottom Rules, Data Bars, Color Scales, and Icon Sets to selected cells based on criteria
Cells Group		
Insert ▼ /Insert Cells		Inserts blank cells, shifting existing cells down

EXCEL 2013 COMMAND SUMMARY

COMMAND	SHORTCUT	ACTION
Insert ▾ /Insert Cut Cells		Inserts cut row of data into new worksheet row, shifting existing rows down
Insert ▾ /Insert Copied Cells		Inserts copied row into new worksheet row, shifting existing rows down
Insert ▾ /Insert Sheet		Inserts a new blank worksheet in workbook
Insert ▾ /Insert Sheet Rows		Inserts blank rows, shifting existing rows down
Insert ▾ /Insert Sheet Columns		Inserts blank columns, shifting existing columns right
Delete ▾ /Delete Sheet		Deletes the active worksheet
Delete ▾ /Delete Sheet Rows		Deletes selected rows, shifting existing rows up
Delete ▾ /Delete Sheet Columns		Deletes selected columns, shifting existing columns left
Delete ▾ /Delete Sheet		Deletes entire sheet
Format ▾ /Row Height		Changes height of selected row
Format ▾ /AutoFit Row Height		Changes row height to match the tallest cell entry
Format ▾ /Column Width		Changes width of selected column
Format ▾ /AutoFit Column Width		Changes column width to match widest cell entry
Format ▾ /Default Width		Returns column width to default width
Format ▾ /Rename Sheet		Renames sheet
Format ▾ /Move or Copy Sheet		Moves or copies selected sheet
Format ▾ /Tab Color		Changes color of sheet tabs

Editing Group

COMMAND	SHORTCUT	ACTION
Σ ▾ Sum		Calculates the sum of the values in the selected cells
Σ ▾ Sum/Average		Calculates the average of the values in the selected range
Σ ▾ Sum/Max		Returns the largest of the values in the selected range
Σ ▾ Sum/Min		Returns the smallest of the values in the selected range

EXCEL 2013 COMMAND SUMMARY

COMMAND	SHORTCUT	ACTION
Fill/Right	Ctrl + R	Continues a pattern to adjacent cells to the right
Clear		Removes both formats and contents from selected cells
Clear/Clear Formats		Clears formats only from selected cells
Clear/Clear Contents	Delete	Clears contents only from selected cells
/Find	Ctrl + F	Locates specified text, numbers, and/or formats
/Replace	Ctrl + H	Locates specified characters or formats and replaces them with specified replacement characters or format
/Go To	Ctrl + G	Goes to a specified cell location in worksheet

Insert Tab

Illustrations Group

Pictures		Inserts a picture from a file on your computer or a local network
Online Pictures		Finds and inserts pictures from online sources

Charts Group

Recommended Charts		Displays several recommended chart types for selected data
		Inserts a column chart
		Inserts a pie chart
		Inserts a combo chart

Sparklines Group

Line		Inserts sparkline in the selected cell

EXCEL 2013 COMMAND SUMMARY

COMMAND	SHORTCUT	ACTION
Text Group		
Header & Footer		Adds header or footer to worksheet
Page Layout Tab		
Themes Group		
Themes		Applies selected theme to worksheet
Themes /Save Current Theme		Saves modified theme settings as a custom theme
Colors ▾		Changes colors for the current theme
Page Setup Group		
Margins /Narrow		Changes margin settings
Margins /Custom Margins/Horizontally		Centers worksheet horizontally on page
Margins /Custom Margins/Vertically		Centers worksheet vertically on page
Orientation /Landscape		Changes page orientation to landscape
Print Area ▾ /Set Print Area		Sets print area to selected cells
Breaks /Insert Page Break		Inserts page break at cell pointer location
Breaks /Remove Page Break		Removes page break at cell pointer location
Breaks /Reset All Page Breaks		Restores automatic page breaks
Scale to Fit Group		
Width:		Scales worksheet width to specified number of pages
Height:		Scales worksheet height to specified number of pages

EXCEL 2013 COMMAND SUMMARY

COMMAND	SHORTCUT	ACTION
🔼🔽 Height: /1 page		Scales worksheet vertically to fit one page
Scale:		Scales worksheet by entering a percentage
Scale: /Fit To		Scales the worksheet to fit a specified number of pages
Sheet Options Group		
Gridlines ☑ View ☑ Print		Displays/hides gridlines for viewing and printing
Formulas Tab		
Function Library Group		
Σ AutoSum ▾		Enters Sum, Average, Minimum, Maximum, or Count function
Formula Auditing Group		
Show Formulas	Ctrl + '	Displays and hides worksheet formulas
✓! ▾ Error Checking		Checks worksheet for formula errors
Watch Window		Opens Watch Window toolbar
Data Tab		
Data Tools Group		
What-If Analysis ▾ /Goal Seek		Adjusts value in specified cell until a formula dependent on that cell reaches specified result
Review Tab		
Proofing Group		
ABC ✓ Spelling	F7	Spell-checks worksheet
Thesaurus	Shift + F7	Opens the Thesaurus for the selected word in the Research task pane
View Tab		
Workbook Views Group		
Normal		Changes worksheet view to Normal
Page Break Preview		Displays where pages will break when a worksheet is printed
Page Layout		Displays worksheet as it will appear when printed

EXCEL 2013 COMMAND SUMMARY

COMMAND	SHORTCUT	ACTION
Show Group		
☑ Gridlines		Turns on/off display of gridlines
☑ Headings		Turns on/off display of row and column headings
Zoom Group		
🔍 Zoom		Changes magnification of window
Window Group		
Freeze Panes ▾ /Freeze Panes		Freezes top and/or leftmost panes
Freeze Panes ▾ /Unfreeze Panes		Unfreezes window panes
Split		Divides window into four panes at active cell or removes split
Picture Tools Format Tab		
Picture Styles Group		
✎ Picture Border ▾		Specifies color, width, and line style for outline of shape
Picture Effects ▾		Adds glow, shadow, and other effects to pictures
Picture Layout ▾		Converts selected picture to a SmartArt graphic
Chart Tools Design Tab		
Chart Layouts Group		
Add Chart Element ▾ /Chart Title		Adds, removes, or positions the chart title
Add Chart Element ▾ /Axis Titles		Adds, removes, or positions the axes titles
Add Chart Element ▾ /Legend		Adds, removes, or positions the chart legend
Add Chart Element ▾ /Data Labels		Adds, removes, or positions the data labels
Quick Layout ▾		Changes the overall layout of the chart

EXCEL 2013 COMMAND SUMMARY

COMMAND	SHORTCUT	ACTION
Chart Styles Group		
Change Colors		Changes colors associated with chart styles
Data Group		
Switch Row/ Column		Swaps the data over the axes
Select Data		Changes the data range included in chart
Type Group		
Change Chart Type		Changes to a different type of chart
Location Group		
Move Chart		Moves chart to another sheet in the workbook
Chart Tools Format Tab		
Current Selection Group		
Chart Area		Selects an element on the chart
Format Selection		Opens Format dialog box for selected element
Shape Styles Group		
More		Opens Shape Styles gallery
Shape Fill ▾		Adds selected fill to shape
Shape Outline ▾		Specifies color, weight, and type of outline
Shape Effects ▾		Adds selected effect to shape
Sparklines Tool Design Tab		
Style Group		
More		Opens sparkline style gallery
Clear ▾		Removes sparkline

WWW.MHHE.COM/OLEARY

b

Backstage: Contains commands that allow you to work with your document, unlike the Ribbon that allows you to work in your document; contains commands that apply to the entire document.

Buttons: Graphical elements that perform the associated action when you click on them using the mouse.

c

Character effects: Enhancements such as bold, italic, and color that are applied to a selected text.

Clipboard: Where a selection is stored when it is cut or copied.

Cloud: Any application or service hosted and run on servers connected to the Internet.

Commands: Options that carry out a selected action.

Context menu: Also called a shortcut menu; opened by right-clicking on an item on the screen.

Contextual tabs: Also called on-demand tabs; tabs that are displayed only as needed. For example, when you are working with a picture, the Picture Tools tab appears.

Cursor: The blinking vertical bar that marks your location in the document and indicates where text you type will appear; also called the insertion point.

d

Database: A collection of related data.

Default: The standard options used by Office 2013.

Destination: The new location into which a selection that is moved from its original location is inserted.

Dialog box launcher: A button that is displayed in the lower-right corner of a tab group if more commands are available; clicking opens a dialog box or task pane of additional options.

Document window: The large center area of the program window where open application files are displayed.

e

Edit: To revise a document by changing the parts that need to be modified.

Enhanced ScreenTip: Displayed by pointing to a button in the Ribbon; shows the name of the button and the keyboard shortcut.

f

Field: The smallest unit of information about a record; a column in a table.

Font: Type style; also called typeface.

Font size: Size of typeface, given in points.

Format: The appearance of a document.

g

Groups: Part of a tab that contains related items.

h

Hyperlink: Connection to information located in a separate location, such as on a website.

i

Insertion point: Also called the cursor; the blinking vertical bar that marks your location in a document and indicates where text you type will appear.

k

Keyboard shortcut: A combination of keys that can be used to execute a command in place of clicking a button.

Keyword: A descriptive word that is associated with the file and can be used to locate a file using a search.

l

Live Preview: A feature that shows you how selected text in a document will appear if a formatting option is chosen.

m

Metadata: Details about the document that describe or identify it, such as title, author name, subject, and keywords; also called document properties.

Mini toolbar: Appears automatically when you select text; displays command buttons for often-used commands from the Font and Paragraph groups that are used to format a document.

O

Office Clipboard: Can store up to 24 items that have been cut or copied.

On-demand tabs: Also called contextual tabs; tabs that are displayed only as needed.

p

Paste Preview: Shows how a Paste Option will affect a selection.

Properties: Shown in a panel along the right side of the Info tab, divided into four groups; information such as author, keywords, document size, number of words, and number of pages.

q

Quick Access Toolbar: Located to the right of the Window button; provides quick access to frequently used commands such as Save, Undo, and Redo.

r

Records: The information about one person, thing, or place; contained in a row of a table.

Ribbon: Below the title bar; provides a centralized location of commands that are used to work in your document.

s

ScreenTip: Also called a tooltip; appears with the command name and the keyboard shortcut.

Scroll bar: Horizontal or vertical, it is used with a mouse to bring additional information into view in a window.

Selection cursor: Cursor that allows you to select an object.

Shortcut menu: A context-sensitive menu, meaning it displays only those commands relevant to the item or screen location; also called a context menu, it is opened by right-clicking on an item on the screen.

Slide: An individual page of a presentation.

Slide shows: Onscreen electronic presentations.

Source: The original location of a selection that is inserted in a new location.

Status bar: At the bottom of the application window; displays information about the open file and features that help you view the file.

t

Table: A database object consisting of columns and rows.

Tabs: Used to divide the Ribbon into major activity areas.

Tag: A descriptive word that is associated with the file and can be used to locate a file using a search; also called a keyword.

Task pane: A list of additional options opened by clicking the dialog box launcher; also called a dialog box.

Template: A professionally designed document that is used as the basis for a new document.

Text effects: Enhancements such as bold, italic, and color that are applied to selected text.

Tooltip: Also called a ScreenTip; appears displaying a command name and the keyboard shortcut.

Typeface: A set of characters with a specific design; also commonly referred to as a font.

u

User interface: A set of graphical elements that are designed to help you interact with the program and provide instructions for the actions you want to perform.

v

View buttons: Used to change how the information in the document window is displayed.

w

Worksheet: An electronic spreadsheet, or worksheet, that is used to organize, manipulate, and graph numeric data.

z

Zoom slider: Located at the far right end of the status bar; used to change the amount of information displayed in the document window by "zooming in" to get a close-up view or "zooming out" to see more of the document at a reduced view.

3-D Reference: A formula that contains references to cells in other sheets of a workbook; allows you to use data from multiple sheets and to calculate new values based on this data.

a

Absolute Reference: A cell or range reference in a formula whose location does not change when the formula is copied.

Active Cell: The cell your next entry or procedure affects, indicated by a black outline.

Active Sheet: The sheet in which you can work, the name of which appears bold.

Adjacent Range: A rectangular block of adjoining cells.

Alignment: The settings that allow you to change the horizontal and vertical placement and the orientation of an entry in a cell.

Antonym: A word with an opposite meaning.

Area Chart: Shows the magnitude of change over time by emphasizing the area under the curve created by each data series.

Argument: The data a function uses to perform a calculation.

AutoCorrect: A feature that makes some basic assumptions about the text you are typing and, based on these assumptions, automatically corrects the entry.

AutoFill: A feature that makes entering a series of headings easier by logically repeating and extending the series. AutoFill recognizes trends and automatically extends data and alphanumeric headings as far as you specify.

AutoFit: Automatically adjusts the width of the columns to fit the column contents.

AutoRecover: A feature that, when enabled, will automatically save your work and can recover data if the program unexpectedly closes.

Axis: A line bordering the chart plot area used as a frame of reference for measurement.

b

Bar Chart: Displays data as evenly spaced bars. The categories are displayed along the Y axis and the values are displayed horizontally, placing more emphasis on comparisons and less on time.

Bubble Chart: Compares sets of three values. They are similar to a scatter chart with the third value determining the size of the bubble markers.

c

Category Axis: The X axis, usually the horizontal axis; contains categories.

Category-Axis Title: Clearly describes the information on and/or format of the X axis.

Cell: The intersection of a row and a column.

Cell Reference: The column letter and row number of the active cell (e.g., A1).

Cell Selector: The black border that surrounds the active cell.

Cell Style: A defined theme-based combination of formats that have been named and that can be quickly applied to a selection.

Character Effect: Font formatting, such as color, used to enhance the appearance of the document.

Chart: A visual representation of data in a worksheet.

Chart Area: The entire chart and all its elements.

Chart Elements: The different parts of a chart that are used to graphically display the worksheet data.

Chart Gridlines: Lines extending from the axis line across the plot area that make it easier to read the chart data.

Chart Layout: A predefined set of chart elements that can be quickly applied to a chart. The elements include chart titles, a legend, a data table, or data labels.

Chart Object: A graphic object that is created using charting features. An object can be inserted into a worksheet or into a special chart sheet.

Chart Style: A predefined set of chart formats that can be quickly applied to a chart.

Chart Title: A descriptive label displayed above the charted data that explains the contents of the chart.

Chart Type: The different chart types, such as bar, area, and line, that represent data in different ways.

Clip Art: Royalty-free drawings and photographs.

Column: The vertical stacks of cells in a workbook.

Column Chart: Displays data as evenly spaced vertical columns. They are similar to bar charts, except that categories are organized horizontally and values vertically to emphasize variation over time.

Column Letter: Located across the top of the workbook window; identifies each worksheet column.

Combo Chart: Combines two or more chart types to make comparisons easy when you have two types of data or the data values vary widely.

Column Width: The size or width of a column that controls the number of characters that can be displayed in a cell.

Conditional Formatting: Changes the appearance of a range of cells based on a condition that you specify.

Constant: A value that does not begin with an equal sign and does not change unless you change it directly by typing in another entry.

Copy Area: Range of data to be copied and pasted.

Custom Dictionary: In the spelling checker, holds words you commonly use but that are not included in the main dictionary.

d

Data: The information entered in a cell. It can be text, numbers, dates or times.

Data Label: Label that corresponds to the data points (values) that are plotted along the X axis.

Data Marker: A bar, area, dot, slice, or other symbol in a chart, representing a single data point or value that originates from a worksheet cell.

Data Series: Related data markers in a chart.

Default: Predefined settings, used on new blank workbooks.

Depth Axis: The Z axis; a third axis, in a 3-D column, 3-D cone, or 3-D pyramid chart; allows data to be plotted along the depth of a chart.

Destination File: The document into which an object is inserted.

Doughnut Chart: Similar to pie chart except that it can show more than one data series.

Drawing Object: A graphic element.

e

Embedded Chart: Chart that is inserted into a worksheet; it becomes part of the sheet in which it is inserted and is saved as part of the worksheet when you save the workbook file.

Embedded Object: An object, such as a graphic, created from another program and inserted in the worksheet, becoming part of the sheet in which it is inserted; it is saved as part of the worksheet.

Explode: Separation between the slices of a pie chart to emphasize the data in the categories.

External Reference: References the location of a source file and the selection within a document that is linked to the destination file.

f

Fill Handle: The green box in the lower-right corner of a selection.

Find and Replace: A feature that helps you quickly find specific information and automatically replaces it with new information.

Footer: Provides information that appears at the bottom of each page; commonly includes information such as the date and page number.

Formula: An equation that performs a calculation on data contained in a worksheet. A formula always begins with an equal sign (=) and uses arithmetic operators.

Formula Bar: Below the Ribbon; displays entries as they are made and edited in the workbook window.

Freeze Panes: Prevents the data in the pane from scrolling as you move to different areas in a worksheet.

Function: A prewritten formula that performs certain types of calculations automatically.

g

Goal Seek: A tool used to find the value needed in one cell to attain a result you want in another cell.

Gradient: A fill option consisting of a gradual progression of colors and shades that can be from one color to another or from one shade to another of the same color.

Graphic: A nontext element or object such as a drawing or picture that can be added to a document.

Group: Two or more objects that behave as a single object when moved or sized. A chart is a group that consists of many separate objects.

h

Header: Information appearing at the top of each page.

Headings: Entries that are used to create the structure of the worksheet and describe other worksheet entries.

k

Keyword: Descriptive term associated with a graphic.

l

Legend: A box that identifies the chart data series and data markers.

Line Chart: Displays data along a line; used to show changes in data over time, emphasizing time and rate of change rather than the amount of change.

Link: Contains references to the location of a source file and the selection within a document that is linked to the destination file.

Linked Object: Information created in one application that is inserted into a document created by another application.

Live Link: A link that updates the linked object when changes are made to the source file.

m

Main Dictionary: The dictionary that is supplied with the spelling checker program.

Margin: The blank space outside the printing area around the edges of the paper.

Merged Cell: Two or more cells combined into one.

Mixed Reference: In a formula, either the column letter or the row number is preceded with the $. This makes only the row or column absolute. When a formula containing a mixed cell reference is copied to another location in the worksheet, only the part of the cell reference that is not absolute changes relative to its new location in the worksheet.

n

Name Box: Displays the cell reference.

Nonadjacent Range: Two or more selected cells or ranges that are not adjoining.

Number: The digits 0 to 9.

Number Format: Formatting that changes the appearance of numbers onscreen and when printed, without changing the way the number is stored or used in calculations.

o

Object: An element that is added to a document.

Operand: The values on which a numeric formula performs a calculation, consisting of numbers or cell references.

Operator: A symbol that specifies the type of numeric operation to perform, such as + (addition), − (subtraction), / (division), * (multiplication), % (percent), and ^ (exponentiation).

Order of Operations: In a formula that contains more than one operator, Excel calculates the formula from left to right and performs the calculation in the following order: percent, exponentiation, multiplication and division, and addition and subtraction.

p

Page Break: The place where one printed page ends and another starts.

Pane: A section of the workbook window when using the Split command.

Paste Area: Location you paste material you have copied.

Picture: A graphic element.

Picture Style: Adds a border around a graphic object that consists of combinations of line, shadow, color, and shape effects.

Pie Chart: Displays data as slices of a circle or pie; shows the relationship of each value in a data series to the series as a whole. Each slice of the pie represents a single value in the series.

Plot Area: The area within the X- and Y-axis boundaries where the chart appears.

Print Area: The area you selected for printing; surrounded by a heavy line that identifies the area.

q

Quick Analysis Tool: A feature that displays a gallery of likely formatting or analysis commands for the current selection.

Quick Style: A named group of formatting characteristics that allow the user to apply various formats to a selection.

r

Radar Chart: Displays a line or area chart wrapped around a central point. Each axis represents a set of data points.

Range: A selection consisting of two or more cells on a worksheet.

Range Reference: Identifies the cells in a range.

Recalculation: When a number in a referenced cell in a formula changes, Excel automatically recalculates all formulas that are dependent upon the changed value.

Relative Reference: A cell or range reference in a formula whose location is interpreted in relation to the position of the cell that contains the formula.

Row: Horizontal string of cells in a workbook.

Row Height: The size or height of a row measured in points.

Row Number: Along the left side of the workbook window; identifies each worksheet row.

s

Sans Serif: Fonts that do not have a flare at the base of each letter, such as Arial and Calibri.

Scaling: Reducing or enlarging the worksheet contents by a percentage or to fit it to a specific number of pages by height and width.

Scatter (XY) Chart: Used to show the relationship between two ranges of numeric data.

Selection Rectangle: Box that surrounds a selected object, indicating that it is a selected object and can now be deleted, sized, moved, or modified.

Serial Value: Data stored as consecutively assigned numbers, such as dates where each day is numbered from the beginning of the 20th century. The date serial values begin with 1.

Series Axis: The Z axis; a third axis, in a 3-D column, 3-D cone, or 3-D pyramid chart; allows data to be plotted along the depth of a chart.

Series Formula: Links a chart object to the source worksheet.

Serif: Fonts that have a flare at the base of each letter that visually leads the reader to the next letter. Two common serif fonts are Cambria and Times New Roman.

Sheet: Used to display different types of information, such as financial data or charts.

Shape Style: Predefined combinations of fills, outlines, and effects that can be applied to the selected chart element.

Sheet Name: Descriptive name that can be assigned to each sheet in a workbook. A sheet name helps identify the contents of the sheet.

Sheet Reference: The name of the sheet, followed by an exclamation point and the cell or range reference, in a formula.

Sheet Tab: Where the name of each sheet in a workbook is displayed, shown at the bottom of the workbook window.

Size: The width of a column.

Sizing Handles: Eight squares and circles located on the selection rectangle that allow the object to be resized.

Source File: The document that houses information that is referenced elsewhere.

Source Program: The program in which an object was created.

Sparkline: A tiny chart of worksheet data contained in the background of a single cell.

Spelling Checker: Locates misspelled words, duplicate words, and capitalization irregularities in the active worksheet and proposes the correct spelling.

Split Window: A feature that allows you to divide a worksheet window into sections, making it easier to view different parts of the worksheet at the same time.

Spreadsheet: A worksheet; a rectangular grid of rows and columns used to enter data.

Stacked Column Chart: Displays data as evenly spaced columns; this type of chart also shows the proportion of each category to the total.

Stock Chart: Illustrates fluctuations in stock prices or scientific data; requires three to five data series that must be arranged in a specific order.

Stops (Gradient Stops):   Specific points where the blending of two adjacent colors in the gradient ends.

Surface Chart: Displays values in a form similar to a rubber sheet stretched over a 3-D column chart. These are useful for finding the best combination between sets of data.

Synonym: A word with a similar meaning.

Syntax: Rules of structure for entering all functions.

t

Tab Scroll Buttons: Located in the sheet tab area; used to scroll tabs right or left when there are more sheet tabs than can be seen.

Template: A file that contains settings that are used as the basis for a new file you are creating.

Text: Any combination of letters, numbers, spaces, and any other special characters.

Text Box: A graphic element that is designed to contain specific types of information.

Theme: A predefined set of formatting choices that can be applied to an entire worksheet in one simple step.

Thesaurus: A reference tool that provides synonyms, antonyms, and related words for a selected word or phrase.

Thumbnail: Miniature representations of graphic objects.

V

Value Axis: The Y axis, usually the vertical axis; contains data.

Value-Axis Title: Describes the information on and/or format of the Y axis.

Variable: A value that can change if the data it depends on changes.

W

What-If Analysis: A technique used to evaluate the effects of changing selected factors in a worksheet.

Workbook: An Excel file that stores the information you enter using the program.

Workbook Window: The large center area of the program window.

Worksheet: Also commonly referred to as a spreadsheet; a rectangular grid of rows and columns used to enter data.

X

X Axis: Also called the category axis; usually the horizontal axis and contains categories

Y

Y Axis: Also called the value axis; usually the vertical axis and contains data.

Z

Z Axis: Also called the depth axis or series axis; a third axis, in a 3-D column, 3-D cone, or 3-D pyramid chart; allows data to be plotted along the depth of a chart.

Index

Credits

EX1.2   TRBfoto/Getty Images

EX2.2   BlueMoon stock/agefotostock

EX3.2   Hill Street Studios/Getty Images

Notes

Notes

Notes

Notes

Notes

Notes

Notes

Notes

Notes

Notes